**Keep this book. You will
need it and use it throughout
your career.**

About the American Hotel & Lodging Association (AH&LA)

Founded in 1910, AH&LA is the trade association representing the lodging industry in the United States. AH&LA is a federation of state lodging associations throughout the United States with 11,000 lodging properties worldwide as members. The association offers its members assistance with governmental affairs representation, communications, marketing, hospitality operations, training and education, technology issues, and more. For information, call 202-289-3100.

LODGING, the management magazine of AH&LA, is a "living textbook" for hospitality students that provides timely features, industry news, and vital lodging information.

About the Educational Institute of AH&LA (EI)

An affiliate of AH&LA, the Educational Institute is the world's largest source of quality training and educational materials for the lodging industry. EI develops textbooks and courses that are used in more than 1,200 colleges and universities worldwide, and also offers courses to individuals through its Distance Learning program. Hotels worldwide rely on EI for training resources that focus on every aspect of lodging operations. Industry-tested videos, CD-ROMs, seminars, and skills guides prepare employees at every skill level. EI also offers professional certification for the industry's top performers. For information about EI's products and services, call 800-349-0299 or 407-999-8100.

About the American Hotel & Lodging Educational Foundation (AH&LEF)

An affiliate of AH&LA, the American Hotel & Lodging Educational Foundation provides financial support that enhances the stability, prosperity, and growth of the lodging industry through educational and research programs. AH&LEF has awarded hundreds of thousands of dollars in scholarship funds for students pursuing higher education in hospitality management. AH&LEF has also funded research projects on topics important to the industry, including occupational safety and health, turnover and diversity, and best practices in the U.S. lodging industry. For information, call 202-289-3180.

TOURISM
and the
HOSPITALITY
INDUSTRY

Educational Institute Books

TOURISM
and the
HOSPITALITY
INDUSTRY

Joseph D. Fridgen, Ph.D.

EDUCATIONAL INSTITUTE
American Hotel & Lodging Association

Disclaimer

This publication is designed to provide accurate and authoritative information in regard to the subject matter covered. It is sold with the understanding that the publisher is not engaged in rendering legal, accounting, or other professional service. If legal advice or other expert assistance is required, the services of a competent professional person should be sought.
> —*From the Declaration of Principles jointly adopted by the American Bar Association and a Committee of Publishers and Associations*

The author, Joseph D. Fridgen, is solely responsible for the contents of this publication. All views expressed herein are solely those of the author and do not necessarily reflect the views of the Educational Institute of the American Hotel & Lodging Association (the Institute) or the American Hotel & Lodging Association (AH&LA).

Nothing contained in this publication shall constitute a standard, an endorsement, or a recommendation of the Institute or AH&LA. The Institute and AH&LA disclaim any liability with respect to the use of any information, procedure, or product, or reliance thereon by any member of the hospitality industry.

Project Editor: Ann M. Halm
Editors: Timothy J. Eaton
       John Morier
       Jim Purvis

Contents

Congratulations. . .

You have a running start on a fast-track career!

Developed through the input of industry and academic experts, this course gives you the know-how hospitality employers demand. Upon course completion, you will earn the respected American Hotel & Motel Association certificate that ensures instant recognition worldwide. It is your link with the global hospitality industry.

You can use your AH&MA certificate to show that your learning experiences have bridged the gap between industry and academia. You will have proof that you have met industry-driven learning objectives and that you know how to apply your knowledge to actual hospitality work situations.

By earning your course certificate, you also take a step toward completing the highly respected learning programs—Certificates of Specialization, the Hospitality Operations Certificate, and the Hospitality Management Diploma—that raise your professional development to a higher level. Certificates from these programs greatly enhance your credentials, and a permanent record of your course and program completion is maintained by the Educational Institute.

We commend you for taking this important step. Turn to the Educational Institute for additional resources that will help you stay ahead of your competition.

Foreword

Modern tourism has the ability to transport and provide for millions of tourists most anywhere in the world—and to do so efficiently, safely, and comfortably. As an industry, tourism consists of an enormous network of people, places, and services that affect relationships within a country's borders and between nations. The importance of tourism should not be understated. In the United States, it is our number-one export earning, bringing in more than $44 billion in new currency, ... our second largest employer, providing jobs for nearly 6 million citizens, ... and our third largest retail industry, accounting for more than $350 billion in revenues to our economy in 1990.

Joseph D. Fridgen and the Educational Institute of the American Hotel & Motel Association have developed a text that approaches tourism from various angles, including the impacts that tourism has on cultures, societies, the environment, and economies worldwide.

In recent years, global tourism accounted for more than $2 trillion in expenditures, or about 10% of the world's gross national product. And, if we look at physical structures, more than 4 million miles of roads, 16,000 airports, and 44,000 lodging properties serve the pleasure-seeking tourist in the United States alone. Such immense figures do more than imply the significance of tourism—they spell it out. More and more, tourism is becoming a giant among industries that shape the health, well-being, prosperity, and social consciousness of the world.

The future of tourism holds many promises—tourism as a force for world peace being one of the greatest. As international barriers to travel continue to fall, and as tourists broaden their travel patterns to learn more about cultures and environments, understanding between peoples of different nations and regions should increase. Travel for other reasons—escape from the stress of daily routine, search for fun and excitement—will continue as dual-income families with discretionary income and leisure time prevail.

Tomorrow's tourism professionals face many challenges. They must be prepared to meet them wisely with an eye toward the future life of the industry and of generations to come.

—Rockwell A. Schnabel
Under Secretary of Commerce
for Travel and Tourism

Preface

Tourism is rapidly becoming one of the largest industries in the world. As tourism continues to grow over the next five to ten years, industry professionals must also expand and fine-tune their knowledge and expertise. *Tourism and the Hospitality Industry* is designed to introduce the basic concepts of tourism to beginning professionals, and to serve as a comprehensive resource for the seasoned manager, supervisor, or executive. Some readers, too, may use this text as a bridge to further analysis and advanced study of tourism.

Tourism and the Hospitality Industry approaches tourism from a social science perspective. Discussions focus on tourism positives and negatives in order to give the reader a clear and objective view of the industry. The text addresses various factors that influence tourism—as well as how tourism affects certain elements in today's world.

The book consists of two parts. Part I looks at six dimensions of tourism: historical, psychological, social and cultural, international, economic, and environmental. Together, these chapters emphasize that many factors influence the decisions, families, social situations, dispositions, and orientations of tourists around the world. Part II examines the services and tools available to assist industry professionals in managing and understanding tourism activity. These six chapters focus on services for the traveler, planning and development, marketing, research and measurement, and tourism policy.

It cannot be said enough—or too strongly—that hospitality operations, attractions, transportation systems, and other tourism-related endeavors do not exist in a vacuum. Decision-makers from the public and private sectors, citizens from tourism destinations, businesspersons from domestic and international firms, and tourists from all points on the globe all work together to shape tourism.

Many people contributed to the development and completion of this project. Industry and academic colleagues took the time to read the manuscript and offer insightful comments. The professional staff of the Educational Institute of the American Hotel & Motel Association were most patient and helpful in keeping the ideas churning.

Special thanks go to **Tom Berrigan,** Director of Communications, Travel Industry Association of America, Washington, D.C., **Suzanne D. Cook,** Ph.D., Executive Director, U.S. Travel Data Center, Washington, D.C., and **Charles J. Metelka,** Ph.D., University of Wisconsin-Stout, Menomonie, Wisconsin, for reading and commenting on selected chapters. I also extend my thanks to my colleagues, **Donald F. Holecek,** Ph.D., and **Dennis B. Propst,** Ph.D., both from the Department of Park and Recreation Resources at Michigan State University. Dr. Holecek contributed to the chapter on research and measurement and Dr. Propst contributed the chapter on economics. I sincerely appreciate and acknowledge their hard work under tight deadlines. Most important, I wish to thank my editor, **Ann M. Halm,** who day in and day out required that creative ideas be put on paper. Consistently, she made a good idea even better with tight, clean editing. Finally, I thank my wife, **Cynthia Fridgen,** whose patience and support helped bring this project to fruition.

—Joseph D. Fridgen, Ph.D.
Associate Professor
Department of Park and
Recreation Resources
Michigan State University
East Lansing, Michigan

Study Tips for Users of
Educational Institute Courses

Learning is a skill, like many other activities. Although you may be familiar with many of the following study tips, we want to reinforce their usefulness.

Your Attitude Makes a Difference

If you want to learn, you will: it's as simple as that. Your attitude will go a long way in determining whether or not you do well in this course. We want to help you succeed.

Plan and Organize to Learn

- Set up a regular time and place for study. Make sure you won't be disturbed or distracted.

- Decide ahead of time how much you want to accomplish during each study session. Remember to keep your study sessions brief; don't try to do too much at one time.

Read the Course Text to Learn

- *Before* you read each chapter, read the chapter outline and the learning objectives. If there is a summary at the end of the chapter, you should read it to get a feel for what the chapter is about.

- Then, go back to the beginning of the chapter and *carefully* read, focusing on the material included in the learning objectives and asking yourself such questions as:

  —Do I understand the material?

  —How can I use this information now or in the future?

- Make notes in margins and highlight or underline important sections to help you as you study. Read a section first, then go back over it to mark important points.

- Keep a dictionary handy. If you come across an unfamiliar word that is not included in the textbook glossary, look it up in the dictionary.

- Read as much as you can. The more you read, the better you read.

Testing Your Knowledge

- Test questions developed by the Educational Institute for this course are designed to measure your knowledge of the material.

- End-of-the-chapter Review Quizzes help you find out how well you have studied the material. They indicate where additional study may be needed. Review Quizzes are also helpful in studying for other tests.

- Prepare for tests by reviewing:

  —learning objectives

  —notes

  —outlines

  —questions at the end of each assignment

- As you begin to take any test, read the test instructions *carefully* and look over the questions.

  We hope your experiences in this course will prompt you to undertake other training and educational activities in a planned, career-long program of professional growth and development.

Part I

Chapter Outline

Travel in Prehistoric Times
Travel in Neolithic Times
Travel in Ancient Civilizations
    Conditions for Travel
    Early Pleasure and Religious Travel
Travel in the Middle Ages
    The Crusades and Pilgrimages
Travel in the Renaissance
    The Grand Tour
Travel in the Industrial Age
    Travel Motivations
    Transportation
    Cook's Tours
The Emergence of Modern Mass Tourism
    The Automobile
    The Airplane
    Leisure Time
    Beyond the 1960s

Learning Objectives

1. Describe travel conditions and methods during the Paleolithic age.

2. Point out the innovations and changes in community structure which affected the nature of travel during the Neolithic age.

3. Identify the conditions which fostered the growth of travel in ancient civilizations.

4. Analyze the effect that religious beliefs and practices had on travel in the Middle Ages.

5. Describe two major forms of travel in the Middle Ages.

6. Summarize the purpose, scope, and history of the Grand Tour.

7. Identify the advances in transportation which affected travel during the industrial age.

8. Analyze the factors which contributed to the success of Cook's Tours.

9. Describe the roles of the automobile and the airplane in fostering modern mass tourism.

10. Identify key labor trends and legislation which facilitated mass tourism.

11. Identify several factors which have shaped tourism in recent years.

Historical Dimensions

MODERN SOCIETIES HAVE many legacies—including those associated with travel. Since travel is an ancient behavior, any study of tourism is incomplete without a historical perspective. History provides a context for current tourism activity and policy. Without looking back, it would be easy to imagine that most people have always been able to travel freely and safely from country to country. But upon closer scrutiny, we see that freedom to travel for people of modest means is a very current privilege.

Even as recently as the mid-1800s, most travel was reserved for the well-to-do, the powerful, and the determined or curious explorer. Middle- to lower-income citizens stayed at home and tended to their lives and businesses. For these people, travel was an occasional trip to a neighboring community or an infrequent trip to a larger city hosting a state fair or religious meeting. International travel was rare and usually impossible due to lack of resources or to policy restrictions. History also reveals the harsh realities of travel in earlier times and civilizations. Accommodations—if even available—were minimal, foods were basic and meager, and a sense of hospitality was often lacking.

Tourism has a history colored with both success and failure. For the most part, tourism is a story of rapid change effected by industrial and technological advances. Most of tourism's success is epitomized by a single, symbolic measure: the rapidly decreasing amount of time it takes to travel from one place to another. Today, a person can cross the country by air from New York to Los Angeles in four to five hours. Just 100 years earlier, such a trip would be stretched from days into weeks—and would be accompanied by frustration and hardship over rough or nearly impassable roads. From a historical point of view, advances in tourism have been spectacular. This chapter will examine the evolution of tourism as well as anticipate some of the changes we can expect in the travel world.

Travel in Prehistoric Times

Early humans lived hard lives. Evidence from the latter part of the **Paleolithic age** (roughly 32,000 B.C. to 10,000 B.C.) suggests that all human activity focused upon day-to-day survival. The search for basic necessities—food, water, and shelter— kept early hunters and gatherers on the move. This often meant difficult and dangerous travel for families or entire communities.

People traveled by foot over paths, open fields, forests, and low marsh lands. Foot trails were useful when available. More often, early humans had to travel to new, unfamiliar locations—which meant breaking new trails. Movement across the landscape was a perilous adventure that required caution and skill. Like the animals they hunted, prehistoric humans had to cope with dangerous predators—including other hunting and gathering tribes. Once a hospitable region was explored, foot paths were developed that led to hunting grounds and to seasonal sources of food and water.

The discovery and control of fire, the use of tools, and the ability to build shelters broadened the range of travel. Fire gave early travelers protection and warmth in different environments. The ability to use tools and build shelters permitted prehistoric humans to travel to new hunting grounds and food gathering locations even in extreme or unpredictable weather.

It is important to note that prehistoric humans did not transport their tools. These nomadic people fashioned tools from natural resources and materials found in their new surroundings such as stone, wood, and bones. Carrying any objects on a trip was probably difficult since animals of burden were not domesticated until 10,000 B.C. to 9000 B.C.

Although traveling was rigorous and unsafe, it did not stop early people from migrating all over the globe. Today, humans occupy all the major land masses. As one source notes: "… most families of mammals are less than worldwide in their distribution. Man shares his very unusual cosmopolitan distribution with only three families of bats and some mice and rats."[1] Although we may be uncomfortable with the company we keep as world travelers, the point is reaffirmed: humans have traveled since the beginning of time.

Travel in Neolithic Times

The **Neolithic age** refers to a time of change which began about 10,000 B.C. During this period, primitive people settled in more permanent areas, formed agricultural communities, and developed elementary cultures. These agricultural communities had many advantages over the nomadic tribes of the Paleolithic era. For one, the community was more likely to have a reliable food source. In addition, food could be stored and consumed at a later date—which reduced the need to migrate to new hunting grounds.

Several innovations during the Neolithic age changed the nature of travel forever. Sailing vessels were built in Egypt around 4000 B.C.[2] During this period, animals were being domesticated and trained to carry supplies, community members, weapons, and tools. Third, the Sumerians invented the wheel around 3500 B.C. and used it to move materials, people, military might, and to make pottery and tools. Each development alone, and in combination, dramatically affected travel. The burdens of travel were considerably reduced and the distance which a person, group, or whole community could travel expanded from a few miles to hundreds.

Most early travel was associated with the trade and exchange of goods. Growing agricultural communities were able to maintain reliable sources of food and water and offered some measure of safety and stability for travelers. This security fostered exchanges of surplus food, artifacts, tools, and weapons among neighboring communities and cultures. Innovations in the means of travel also made trading a realistic venture for some community members.

Related to the rise of travel for trade was the development of media of exchange between communities. Before coins were invented, valuables such as attractive

Key Events in Travel and Tourism

Events: B.C.

9000	Animals are domesticated, used in transportation
4000	Sailing crafts used in Ancient Egypt
3500	Wheel invented and used by Sumerians
776	First Olympic Games held in Ancient Greece
700	Homer writes *Iliad* and *Odyssey,* ancient literature with tales of travel
680	First coins used by people of Lydia

Events: A.D.

476	Approximate fall of the Roman Empire
1492	Columbus discovers the New World
1669	Early scheduled coach service arranged in England
1787	Early form of steamboat used on the Potomac
1796	U.S. issues first passport without personal description
1820	Horse-drawn carriage rentals available for touring in France
1825	Erie Canal completed, connected Great Lakes and Hudson River; passenger trains open in England
1827	U.S. passport contains description of traveler
1828	Pioneer U.S. railway established—the Baltimore & Ohio
1829	Early "all inclusive" tours packaged for Switzerland
1838	First ocean going service routes between England and India
1841	Thomas Cook arranges first group tour for Temperance Society
1845	Cook conducts tours as a commercial business
1862	U.S. government begins charging for passports
1864	First Pullman sleeping train car called the *Pioneer*
1866	First Cook's Tour in the United States after the Civil War
1867	Cook introduces hotel coupon
1869	Union and Central Pacific Railroads meet in Utah
1869	Suez Canal completed
1871	Dean and Dawson tour company formed in England
1871	Bank holidays introduced in England for workers
1871	Cook opens office in New York
1872	Cook leads the first around the world tour
1873	Cook issues *Circular Notes*—an early type of traveler's check
1875	Cook provides the first short duration boat tour
1876	Development of the telephone
1876	Internal combustion engine developed
1879	Discovery of electricity
1894	Labor Day proclaimed a national holiday in the United States
1895	American Express opens first foreign office in Paris
1902	American Automobile Association formed
1903	First automobile crosses the United States
1903	Wright brothers' historic, short air flight
1911	America crossed for first time by airplane
1912	Titanic sinks in Atlantic

(continued)

1916	U.S. National Park Service established
1919	Cook offers one of the first tours by airplane
1920	Prohibition becomes law in the United States
1924	British form Imperial Airways after World War I
1927	Lindbergh crosses the Atlantic from the United States to France
1929	Stock market crash in the United States
1930	First stewardess on planes
1937	Hindenburg crashes in New York after Atlantic flight
1938	Fair Labor Standards Act passed in the United States; 40-hour workweek established
1941	Japanese attack Pearl Harbor; U.S. enters World War II. Through 1945, the impacts of World War II on travel include: gas rationing; disruption of family life; shutdown of certain resorts; and use of hotels for hospitals. War effects improvements in travel technology for automobiles, trucks, airplanes, and ships.
1945	World War II ends
1957	Air travelers surpass ship traffic across Atlantic
1958	Economy class of airline travel introduced
1967	U.S. Department of Transportation established
1970	Amtrak rail system established
1975	First OPEC oil embargo
1976	Atlantic City, New Jersey permits gambling
1976	The U.S. holds national bicentennial celebration
1978	Airline deregulation put into effect in the United States
1979	Second OPEC oil embargo
1981	U.S. Travel and Tourism Administration established
1985	Civil Aeronautics Board of the United States terminated
1989	France celebrates 200th anniversary of the French Revolution

Sources: The Queensbury Group, *The Book of Key Facts* (New York: Paddington Press Ltd., 1978); C. Harold King, Arthur J. Fletcher, *A History of Civilization: The Story of Our Heritage* (New York: Scribner, 1969); J.E. Spencer and W.L. Thomas, *Introducing Cultural Geography* (New York: Wiley, 1973); Maxine Feifer, *Going Places: The Ways of the Tourist from Imperial Rome to the Present Day* (London: Macmillan London Ltd., 1985); Horace Sutton, *Travelers: The American Tourist from Stagecoach to Space Shuttle* (New York: Morrow, 1980); Edmund Swinglehurst, *Cook's Tours: The Story of Popular Travel* (Dorset, U.K.: Blandford Press, 1982).

jewelry, knives, and implements for lighting fires served as exchange media. The first coins were developed around 680 B.C.[3] They were irregular and round in shape with official imprints stamped by the issuing government. With the coin, travel costs could be managed without transporting cumbersome, perishable, and often heavy bundles of valuables for barter.

The unique cultures and religions which emerged during the Neolithic revolution fostered travel for religious and spiritual purposes. While earlier hunters and gatherers traveled to survive, the people of primitive agricultural communities were able to set aside regular times for spiritual events and festivals. Some members of the community traveled to shrines, burial grounds, sacred locations, and places of exceptional beauty or mystery.

The leisure time required for pleasure travel was very scarce in primitive societies—even in the first agricultural communities. As these communities stabilized, and as surplus food supplies and trade increased, leisure time did appear for some people. The quality of life for community members was significantly higher than for members of earlier hunting and gathering tribes. Gradually, the number of options increased in terms of how people could choose to spend their time and their resources.

Travel in Ancient Civilizations

Many historians and anthropologists consider travel for trade and commerce a common activity in ancient civilizations. Civilizations of great power, long duration, and extensive dominion were also known for sophisticated levels of commerce. As commerce grew, so did travel for pleasure. The societies of Greece, Egypt, and Rome openly encouraged pleasure travel by providing necessary ways and means. With such support, travel contributed to the success of each of these great empires.

Conditions for Travel

The ever-increasing **specialization of labor** within ancient civilizations fostered the growth of travel. As ancient communities grew in size, the tasks and roles of the population became more specialized and skilled. This made it possible for communities to develop an array of products that increased in quality with each generation. Craftspersons honed their skills and passed them on to family members or others willing to learn. Such division of skills meant that people needed to exchange goods to survive. For example, a craftsperson busy producing pottery would not have time to plant and harvest crops for food. This scarcity of time required the craftsperson to obtain such necessities through barter and trade with a person who specialized in planting and harvesting crops.

The exchange of products and currency required travel. Caravans and trade expeditions moved people, products, and ideas between cultures. The oceans provided the major routes of travel for the cultures centered in the Mediterranean— particularly the Greek, Egyptian, and Roman empires. Roads, too, supported the swift deployment of military power and facilitated the exchange of goods over vast distances. Over time, the earliest foot trails became overland trade routes. As these routes were maintained and improved, they became the basis for extensive road systems.

Road systems were quite advanced in several ancient civilizations. The Romans were excellent road builders. Well-maintained road systems were extremely important to the Roman Empire because they supported rapid communication across the republic. Road systems, too, enabled swift and effective military movement which kept the empire intact. In fact, the quality of life for citizens within the Roman Empire was partly due to the diversity of goods, foods, and services made possible by an effective road system.

Based upon the history and quality of these road systems, we can assume that travel was an important part of commerce, government, and cultural exchange during the rule of the Romans. In the latter years of the Roman Empire, the road system included inns, stables for animals, and crude maps or itineraries. Travel was on foot, on horseback, in carriages of various types, or in a litter—a covered or curtained couch carried by slaves or servants.

Travel technologies and the ability to support commerce and trade over long distances resulted in improvements for travel of all types—including pleasure, communications, and military travel. After conflicts and wars, the victor usually absorbed the best innovations, social behaviors, tools, and implements of the conquered. Conquered lands had to be managed, controlled, and supplied—and that required those in power to settle within the new lands and adapt to a new setting, new land, and people. Travel blossomed as those in power and the new citizens moved back and forth between territories. With peace established, military routes became routes of commerce, and of political, social, and religious exchange.

Early Pleasure and Religious Travel

While military and commercial goals may have been major stimuli for early travel, the wonders of travel itself were not lost on the peoples of ancient societies. Ancient travelers were lured to new lands to discover beautiful places, to experience natural attractions, and to obtain curios. However, the majority of pleasure travel was allowed or affordable only to those in power or with sufficient resources.

Those with the necessary resources frequently traveled for religious purposes. The monuments to the gods became travel destinations that people visited out of religious motives or curiosity. Ancient Egyptians traveled to religious centers up and down the Nile, Greeks traveled to Mt. Olympus, and the early Christians traveled to the holy cities of Jerusalem and Rome.

Cultural events often developed from religious festivals and became attractions in their own right. Examples from Greece include classical drama and the Olympic games. These popular events attracted local residents from the countryside and the foreign visitor. Some Greek plays had religious overtones while the games originated in a spiritual festival in honor of Zeus. Greek literature and philosophy also underscored leisure and travel in the pursuit of self-enrichment and exploration. Philosophers Plato and Aristotle both stressed the importance of leisure to society, arguing that such activities helped develop better citizens and political leaders. Nowhere is the Greek fascination for travel more clearly illustrated than in the *Iliad* and the *Odyssey*—epics written by Homer around 700 B.C.

The Romans, too, traveled for a variety of reasons and enjoyed such attractions as natural beauty, creations of artists, and the infamous colosseum games. The Romans had safe access to Egypt, Asia Minor, Greece, and extensive parts of present-day Europe and Africa. Travel for business, pleasure, religion, and sport was recognized as an important use of a well-to-do Roman's leisure time and discretionary resources.

The primary conditions that nurtured travel were present during the time of the Roman Empire. The Roman citizen had the resources and time for travel. The empire, too, provided the support services such as roads, inns, slaves, and a host of consumer goods. Holidays were plentiful. All the gods needed to be celebrated and, of course, a military victory was an excellent reason for celebration. At one point, nearly a third of the days in a year were set aside for holidays.

With time and funds, the rich could travel—and they did. They were off to the sea, to Egypt to see the Pyramids, or to Greece to soak in the art and culture of the land. One researcher captures the moment:

> The year is AD 130. The place is Thebes, in Egypt, by the colossal broken stone statue of Pharaoh Amenhotep III. The hour is shortly after dawn. Even though it's early, a crowd of souvenir merchants is pressing forward. They proffer the usual mementoes: little flasks of Nile water, terracotta replicas of the statue. But the merchants are elbowed aside to make way for a royal party: Emperor Hadrian, his queen Sabina, and assorted companions, attendants and guards. The Roman visitors have sailed all the way up the Nile to see Egypt's most talked-about sight, the speaking statue. Every morning at this time, since the earthquake of 27 BC when its top fell off, the statue has emitted a cry, something like the snapping of a lute string. It must be the gods talking, or at least a freak of nature—either way, not to be missed.[4]

This scene is a snapshot of the sights that attracted the rich Roman. Romans of wealth traveled within the empire, taking trips to villas owned by family or friends. Rome itself was an attraction, as were various seaside facilities. Even in these ancient times, the "second home" by the seaside was available to the wealthy, just as it often is today.

The Roman of less means could also get away for an occasional pleasure trip. Boarding houses and inns were available to lodge travelers at popular locations such as the seashore. Such accommodations, however, did not include the comforts afforded the rich or well-to-do. Most such establishments were not the ideal place for a "family vacation" given the company of bedbugs, prostitutes, and gamblers.[5]

As the Roman Empire was awash in the pleasures of games, festivals, and leisure, another movement was emerging as the next dominant force to control leisure and travel behavior—Christianity. The stability of the Empire permitted relatively free flow of travel for the teachers of this new religion. In the time immediately after the life of Christ, the Apostles moved about the Roman Empire, taking advantage of the safe, quality road system.

The fall of the Roman Empire retarded the development of travel in old Roman territories, across Europe, and in parts of Asia minor for centuries. The social, political, architectural, and philosophical excellence of Roman society were vanquished, set aside, and, in many cases, destroyed. So, too, were the excesses and the monstrous exhibitions of cruelty and abuse shown for the pleasure of the masses. The power of the Church in the centuries after Christ became a force that dictated social and moral norms.

Travel in the Middle Ages

The fall of the Roman Empire between A.D. 400 and A.D. 500 ushered in changes that profoundly affected travel. In the centuries that followed, to about A.D. 1000, the safety, services, and comforts of travel disappeared. Local travel continued in response to limited bartering and trade. However, civil wars, changes in leadership, and shifting political and military boundaries made travel difficult and dangerous. Limited trade among the European feudal communities represented most of the significant travel that occurred.

Rome: The Attraction

In ancient times, the city of Rome became a seat of power, trade, culture, and travel. A visitor to the city would see people of all nationalities on the streets—as well as merchants and vendors selling items from all corners of the known world. The Roman citizen stood apart with the common Roman dress of the time; but the visitors, slaves, servants, and traders presented a very worldly, cosmopolitan image.

By far, the games were the most notable attractions for the excitement-seeking Roman or traveler. The games were dark and blood-thirsty events fueled by the mass hysteria and excesses of the crowd. The structures which housed the events were in themselves testament to the popularity of these games. Theaters held a few thousand in attendance, the colosseum held approximately 50,000, while the Circus Maximus— the very large stadium built for races and games—held up to 180,000.

The games became an attraction known throughout the Roman world. Visitors came from across the empire to be part of these events in all their splendor, gore, and savagery. Many, too, attended the games while in Rome for commercial, military, or political purposes.

The animals and people performing in the games also gave witness to travel. The elephants, lions, tigers, ostriches, and apes used in combat came from the far reaches of Africa and India. And the prisoners, gladiators, and slaves condemned to perform were people from territories far away from the city of Rome.

The Romans provided for mass leisure and developed some of the earliest and most impressive travel attractions in the history of civilization. From the games to competitive sports festivals, the leaders of the Roman Empire continued to affirm the philosophy that free time was to be used in an enjoyable manner. While the Greeks argued that free time should be used for personal development, the Romans promoted spectacular events and attractions in the pursuit of pleasure. An important new feature was that these attractions and events were attended by the common person, the unemployed, the ordinary citizen, or the foreign traveler. The games of Rome represent some of the first large-scale travel attractions provided for the masses.

These **Middle**—or **Dark**—**Ages** were indeed dark times for travel. The luxury of vacation travel disappeared. Resources required for the common person to travel were no longer available. The new rulers of the old Roman lands did not continue to develop leisure activities for the masses. The common person was subjected to a life of toil in the service of land owners in return for food, shelter, and protection.

During these times, the Roman Catholic Church became a central force throughout Europe. At first, the Catholic Church was one of many religions. But as wars continued, the Catholic Church remained constant and became a comfort to individuals in a dangerous and warring world. Gradually, Catholicism replaced pagan religions and rituals. The Roman festivals, games, and holidays gave way to Catholic holy days. These holy days were just as plentiful as their Roman counterparts, but more sober in vein. They required solemn reflection—not the gay revelry of times past. Furthermore, the Catholic Church interpreted Christ's teachings to mean that the pleasures of this earth were to be denied and scorned. A person's time was to be spent in religious thought of heavenly rewards—not in worldly pleasure.

Civil strife, wars, and the Church's interpretation of social and personal behavior made the early Middle Ages a time of little travel and exploration. Communities became isolated, as did entire countries. Exchange of any type was extremely restricted. The only major travel activities of the period included the Crusades and pilgrimages.

The Crusades and Pilgrimages *major travel activity for the middle ages*

The Crusades consisted of several military expeditions between 1095 and 1291 in which Christian powers attempted to regain the Holy Land from the Muslims. From a military standpoint, the Crusades were less than successful for the Christian warriors. From a cultural standpoint, the Crusades not only enabled an exchange of ideas and the continuation of trade, but also represented a major form of travel across Europe and into the Middle East. The Crusades drew upon the wealthy and the poor, the young and the old—offering individuals a chance for travel and adventure beyond the walls of the local burg or castle.

During the Middle Ages, **pilgrimages** were undertaken for a variety of purposes. Some individuals traveled to religious sites for the forgiveness of their sins, others to receive a divine cure for their health problems. While religion was the primary purpose for a pilgrimage, adventure, learning, and merriment were also enjoyed on the trip.

Several shrines or churches shaped a common itinerary. The most popular sites included Santiago de Compostela in Spain, the famous churches of Paris, the seat of the Roman Catholic Church in Rome, and the Holy Land—particularly Jerusalem. Since the pilgrim was in search of forgiveness or indulgences (years of forgiveness), proof had to be obtained. This was often provided in the form of a pendant or pin—a kind of "holy souvenir."

Travel was by foot or horseback; when possible, pilgrims traveled by boat or horse-drawn coach. The mass pilgrimages required communities near the shrines or along popular routes to provide accommodations for these spiritual travelers. Some inns catered only to particular nationalities; others varied by location and in terms of the resources of the traveler. Very popular sites had an array of inns and hostels to accommodate weary travelers in search of salvation—as well as those in search of earthly pleasures and curiosities.

People traveled in groups to guard against robbers and muggers, and for comfort and merriment. In the *Canterbury Tales*, Chaucer captures the atmosphere of a merry, unique band of travelers on their way to Canterbury. All types of people made pilgrimages, but the trip was most pleasant for those of means. Travelers who could afford the expense took servants along, much like the travelers of ancient times. Those less affluent walked and carried their own belongings, and sought out inexpensive inns and food.

England imposed some restrictions on travel at various times during the pilgrimages. Usually, these restrictions weighed most heavily upon the poorer travelers. At one point, Parliament passed a law requiring that pilgrims be checked to ensure that they were travelers on a holy mission. Students traveling without documents from their school's chancellor, or pilgrims without letters or passes from their local priest, were to be arrested, beaten, and returned home.[6] This was done to control the movement of laborers and skilled workers and to control vagrancy, loitering, and begging.

Services were developed to cater to the pilgrim. Inns provided accommodations, food, and drink, as they did during the reign of ancient civilizations. Other services included the provision of souvenirs, the sale of religious objects, and ample opportunities to engage in common vices of the day, such as gaming. Guides were available to assist the traveler in understanding major secular and sacred attractions. Some guides were paid, others were made available to enhance the experience of the traveler.

The search for the authentic did not seem to be a primary concern for the pilgrim. Often, more than one shrine or chapel had the same sacred relic or religious artifact. Then, as now, "tourist traps" were prevalent. Scenarios like the following were common along routes used by pilgrims:

> The cavalcade of miraculous relics was not slow to present itself. After three days' walk, the pilgrim came to the first great stopping place on the itinerary, Amiens Cathedral, where the skull of John the Baptist was kept. He bought a brooch representing the venerated head and triumphantly pinned it to his hat.
>
> A few days more brought the pilgrim to Paris, where the great attraction was Sainte Chapelle, whose reliquary held bits from the sponge, reed, and cloak used in Christ's walk to Calvary; the Crown of Thorns; breast milk and hair from the Virgin Mary; and more fragments of the True Cross. To the south was Orleans, with even more fragments of the True Cross. Later scholars reckoned that if all the fragments of the True Cross displayed in the fifteenth century were assembled, there would be enough wood to build three ocean liners. Not far beyond Orleans was St. Jean d'Angely, where one hundred monks stood perpetual guard over the skull of … John the Baptist.
>
> For those who had just recently been at Amiens, an explanation was in order. One curate used to tell the pilgrims that the first relic "must have been the skull of the saint as a young man." This was not the only duplicate relic the pilgrim would run into: no less than five shrines, for instance, claimed to possess the body of St. Gilles…. Both St. Jean d'Angely and Amiens remained venerated shrines throughout the Middle Ages. Full of belief, the pilgrim made an ideal tourist.[7]

By the thirteenth and fourteenth centuries, pilgrimage was a mass phenomenon. A growing industry of charitable hospices and mass-produced indulgence handbooks served the travelers. Eventually, the religious nature of travel gave way to more secular pleasures, education, and sight-seeing. Significant social changes began to shape a new sense of the individual. People began to search for a better quality of life, and acknowledged the importance of education, culture, art, and science. This important period was called the Renaissance.

Travel in the Renaissance

The Renaissance was a time of enlightenment, change, and exploration from the fourteenth to the seventeenth century. During this period, the Grand Tour of Europe emerged as one of the first manifestations of upper-class travel. It is here, too, that we see the beginnings of modern tourism.

The Grand Tour

The Grand Tour began as an educational experience for the sons of the English aristocracy. Generally, the tour started in England and had the major cultural cities of Italy as its ultimate destination. A typical tour took the young traveler, his servants, and tutors to France, to Rome, and then back to England via Germany and the Netherlands.

The Grand Tour encompassed the period from 1500 to about 1820. During its early years, the Grand Tour could last as long as 40 months because of the extensive amount of study involved. For example, the young aristocrat could spend an entire year studying a new language or a particular type of literature.

In the time of the Grand Tour, travel purposes went beyond commerce, trade, religion, and military expeditions. Education, culture, health, pleasure, curiosity, science, career development, art, and scenery became motives for traveling—motives very different from those of the Middle Ages. People traveled to experience culture, and to learn about the new scientific discoveries. These same scientific findings turned into technologies that facilitated travel. Ship building, geographical analyses, navigational skills and training, and mapmaking were making travel safer over longer distances. Traveling to observe scenery also emerged as an important travel motivation in the latter part of the Grand Tour era. In the late 1700s, writers, artists, and philosophers began to argue for the value, inherent beauty, and the sublime characteristics of nature which all people could see and appreciate.

Near the end of the Grand Tour era, the trip lasted a mere four months, and the age of the average traveler had increased. By the 1800s, the Grand Tour, for the most part, was taken by members of the upper and middle classes. These individuals traveled more for pleasure than for an extended educational tour.[8] Exhibits 1 and 2 show the average length of the tour and age of the traveler over an extended period.

Lodging, Services, and Transportation. In the early stages of the Grand Tour, the young man, his tutors, and servants used the better of the accommodations which had been offered to the pilgrims in earlier times. By the seventeenth and eighteenth centuries, certain cities along the tour were becoming known for their excellent hotels and services. However, in the rural parts of Europe, the tourist had to use what was available. Sometimes these lodgings were very unpalatable to the young student. Services of other types also became available to the traveler. Peddlers sold souvenirs, and taverns and inns offered food and drink to those on the road. Armies of servants and porters were available for hire to assist tourists at hotels, river crossings, and mountain passes.

Transportation was always a concern for the traveling party. Crossing the Alps drained the most devoted travelers. Marshes, waterways, and poor roads yielded physical punishment. Road villains and thieves also posed a constant threat. The traveler could cross Europe via postal or mail coach system, canal or river vessel, on horse, or by foot. By the time the steamboat and railroads revolutionized travel in the early 1800s, the Grand Tour was fading as a phenomenon.

Exhibit 1   Average Length of the Grand Tour

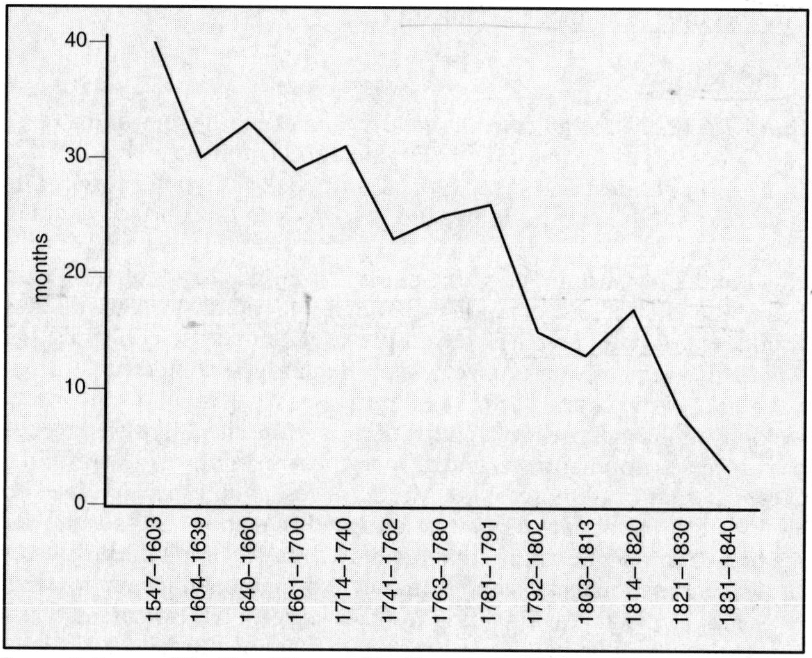

Source: J. Towner, "The Grand Tour: A Key Phase in the History of Tourism," *Annals of Tourism Research* 12 (1985): p. 316, Fig. 5.

During the latter part of the Grand Tour, travel was facilitated by transportation rentals. An important transportation advance in the 1700s was the "all-inclusive" rental or purchase agreement. Upon arriving on the continent, English tourists could purchase or rent a carriage that they later returned or sold back to the original establishment. In 1820, carriages could be rented at hotels for travel throughout Europe—much like rental cars can today. In 1829, a travel merchant in London offered one of the first all-inclusive trips to Switzerland for 16 days covering all transportation, food, and lodging.[9] Thus, the all-inclusive package tour was born.

Travel in the Industrial Age

During the industrial age, the economies of nations shifted from rural agriculture to urban-based industry. The structure of employment, class, and affluence shifted as well. More and more people were able to travel for health, pleasure, and curiosity. Expanding railroads, distant travel by sea, and the coach system all contributed to the democratization of travel.

Travel Motivations

Health and pleasure were strong travel motivations during the seventeenth and eighteenth centuries. The Grand Tour gave way to vacation types of travel for family and friends. Across Europe, the wealthy traveled to spas to experience the curative

Exhibit 2   Average Age of the Grand Tour Traveler

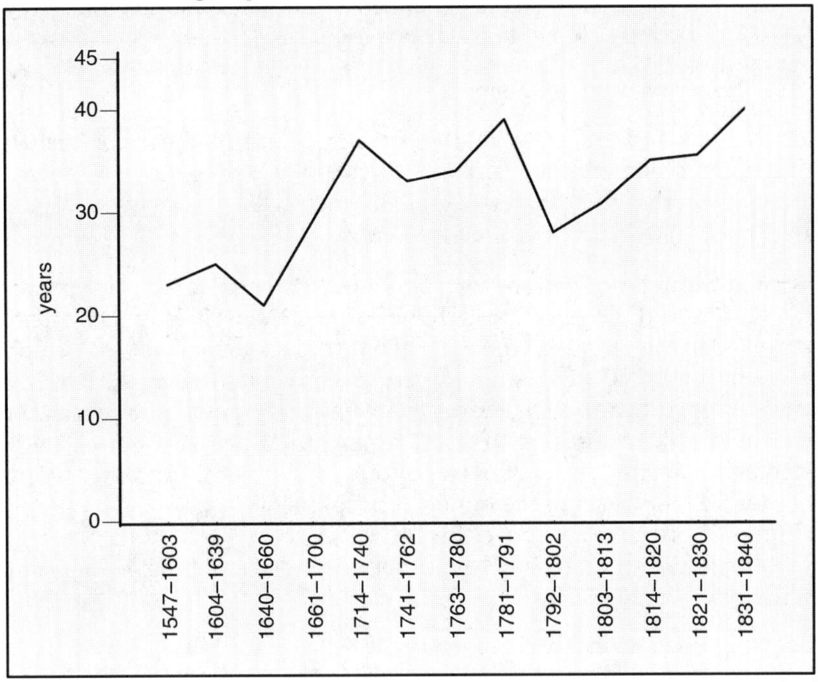

Source: J. Towner, "The Grand Tour: A Key Phase in the History of Tourism," *Annals of Tourism Research* 12 (1985): p. 306, Fig. 3.

effects of hot mineral springs. Spas became major travel attractions for the rich who sought good health, good company, and good fun. Over time, spas expanded their facilities and became less exclusive and more available to the common traveler.

Before the Revolutionary War in the United States, residents of the American colonies traveled to seaside resorts and spas much like their European counterparts. Popular sites included Yellow Springs near Philadelphia, Stafford Springs in Connecticut, and Berkeley Springs in Virginia. Like the European spas, the American spas attracted the rich and famous, including early presidents such as George Washington and John Adams. American spas grew in size and popularity well into the 1800s.[10] Cheaper travel accommodations and the increasing ability to serve more guests made the spas and seaside resorts accessible to the expanding population of travelers. Also, as the Puritans lost some of their control over colonial social life, the taboos against such light-hearted activities waned.

As the social climate changed and the validity of the "cures" provided by spas were challenged, the more forthright motivations for these vacation trips surfaced. Most came for a good time, to meet new people, and to be seen with those of wealth, fame, and status. To our modern minds, the kinds of illnesses supposedly cured by the spring waters reads like a list of ancient mystical spells. Consider the following passage from an 1821 guidebook which lists the benefits of Saratoga baths and mineral waters:

Jaundice and bilious affections generally, Dyspepsia, Habitual Costiveness, Hypochondrical Complaints, Depraved appetite, Calculous and nephritic complaints, Phagedenic or ill-conditioned species or states of gout, some species of dropsy, Scrofula, paralysis, Scorbutic affections and old Scorbutic ulcers, Amenorrhea, Dysmenorrhea and Chlorosis.[11]

Modern spas and resorts still attract the rich and famous, but their health claims are more in line with the trim and fit consciousness of our society. Few resorts would claim that their waters could cure tuberculosis, scurvy, ulcers, bleeding gums, and iron deficiencies in teenage girls.

Romanticism. Strong motivations for travel were also generated through a movement in literature and the arts. Through the early 1800s, writers, poets, artists, and explorers extolled the virtues of the natural world. This love of nature, beauty, and the sublime represented the romantic period—or **romanticism**—in Europe and America. Stories of beautiful landscapes, majestic mountains, and vast oceans were passed on to the masses for their enjoyment; through these stories, the public developed an interest in faraway places and unknown lands. In other words, the precursor for travel was set in the minds of people.

In Europe, Lord Byron wrote of his travels in poetry. A famous passage from Byron illustrates his strong feelings about nature and echoed the feelings of many artists and writers in the 1800s:

There is a pleasure in the pathless woods,
There is a rapture on the lonely shore,
There is society, where none intrudes,
By the deep sea and music in its roar:
I love not Man the less, but Nature more,
From these our interviews, in which I steal
From all I may be, or have been before,
To mingle with the Universe, and feel
What I can ne'er express, yet cannot all conceal.[12]

For the romantics, nature was difficult to express since it filled one with such joy and mystery. In the United States, writers claimed that the stresses of the city were unhealthy for body and mind; to be closer to God, one needed to be with nature. For the well-off and members of the arts, nature appreciation was a reason to travel, to tour, and to see the landscapes of America and Europe.[13] Through painting and writing, the artists of the romantic period generated an interest in landscapes, primitive peoples and living conditions, and travel for the adventure of it.

Transportation

The most important travel developments during the industrial age occurred in transportation. The expansion of the coach system was as much a by-product of the development of the postal service as it was a response to the increasing demands of tourism and business travel. In England, early attempts to schedule coach service between two cities began around 1669. Nearly 100 years later, England had a fairly comprehensive postal service and a nearly complete coach service between cities.

by 1770

However, not all cities were connected nor was travel easy and convenient. Similar developments in coach travel occurred in America before and after the revolution.

Stagecoach travel required roads and accommodations such as inns where both horses and travelers could eat and rest. The inns of Europe and America had improved since the time of pilgrimages—but not to the point of making a stay a complete pleasure. The accounts of those on the road attest to poor food and occasional rude service. During the late 1700s and early 1800s, the stagecoach ride itself was oppressive. Those who traveled expressed displeasure at the physical abuse they experienced on the hard seats as the coach traveled over the deep holes and ruts in the roads. Schedules were unpredictable, and the time en route was variable. The ride was not only hard on the kidneys, but sometimes uncomfortably hot or cold—depending on the season.

Travel by water offered more alternatives than coach travel, and was considered more pleasurable. Migration by ship to new lands such as Africa, North America, South America, and Asia was well underway in the eighteenth century as England and other European countries expanded their worldwide colonization. England, Spain, France, and the Netherlands sponsored travel on the high seas in search of new trade routes, trade products, and lands to colonize. Travel on the high seas was advancing in terms of technology, safety, speed, and convenience, but even in the 1800s, sea travel was still an ordeal.

In the 1820s, regular ferry service was initiated across the English Channel.[14] Before this time, steamboats traveled on the rivers of France and America. In 1787, a steamboat was tested on the Potomac. This foreshadowed the extensive use of America's waterways as courses of commerce, as boundaries for settlements, and as a relatively smooth means of travel. By 1800, many rivers were essentially the "highways" of the new world.

Travel by ship soon became an important means of travel for the Europeans. Ship travel became a necessity to the expanding European powers who needed to stay in touch with their new colonies. Significant events included regular long-distance service which began in 1838 in England with routes to India and the Far East. In 1840, the Cunard Steamship Company started regular service to America. Postal service needs also pushed the development of reliable transportation.

As the ships plowed the seas, the steam engine made railroads the symbol of mass travel by land. The Liverpool and Manchester Railway opened in England in 1830. In 15 years, rail connected London with several surrounding cities.[15] Railroads were also expanding in America, providing access to the West and to the new states. It is ironic that the very same year the first passenger train began service in England, the Erie Canal opened in America for shipping via water. The canal was developed to transfer goods and people, but soon faced heavy competition from the train which began service in America only five years later. The competition was fierce, but trains soon overtook the canal trade to become a major force in travel and development.

Cook's Tours

The fine art and business skill of developing the inclusive group tour can be credited to Thomas Cook of England. While others may have used the concept earlier,

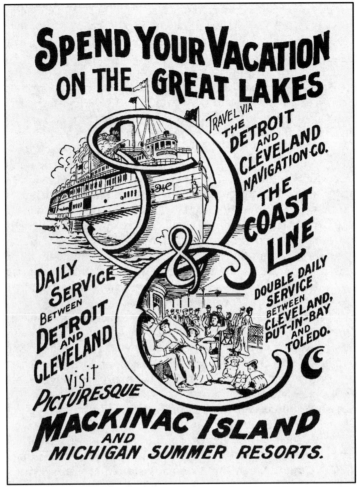

An early advertisement shows the appeal of boat travel for the nineteenth and early twentieth century tourist. (Courtesy of the State Archives of Michigan)

Cook made the group tour a true business venture that appealed to the public. As an active member of the Temperance Society, he put together the first group trip by train in July 1841. He arranged a trip by rail of nearly 600 people to a large temperance meeting—at a reduced rate.

Some four years later, Cook began arranging tours as a commercial business.[16] He began with small tours within England, taking school children, mothers, women, couples, and common people to places they had not been able to visit before the development of the train and inexpensive tours. Cook knew that the newer trains could carry many passengers—and needed to fill their seats to remain profitable. Cook negotiated prices with the rail owners. He then drummed up business by distributing flyers that he had produced through his own printing house.

Cook's success rested in his ability to understand the travel possibilities of his time. He saw the need, the desire, and the motivations for travel—and capitalized on all three through his tours. Cook recognized how new industries were changing the social and economic structure of his day. He saw how people were moving off the land and into the cities for employment and livelihood. He saw how rails and waterways moved manufacturing materials in and out of the cities. And finally, Cook saw how these same rails and waterways could be used to move people.

Cook made travel possible for people with limited opportunities to travel. The person of modest means could take a short trip to a nearby attraction or a destination. At first, the arrival of tourists was a noteworthy event for the host communities. Most communities were unaccustomed to the arrival of so many new people all at once. As one historian writes:

> In a country where the population consisted of small communities that had little contact with each other, the appearance of groups of tourists who had come from hundreds of miles away was amazing, and the citizens of the towns visited would show their astonishment and excitement by turning out in force to see the Cook tourists; waving flags, firing cannons and playing them in with the local brass band.

> Such spectacles as those which greeted Cook's Tours are never likely to be witnessed again, unless we are visited by beings from outer space, and they generated a curiosity and excitement about travel that soon swept through the whole nation.[17]

Services. As part of his service, Cook handled all the matters related to tours such as connections, tickets, and timetables. He handled currency exchanges for trips abroad and even published travel guides and tour timetables at his printing company. Cook also developed the guided—or Cook's—tour which he led himself or delegated to his son. By doing so, Cook developed strong loyalties with his customers. These customers, in turn, would tell friends or relatives about the joys of a **Cook's Tour**. By today's jargon, what Cook had done was to build for himself an effective "word-of-mouth" marketing program.

Not only was Cook sensitive to service, he was also sensitive to providing convenience at a reasonable cost. In the early days of rail, each line was often a separate company with its own schedule and fares. Lines could be short or long, up to but not through a city, or connected with other lines. Cook pulled together the tickets required to complete particular itineraries—sometimes including stage or steamer—and called the package the *Circular Ticket*. Any unused tickets were refunded.

Cook also introduced the *Cook Coupon*. These coupons were used by his tourists for meals and rooms at participating hotels. In 1873, Cook expanded the idea behind the coupon and introduced *Circular Notes*—an early form of the traveler's check.[18] Cook took cash from tourists and issued Circular Notes which the tourists could cash at hundreds of hotels on Cook's list. These notes ensured that the establishments on his list would be patronized by his tours; provided a safe means for tourists to carry funds; and offered a convenient means for tourists to avoid the complications of currency exchanges. At the time he started this practice, Cook had approximately 200 hotels in the program. By 1890, Cook's tours extended across the globe, with nearly 1,000 participating hotels.

(Further Expansion) Cook's desire to make tourism possible for the masses foreshadowed the tourism explosion which occurred over the next 100 years. Cook arranged tours all over the world. His son led the first U.S. tour in 1866. Cook brought travelers from Britain to America and Canada. By 1871, he had established an office in New York. By 1880, he had 60-some offices located around the world.

Cook, his son, and eventually his three grandsons explored the world with tours and tourists, mostly from the middle class. Major events such as world fairs and exhibitions, exotic scenery and cultures, and the romance of travel itself gave his company the corner on the tourism market. Exhibitions in Paris, London, Chicago, and St. Louis became attractions for the Cook's Tour company. In 1872, Cook took his first world tour with 11 tourists. Cook published on-site written accounts of some of these trips in *The Times* newspaper in London—thus giving the masses an even larger window on the world.

Cook conducted one of the first short tours by ship in 1875. He and a small band of tourists went on a seven-day tour in Scandinavia to enjoy the midnight sun of the summer. The tour was appropriately called the "Midnight Sun Voyage." This early sea tour foreshadowed the "cruise" which appeared as a prominent travel choice around the turn of the century. The demand generated by tour companies like Cook's eventually created a competitive atmosphere among luxury ships. The more luxurious ones were commissioned between 1888 and 1896 by several countries including the United States, Britain, and Germany. The competition for speed and luxury continued until World War II.

The Cook's Tours between 1850 and 1900 foreshadowed the true age of travel for the masses. However, it is difficult to say exactly when such tourism and travel truly became available. Certainly, the advent of railroads, large safe ships, and Cook's packaged tours gave millions of middle-class people an opportunity to travel beyond their own communities. A world was now open to the middle class that was once open only to the very rich. But even so, tourism required more than money—it required time. Time has always been a scarce resource for working people—even when money for travel is not an object.

The Emergence of Modern Mass Tourism

A series of key technological, political, and social events during the first 50 years of the twentieth century finally made tourism a major worldwide business and leisure experience for the middle class. While travel was greatly limited during the two world wars, the desire to travel seemed to increase. Following each of these wars, people were anxious to travel and put their wartime anguish and concerns behind them. This suggests that travel increases when conflict subsides and normalcy is re-established between nations.

The two world wars hastened technological advancement—primarily in the interest of weaponry. Some wartime innovations benefited tourism. For example, after World War I, surplus ships were converted to ocean liners—thus prompting the growth of world travel by ship. In 1928, a reported 437,000 Americans sailed abroad.[19] First and second class travel became popular on ships crossing the Atlantic and Pacific. Some have called this period a glorious time for travel—a time that

Group tours by motor coach were a fashionable form of entertainment for the turn-of-the-century sightseer. (Courtesy of the State Archives of Michigan)

reflects the excitement of the 1920s before the stock market crash of 1929 and the Great Depression.

However, it was not so much the economy that reduced sea travel as it was the emergence of the automobile and the airplane. Both became reliable modes of travel for a large middle class—a middle class which had the financial means and leisure time for travel. In this sense, modern **mass tourism** had come into its own.

The Automobile

The automobile is one of the most revolutionary technological advances in the history of travel. Ironically, the first automobiles met with the same disdain as the first trains. Cars were seen as disruptive, dirty, unreliable, and a dead end with respect to travel. Despite these early perceptions, the automobile revolutionized travel and tourism across the world.

As early as 1903, an automobile crossed the United States in 52 days.[20] Although the time was not fast, the trip became a landmark reflecting freedom of choice for the individual traveler. But even more than offering freedom of choice, cars broadened people's worlds. Distance was no longer a huge obstacle for the traveler. And in a sense, cars represented a return to "the familiar." As two researchers observe:

Fortunately for the motorist, the road system has evolved from the unpaved and rutted to the efficient and smooth surfaces of the modern freeway. (Courtesy of the State Archives of Michigan)

Until the eighteenth century the most usual form of transport was the horse, and on horseback nearly all individual travel was performed. Today, when public transport in large vehicles is perfectly familiar, it is easy to overlook the fact that historically the one-man one-vehicle principle predominates. The multi-passenger vehicle is one of the ways in which the modern world differs structurally from its predecessors. With the widespread ownership of cars, there is now a return to the historical norm of individual transport. What needs explaining is not the private car, but the train, the coach, and the aircraft.[21]

More automobile use after World War I generated the need for better roads and accommodations. As local, state, and federal governments began to expand and improve the quality of the road system, accommodations were needed in remote and distant places. Between the world wars, "bungalow camps" surfaced in the United States to serve the needs of the new auto traveler.[22] These wayside camps provided few amenities but, nonetheless, offered a clean bed and the opportunity to freshen up. In Europe, the "holiday camp" served the auto traveler—especially the tourist of modest means. While bungalow camps were simply overnight stops en route to primary destinations, holiday camps were themselves considered primary destinations.[23] The holiday camp provided reasonably priced accommodations, entertainment, and child care. Both the bungalow and holiday camp can be seen as the forerunner of the motor hotel or motel—as well as the reasonably-priced, all-inclusive, entertainment-oriented resort.

The Airplane

The first U.S. crossing by air occurred before World War I in 1911. The trip was long and difficult, taking 82 hours of air time, plus the time to get up and running after several crashes. After the war, the U.S. Army sent a plane cross-country in 1924 in 21 hours and 48 minutes.[24] In England, Cook's travel service offered tours by airplane as early as 1919; business service soon followed. Limited air service began in the United States about the same time. Commercial and personal air travel in the United States received its greatest impetus after Charles Lindbergh crossed the

Campgrounds were popular stopovers for the new auto traveler. (Courtesy of the State Archives of Michigan)

Atlantic in 1927. Following this historic flight, America became serious about air travel for the citizen as well as for the military.

Early air travel was expensive, difficult, and somewhat dangerous. At first, air travel was merely a novelty for the rich. In time, it became the major type of international travel for millions of people. Noticeable changes occurred around 1930 that primed the world for air travel. Planes became larger, the distances between refueling longer, and the services more luxurious. Many flights featured food services, restrooms, and flight attendants.

Novel adaptations of air travel were also explored. The sea plane, which landed on water and crossed the oceans in measured stops for refueling, began regular service in the late 1930s before the war. Among short-term travel innovations were zeppelins—huge airships named after their German designer. These airships flew across Europe and the Atlantic from before World War I up to the 1937 crash of the Hindenburg in New Jersey. The demise of airships can be attributed to World War II and to the development of fast, pressurized, and modern aircraft that could cross oceans without refueling.

Air travel blossomed after World War II. Competition for tourism business required that air travel be as luxurious as travel by train or ship. Planes used for early trans-Atlantic flights were fitted with tables, chairs, and sleeping berths. Food service, sleeping accommodations, and well-appointed cabins were also part of the emerging air travel.

The habits and tastes of a growing motoring public prompted the evolution of roadside inns and motels. (Courtesy of the State Archives of Michigan)

In 1958, two events heralded the age of mass tourism in the international sense: jet travel and "economy" class air travel.[25] National mass tourism was generated by a third event: the boom of prosperity following World War II. Most of America and Europe were now able to take a Sunday drive to visit relatives in the next town, drive to a nearby river or lake for a picnic or outdoor event, or just get on the road and travel. Truly, mass tourism had arrived.

Leisure Time

Historically, holy days created free time for the masses to travel, relax, and be away from work. After World War I, industries within several countries considered granting holidays for their employees. In England, while labor unions were obtaining benefits such as paid holidays, youth movements—such as the Co-operative Holidays Association, and the Workers Travel Association—were organizing for travel to foster personal development and culture.[26] In the United States, the workweek was shrinking, holidays were expanding, and the paid vacation was being considered.

Throughout the history of tourism, the common theme has been that the phenomenon affects the rich first, the middle class second, and the working class third. This theme also applies to the availability of leisure time as well. The public began to travel in earnest when paid vacations and holidays became available for all classes of workers. Throughout the industrial age, workweeks were long and hard with only Sundays off to rest. In the mid- to late-1800s, a laborer could work as many as 60 to 70 hours per week. The 40-hour workweek was not established until the Fair Labor Standards Act in 1938.

By the 1920s, the two-week vacation was being accepted for middle-class workers, but not yet for the working class. In 1968, legislation was passed in the United States for four permanent federal holidays each year. Each holiday was slated to fall on a Monday—thus resulting in a "three-day weekend." In Spain and France, more holidays exist—as many as 12 or 13 per year. And, in some countries, like France, employees have more paid vacations than their counterparts in the United States.

The shorter workweek, paid holidays, and longer vacations were conditions that facilitated mass tourism. In addition, the increase in real incomes for the working and middle class contributed to the arrival of mass leisure and tourism after World War II.

Beyond the 1960s

Travel and tourism has continued its transformation in more recent times. As general travel took off with the airlines in the 1960s, other changes occurred around the world that altered the course of tourism. Two important social and economic events that influenced the world in a dramatic way were the oil crisis of the mid- to late-1970s and the recession of the early 1980s. In each event, travel and tourism were challenged by costs and policy. Potential automobile tourists faced fuel shortages, higher costs at the pump, and the uncertainty of whether fuel would even be available. Needless to say, travel volume diminished in the United States during each of these crises. In addition, U.S. policy addressing fuel shortages was often directly aimed at the leisure use of the automobile, boats, and recreation vehicles. Weekend closing of gas stations and allocation programs fell most heavily upon the tourist.

With the 1979 oil embargo, the world also entered into a recession. Not only were fuel prices high, but so were the costs of many other goods and services—including tourism. Inflation pushed prices higher month by month. The vacation dreamed of during the winter could be beyond reach by the time summer arrived. Many people, too, feared unemployment. This discouraged traveling great distances at high prices. It took several years before people felt confident about traveling again and before tourism recovered from the effects of the recession.

Other major factors and events which shaped tourism in recent years included shifts in tourism policy, advances in technology, and the growth of theme parks.

Tourism Policy. Major shifts in tourism policies occurred in the late 1970s and early 1980s. In 1978, the United States deregulated the airline industry. While no consensus exists on the full benefits or costs of this action, the impacts were felt immediately. For one, large travel markets felt the influences of increased competition. As a result of "fare wars," more flights were available at lower prices. Smaller communities, too, lost air service from the major airlines. This spurred the formation of "commuter" or "feeder" airlines to fill the needs of tourists from remote or smaller population areas. By 1990, many airlines had come and gone. Some fell to bankruptcy, others merged with larger airlines. The jury is still out on how well deregulation actually contributed to airline diversity and competition. Today, a majority of all air travel is controlled by a handful of very large airline companies. Europe, too, is undergoing a deregulation—or liberalization—process.

The U.S. Department of Transportation manages most of the plans and impacts of deregulation. This department, in itself, is relatively new, having been established in 1967 in an effort to put most of the U.S. transportation matters under one agency. In 1985, this agency received the duties and functions of the defunct Civil Aeronautics Board—a government agency which controlled and monitored the air industry through regulated rates and routes.

In another policy move, Congress established the U.S. Travel and Tourism Administration (USTTA) within the Department of Commerce in 1981. This organization replaced the U.S. Travel Service (USTS) which was established in 1961. The USTS had aimed to promote and develop travel to the United States by tourists from abroad. When this unit was replaced by the USTTA and elevated to a higher level in the bureaucracy, it signaled a renewed focus upon international tourism. Although its budgets have traditionally been meager, the USTTA has helped the United States gain exposure in a very competitive travel world. Among the innovative efforts of the USTTA are joint studies with Tourism Canada on specific international tourism markets in eight different countries.

Technology. The last 20 to 30 years have brought dramatic technological changes which have left no sector untouched—including travel and tourism. Advances in aviation and rail have fostered high speed transportation that makes our world seem even smaller. Regularly scheduled commercial flights for supersonic transport (SST) began in Europe in 1976. Air France and British airways found the SST a viable means of transport for jet setters and business travelers. In Europe and Japan, "fast trains" are being planned, developed, and in some instances, in operation. These rail systems will offer an attractive alternative to the congested roads and airports of major European cities—and will play a role in the unified Europe of the 1990s. Advances in architecture have brought new and sophisticated design to hotels. Some hotels boast airy or spacious atriums blended with shopping complexes. More and more, computer electronics are integrated into a property's design and help to increase staff productivity.

Theme Parks. Theme parks have grown and become destinations in and of themselves within the last 20 years. Disney World in Florida is a center of high technology and speaks of the benefits of detailed planning and excellent crowd management. Disney's success in America inspired new Disney parks in Japan and in France. Other parks boomed in the 1970s and 1980s, namely Six Flags, Tampa Gardens, and Cedar Point. Attendance in the nation's national and state park system—as well as independent wilderness areas—peaked in the late 1970s and early 1980s. Much of the interest in the outdoors was fostered by the environmental movement. During this time, the more famous or popular parks took certain measures to deal with the growing number of visitors. For all practical purposes, parks became major tourism destinations for Americans and foreign guests alike.

In summary, the history of tourism is filled with social, economic, and political currents that move the industry forward. Central to understanding tourism's history are the mix of people's motivations and the availability of attractions. Travel patterns change with the times, technology, and policies, but do not stop. The spark of adventure first experienced by prehistoric travelers has been passed from the visitors to the Nile, to pilgrims and crusaders, to the first tourists on a Cook's tour, and on to the modern day traveler who enjoys the luxury of cruising or flying by supersonic jet.

Endnotes

1. J. E. Spencer and W. L. Thomas, *Introducing Cultural Geography* (New York: Wiley, 1973), p. 66.
2. The Queensbury Group, *The Book of Key Facts* (New York: Paddington Press Ltd., 1978), p. 6.
3. C. Harold King, Arthur J. May, and Arnold Fletcher, *A History of Civilization: The Story of Our Heritage* (New York: Scribner, 1969), p. 43.
4. Maxine Feifer, *Going Places: The Ways of the Tourist from Imperial Rome to the Present Day* (London: Macmillan London Ltd., 1985), p. 7.
5. Feifer, p. 12.
6. Judith Adler, "Youth on the Road: Reflections on the History of Tramping," *Annals of Tourism Research* 12 (1985): p. 338.
7. Feifer, p. 34.
8. John Towner, "Approaches to Tourism History," *Annals of Tourism Research* 15(1) (1988): p. 301.
9. Towner, p. 323.
10. Horace Sutton, *Travelers: The American Tourist from Stagecoach to Space Shuttle* (New York: Morrow, 1980), pp. 11–34.
11. Sutton, pp. 29–30.
12. From Lord Byron's "Childe Harold's Pilgrimage—A Romaunt," from Canto VI, 178. As it appears in M.H. Abrams, General ed., *The Norton Anthology of English Literature—* rev. ed., Vol. 2 (New York: Norton, 1968), p. 315.
13. Roderick Nash, *Wilderness and the American Mind*, 3d ed. (New Haven: Yale University Press, 1982), p. 44.
14. J. Christopher Holloway, *The Business of Tourism*, 2d ed. (Estover, Plymouth, England: Macdonald and Evans Ltd., 1983), p. 32.
15. A. J. Burkart and S. Medlik, *Tourism: Past, Present, and Future* (London: Heinemann, 1984), p. 12.
16. Edmund Swinglehurst, *Cook's Tours: The Story of Popular Travel* (Dorset, U.K.: Blandford Press, 1982), p. 15.
17. Swinglehurst, p. 17.
18. Swinglehurst, p. 25; 65.
19. Sutton, p. 134.
20. Sutton, pp. 100–115.
21. Burkart and Medlik, p. 7.
22. Sutton, p. 148.

23. Holloway, p. 35; 42.
24. Sutton, p. 128; 158.
25. Sutton, p. 247; 248.
26. Swinglehurst, p. 151.

Key Terms

Cook's Tour
The Crusades
The Grand Tour
mass tourism
Middle Ages
Neolithic age

Paleolithic age
pilgrimage
The Renaissance
romanticism
specialization of labor

Discussion Questions

1. What discoveries broadened the range of prehistoric travel?

2. What innovations from the Neolithic age affected the nature of travel?

3. What conditions stimulated the development of pleasure and religious travel in the Greek and Roman empires? Who was most able to participate in these forms of early travel?

4. How did religious beliefs and practices affect travel in the Middle Ages? What were the two major activities of this period?

5. What was the Grand Tour?

6. How did advances in transportation affect travel in the industrial age?

7. What services and approaches to travel contributed to the success of Cook's Tours?

8. What key technological events in the first 50 years of the twentieth century made tourism a major worldwide business?

9. What key labor trends and legislation facilitated mass tourism in the twentieth century?

10. What major shifts in tourism policy in the 1970s and 1980s continue to affect travel today?

REVIEW QUIZ

When you feel you have covered all of the material in this chapter, answer these questions. Choose the *best* answer. Check your answers with the correct ones found on the Review Quiz Answer Key at the end of this book.

True (T) or False (F)

T F 1. Most people traveled by horse during the Paleolithic age.

T F 2. The security of the growing agriculture communities fostered the exchange of foods, artifacts, and materials.

T F 3. The earliest foot trails became the basis for extensive road systems.

T F 4. The purpose of the Crusades was to regain the Holy Land from the Christians.

T F 5. Crossing the Alps did not pose much of a major obstacle for Grand Tour travelers.

T F 6. Stagecoach rides were generally comfortable, efficient, and predictable.

T F 7. By today's jargon, what Cook did for himself was to build an effective "word-of-mouth" marketing program.

T F 8. One of the earliest methods of flying over the Atlantic was by a huge airship called the zeppelin.

T F 9. Shorter workweeks, paid holidays, and longer vacations were conditions that hindered the growth of mass tourism.

T F 10. Among the efforts of the United States Travel and Tourism Administration are joint studies with Canada on international tourism markets.

Alternate/Multiple Choice

11. In the Middle Ages, _____ became the central religious force throughout Europe.

   a. paganism
   b. Roman Catholicism

12. The very same year the first passenger train began service in England:

   a. the Erie Canal opened in America.
   b. the steam engine was developed.

13. The availability of leisure time, which permitted more time to travel, affected the _____ first.

   a. rich
   b. middle class

14.   Which of the following countries sponsored travel on the high seas in search of new trade routes, products, and lands?

    a. England
    b. Spain
    c. France
    d. all of the above

15.   Cook developed an early form of the traveler's check called:

    a. Circular Notes.
    b. Cook Coupons.
    c. Circular Tickets.
    d. Circular Coupons.

Chapter Outline

Tourism as Behavior
Perception
    The Action of Perception
    General Perceptual Principles
    Elements of Perception
    Environmental Perception
    Social Perception
Attitudes
    Affective Component
    Cognitive Component
    Behavioral Component
    Stereotypes
    Attitudes and Persuasion
    Attitudes and Tourism Development

Learning Objectives

1. Define psychology and how it relates to the study of travel and tourism.

2. Compare the internal and external forces which influence the traveler and travel decisions.

3. Explain the process of perception and identify nine general perceptual principles.

4. Describe three fundamental elements involved in perception.

5. Distinguish between environmental perception and social perception.

6. Explain how three forms of social perception—impression formation, verbal and non-verbal cues, and attribution—affect tourism.

7. Describe the three basic components which constitute attitudes.

8. Analyze how stereotypes can affect a tourism destination and its tourists.

9. Identify the variables which contribute to the effectiveness of a persuasive message.

10. Point out why attitudes are becoming a major focus in the study of travel and tourism.

2

Psychological Dimensions: Perception and Attitudes

Scholars of various disciplines have studied tourism from a number of angles. Many of these studies are economic-based, involving counts of people, travel patterns, or expenditures. While such counts are valuable to the agencies or countries involved, they shed little light on the psychology of tourism. Twenty thousand people may attend a festival and spend thousands of dollars. But knowing "how many" and "how much" does not reveal "why" people traveled to the festival—or if they were satisfied with their experiences.

Psychology is the study of human behavior, or more specifically, the study of thoughts, feelings, and actions of the individual.[1] Day-to-day experiences reveal just how diverse human behavior can be. The process of getting to work or school on time involves a complex set of behaviors which occur within a fast-changing set of circumstances. For example, driving in traffic involves observing and responding to traffic lights, other motorists, the weather, and road conditions. Maneuvering through the streets entails putting thousands of decisions into action through coordinated hand and eye movements. While these actions may interest the psychologist concerned with hand and eye coordination, little is revealed about what prompted the person to go out the door in the first place.

A knowledge of psychology basics can contribute to understanding travel and tourism behavior. The psychology of tourism relates to individual travelers. Individuals make travel decisions based on a complex and interrelated set of personal, social, and environmental factors. This chapter examines two psychological dimensions of tourism—perception and attitudes.

Tourism as Behavior

Tourism is a purposeful, planned, and motivated **behavior**. The central character is the tourist—a person engaged in travel. A model of the forces influencing the individual can be seen in Exhibit 1. In this model, the travel decision-maker is subject to psychological, social, cultural, and environmental forces. Travel decisions are influenced most directly by internal factors.

As the model shows, *internal forces* are often considered *part* of the person. In contrast, *external forces* exist *outside* the person. Most people are born into external situations such as a social class or a particular culture. Little can be done to change external forces. Both internal and external forces can influence the traveler and his/her subsequent decisions. Internal forces include attitudes, values, perception,

Exhibit 1   Influences Upon the Travel Decision-Maker

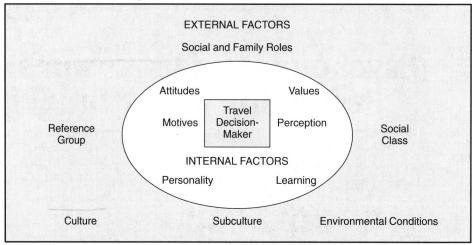

Based on Edward J. Mayo, Jr. and Lance P. Jarvis, *The Psychology of Leisure Travel: Effective Marketing and Selling of Travel Services* (Boston, Mass.: CBI Publishing Company, Inc., 1981), p. 20.

learning, personality, and motives. External forces which shape travel include social and family roles, social class, environmental conditions, the surrounding culture and subculture, and reference groups.

All these factors interact in complex ways to shape travel and tourism behavior. As an example, consider a person from an urban background whose lifestyle revolves around drama and art. This individual is more likely to visit the theater while vacationing in London than an individual from a rural area who has had little or no exposure to drama and no interest in it. The selection of accommodations is another case in point. As a traveler learns more about the rates and amenities of certain hotels, the type of hotel he/she chooses may vary depending upon the purpose of the trip. In other words, social, developmental, and learning experiences interact with personal preferences in the decision-making process.

Perception

While observing and recognizing a building or another person may seem like a simple act, it is actually a complicated process—the eyes respond to the configuration of light reflected from the object. The sensory stimuli are then passed along to the brain for interpretation. Translating sensory data into meaningful information that can be used and acted upon is the process of **perception**. Through perception we make sense of the world.

The Action of Perception

Perception is an active process. People do not merely passively receive sensory input from the environment, they actively seek it out. For example, people explore their neighborhoods, communities, and other countries for new and different information. The types of information obtained depend on the situation or

[handwritten margin notes:] Perceptions 100% your reality

Influences - personal experiences cultural backrounds, Training.

Social norms.

A person's perception of a dining establishment will be shaped by learning, experience, and the service itself.

environment in which perception takes place, as well as the perceiver's personality, motivations, and social background.

Perception is not only active, it is selective. Of all the information that is potentially available, only a portion of it is useful or meaningful at any one time. Perception is influenced by learning and past experience. Over time, a person develops ways of perceiving the world. As a perceiver learns more about a person or a situation, perceptions become keener. Consider how someone might learn about dining in fine restaurants. At first the subtleties of the service, the menu, and the meal are lost on the novice. With time, the person learns what to look for. In fact, this same person might, over time, become a connoisseur of fine dining, able to detect spices and seasonings that go unnoticed by those with less experience. Learning and experience also guide perceptions of hotels and related travel services. With more experience, people are able to differentiate between quality and "merely average" accommodations.

General Perceptual Principles

Early studies revealed general principles that operate during the perceptual process. Travel and tourism professionals use these same principles in designing attractions and properties, marketing, quality control, and pricing. Several of these principles are discussed in the following sections.[2]

Sensory Adaptation. People get used to stimuli, events, and objects that they see or experience repeatedly. Getting used to things and taking them for granted is called sensory adaptation. In many ways, this process drives the tourism industry to find and offer new attractions, events, packages, destinations, and experiences. Hotels across the country are constantly changing packages, rates, amenities, room design,

---

34 *Chapter 2*

Exhibit 2   Context Effect

A	B	C	D	E	F
11	12	13	14	15	16

Source: Terrell G. Williams, *Consumer Behavior: Fundamentals and Strategies* (St. Paul, Minn.: West Publishing Co., 1982), p. 65.

and on-site activities in order to counter the public's tendency to do the "same old thing." While sensory adaptation is not the sole reason for changes in business strategies, it is a perceptual reality that the tourism profession should appreciate.

Color and Contrast. One way to deal with sensory adaptation is to change the stimulus and offer something "new." People are sensitive to colors and particularly to bright colors, contrasts, and unusual arrangements. If something stands out, a person is more likely to notice it. In advertising, it is suggested that color advertisements draw more attention than black and white. On the other hand, a black and white ad may draw attention when positioned among color advertisements. Tourism promotions frequently apply the concept of contrast. Consider the effect of a promotional piece that features warm beach scenes—particularly one that runs in publications distributed in the Northern United States during the winter.

Context. Through learning and experience, a person develops expectations about what things go together. If you are going to a movie, you expect to view a film on a big screen in a darkened auditorium while snacking on popcorn or candy. In the same way, a guest expects certain amenities and services from a hotel. A guest, however, would not expect the same level of service or the same amenities from a seaside resort, a campground, and a restaurant.

The role of context is important in understanding the world. Context is the setting or the interrelated conditions in which something exists or occurs. Context sets up expectations and perceptions. Certain things are expected to go together. When expectations are broken, it can lead to disorientation. Exhibit 2 demonstrates the principle of simple visual context. In the top row of the exhibit, a graphic is seen as the letter B when it appears within the context of the alphabet. Now look at the second row in the exhibit. That same graphic appears as the number 13 when it is placed within a familiar series of numbers. Note again that the graphic details of the B and the 13 are exactly the same. The interpretation of what the graphic stands for is based entirely upon the context in which it appears.

The hotel stay has become an experience that carries a number of expectations—particularly in terms of amenities. Millions of tourists now expect lodging operations to provide a phone, television, personal hygiene items, and in some markets, a free morning paper, complimentary breakfast, and drinks during the late afternoon cocktail hour. Indeed, the industry has established these expectations. More than 40% of U.S. hotels have the following services available above and beyond the phone and television: bathroom amenities, free parking, dry cleaning, audiovisual equipment for business meetings, outdoor pool, transportation to the airport, a newsstand, gift shop, multilingual staff, and auto rental services.[3] These expectations become the norm and establish the context for a hotel stay. Should the context be changed, the perception of the property and the service would be altered—and occupancy and repeat business could be affected.

Figure-Ground. To viewers, some objects are more important than others in the surrounding environment. Like a camera, a person will focus upon a particular object within his/her field of vision and blur others into the background. In advertising, it is important that the perceiver be able to differentiate between the foreground and background. A tourism promotion may paint a tantalizing picture of beach life but may obscure the actual name and location of the resort if the ad is not produced properly.

Closure. Closure refers to the tendency we have as perceivers to complete an image if only part of it is present. Partial pictures of something familiar like a cat will be seen as a cat even though the drawing or artwork may not be complete. As perceivers, we strive for a complete, comprehensive picture of our world and go the next step of completing it if need be.

Consider how some tourism advertisements do not provide details of a property's interior. Often it is enough to show the beautiful exterior, the lovely natural surroundings, and the exquisite service at the poolside. The viewer automatically assumes that the rooms, lobby, and dining areas are of similar quality. Here, the implied message of complete quality is provided by the viewer through the perceptual process of closure.

Proximity. Objects, events, or actions occurring closely in time or appearing together are assumed to be related in some way. This perceptual principle helps to organize the world, but can lead to faulty conclusions. Association does not prove that things are truly related or connected. For example, we may learn in school that when the bell rings, students enter the classroom and class begins. Mere association may suggest that the bell brings students into the classroom. But, in reality, other motivations—not the bell—prompt the student to attend the class.

Proximity means closeness—or the quality or state of being very near or close. Proximity is used as a perceptual principle in tourism promotions. The tourist is often portrayed as enjoying scenery, attractions, and companionship while in exotic places. The proximity of the tourist to a resort or setting implies that the resort and setting creates the sense of enjoyment. In reality, a host of factors—including the resort—contribute to enjoyment.

Perceptual Constancy. People have the ability to view an object as the same object even though the actual stimulus may be changing. For example, if the amount of light falling on the surface of a red table cloth is reduced, we still see the cloth as red just as we saw it as red in the full light of day. This ability is referred to as color constancy. Constancy applies to size, brightness, form, and movement. Through our perceptual processes we are able to see the same object in bright light or shadows, while moving or still, and from a distance or up close. The variations of sensory stimuli do not alter our interpretation of the same target.

Selective perception allows people to carry on one-on-one conversations even in large groups. (Courtesy of Disneyland Hotel, Anaheim, California)

Selective Perception. Perception is selective for many reasons, including the perceiver's inability to cope with all the information in the environment. The perceiver screens out or selects specific types of information due to motivations, experiences, or cultural history. Perceivers regularly select or ignore information as needed. Some go so far as to selectively ignore negative information about themselves. A party is a common experience at which a great deal of selective perception occurs. Here we see a room full of people and many one-on-one conversations taking place. Without selective perception, it would be impossible for a person to have a discussion with just one other person.

Selective perception applies to tourism as well. Consider the situation in which a tourist chooses a less-than-perfect destination. After the commitment is made—and after the traveler arrives—the tourist may ignore the negative side of the accommodations, amenities, or service through the process of selective perception. This way, the trip may be seen as successful in the mind of the perceiver.

Weber/Fechner Law. An interesting perceptual "law" discovered a century ago was that people's perception of change was relative to the amount of the initial stimulus. If a person was used to seeing a room with one light on, only a small amount of extra light would have to be added before the person would say that the illumination in the room increased. On the other hand, if the room was very well lit, the amount of additional light required for the person to notice a difference would be larger. In other words, to notice a difference in a stimulus (light, weight, smell, or taste), the amount of change required is relative to the amount of initial stimulus that the person was familiar with or was judging. This is called the Weber/Fechner law of different thresholds.

Although it is often overlooked, this principle has many potential applications in travel and tourism. One obvious situation is pricing. If a property owner wants to increase the price for rooms, the amount that will be tolerated and noticed is dependent to some extent upon the original price. Large increases are resisted to some degree by the market, but resistance can be stronger when original prices were small to begin with.

Elements of Perception

The fundamental elements involved in perception are the perceiver, the target, and the situation. For our purposes, the perceiver is a person. This person could be a tourist, a guest, a hotel employee, or a local resident in a tourist community. Since people are involved in perception, the characteristics of the individual influence the resulting perceptions. A person's experiences, cultural background, training, social norms, and personal preferences can influence perception. Motivations, for example, can shape how a restaurant server perceives and responds to guests. If the server needs money or wants to advance within the organization, each guest could represent a source of income or an aid to career development and personal success. Another server may perceive guests as just another source of work to avoid or ignore. These different perceptions will have very different outcomes for the restaurant and the tourist.

The target of perception can be almost anything—other people, a beach, a resort, a hotel, a whole island, a city, or the pencil on your desk. Like the perceiver, the target has characteristics that influence perception. Characteristics may be the scenery at a resort, the color and composition of a travel advertisement, the personality of the taxi driver, or the colors and design of a hotel lobby. People and large-scale environments as targets of perception will be discussed in more detail later in this chapter.

The situation refers to the context in which perception takes place. A physical situation could be a room, church, hotel, taxi cab, or the edge of the Grand Canyon. Perception takes place within social situations as well. Social situations are as varied as physical settings. The tones of social situations fall within a wide range of human emotions. Imagine the differences in perceptions which can occur under the influences of anger, sadness, excitement, or happiness. The perceived notes of the church organ at a funeral are very different from those at a wedding—and these perceptions go beyond the meanings of the words or nature of the music played.

Tourism offers a unique and varied range of situations for perceptions. Consider the different perceptions you might have when reviewing a travel brochure in a travel agency or in the comfort of your own home. Consider, too, how the perceptions of family members while having dinner together on vacation might compare with their perceptions while having dinner together at home. As a final example, imagine yourself in a familiar room among friends, relatives, and neighbors. Here, the perception you have about a neighbor who is an airline pilot is one thing. The next day when you board that neighbor's jet to embark on a vacation, the situation is very different—and your perceptions will be different as well.

Environmental Perception

Early studies of perceptual processes focused upon how people came to know objects as meaningful things. In reality, people move about in large-scale environments that are both familiar and novel. A holistic approach which considers perception of the larger environment is called **environmental perception**. Environmental perception is ongoing and applies to environments from all parts of life including neighborhoods, our home, travel destinations, and tourism attractions.

The characteristics of the environment and how they are perceived make environmental perception directly applicable to the study of travel and tourism. Environments surround, demand participation, engage a person's senses, and involve a social and aesthetic atmosphere.[5] In other words, a person becomes actively involved in a setting when he/she moves through an environment. The entirety of a tourist attraction—such as a beach resort—is not perceived at a glance but through exploration. The experiences a guest has with the resort's facilities, activities, employees, and other guests will influence how the guest perceives the resort's style, service, and ambience. The physical and natural resources surrounding the resort also contribute to the guest's perception. Rooms with a spectacular view of the ocean at sunset or mountains in the morning mist are more than "nice rooms with a view at a reasonable rate." The total image, feeling, atmosphere, and quality implied in such a room is what counts—and is essentially what the tourist pays for.

Environmental perception is closely tied to land use, planning, tourism development, and tourism destination preferences.

Social Perception

The perception of other people is formally called **social perception**. Like perception in general, the same sense organs are at work, but the target now is another person. Since we are social beings, other people are among the most powerful stimuli we encounter on a daily basis.

Much of what goes into the tourism experience is dependent upon social interaction. While the travel experience may be personal, the activity itself usually involves social contact. People travel together and interact with other tourists, local citizens, and service employees on airlines and in hotels. Tourism is made possible through the efforts of many individuals behind the scenes making sure that the service—be it air travel, hotel accommodations, or some other recreational activity—is carried out to the tourist's satisfaction. From the perspective of the tourist, face-to-face interactions generate the experience, the impressions, and the perceptions of quality.

The perceptions we have of people are somewhat different from those we have of objects like trees or pencils. Like objects, people present an array of physical characteristics to be perceived and analyzed. In addition, people display overt behavior which has to be interpreted. What is interesting and important is that the perceiver goes beyond the physical data presented by the person and makes

The employees of hospitality operations are links in a traveler's chain of first impressions.

inferences about the person's motives, intentions, background, and personality. By observing behavior, the perceiver develops impressions and infers what the person is really like inside.

Researchers have outlined several unique characteristics of social perception.[6] First, as social objects of perception, people are centers of action and intention. Second, what we know about a person is only partially revealed by external characteristics and behaviors. A person's appearance yields some information, but does not reveal what a person is truly like inside. Third, the target of perception is similar to the perceiver—each is a human being. This, of course, may cause the "target" to alter his/her behaviors because of the mere presence of the perceiver. Further, the perceiver may interact with the target, causing his/her perception to change.

Finally, much of what we infer about others is based upon selective perceptions. Knowing very little about a person generates a number of assumptions. **Attribution** helps the perceiver make sense out of the actions of others. Seeing a person drinking water allows one to assume that the other person is thirsty. If a person appears friendly, the perceiver often assumes that this person is warm and congenial, and would be worthwhile to visit with again. Yet often, so little information is actually exchanged that assumptions can be inaccurate. The following sections discuss impression formation, verbal and non-verbal cues, and attribution in more detail.

Impression Formation. What a person thinks about another after a first encounter is a **first impression**. Many first encounters are brief and permit only limited information to be exchanged between people. These exchanges, however, form impressions that people use to make important subsequent decisions. In our daily lives, we may decide not to pursue a friendship with another individual due to a first impression, or a first impression may be so positive that a friendship develops immediately.

A vacation or business trip is often a long series of first impressions. Encounters may begin with the taxi driver that takes the tourist to the airport. From this point on, no fewer than 10 to 15 brief social exchanges will occur between leaving home and turning on the television set in the hotel room. Imagine it: after the taxi driver, there are airline ticket counterpersons, security and gate personnel, airline hosts, fellow passengers, baggage assistants, another taxi or van driver, hotel baggage assistants,

Exhibit 3   Communication and Non-Verbal Cues

Category	Examples
Physical	
Body	Color of hair, attractiveness
Appearance	Dress, uniform, makeup, hairstyle
Kinesic Cues	
Gestures	Shaking head, thumbs up, fidgeting
Postures	Arms folded, slouching, standing
Gaze	Staring, eye contact
Facial	Frown, smile
Touch	Kiss, slap, handshake
Paralanguage	Tone of voice, mumbling, scream
Proxemics	Seating arrangements, spacing at party

Adapted from *Social Psychology* by Donelson Forsyth (Pacific Grove, Calif.: Brooks/Cole, 1987), p. 101.

and finally registration staff. Each social interaction generates impressions of the person and also of the business and service the person represents. These impressions are the result of perception. The exchange can be seen as positive, neutral, or negative. In the case of travel—especially vacation travel—positive exchanges enhance the travel experience and the value of the vacation. Negative encounters detract from the vacation experience and, of course, reflect poorly upon the service staff and the business.

Recently, service encounters have received extensive attention by experts concerned with the quality of service provided by different businesses across the world. For now, it is important to note that these service encounters generate impressions based upon verbal and non-verbal cues.

Verbal and Non-Verbal Cues. In social exchanges, people provide perceptual information through **verbal** and **non-verbal cues**. Verbal cues include the tone and method of speech delivery as well as the content. Non-verbal cues include dress, personal appearance, hand gestures, body movement, stance, and facial expressions.

A summary of the different types of information obtained in a social exchange can be seen in Exhibit 3. The table shows that a person provides information to another through various non-verbal channels. Some of these are related to physical traits such as ethnicity, height, weight, and attractiveness. Others relate to how people alter their appearance through dress, makeup, and hair style. In tourism, some of these variables are controlled through the use of required uniforms.

The table also shows several kinesic cues that provide information to the observer. **Kinesics** involves the study of the relationship between communication and non-verbal body motions such as blushes, shrugs, and eye movements. Facial expressions and hand motions are very powerful and common components of any social exchange. Additional kinesic cues provide information about feelings, attitudes, and personal disposition. How often have you seen someone trying to "stare down" the ticket agent in an effort to get relief from a scheduling problem? These non-verbal cues send strong messages to another about how one feels and reacts to a situation.

Related to kinesic cues are **proxemic** cues—or the spatial orientation of individuals in social and interpersonal situations. In the same heated argument at the ticket counter, the parties are usually standing very close together—sometimes even leaning across the desk in a face-off. The use of proxemics are common in both positive and negative social exchanges. In contrast to the ticket counter event, consider how a couple might sit very close together as they fly off to their honeymoon retreat.

Finally, our voices carry more information than just the meaning of the words. It is *how* something is said that adds extra meaning to the words. These paralanguage cues are subtle but influential. The tone of voice we use is monitored closely by those with whom we interact. People are adept at using such cues to defy or to enhance the true meaning of the spoken word. If the hotel clerk says "thanks for staying" and accompanies the phrase with a smile, eye contact, and pleasing tone of voice, the feeling of sincerity is transmitted.

Through verbal and non-verbal channels the tourist—or perceiver—comes to understand the message another is trying to convey. Accuracy can be a problem since non-verbal cues such as appropriate social distance can vary from country to country. For the most part, the result of an encounter will be an impression that lingers and influences later decisions and perceptions. First impressions are accumulative and become integrated components of a person's past experience. In the case of tourism, if most of the accumulated experiences are developed through brief first impressions, then negative experiences and misinterpretation can be a problem. Negative encounters can result in the perceiver assigning dubious traits to the company or hotel itself through the process of attribution.

Attribution. Attribution is a pervasive, common activity that people use to understand the behaviors of others and themselves in a range of situations. It is central to quality control of service in the tourism industry. Take the case of a rude hotel employee behind the registration desk. If lines are long and everyone seems to be pressed for time, a bit of rudeness could be understood and possibly tolerated. The curtness of people behind the desk might be further explained if the manager comes out to help and points out that the staff has volunteered to stay on extra time to help with the crowds. Given these circumstances, the tourist might attribute the employee's rude behavior to fatigue. The tourist, too, may respect the hotel for the good intentions of the staff and the manager. For the most part, the situation, circumstances, and social pressures explain the unfolding behavior. Tourists, in this instance, will probably assign neutral to positive attributes to the hotel and staff even though negative exchanges occurred.

Now consider the same situation with a few additional variables. This time, the manager does not appear to help out. The tourist is mildly offended by the brusque treatment received from front desk staff. Yet, because of the pressure of the long lines and the late hour, the tourist can still understand a bit of rudeness. This same tourist then seeks information about the city from the information desk.

Here, the tourist is treated rudely again—even though the desk is not busy. Now, the tourist's attribution about the staff and the hotel turns sour. The rude treatment at the information desk could not be explained by external circumstances. Most likely, the tourist will not return to the property again—or, if the case may be, to others in the chain.

In these brief examples, the behavior and circumstances started out the same. However, in the second scenario, the tourist had the opportunity to further interact with hotel staff at the information desk. In terms of social perception, the tourist gained consistent information (rudeness) across two different situations (the busy front desk and the quiet information desk)—which led the tourist to attribute negative characteristics to the staff and the hotel.

These encounters illustrate the effect that timing and context can have on impression formation. In many situations, more importance is placed on information gained early on than on information received later. In psychological terms, this is called the *primacy effect*. If more importance is placed on information received later than on information received early on, it is called the *recency effect*. Generally, primacy effects are more influential than recency effects.[7]

With travel, there is generally no "second chance" to fix a negative exchange by providing a new and better exchange later on. Industry employees should strive to make that good impression on the tourist in each and every encounter.

Attitudes

Central to preference, feelings, and actions is the concept of attitudes. In daily usage, the concept of an attitude may be familiar, but its meaning is complex. **Attitudes** are intellectual, emotional, and behavioral responses to events, things, and persons which people learn over time.[8] A common view suggests that attitudes are composed of at least three components: affective, cognitive, and behavioral.[9]

Affective Component

The affective component refers to a person's emotional response to an object or process. Emotions may be strong or weak, positive or negative. Liking, loving, and caring are positive emotions which can vary in strength. Fear is unpleasant and can be very powerful. For example, a person could say that "I am afraid of flying on large jets," or "I dislike the way my baggage is being handled in airports these days." These are emotional responses toward an object or process—both negative. An example of a positive response might be "I love vacationing on Cancun."

Cognitive Component

The cognitive component of attitudes refers to beliefs—assumed facts about an attitude target. Beliefs represent knowledge about most anything—hotel clerks, a theme park, a vacation destination, or a mode of transportation. A person who fears flying could state: "I believe that flying on large jets is dangerous." Such a person may have a collection of beliefs about flying that form part of the foundation for this attitude. Cognitions could include not only assumptions of risk and

Exhibit 4   Percent Change in U.S. Vacation Travel

Time Period	Predicted Increase	Actual
Summer 1988	3%	9%
Summer 1987	4%	4%
Summer 1986	5%	4%
Summer 1985	5%	2%

Based upon data from U.S. Travel Data Center, "Summer Vacation Travel Forecast," *Special Studies in Travel Economics and Marketing* (Washington, D.C.: U.S. Travel Data Center, selected years—1989, 1988, 1986).

danger, but beliefs about inferior jet motor production, poorly trained pilots, and overworked air traffic controllers. All these beliefs shape the resulting attitude toward flying.

Behavioral Component

Finally, the behavioral component refers to the person's actual behavior *or* intended behavior regarding the attitude's target. For tourism, it is what the potential traveler actually does that is important. In the previous example, the person may decide not to travel by jet for vacation or business. In the end, this person may elect to use trains and automobiles whenever possible; if a plane is required, a propeller plane may be the only type that will be tolerated. Furthermore, this person could state that he/she will not travel by jet even if safety records improve. This latter statement is a behavioral intention.

It would be convenient for students of marketing and tourism if attitudes were excellent predictors of behavior. Attitudes *do* predict behavior under certain circumstances. The relationship is rarely one-to-one, but nonetheless, a relationship has been found. Consumer behavior studies illustrate the complexities of this relationship. Among the findings are:[10]

1. Attitudes can best predict consumption when the attitude is specifically related to a particular product (a watch) and behavior (purchasing a watch). Panel studies reveal that attitudes are good predictors when consumers are asked to state intended purchase behavior toward a specific product.

2. Many factors can intervene between the attitude and behavior and negate the predictive relationship. For example, an unexpected price increase in a product or service can change a consumer's attitude toward that product or service.

Attitudes and behavioral intentions can be of value in predicting travel and tourism behaviors. The U.S. Travel Data Center (USTDC) conducts a survey each spring to predict the volume of summer travel. Exhibit 4 compares the predicted and the actual percent change in summer travel for a four-year period. For the most part, the predictions—which are based upon attitudes and behavioral intentions—have been quite accurate. The USTDC predicted a 4% increase in travel for the summer of 1987. Subsequent analysis of the 1987 summer travel revealed that, indeed, summer travel was up 4%.[11] In the spring of 1986, the USTDC predicted that the summer vacation volume would be up 5% for the summer months of June, July, and August. An analysis of vacation travel during that time indicated that vacation volume did, in fact, increase 4%.[12] In 1985, predictions were at 5%.[13] Actual travel turned out to be 2%—which is still a reasonable prediction.

The 1988 summer vacation season reminds us how attitudes and behavioral intentions do not always correspond one-to-one. The predicted increase in summer travel was 3%. This prediction was based on the reported intentions of the surveyed potential travelers and an analysis of the U.S. economic conditions at the time. The outcome for the summer revealed an increase of nearly 9%—a difference somewhat larger than those of recent years. The 1988 summer travel season followed the stock market crash of late 1987 which undercut consumer confidence. This major event on Wall Street may have depressed people's future travel plans. In addition, analysts were cautious about the consumer through the first part of 1988. By the time summer rolled around, consumer confidence regained its strength and travel rebounded.

Predictions for travel as well as for the purchase of durable consumer goods cannot ignore the role of unexpected economic or pricing effects. The recession of the late 1970s and early 1980s had a depressing effect upon travel. After the recession, people did begin to vacation again, but the return to the level known in the late 1970s was slow in coming. It was not that people had turned away from travel. Rather, the purchase of durable goods which had been postponed during the recession placed a demand on discretionary dollars that could have been used for travel.[14] After the pent-up demand for these goods had been satisfied, travel began to recover and increased during the second half of the 1980s.

Stereotypes

As we have seen, tourists and residents of tourism communities have very strong perceptions about each other. These perceptions are part of the complex interaction between the host and the guest. Perceptions and attitudes can be positive and caring, or sometimes negative and hostile. Perceptions generate impressions which foster strong beliefs about others. These beliefs, as part of an attitude, can often become **stereotypes.**

Stereotypes are characteristics which people assign to a certain type of person, a group, or a set of objects. Stereotypes have been applied to people on the bases of race, sex, religious belief, group affiliation, manner of dress, and physical characteristics. Stereotypes have also been applied to behavioral roles, such as the role of children, mothers, and fathers. Stereotypes are often negative, inaccurate, and the result of overly simplified attempts to place people, objects, or groups into categories.

Stereotypes can lead to discrimination and defamatory behavior—in school, at work, in government, or in tourist settings. In the case of tourism, stereotypes develop for tourists and hosts alike. In Michigan, for example, visitors to the northern parts of the state during the summer are referred to as "fudgies"—a stereotype for summer tourists who visit the many fudge shops in tourist-oriented communities. In Arizona and Florida, winter visitors are called "snowbirds"—a label for the non-residents visiting those sunny states. In reverse, tourists have stereotypes for the hosts in particular countries or regions. Consider how many times you've heard a destination called a "tourist trap." This label certainly carries a negative connotation that may not be totally accurate.

Stereotyping involves more than labeling persons, groups, or tourists. Behaviors toward the target group are often discriminatory, condescending, rude, and sometimes directly hostile. Avoidance is another behavioral by-product of stereotypes. Since the people holding stereotypes are the ones most likely to avoid the target group, it becomes very difficult to foster interaction which could change perceptions and the faulty stereotype itself.[15] In sum, stereotypes are very resistant to change and modification.

Attitudes and Persuasion

New and different information influences what we believe and the attitudes that we hold. Attitudes can be changed through **persuasion.** Attempts to influence people through the media, personal communication, or advertising are examples of persuasion. Information is used in a manner designed to convince others to change their attitudes toward some object, person, or event.

The effectiveness of the persuasive message is dependent to a great extent on the source or communicator. Persuasive attempts made by family or friends are usually stronger than those made by strangers. Personal sources are seen as more believable and trustworthy. Communicators who are perceived as friendly and likable can be more influential than those who are perceived as disagreeable and rude. Also, individuals perceived as similar to oneself can be more effective in changing attitudes than individuals perceived as dissimilar. Tourism advertisements sometimes depict the "regular-type family" suffering the strains of daily life. An ad of this nature suggests that a family can get in touch with each other again by taking a well-deserved vacation at a family resort. Ads sponsored by the government also carry a degree of credibility and trustworthiness. Such sponsorship implies that the information is true since the government has traditionally been seen as an honest source.

Persons with credentials also carry credibility. Government officials, academic scholars, and individuals with extensive experience are seen as experts; their messages can be more persuasive than the words of those perceived as less informed and knowledgeable. Persuasion can be effective if the source holds some type of control or power over those being persuaded. As one might expect, reinforcements, incentives, and punishments can foster attitude change.

In tourism, persuasion is not inexpensive. Across the United States, individual states spent $71.5 million in advertising alone in 1988. Other U.S. destinations, communities, and regions spent another $58.5 million in major media advertising.[16] These figures do not include the operation and manning of all 50 state travel offices and the associated expenses that surround tourism promotion. Entire countries spend extensive amounts on promotional campaigns to solicit both domestic and international travel. Canada and Mexico invest heavily in major media promotion within the United States to attract the U.S. tourist. In 1988, Canada spent $11.1 million and Mexico spent $10.5 million. The total amount spent in 1988 on advertising to reach the American public was estimated to be $1.1 billion—a figure that was up some 30% over 1984 figures.[17]

Different media can be used in persuasion. It is important to understand the strengths and weaknesses of each type and develop ads that work within those parameters. Television is often considered the medium of choice, but is very expensive. Research has also raised some questions about the effectiveness of televised promotions versus promotions through other media. Another variable to consider is the persuasive message itself. Some messages appeal to basic needs, some promote fear, while others invoke warmth and charm. The art and science of advertising focuses upon developing messages that are appealing, stimulating, and persuasive.

It is important, too, to understand the characteristics of the audience when developing a persuasive message. In mass consumer markets, persuasion often involves appealing to the general public to get their attention, inform them, and eventually convince them to purchase a product or service. Individuals who make up tourism markets, however, are not considered to have the same needs, wants, and travel desires. Marketers recognize that different properties appeal to different groups of travelers—and that it is best to direct a persuasive message to those most likely to enjoy a particular type.

Attitudes and Tourism Development

The attitude of host communities toward tourists and the tourism industry is fast becoming a major issue across the world. Residents may form specific negative attitudes about tourism and travelers for several reasons. These include automobile and foot traffic congestion, increased commercialism, loss of community identity, increased taxes and costs, litter, and vandalism.[18] Conversely, those employed in tourism find positive benefits associated with the industry as do general retail merchants and developers. Jobs, benefits, and contributions to a community's quality are just a few of the positive effects tourism can have. In some parts of the world, tourism provides precious foreign capital that is needed to purchase other imports, manage debt, and provide employment.

Residents living in core tourism areas may feel oppressed by the growth of tourism and develop negative attitudes toward the industry. Some researchers have found that a resident's level of attachment to a destination is related to negative attitudes toward tourism. Residents who have the strongest attachment to the community are more likely to have negative attitudes toward tourism than those who are less attached.[19]

Tourists, too, have attitudes and perceptions about the destination and the local residents. The tenor of these attitudes and perceptions can swing between good and bad depending upon the interpersonal relationship which develops between the traveler and the resident. Excellent hospitality—or in contrast, rude treatment—by local residents or travel-related personnel can have a significant influence on the trip and the traveler's propensity to return to the destination.[20]

An excellent example of attitude change that occurred in response to tourism development and activity is provided by a major tourism event: the 1988 Winter Olympics held in Calgary. From 1983 to 1986, citizens of Calgary were monitored to track shifts in perceptions and attitudes toward the games, the organizers, and

Exhibit 5   Resident Ratings of Organizations Involved in the 1988 Winter Olympics

Organization	Survey	Poor	Fair	Good	Excellent	Uncertain
				Percent		
Federal	1986	12	23	29	2	34
Government	1985	13	36	22	1	29
	1984	46	26	8	1	19
	1983	37	31	12	1	19
Provincial	1986	5	17	48	6	24
Government	1985	10	30	36	4	20
	1984	11	37	33	3	16
	1983	19	40	25	3	13
City of	1986	2	5	49	32	11
Calgary	1985	2	16	52	18	11
	1984	3	15	53	20	10
	1983	5	16	49	19	12
Organizing	1986	6	14	37	27	16
Committee	1985	5	15	46	19	15
	1984	5	12	42	26	16
	1983	6	15	42	19	17

Source: J. R. Brent Ritchie and Marcia M. Lyons, "Olympulse III/Olympulse IV: A Mid-Term Report on Resident Attitudes Concerning the XV Olympic Winter Games," *Journal of Travel Research*, Summer 1987, p. 24.

the role of the city, provincial, and federal governments in preparing for the games.[21] In general, the citizens expressed support and awareness for the event from the beginning. More than 84% of residents voiced support for the games in 1983 and continued to do so throughout the study. Attitudes and perceptions shifted over time toward the various government roles. While a modest percentage rated the city's performance as excellent in the early polls (18.5%), nearly a third (32.1%) rated the city as doing an excellent job by 1986 (see Exhibit 5). By comparison, increasing numbers of people were willing to rate the provincial and federal governments as "good" in 1985 and 1986; but few were willing to say that the performance of these entities was "excellent." This study provides a clear example of attitude change—as well as stability—in a community preparing to host a major tourist event.

Another illustration of the relationship between attitudes and perception is seen in recent studies conducted by the U.S. Travel and Tourism Administration in cooperation with Tourism Canada.[22] Individuals in Japan—who fit the profile of a potential long-distance traveler—were asked to rate the importance of selected attractions and attributes of an overseas vacation. Then they were asked to rate how well the United States and Canada met the criteria compared to other destination countries. These relationships were plotted on a graph, and various strengths and weaknesses were noted. For example, the Japanese considered "outstanding scenery" to be important when on vacation; the United States and Canada were seen as doing well in this area. Personal safety also gained high marks. Respondents viewed Canada as better able to provide for personal safety compared with the United States. This example shows how travelers can form images of destinations based upon perceptions and attitudes.

Tourism decisions are based upon tourists' perceptions and attitudes toward destinations, attractions, tourism service industries and employees, and residents. Although these impressions may be inaccurate or overstated, the student of tourism should recognize that these impressions form the bases for tourist decisions. With this in mind, tourism promotional efforts should strive to generate positive images of destinations and attractions in order to enhance or modify perceptions, attitudes, and actual travel behavior.

Endnotes

1. Albert A. Harrison, *Individuals and Groups: Understanding Social Behavior* (Monterey, Calif.: Brooks/Cole, 1976), p. 601.

2. This discussion on general perceptual principles is drawn from the following: Charlotte L. Doyle, *Explorations in Psychology* (Monterey, Calif.: Brooks/Cole, 1987), pp. 46–97; Edward J. Mayo, Jr. and Lance P. Jarvis, *The Psychology of Leisure Travel: Effective Marketing and Selling of Travel Services* (Boston, Mass.: CBI Publishing Co., Inc., 1981), pp. 22–71; Terrell G. Williams, *Consumer Behavior: Fundamentals and Strategies* (St. Paul, Minn.: West Publishing Co., 1982), pp. 57–79.

3. Chuck Y. Gee, James C. Makens, and Dexter J.L. Choy, *The Travel Industry,* 2d ed. (New York: Van Nostrand Reinhold, 1989), p. 300.

4. Harrison, pp. 88–89.

5. William H. Ittelson, "Environmental Perception and Contemporary Perceptual Theory," in *Environmental Psychology: People and Their Physical Settings,* 2d ed., edited by Harold M. Proshansky, William H. Ittelson, and Leanne G. Rivlin (New York: Holt, Rinehart & Winston, 1976), p. 149.

6. Edward E. Jones and Harold B. Gerard, *Foundations of Social Psychology* (New York: Wiley, 1967), pp. 258–259; 261–262.

7. Donelson R. Forsyth, *Social Psychology* (Pacific Grove, Calif.: Brooks/Cole, 1987), p. 118.

8. Harrison, p. 192.

9. Forsyth, p. 192.

10. Martin I. Horn and William D. Wells, "Do Trends in Attitudes Predict Trends in Behavior?" in *Personal Values and Consumer Psychology,* edited by Robert E. Pitts, Jr., & Arch G. Woodside (Lexington, Mass.: Lexington Books, 1984), pp. 187–198.

11. Suzanne D. Cook, "1987 Domestic Travel in Review," in *Second Annual Travel Review Conference Proceedings: The 1987 Experience—A Basis for Planning* (Salt Lake City, Utah: Travel and Tourism Research Association, 1987), p. 1.

12. Douglas Frechtling, "1986 U.S. Travel Activity and Industry Trends: Part I," in *First Annual Travel Review Conference Proceedings: The 1986 Experience—A Basis for Planning* (Salt Lake City, Utah: Travel and Tourism Research Association, 1987), p. 8.

13. *Travel Printout,* May 1985, Vol. 14 (5), p. 1. A newsletter published by the U.S. Travel Data Center, Washington, D.C.

14. Cook, p. 4.

15. Daniel M. Wegner and Robin R. Vallacher, *Implicit Psychology: An Introduction to Social Cognition* (New York: Oxford University Press, 1977), p. 22.

16. *Trends in Travel and Tourism Advertising Expenditures in United States Measured Media 1984–1988.* A special report for Ogilvy and Mather (New York: Ogilvy and Mather, July 1989), p. IV-1.

17. Ogilvy and Mather, p. V-3.

18. Peter E. Murphy, *Tourism: A Community Approach* (New York: Methuen, 1985), pp. 119–151.

19. Seoho Um and John L. Crompton, "Measuring Residents' Attachment Levels in a Host Community," *Journal of Travel Research,* Summer (26, 1) 1987, pp. 27–29.

20. Dennis L. Hoffman and Stuart A. Low, "An Application of the Probit Transformation to Tourism Survey Data," *Journal of Travel Research,* Fall (20, 2) 1981, pp. 35–38.

21. J. R. Brent Ritchie and Marcia M. Lyons, "Olympulse III/Olympulse IV: A Mid-Term Report on Resident Attitudes Concerning the XV Olympic Winter Games," *Journal of Travel Research,* Summer 1987, pp. 18–26.

22. *Highlights Report—Pleasure Travel Markets to North America: Japan, United Kingdom, West Germany, France.* Report prepared for U.S. Travel and Tourism Administration and Tourism Canada by Market Facts of Canada Limited, August 1987, p. 14.

Key Terms

attitudes	perception
attribution	persuasion
behavior	proxemics
environmental perception	psychology
first impression	social perception
kinesics	stereotypes
non-verbal cues	verbal cues

Discussion Questions

1. What are some of the internal forces which can influence tourism behavior? What are some of the external forces?

2. Is perception an active or passive process? Why?

3. What are some of the general principles that operate during the perceptual process?

4. What are the three fundamental elements of perception?

5. How does environmental perception differ from social perception?

6. How do verbal and non-verbal cues affect social perception?

7. What three components constitute an attitude? What does each component refer to?

8. How can stereotypes affect a tourism destination and its tourists?

9. What variables determine the effectiveness of a persuasive message?

10. Why are attitudes becoming a major focus in the study of travel and tourism?

REVIEW QUIZ

When you feel you have covered all of the material in this chapter, answer these questions. Choose the *best* answer. Check your answers with the correct ones found on the Review Quiz Answer Key at the end of this book.

True (T) or False (F)

T   F   1. A knowledge of the basic elements of psychology can add to the understanding of travel and tourism behavior.

T   F   2. External forces include values, attitudes, and motives.

T   F   3. Sensory adaptation means getting used to things and taking them for granted.

T   F   4. Proximity is used as a perceptual principle in tourism promotions.

T   F   5. The fundamental elements of perception are the perceiver, the target, and the situation.

T   F   6. Attribution helps the perceiver make sense out of others' actions.

T   F   7. First impressions can be the basis for impression formation.

T   F   8. In the travel industry, there is usually a "second chance" to fix a negative first impression.

T   F   9. Attitudes and behaviors are valuable in predicting travel and tourism behaviors.

T   F   10. Stereotypes often carry a positive and accurate portrayal of people and situations.

Alternate/Multiple Choice

11.   Perception is a(n) _____ process.

    a. active
    b. passive

12.   Closure refers to a perceiver's tendency to:

    a. complete an image.
    b. imply a message.

13.   The affective component of an attitude refers to a person's:

    a. emotional response to an object.
    b. negative response to an object.

14.   An example of a negative stereotype of a tourist is the term:

    a. fudgies.
    b. a tourist trap.
    c. residents.
    d. commuters.

15. In tourism, persuasion is:

   a. inexpensive.
   b. ineffective.
   c. expensive.
   d. trustworthy.

Chapter Outline

Motivation
    Types of Motivation
    Theories of Motivation
Personality
    Personality and Tourism
    Personality Traits
    Personality Measures
    Psychographic Research
Values
    Need-Driven
    Outer-Directed
    Inner-Directed
    Combined Inner- and Outer-Directed
    Application to Tourism
Learning
    Learning and Tourism

Learning Objectives

1. Analyze why motivations are so difficult to measure.

2. Compare the different types of motivation in terms of their application to travel and tourism.

3. Describe two theories of motivation as they relate to travel and tourism.

4. Explain how personality traits affect travel and tourism.

5. Compare three types of personality measures.

6. Differentiate between allocentric and psychocentric travelers and destinations.

7. List eight basic values and the implications these values have for marketing.

8. Identify the four basic groupings that correspond to the lifestyle segments used in the VALS system.

9. Examine how shifting values within the VALS system might affect travel and tourism.

10. Describe how the process of learning can be applied to travel and tourism.

11. Identify four learning methods appropriate to the study of travel and tourism.

3

Psychological Dimensions: Motivation, Personality, Values, and Learning

IF YOU WERE TO ASK a friend why he/she is taking a vacation, that friend could probably give you a long list of very good reasons. On that list might be relaxation, sun and surf, or seeing different places; other reasons might include being with the family and meeting new people. In the study of tourism, it is important to differentiate between *stated reasons* and *motivations* for travel. Not all reasons for travel listed by tourists are motivations; many are descriptions of the destination, its image, amenities, and characteristics. While informative, these reasons are not motivations.

Personality—as expressed in behavior and communication—also affects travel and tourism. While personality may be difficult to measure and interpret, personality certainly manifests itself through the travel decisions a tourist makes, and in the way a tourist handles travel experiences. Personality, in part, is reflected by the values an individual holds and expresses. Values are deeply personal and strong convictions about what a person views as right and wrong. Values may influence the types of vacations a person takes and how that person behaves during vacations.

The transformation of data into information and knowledge can be thought of as learning. Learning to travel and learning about tourism can be enjoyable experiences. This chapter will look at learning in the context of tourism along with three other psychological dimensions: motivation, personality, and values.

Motivation

When your neighbors take a vacation, you instantly make some assumptions about their motivations. The neighbors could be taking the vacation to relax, to be together, or to enjoy the beach or a mountain retreat. You assume that your neighbors are looking for something, that they are trying to satisfy some need or desire. This need may seem simple: to have a good time, to get away from work, or to visit with old friends. Although simple on the surface, such needs actually represent complex psychological motivations.

Motivation is a force within an individual which causes him/her to do something to fulfill a biological need or psychological desire. The human body requires water and food to satisfy biological needs. When we feel hungry, our bodies create a hunger sensation which stimulates a search for and consumption of food. This sequence of sensations and behaviors is associated with biological or primary needs. Motivation also includes secondary needs. Secondary needs are often called social or psychological desires. To mention but a few, social and psychological needs include achievement, success, socialization, and recognition. Needs and desires are developed through learning and social processes. The social and cultural context in which a person develops fosters the learning of various types of secondary needs. As an example, children from families that are strongly concerned about accomplishments and hard work may develop a need for success or achievement.

Of course, these two different need systems do not operate independently of each other. Take eating, for example. Eating is more than satisfying a biological need. The ritual, the social event, and the creativity associated with dining make eating more than simply satisfying biological hunger. Dining satisfies two needs at the same time: socialization and hunger. In this case, the two motivations are complementary. But in the case of travel, motivations sometimes seem to contradict each other. Tourists may seek relaxation and excitement in the same trip. A pair of travelers may start a trip intending to get away from people and to be alone with each other. Yet by the third night, this same couple might be the "life of the party," socializing with everyone in sight. In sum, tourism motivation is complex, unique to an individual, and central to travel behavior.

Because motivations are so personal and subjective, they are difficult to measure. Tourists may not be able to or want to discover their true motivations for a particular outing. Even if they are aware of their travel motives, they may not want or be able to express it in words. Too, cultural and language barriers may prevent tourists from sharing their travel motivations with others.

Tourists might be asked through research studies to discuss their travel motives. But even in personal interviews, the deeper, more profound motivations may not surface. Typical tourists might say that they are on vacation to visit the ocean, to see the sights, and to live a few days in luxury. While these are enjoyable things to do, it is doubtful whether these are the real motives behind a family vacation. Rather, a number of deeper, personal motives probably prompted the vacation. Such needs might include re-establishing family bonds or, in the case of a couple, rekindling love.

Types of Motivation

Both short- and long-term motivation guide travel behavior. After a long week, a busy family might want to spend a quiet weekend together in a setting away from home. Such a feeling could be considered a short-term motivation. In contrast, adventure hikers may regularly seek out the mountains to satisfy a long-term motivation to be with nature, to be challenged, and to be knowledgeable of the outdoors. Over time, this long-term motivation will influence the choice of many destinations, friendships, and vacation travel patterns. The motivations associated with tourism are primarily long-term. The annual family vacation probably satisfies an enduring need to be with family, to get away from work, and to take a break from the daily routine.

Travel decision-making and behavior are also influenced by **intrinsic** and **extrinsic motivations**. If someone is intrinsically motivated, no external rewards are

Intrinsic FINAL!

required. The behavior is carried out and enjoyed for its own sake. Such behaviors are stimulated and reinforced by internal satisfactions such as personal feelings of accomplishment. Other common intrinsic rewards include: achievement, success, or enjoyment. Intrinsic motivations are personal and psychological—which makes them more difficult to understand and more difficult for others to manipulate. Conversely, behaviors stimulated and reinforced by external rewards are considered to be extrinsically motivated. Common external rewards include money and material goods such as televisions, radios, and cars.

Most travel is a function of both intrinsic and extrinsic motivation. Some people travel for personal satisfaction and excitement, while others travel for business, a career, or commercial opportunity. In most travel, a mixture of needs is being satisfied. Most vacations are intrinsically motivated. Normally, no one from "the outside" directs or pays the family to go to a selected vacation site. Generally, the choice of activities and destinations is controlled by the personal motives of family members. The business traveler is at the other extreme. Most of the needs which travel must fulfill are related to the job. A company might expect the traveler to return with a product, a new contract, a business agreement, or new account. But business travel is not all work. About 25% of business travelers extend their business trips to include extra vacation days with family and friends—confirming the idea that travel motivations often mix.[1]

Motivations for travel cover a broad range of human behaviors and human experiences. A brief listing of travel motivations might include: relaxation, excitement, social interactions with friends, adventure, family interactions, status, physical challenges, and escape from routine or stress.

A common set of themes run through the list of motivations. The first is the need to escape from something such as stress or boredom. The stimulation at home or work is too much or, in some cases, not enough. A vacation or trip provides an escape, a change from the routine. Second, travel motives consistently involve social exchanges, which reflects the strong social nature of tourism. Third, many travel motivations involve social and personal comparisons. Tourists may challenge themselves in an activity and measure success in a private and personal way. For example, a person may tackle a resort's jogging trails for the experience—not to compete in a race with other guests. For others, the criteria for success are very public, fulfilling a need to be seen and recognized. A tourist may want to create an image of being a sophisticated traveler, and do so by taking expensive, prestigious vacations. Fourth, many people travel in search of novelty and exploration. The very nature of travel implies a sense of adventure and exploration. This motive is commonly expressed in destination advertisements that attempt to stimulate the desire to explore. Motivations of this type involve a sense of fantasy as well as adventure. But in tourism, once the trip ends, the exploration is over. In other words, few people stay in the jungle beyond the vacation. Vacations and destinations may also facilitate a person's ability and desire to "get in touch with oneself." Quiet vacations in isolated locations, taken alone or with a loved one, can fulfill such exploration needs.

Exhibit 1 lists and defines commonly observed motivations in more detail. While this exhibit does not represent a comprehensive listing of all the motives that

Exhibit 1   Tourism Motivations

Motivation	Definition	Example
Escape	To get away	Weekend holiday
	Get away from stress	Staying on an island
	Being removed from others	Vacation alone
	Being removed from norms	Visit new culture
Social	Being with others	Visiting friends
	Kinship	Visiting family
	Social exploration	Meeting new people
	To be alone	Vacation in solitude
Comparison	Challenge/adventure	Climb a mountain
	Prestige/status	Take an expensive cruise vacation
	Physical challenge	Learn and train to climb mountains
	Internal satisfaction	Private, worldwide rock collecting
Novelty	Exploration	Visit a third world country
	Stimulation	Thrill rides at Disney
	Curiosity	Sight-seeing
	Arousal	White-water raft vacation

This exhibit is based on material from the following resources: Graham M.S. Dann, "Tourism Motivation: An Appraisal," *Annals of Tourism Research* 8, no. 2 (1981): pp. 187–219; Edward J. Mayo and Lance P. Jarvis, *The Psychology of Leisure Travel* (Boston, Mass.: CBI Publishing Co., 1981), pp. 155–176; Seppo E. Iso-Ahola, "Towards a Social Psychology Theory of Tourism Motivation: A Rejoinder," *Annals of Tourism Research* 9 (1982): p. 259; John Crompton, "Motivations for Pleasure Vacations," *Annals of Tourism Research* 6, no. 4 (1979): pp. 414–421.

stimulate travel, it does represent the major types of motives mentioned most often by tourists and tourism researchers.

Theories of Motivation

Many theories of motivation have been advanced. Early philosophical thought implied that people were motivated by a simple pleasure-pain principle. People did things that felt good and avoided those that felt bad. Freud suggested that deep-seated motives were associated with sexual urges and that all behavior could be related to primary sexual needs. Under closer observation, most early theories were found to be too simple or too abstract and could not account for the diverse and seemingly contradictory behaviors of humans.

Maslow's Hierarchy of Needs. A motivational theory which has received considerable attention is Maslow's Hierarchy of Needs.[2] Maslow proposed that needs are ordered in levels of priorities. He suggested that a person will be motivated to fulfill a higher level need only if lower needs have already been fulfilled. Maslow's needs and their order of priority are:

- **Physiological**—food, water, air, shelter, reproduction

- **Safety**—stability, security, structure

- **Love**—affiliation, affection, sense of belonging

- **Esteem**—success, self-worth, achievement

- **Self-Actualization**—self-fulfillment, personal growth

It is not clear whether this hierarchy holds true for travel motivations. Travelers are capable of experiencing, expressing, and pursuing needs from several of the steps in the hierarchy at the same time. Tourists with the financial means may satisfy various needs at the same time by staying in swank lodging accommodations, dining in the area's renowned restaurants, or sharing personal time with a loved one on a romantic beach. And around the world, people of very limited means still travel on holidays and festival days to visit sacred shrines, religious centers, or family and friends. So, it would seem that Maslow's hierarchy is not as rigid as originally proposed. This does not mean that the theory does not provide a viable framework to characterize motivations. What it does show is that travel permits several needs to be fulfilled at the same time. Too, it is important to recognize that those in extreme poverty have few—if any—resources to pursue pleasure travel. But under most conditions, people continuously strive for growth and self-improvement—a point implied in Maslow's theory.

Optimal Arousal Theory. An additional and more recent theory of motivation is the optimal arousal theory.[3] The basic principle behind the theory is that a person seeks out a level of stimulation that is best for him/her as an individual. If a person's life is too quiet, the person may seek out stimulation through activity. If too much is happening in a person's world, then the person seeks to cut off stimulation and find a quieter environment. Tourism provides an excellent means of accommodating a person's need for an optimal level of stimulation. Someone whose day-to-day life is overbearing may choose to visit a remote, peaceful setting to counter the pressures of home and work. Someone whose work and life are boring may want a vacation that supplies adventure and excitement.

The optimal arousal theory considers tourism to be guided primarily by intrinsic motives and the need to escape stress, excessive stimulation, and the mundane. At the same time, the tourist seeks out a situation that is less boring, or less stimulating—whatever the case may be. Through travel, the tourist seeks the stimulation or the peace and tranquility he/she may not have at home or work. Tourists seek out new or different environments that may supply intrinsic rewards such as enjoyment, relaxation, a sense of competence, or a challenge.

Personality

Reflect on vacation stories that you have heard from friends and relatives. Eventually, you will hear about the "character" they met while on vacation. They may tell you how this person behaved, what the person said, and what the person looked like. They may tell you that this person was charming, likeable, friendly, willing to help, and open to discussing a range of subjects. What your friends are sharing with you is the essence of the individual—or that person's **personality**.

People often seek to balance the routine of everyday life through vacations packed with surprise, adventure, and camaraderie. (Courtesy of Texas Department of Commerce, Richard Reynolds, Austin, Texas)

While personality is considered a reflection of the inner self, in most social situations, much of a person's true personality is hidden or masked by socially acceptable behaviors and gestures. For the most part, only intimate relationships —such as those among family members, lovers, and close friends—allow the "real" person to surface.

Even in the clinical and psychological professions, there is disagreement about the best way to define personality. For our purposes, personality will be defined as the manner by which a person's thoughts and actions interact with and modify the conditions of his/her life.[4]

Personality and Tourism

It could be argued that the nature of the trip itself reflects the personalities of travelers. In the case of vacation travel, a family can make very personal decisions about a number of variables: the destination, the mode of travel, the length of stay, and the activities. These decisions could be seen as reflecting the personality of the family members. On the other hand, factors such as expense, popularity of destinations, and pressure from family and friends may blunt some of the influences that personality could have on the vacation decision-making process.

Several personality traits could influence tourism—especially vacation travel. Certainly, a person who is extremely introverted would have a difficult time with a vacation that requires extensive contact with strangers. Individuals who are reluctant to try out new things may also be unlikely to try adventure-related vacations.

In a few cases, personality dimensions have been related to tourism and travel decisions and behaviors. Tourism ads and promotions often imply that such a relationship is alive and well. Consider how many times you have seen ad copy of this tenor: "See these exotic islands, satisfy your deepest fantasies ..." or "Explore this unique culture, the folkways and traditions of this lost civilization." These advertisements assume that certain kinds of people want to travel to specific places and participate in unique activities. It is further assumed that destinations are designed to match both motivational needs and personality traits of individual tourists.

Personality Traits

From ancient times up to the turn of the century, people were thought to be of certain types. During the time of the Greeks, people were slotted into one of four categories—each characterized by a unique temperament: choleric (irritable), sanguine (optimistic and happy-go-lucky), phlegmatic (calm and quiet), and melancholic (depressed). But as more and more complexities were revealed about human nature, it was discovered that such a simple system could not adequately classify or describe individuals.

Modern psychologists have found the concept of traits to provide a more meaningful explanation of personality. People vary in their responses to events and circumstances. As a result, it is easier to see people in terms of possessing degrees of certain traits such as aggression, affiliation, dominance, or need for recognition—rather than in terms of being a specific type. This seems to fit more closely with what we actually observe in people. People do not fall exclusively into one type or another. For example, an individual may be aggressive given particular circumstances—even though he/she is not considered to be an aggressive person in other circumstances. What this means is that people vary by degree in terms of specific personality traits.

Personality Measures

Traditionally, personality was studied by the clinical psychologist, medical doctor, or the psychiatrist concerned with mental well-being. In the twentieth century, the study of individuals as consumers spawned an interest in **psychographics**—the measurement of personality, attitudes, and values from a marketing perspective. Psychographics goes beyond the standard demographic measures such as age, profession, and sex by including information on personal attitudes, activities, interests, values, and personality.[5]

Lifestyle measures are closely related to psychographics. Whereas psychographic measures have a stronger personality element, lifestyle measures examine how daily lives unfold. In a simple sense, people *live* a lifestyle. They own homes and cars of certain types, are involved in certain types of activities, and have certain socioeconomic characteristics. Lifestyle measures also look at a person's interests, activities, and opinions regarding a range of national and personal family issues. Psychographics and lifestyle measures are often blended together. Demographics

Exhibit 2   Components of Lifestyle Dimensions

Activities	Interests	Opinions	Demographics
Hobbies	Job	Themselves	Education
Work	Family	Politics	Age
Social events	Home	Business	Income
Vacations	Recreation	Economics	Family size
Entertainment	Community	Social issues	Occupation
Community	Food	Products	Housing
Sports	Fashion	Future	Geography
Clubs/Associations	Media	Culture	City size
	Achievements	Education	Life cycle stage

Source: Joseph T. Plummer, "The Concept and Application of Life Style Segmentation," *Journal of Marketing* 38 (January 1974): p. 34.

are added to provide a more complete picture of what the person—or potential consumer—is like.

Exhibit 2 lists a collection of lifestyle components: activities, interests, opinions, and related demographics. Many of these lifestyle characteristics would be measured and evaluated in a psychographic study of a travel market. The purpose of such a study would be to develop a profile of potential travelers by listing their likes and dislikes. Standard demographic characteristics are added to the profile so that destinations, promotions, and travel packages can be matched to appropriate markets. Psychographic analyses assume that the more you know about various facets of a person's life, the more you can assess what that person sees as worth doing or purchasing. Certainly, a number of activities mentioned under the activities heading would apply to a study of a tourism market. For example, the preferences and participation rates in various sports, vacations, and entertainment activities would provide useful information that could help assess travel propensities. The same is true of interests and opinions. People with a strong interest in family, community, and home life would probably have different vacation preferences than those interested in fashion, personal achievements, and media attention.

Values shape lifestyles and are central to a person's personality. Values are socially and culturally defined and form the criteria which guide behavior. Values generally fall into two types. First are instrumental or doing values. These represent a person's enduring belief that a specific mode of conduct is personally or socially preferable. Second are terminal or being values. These represent a person's enduring belief that a specific way of living is personally or socially preferable. An individual's ranking of the values represents his/her personal value system.[6] Values affect not only general consumer decisions, but tourism and travel decisions as well. Values and their impact on tourism will be discussed later in this chapter.

Psychographic Research

Psychographic research conducted in the late 1960s and early 1970s suggests that people vary in systematic ways with respect to their propensity to travel.[7] Researcher Stanley Plog developed a scale along which to plot varying personality

Exhibit 3   Allocentric and Psychocentric Travelers

Allocentric	Psychocentric
More frequent travel	Less travel
Venturesome	Less venturesome
Self-confident	Less self-confident
Less inhibited	More inhibited
Less anxious	More anxious in daily life
Travel by various means	Most likely to travel by car
Select more "exotic" destinations	Select familiar and "safe" destinations
Spend more money while on vacation	Spend less money on travel while on vacation

Source: Plog Research, Inc. "California Travelers' Perceptions of British Columbia and Vancouver: Results of the Research." Prepared for British Columbia, Ministry of Tourism, Recreation and Culture, May 1987, pp. 33–35.

ALL- Allocentric.

traits and lifestyle preferences. Plog theorized that travelers can be categorized at or between one of two extremes: psychocentric or allocentric.

 A person on the **allocentric** end of the scale was found to be more adventuresome and willing to travel to exotic destinations. The allocentric is more likely to travel by airplane and to travel more often. Allocentrics, too, tend to spend more when traveling—which is important to the tourism industry. In contrast, the **psychocentric** is less of a traveler. When traveling, the psychocentric is more likely to go by car, to seek out "safe" and familiar destinations, and to spend less in the process. Exhibit 3 summarizes characteristics associated with allocentric and psychocentric travelers.

Such an analysis can be extended to travel destinations. Destinations change in their appeal and can be plotted along the allocentric-psychocentric scale. For example, new destinations appeal to the allocentric seeking out the novel and exotic. Presumably, they tell others about the destination and it grows in popularity—drawing larger and larger numbers of tourists. What this does, however, is reduce the destination's popularity for the allocentric and increase its popularity for the psychocentric. Over time, the destination draws a different type of market. If one assumes that people are distributed along the allocentric-psychocentric scale (see Exhibit 4), the destination will eventually draw fewer people as it becomes the attraction solely for the psychocentric. The destination will be popular, but only to a small number of people who also tend to spend less money.

The best position for a destination to fall in is near the "mid-centric" section of the graph. This is where the largest percentage of travelers is located. People in these personality groups are not frightened of new travel experiences—as long as they are not too unusual or taxing. These travelers, too, tend to spend more while traveling than a group of pure psychocentrics.

In addition to allocentric-psychocentric traits, another measure can be added to help understand travel markets. The **energy-lethargy dimension** is designed to describe the varying energy and lethargy levels of individuals. When these two dimensions are plotted together, four kinds of travelers emerge:[8]

Exhibit 4   Distribution of Allocentric-Psychocentric Dimension

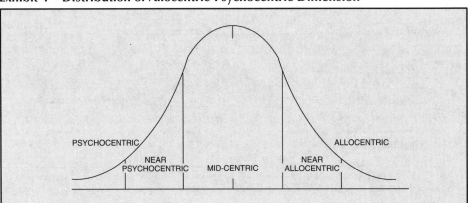

Based upon Plog Research, Inc. "California Travelers' Perceptions of British Columbia and Vancouver: Results of the Research." Prepared for British Columbia, Ministry of Tourism, Recreation and Culture, May 1987, p. 34.

1. *High-energy allocentrics* are frequent travelers who use airlines, spend more, visit the newest attractions and destinations in the world, and strive to have as many new experiences per trip as possible.

2. *Low-energy allocentrics* also travel by air, but are less frequent travelers compared to their high-energy counterparts. They travel more often in fantasy through reading and sharing experiences with friends, rather than being there in person.

3. *High-energy psychocentrics* are fairly active travelers but usually travel via a personal vehicle. This group has a higher recreational vehicle ownership rate than other groups.

4. *Low-energy psychocentrics* prefer to stay home and enjoy their familiar surroundings.

Exhibit 5 shows the different travel planning techniques and package preferences of these different travel personalities. High-energy allocentrics are more likely to be planning a trip by air in the next year compared to the other groups. Both types of psychocentrics are more likely to rely on the travel agent to plan trips and to choose the airline. They like packaged air trips if they travel by air, yet they travel less by air than other groups. This corresponds with the psychocentric need for the familiar since the travel agent does the planning and works out the details.

Values

Values research can be considered another psychographic approach to the study of tourism. The application of values research to tourism has grown along with the study of values in consumer decision-making. Two studies conducted in the United States outlined eight basic values that have implications for consumer marketing. Respondents were given a list of values and asked to indicate which two

Exhibit 5   Allocentric-Psychocentric Travel Characteristics

	Allocentric		Psychocentric	
	Hi	Lo	Hi	Lo
	Energy		Energy	
Leisure Air Trips Last Year (Mean)	3.4	3.0	2.6	2.2
Last Air Trip A Package (% Yes)	20	19	22	33
Cruise Ship/Car Carrier Trip Next Year (% Yes)	50	43	39	35
Plan Leisure Air Trip Next Year (% Yes)	82	65	78	70
Plan Air Trips Through:				
Travel Agent (%)	63	61	71	69
Call Airline Yourself (%)	35	38	27	28
Choose Airline Myself (%)	47	38	30	34
Ask Agent (%)	53	63	70	66

Source: Plog Research, Inc. "California Travelers' Perceptions of British Columbia and Vancouver: Results of the Research." Prepared for British Columbia, Ministry of Tourism, Recreation and Culture, May 1987, pp. 41–43.

values were most important in their lives. The values and the percentage of Americans endorsing them were:[9]

- Self-respect (21%)
- Security (21%)
- Warm relationships (16%)
- Accomplishment (11%)
- Self-fulfillment (10%)
- Being well-respected (9%)
- Belonging (8%)
- Fun, excitement, and enjoyment (4%)

The implications for marketing are that appeals should be directed toward those values with large endorsements—if the product or service matches the social and economic situations of the targeted consumer. For example, the study revealed that a large percentage of those endorsing the value of security had few economic and social resources. In marketing terms, if security products—be it locks, fences, or items promising financial security—were to be sold to this group, the products would have to be priced and positioned appropriately.

Exhibit 6   Values and Lifestyle Segments

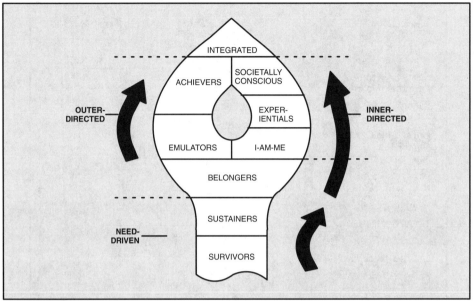

Source: Arnold Mitchell, *Social Change: Implications of Trends in Values and Lifestyles* (Menlo Park, Calif.: SRI International), 1979, p. 9.

With respect to tourism and travel, the group which endorsed fun, excitement, and enjoyment included individuals who sought the good life and placed importance on leisure and vacations. Even though this is a small percentage of the public (4%), it does represent the people who place fun, excitement, and enjoyment among their top two values. Such a finding, of course, is what marketing professionals use to match vacation packages with people who value certain types of vacations.

Recent studies on the role values play in travel decisions suggest that attendance at specific attractions is related to the values of those attending.[10] From a marketing perspective, the values of non-visitors should be studied to understand how the destination might be re-positioned to attract the non-visiting group. To the extent that attractions are perceived as matching personal values, understanding the value systems of target markets is a strategy worth considering by the tourism marketing professional.

A comprehensive system of studying values and lifestyles—**VALS**—has been developed by researchers at SRI International, a research firm located in California.[11] The VALS system places American consumers in four categories and nine lifestyles. Like Maslow's profile, the VALS system has at the bottom those who are need-driven—the poor and less fortunate struggling to make ends meet. The more you move up the diagram in Exhibit 6, the more you see people with lifestyles and values that go beyond day-to-day living. The top of the figure represents people who have achieved an integrated lifestyle.

There are four basic groupings of nine lifestyle segments. First are the *need-driven* individuals who are poverty stricken and often feel that society has left them behind. Next are the *outer-directed*. These are people in the mainstream—or establishment—who are concerned with how they present themselves to others. This group has built and maintained the basic cultural norms. Then, there are the *inner-directed* groups. These include people more concerned with inner values and experiences than traditional material wealth. They are driven more by personal priorities than the wishes or standards of others. Finally, the *integrated group* consists of a combination of inner- and outer-directed individuals. This is a very small group in the United States. The following sections provide more detail on these specific segments.

Need-Driven

1. **Survivors** (4%)—This group includes the poor, the fearful, and the distressed. These people are removed from the mainstream of society and hold out little hope of improvement for their lives. They are older (median age of 66), mostly women, and have little income or education.

2. **Sustainers** (7%)—Hope is still alive in this group, although they have little in the way of material wealth, social status, or education. This group consists of younger people (median age of 28) who are working hard at jobs that are seasonal or subject to the ups and downs of local and regional economies.

Outer-Directed

3. **Belongers** (35%)—The traditional and conventional American makes up this group. As implied by the label, this group likes to belong and to be part of the system. The people in this group are aging (median age of 52), and have modest incomes and a moderate level of education. They represent one of the largest VALS groups—more than a third of all Americans. People in this group adhere to the traditions of U.S. society: community, family, patriotism, and the home.

4. **Emulators** (10%)—This group is ambitious and striving for success in the system. Members are young (median age of 28), with moderate incomes and education levels. They are called emulators because they want to be successful like the achiever group—a group that has made it in the system.

5. **Achievers** (22%)—Members of this group are prosperous—usually the leader type—who are confident and materialistic. They are conservative and conventional, career-oriented, and up to most any challenge. They are a bit older (median age of 42) than the emulator group. Achievers are well educated, although other groups in the VALS system have similar high education levels.

Inner-Directed

6. **I-Am-Me** (5%)—This is a small group of rebellious, single, and young individuals with little earnings who are often attending college. They are also likely to be children of members of the achievers group. This is considered a transition phase. Many Americans move rather quickly through this grouping and outgrow this phase of rebellion and protest.

7. **Experiential** (7%)—The next stage for the I-Am-Me group is often the experiential. Members of this group are young (median age of 28), and focus upon interpersonal relationships, experiences, and gratification gained from other activities besides their jobs. They are less career-oriented and ambitious compared to achievers, although they have well paying jobs which offer career potential.

8. **Societally Conscious** (8%)—This group is even more mature psychologically than those in the experiential group. They are concerned not only about others in their lives, but about society and the world on national and international levels. Their politics are liberal, they have good incomes, and, like the achievers, are a bit older (median age of 37). Members of this group do not take their careers as seriously as achievers. This group has the highest proportion of dual income couples compared to any other VALS segment.

Combined Inner- and Outer-Directed

9. **Integrated** (2%)—The most psychologically mature, this group includes a very small percentage of Americans who are very difficult to classify. They have found a way to merge the two larger types of lifestyles of outer- and inner-directed. They have a broad world view, are tolerant of uncertainties, and have a confident outlook on life.

It should be noted that these VALS segments change over time and that people may move through various segments throughout their lives. These segments are meant to be an approximate classification of Americans at a particular point in time. For marketing applications, marketers generally supplement VALS information with related research on consumer behavior.

Application to Tourism

In 1984, researchers applied the VALS system to tourism in Pennsylvania.[12] Potential travelers to Pennsylvania from neighboring states were classified according to VALS segments. These travelers were asked to rate what criteria were important to them when traveling and to rate Pennsylvania as a destination. This represents one of the first applications of the VALS system to tourism.

It is interesting to note what criteria various segments find important in selecting a destination. First, of the non-business trips made to Pennsylvania, 72% were made by those in the belongers (41%) and achievers (31%) groups. In contrast, most of the business trips were made by achievers (43%), the societally conscious (35%), and belongers (16%). This business travel pattern, in part, reflects the income and occupational status of the particular groups. For belongers, the number of non-business trips is much larger than travel for business.

Among those surveyed, the following items were considered "very important" when selecting a vacation destination:

- Safety
- Reasonable prices
- Good accommodations

Exhibit 7   Vacation Choice Criteria for VALS Respondents

Belongers	Achievers	Societally Conscious
safety	safety	reasonable prices
reasonable prices	good accommodations	relaxing vacations
good accommodations	relaxing vacations	safety
relaxing vacations	good food	good accommodations
good food	reasonable prices	beautiful scenery
friendly people	restaurants	restaurants
restaurants	friendly people	good food
beautiful scenery	beautiful scenery	friendly people

Source: David Shih, "VALS as a Tool of Tourism Market Research: The Pennsylvania Experience," *Journal of Travel Research* 24, no. 4, p. 46.

- Relaxing vacations

- Good food

- Friendly people

- Restaurants/places to dine out

- Beautiful scenery

Exhibit 7 shows that while the same factors are important to belongers, achievers, and the societally conscious group, the order of these items differs. Belongers are concerned with safety, prices, and accommodations. Achievers were also concerned with safety and accommodations, but less so with prices. The societally conscious had a different perspective entirely; they were the most concerned with prices, and less with safety and accommodations. This latter group also placed more emphasis upon scenery and less on the friendliness of the people. These findings suggest that different groups of people have different hierarchies of reasons for selecting vacation destinations.

Finally, a major U.S. consulting firm has extended the research on values and psychographics to industrialized nations in Europe. It was found that people in West Germany and the United Kingdom have experienced shifts in values much like those in the United States.[13] In all three countries, values appear to be shifting from the traditional to those more in line with the inner-directed personality. Exhibit 8 compares the traditional and new values witnessed in industrialized nations today. And as shown in Exhibit 9, the number of people with inner-directed values is projected to grow in all three countries. On the other hand, the proportion of people in the outer-directed grouping is projected to decrease slightly as we move through the 1990s.

While these value shifts are interesting, not all changes will occur at the same time in the same degree for each of these Western nations. These value shifts have implications for tourism in the United States as well as in Europe. Several have the potential to modify the relationship between work and leisure. The growing importance of leisure in some European countries promises to create large blocks

Exhibit 8   Comparison of Traditional and New Values in Industrial Countries

Traditional Values	New Values
Higher standard of living	Better quality of life
Self-denial	Self-fulfillment
Traditional sex roles	Blurring of sex roles
Socially defined success	Individually defined success
Open to technology	Oriented to technology
Industry based	Information/service based
Growth oriented	A sense of limits on growth
Patriotism	Less nationalistic
Expansionism	Pluralism
Hero worship	Ideas oriented
Live to work	Work to live
Traditional family life	Alternative families

Source: Joseph T. Plummer, "Changing Values: The New Emphasis on Self-Actualization," *The Futurist* 23 (January–February 1989): p. 10.

Exhibit 9   Predicted Shifts in Values in Three Industrial Countries

VALUES	U.S.		U.K.		W. GERMANY	
	1984	1990	1984	1990	1984	1990
			Percent			
Tradition-Directed	11	12	33	33	16	16
Outer-Directed	67	62	55	52	72	70
Inner-Directed	22	26	12	15	12	14

Source: Joseph T. Plummer, "Changing Values: The New Emphasis on Self-Actualization," *The Futurist* 23 (January–February 1989): p. 13.

of time for vacations and pleasure travel. In several European countries, four to six weeks of holiday time is presently available through the summer. The availability of free time is not a universal phenomenon for all citizens—especially in the United States. While value changes are important for tourism in the long run, the impacts will be felt differently. The regularly employed person with long paid holidays will be the first to benefit; the underprivileged and unemployed will most likely be the last to benefit—if they benefit at all.

Although American values are shifting, the leisure hours available for travel and recreation have been relatively stable for the last 10 or so years. The major increases in leisure time occurred in the 1960s.[14] Approximately 35 to 40 hours of leisure time are available to Americans each week. Although official reported working hours are seen as increasing,[15] the time at work reported in time diaries is 40 hours a week or less.[16] Despite the numbers, the time pressures perceived by Americans are real and affect prime tourism markets. Time is considered a valuable commodity that should not be wasted by the tourist or those serving the tourist.

This pressure somewhat explains the tension we often see in train stations and airports as vacationers—presumably at leisure—overly concern themselves with arrival times and unexpected small delays.

Two other social trends are influencing tourism. First, an increasing number of women are entering and remaining in the work force. Presently, women comprise nearly half of the civilian work force. This means that travel planning is mediated by two employed spouses in many households. Second, the time crunch is being felt more by the affluent (those earning over $50,000), young professionals, and the more-educated—typically people with college degrees. Unfortunately, these segments are generally the most avid tourists and find vacations an important part of their lifestyles. The prime tourism market in the United States is not only pressed for time, but "stressed out." According to Harris polls, 89% of all Americans say they experience high stress. Again, stress falls most heavily upon prime tourism markets—the educated, higher income professionals and executives.[17]

Other shifts in personal values will affect who is traveling where—and why. These include the growing concern for self-fulfillment, quality of life, and the nature of families. Studies on vacation patterns indicate that travel markets consist largely of people who need a vacation but don't have time to plan one or to go on one. The leisure traveler of the 1990s leads an overcomplicated, highly stressful life in which the scarcest resource is time—not money. In one study, 72% of vacation travelers mentioned "being with family" as the most important reason for taking a vacation.[18]

In these changing times, quality service is essential to meet the needs of pressed travel markets. Some hotel chains have adopted strategies to meet the growing needs of this market. For example, Hilton Hotels Corporation offers the "BounceBack Weekend" while Four Seasons Hotels and Resorts has expanded on an international scale.[19] In the Hilton program, the hotel is trying to appeal to busy, young working couples who are exhausted at the end of a week. They need something to help them "bounce back" and become refreshed. Hilton presents a solution: a weekend escape at a Hilton Hotel. Management at Four Seasons claims that the time-pressed traveler wants hassle-free quality to ease the burden of the business rush and the vacation tension. In its expansion plans, Four Seasons vows to provide luxury and relief for the modern traveler on a world-wide basis.

Concern for the environment and restrictions on development and growth will also influence tourism. Various countries will have to grapple with limited and expensive resources that will have to be shared among tourists and citizens. Finally, the unification of Europe in 1992 interacts in dynamic ways with trade, economic development, tourism supply, and destination access all across Europe.

Learning

When a person acquires knowledge, experiences, and skills that result in changed behavior, learning has taken place. **Learning** can be thought of as "a change or modification in behavior as a result of experience."[20] Learning is a fundamental human process. Without the ability to learn, maturation and mental development would not be possible.

Consider a simple example—you visit your travel agent and mention that you want an island vacation. You add that you want to go someplace warm—and that you want to get there via good airline service. The travel agent takes you to the world map and points out various islands in the Caribbean. What you missed in your geography classes is now filled in by the agent. You cannot make up your mind so the agent provides you with brochures, booklets, and vacation packages and tells you to take them home and review them. After some study, you return and tell the agent that you are ready. You have studied the vacation material, the amenities, and the airline connections, and have made your choice. In other words, you have learned enough to make your decision.

Learning and Tourism

Learning how to act and interact in social situations within society is referred to as **socialization**. As part of the socialization process, children learn about values that are important to their family, community, and nation. During these same early years, children are usually exposed to travel. Since learning is so central to behavior, the relationship between tourism and learning can be complex. There are, however, specific areas of tourism activity where the learning process is critical—and inherent.

Travel Socialization. Travel is a learned behavior just like ways of dressing, talking, dining, and interacting with others. During childhood, the child experiences for the first time how a family uses discretionary time to relax, recreate, and vacation together. Children are exposed to travel modes and means. They learn not only the methods of travel—such as cars, campers, airplanes, or trains—but where to travel and what to observe and enjoy—such as family vacations to national parks and to visit relatives. Some travel widely, others infrequently. In either case, this exposure has the potential to influence the person for a lifetime. Much is learned in these early years of travel, including the perception of distance. The awe and wonder of powerful sights and sounds are also etched into the child's mind—new landscapes and environments, huge city buildings, and vast open roads.

There has been little documentation of how childhood travel experiences influence later tourism activity, travel mode preference, or preferred destinations. Research about people's leisure experiences and activities provides some insight into early childhood experiences and adult leisure pursuits. Some 50% to 60% of leisure activities that people engage in throughout their lives are first learned during childhood.[21] Many of these activities—such as golf, swimming, or fishing—stimulate vacation travel in the later adult years.

The learning process and its effect on later activity is not a simple one-to-one relationship. Over time, some activities cease due to age, while others begin or end due to the person's desire for change or the familiar. This suggests that people add and delete activities depending upon circumstances such as health, interest, and social involvement.[22] As people mature, they modify leisure pursuits, seeking some activities which are novel and stimulating, while continuing old favorites which foster continuity, social contacts, and presumably selected travel patterns.

Childhood travel experiences can determine the nature of travel experiences in adulthood. (Courtesy of the Walt Disney Company, ©1989)

In a recent study of the leisure activities of mature individuals, two kinds of people emerged: *expanders* and *contractors*. Expanders learned a number of activities as children, but they continued to learn and engage in new activities over the course of their lives; a large percentage of people initiated new activities during their 50s and early 60s. This suggests an active pre-retirement and retirement phase of life. By comparison, contractors learned about and initiated activities primarily in their youth; the acquisition of new activities slowed with the acquisition of years.[23]

As groups, contractors and expanders could be compared to the psychocentric and allocentric travel segments. It is worth asking whether psychocentric travelers—those who are reluctant to try new things—are also "contractors"—people who initiate fewer general leisure activities during their lives. This relationship seems logical. If so, it would also seem logical that this group would engage in certain types of leisure activities—some of which stimulate tourism.

Learning Methods. Learning can be broken down into a few selected types which are appropriate to the discussion of tourism. These are conditioning, modeling, and latent learning.

Conditioning. In this type of learning, reinforcement or positive rewards foster the relationship between a stimulus and response. In other words, if a person receives a reward for carrying out a particular act, that person will continue to repeat the behavior. Reinforcement can take many forms: objects, food, money, or social responses like praise and recognition. Consider how a parent might give candy to the kids for being quiet in the back seat of the car while on a trip. This represents a form of conditioning.

Modeling. People also learn by observing others or watching models. If we see how a task is done, it is generally easier to learn and repeat the behavior on our own. This is sometimes referred to as learning by example. Modeling often occurs in tourism situations. Take the case of a bus load of foreign tourists arriving in a strange country. These tourists take instructions from their guide, get settled in the hotel, and then prepare for dinner. At the table, "strange" food is served. These dishes look exciting to the adventurous, but the question remains: How should these foods be eaten properly? A look around the room reveals local residents enjoying these "strange" dishes with a smile. The tourists take a minute or two to observe the local residents—or models—eating; shortly, the tourists are enjoying their new-found cuisine with awkward movements. Through modeling, the tourist learned the "socially accepted" way of dining.

Latent learning. People learn more than they realize through experience. Exploration, travel, and mere day-to-day activity exposes all of us to the realities of the physical and social environment. In the process, people gain information that can be useful at a later time. While traveling by car, the driver will see a number of street intersections, signs, buildings, and landmarks. After arriving at the hotel, checking in, and getting unpacked, the family might decide they would like to go to the city zoo. The family will probably recall the zoo sign observed en route to the hotel. This—and the knowledge of the streets gained through driving—will give the family a good chance of finding their way to the zoo. This represents latent learning. Of course, to reduce the risk of getting lost, this family would be wise to ask the hotel concierge for specific instructions. This scenario illustrates how latent learning can play a role in travel behavior. Also, latent learning fosters repeat visitation and destination loyalty. Remembering positive attributes and potential opportunities about the site will help keep the destination in the mind of the tourist as a possible place to return to.

Other forms of learning. Two other concepts related to learning are *generalization* and *discrimination*. Once people learn something they tend to apply the knowledge to similar situations. They generalize their knowledge and try to use it effectively in what they view as nearly identical situations. In tourism, a common area that people generalize about is the front desk. Tourists practice similar learned behaviors at front desks across the world, such as presenting their credit cards, filling out registration forms, and so on.

The second concept, discrimination, refers to knowing when *not* to apply learned information to a situation that is similar to—but not the same as—the one in which the learning took place. A simple example occurs all the time in very large hotels which have large, long linear front desks. These desks are staffed with employees dressed in similar attire, all waiting to help the tourist. The tourist enters the lobby and seeks to register with the first staff member encountered behind this long desk. Often, to the tourist's surprise, the answer to the registration request is "sorry, registration is to my left; this is the cashier desk." Here, the tourist applied knowledge about registration desks to the similar appearing cashier section. Of course, the cashier sign posted on the wall behind the cashier went unnoticed.

For some individual travelers, a vacation is much more than a two-week break from the office, the shop, or the home. If you look beyond the surface, travel involves a complex set of "inner dimensions" that are played upon by all sorts of forces and conditions.

Endnotes

1. William Niles, "1988 Outlook for Business Travel," in *1988 Outlook for Travel and Tourism,* Proceedings of the U.S. Travel Data Center's 13th Annual Travel Outlook Forum (Washington, D.C.: U.S. Travel Data Center, 1988), p. 90.

2. Abraham H. Maslow, "A Theory of Human Motivation," *Psychological Review* 50 (1943): pp. 370–396.

3. D. E. Berlyne, *Aesthetics and Psychobiology* (New York: Appleton-Century-Crofts, 1972).

4. Walter Mischel, *Introduction to Personality* (New York: Holt, Rinehart & Winston, 1981), p. 2.

5. Edward J. Mayo and Lance P. Jarvis, *The Psychology of Leisure Travel: Effective Marketing and Selling of Travel Services* (Boston, Mass.: CBI Publishing Co., 1981), p. 113.

6. John A. Howard and Arch G. Woodside, "Personal Values Affecting Consumer Psychology," in *Personal Values and Consumer Psychology,* edited by Robert E. Pitts, Jr. and Arch G. Woodside (Lexington, Mass.: Lexington Books, 1984), p. 4.

7. Stanley C. Plog, "Why Destinations Areas Rise and Fall in Popularity," *Cornell Hotel and Restaurant Administration Quarterly* 14 (February 1974).

8. Plog Research, Inc., "California Travelers' Perceptions of British Columbia and Vancouver: Results of the Research." Prepared for British Columbia, Ministry of Tourism, Recreation and Culture, May 1987, pp. 35–36.

9. Lynn R. Kahle, "The Values of Americans: Implications for Consumer Adaptation," in *Personal Values and Consumer Psychology,* edited by Robert E. Pitts, Jr. and Arch G. Woodside (Lexington, Mass.: Lexington Books, 1984), pp. 75–86.

10. Robert E. Pitts and Arch G. Woodside, "Personal Values and Travel Decisions," *Journal of Travel Research* 25 (Summer 1986): p. 24.

11. Rebecca H. Holman, "A Values and Lifestyles Perspective on Human Behavior," in *Personal Values and Consumer Psychology,* edited by Robert E. Pitts, Jr. and Arch G. Woodside (Lexington, Mass.: Lexington Books, 1984), pp. 35–54.

12. David Shih, "VALS as a Tool of Tourism Market Research: The Pennsylvania Experience," *Journal of Travel Research* 24, no. 4, pp. 2–11.

13. Joseph T. Plummer, "Changing Values: The New Emphasis on Self-Actualization," *The Futurist* 23 (January–February 1989): p. 13.

14. John P. Robinson, "Time's Up," *American Demographics* 11, no. 7 (July 1989): pp. 34–35.

15. Louis Harris, *Inside America* (New York: Vantage Books, 1987), p. 17.

16. Robinson, p. 34.

17. Harris, p. 8.

18. "Strictly Business," *Travel People,* May 1989, p. 12.

19. "Strictly Business," *Travel People,* May 1989, p. 12.

20. Albert A. Harrison, *Individuals and Groups: Understanding Social Behavior* (Monterey, Calif.: Brooks/Cole, 1976), p. 140.

21. John R. Kelly, *Leisure* (Englewood Cliffs, N.J.: Prentice-Hall, 1982), p. 172.

22. Seppo Iso-Ahola, *The Social Psychology of Leisure and Recreation* (Dubuque, Iowa: William C. Brown Company, 1980), p. 171.

23. Francis A. McGuire, F. Dominic Dottavio, and Joseph T. O'Leary, "The Relationship of Early Life Experiences to Later Life Leisure Involvement," *Leisure Sciences* 9 (1987): pp. 254-255.

Key Terms

allocentric	personality
energy-lethargy dimension	psychocentric
extrinsic motivation	psychographics
intrinsic motivation	socialization
learning	VALS
lifestyle measures	values
motivation	

Discussion Questions

1. Why are motivations for travel so difficult to measure?

2. Are most vacations considered intrinsically motivated or extrinsically motivated? Why?

3. How do personality traits influence tourism behavior?

4. What is meant by the term psychographics? How can psychographic research be applied to the study of travel behavior?

5. What basic lifestyle characteristics can be used to analyze travel behavior?

6. What is the difference between an allocentric and a psychocentric traveler?

7. What eight basic values have implications for consumer marketing? How do these values affect tourism?

8. What are the four basic lifestyle segments within the VALS system? How might shifting values within these groups influence tourism?

9. How does the process of socialization apply to tourism?

10. How do basic principles of learning apply to tourism?

REVIEW QUIZ

When you feel you have covered all of the material in this chapter, answer these questions. Choose the *best* answer. Check your answers with the correct ones found on the Review Quiz Answer Key at the end of this book.

True (T) or False (F)

T F 1. Travel motivations *always* seem to contradict each other.

T F 2. Behavior that is carried out and enjoyed for its own sake is said to be influenced by intrinsic motivation.

T F 3. Maslow's Hierarchy of Needs clearly holds true for travel motivations.

T F 4. Tourism provides an excellent means of accommodating a person's need for an optimal level of stimulation.

T F 5. Psychographics are measures that look at a person's interests, activities, and opinions.

T F 6. The psychocentric is less of a traveler than the allocentric.

T F 7. Values research is another psychographic approach to the study of tourism.

T F 8. The VALS group that is concerned about others and about society and the world is the societally conscious group.

T F 9. A social trend that is influencing tourism is the increasing number of women entering and remaining in the work force.

T F 10. Learning through experience is called latent learning.

Alternate/Multiple Choice

11. Psychological needs include all of the following *except:*

    a. achievement.
    b. hunger.
    c. success.
    d. socialization.

12. The motivations that influence the choice of many destinations, friendships, and vacation travel patterns are primarily:

    a. long-term.
    b. short-term.

13. The basic principle behind _____ is that a person seeks out a level of stimulation that is best for him/her as an individual.

    a. the Optimal Arousal Theory
    b. Maslow's Hierarchy of Needs

14. Adventuresome tourists who are willing to travel to exotic destinations are considered:

   a. psychocentrics.
   b. allocentrics.

15. Several kinds of learning methods that are appropriate to the discussion of tourism include:

   a. conditioning.
   b. modeling.
   c. latent learning.
   d. all of the above.

Chapter Outline

Societies, Culture, and Tourism
Social and Cultural Behaviors
    Socialization
    Social Norms
    Status and Roles
    Groups
    Social Stratification
    Family Life Cycles
Social Interactions
Social Impacts
    Limitations Affecting Impacts
    Response Models
Cultural Impacts

Learning Objectives

1. Distinguish between societies and cultures.

2. Define cultural tourism and provide some common examples.

3. Indicate how various forms and functions of socialization affect tourism.

4. Explain how social norms affect tourism.

5. Analyze how a person's status and role in society affects travel behavior.

6. Identify the characteristics of four groups that are particularly relevant to the study of tourism.

7. State what is meant by social stratification and its relationship to travel.

8. Examine how stages and elements of the family life cycle affect tourism.

9. Describe the significance of social interactions.

10. Identify four characteristics that limit the quality of social interactions between tourists, providers, and hosts.

11. Compare three models used to explain the social impacts of tourism.

12. Distinguish between a social and a cultural impact.

Property that is owned and is of some assessed value is known as wealth. -

4

Social and Cultural Dimensions

TOURISM EXPERIENCES are personal. But because tourism involves travel, tourism is a true social phenomenon. For the most part, travel is a group endeavor which involves contact with other people. People may travel as families, couples, tour groups, or as delegates to a conference. Social exchanges occur among travelers and others for many reasons. While on a trip, a traveler may buy something, seek information, or just exchange pleasantries with fellow tourists or residents. These encounters are social interactions which provide impressions and images for each person involved. Since travel takes the tourist to distant places, social interactions may include exchanges among people from different cultures. For many, cross-cultural exchange is exactly what makes tourism exciting. This chapter explores the nature of cross-cultural exchange and the relationship of other social behaviors to tourism.

Societies, Culture, and Tourism

When approaching tourism from a social science perspective, it is difficult—but important—to distinguish between the terms society and culture. For example, when an American visits Spain, two different societies *and* cultures come in contact. But what happens when a rural American visits New York? Is the rural visitor from the same society and culture, or is that visitor actually from the same society but a different subculture? This would definitely be the case if the rural visitor were Amish. Amish are American, but are from a distinct subculture within the larger society.

Sociologists and anthropologists have debated the distinction between society and culture for decades. For our purposes, **society** refers to an organized, independent, continuing number of people living in a specific area.[1] **Culture** includes the unique traditions and beliefs that hold these people together. More specifically, culture is a complex set of learned beliefs, customs, skills, habits, traditions, and knowledge shared by members of a society.[2] From an anthropological perspective, culture is much more than the rituals, ceremonies, and dances residents might perform for tourists at culture centers. The richer meaning of culture refers to those activities plus many private and unknown traditions that are part of the local person's daily life.

For outsiders, the culture of an area can represent an attraction in and of itself. This is sometimes called **cultural tourism**. Tourists interested in culture may seek exposure to local behaviors and traditions, to different ways of life, or to vestiges of a vanishing lifestyle. Yet tourism only permits selective exposure to other cultures. Frequently, an area's culture is displayed through stage presentations—often for pay. Because tourists generally stay in an area for a short time, what the tourist actually sees is just a faint reflection of the true culture.

Social and Cultural Behaviors

To fully appreciate the complexities of societies and cultures, it is important to discuss some basic social behaviors. In every society, people learn how to function effectively as a social unit, how to behave on a daily basis, and how to maintain values over generations. Without such capabilities, societies could not form and unique cultures would be lost.

Sociology is the study of the development and organization of societies. The sociologist studies the behavior of groups, the interactions of individuals, and the structure of society. Many of the social behaviors central to sociology are relevant to the study of tourism. Societies offer members predictability. In a society, behavior patterns are developed and people are expected to act accordingly. The development and maintenance of these behaviors form the cultural cornerstones—or belief system—of a society.

A society's culture can be the focus of social and anthropological study as well as a tourist attraction. Such situations abound across the world. Consider how Native American culture attracts tourists in many parts of the United States. In the Southwest, Navajo and Pueblo artists carry on business with the traveler. Arts and crafts, agriculture, and fishing are typical areas of commerce for Native Americans of the Northwest, Midwest, and Plains. For example, tribes in northern Minnesota sell wild rice to tourists and visitors, while tribes in Michigan sell fresh fish from the Great Lakes through retail outlets or local restaurants.

The exchange between tourists and Native Americans involves more than commerce. Tourists are also seeking exposure to the native culture. However, according to anthropologists, tourists come ill-prepared. Tourists lack information about Native American culture and are usually naive about what to expect and how to behave. For the most part, tourists act upon inaccurate and dated stereotypes. Conversely, Native Americans have their own impressions and stereotypes of tourists. These people feel tourists are only interested in purchasing artifacts and Native American art, and in taking pictures.[3] The perceptions held by both groups are misleading and do not truly depict tourists and Native Americans. But, in encounter after encounter, these false images prevail and are passed along.

Cultural tourism flourishes around the world. The festivals of Germany, the history of Rome, and the ceremonies of African bush tribes attract international travelers. To better understand cultural tourism, we must understand a little of what makes and sustains a culture.

Socialization

As a baby grows and matures into an adult, society, the family, and peers influence and teach the child about life and about appropriate behavior. In other words, the

Native American culture attracts tourists in terms of commerce and in terms of special events such as this inter-tribal pow-wow. (Courtesy of the Manhattan Convention & Visitors Bureau, Manhattan, Kansas)

person undergoes the process of **socialization.** Behavior patterns can vary among families, geographic regions, and subcultures. For example, selected patterns of social behavior at the dinner table may vary from the Midwest to the East Coast or from one side of town to the other. By most measures, a person of high school age has learned how to behave in public, eat properly at dinner functions, and visit with others of varying ages.

Tourism is subject to the same socialization process that guides behavior within and between groups. Just as people learn manners at an early age, children also learn tourism and travel behaviors during their first exposures to travel. New, often young, travelers learn how to behave in a broad range of travel situations, from traveling by air to buying souvenirs at local shops. For example, modern air travelers must learn how to purchase an airline ticket and check their baggage. The experience of waiting in line for tickets or luggage in an airport can vary dramatically from place to place and culture to culture. In the United States and some countries in Northern Europe, a proper queue—or waiting line—is important and respected. In some countries in Southern Europe, the queue has much less respect; a person not paying attention to his/her place in line may lose it.

New travelers also learn from others how to work with a travel agent and how to interact with taxi drivers, hotel staff, and other tourists. Travelers are constantly encountering new people from unique cultures in different settings. These exchanges are social learning experiences. As such, they are stored in memory and recalled when traveling to new destinations.

Socialization Functions. Through socialization, individuals learn basic survival functions, societal goals and objectives, living skills, and social roles.[4] People are taught basic personal and social behaviors that are required for acceptance, safety, health, sexuality, and social orientation. The young learn what society considers important through family, peers, and formal education. In most countries, the school system reflects and instills the primary values of the society. In the United States, for example, the goals of capitalism and democracy are learned at home, but refined and reinforced in school. Basic career skills such as reading, writing, math, and science are conveyed through formal education. More personal goals such as self-worth, ambition, and personal fulfillment are also part of socialization. Finally, role behaviors are learned and defined through socialization. The part one plays in society relates to one's role in life. Many behaviors—especially those defining social interaction—are guided by the positions and roles people assume.

Consider how the tourist comes to expect certain behaviors—that servers will serve the food, make suggestions, and see to the needs of the guests, for example. At the same time, tourists act out the role of visitors to a destination: they ask questions, take in the sites, stay at hotels or camp sites, and so on. Through a range of travel experiences and observations, those new to travel learn how to be tourists—or to play out the expected role.

The effect of socialization on other parts of a person's life relate directly to tourism. The well-rounded traveler is often a knowledgeable, skilled, and employed citizen. Skills and talents developed through socialization are used in most tourism experiences. For example, basic skills are used at dining functions while complex skills are used to adapt to new environments, convert currency, and coordinate air flight and hotel arrangements.

Modeling and Imitation. Modeling and imitation are other forms of socialization that shape tourism perceptions. For instance, parents act as models. Children learn by observing and repeating what they see their parents doing. Children who travel with their family are socialized into the proper travel behaviors at hotels, resorts, the beach, and in restaurants. Those exposed to more rural vacations through camping learn yet another set of travel behaviors.

Lessons in tourism take place as people of any age watch others in various travel situations. New travelers learn by observing how other tourists cross the border, exchange currency, or interpret directional signs or maps. Travelers, too, can augment socialization by seeking other sources of information such as travel books, brochures, travel advisors, or other travelers. Staff at the hotel information desk can help the guest understand the proper behavior and dress of the locality or region, the proper way to order a meal or secure a taxi, and even how to avoid insulting someone through a misplaced hand gesture (friendly gestures in one culture may not be friendly in another).

Peer pressure also influences how potential tourists use their free time and discretionary funds. Sharing tourism experiences with friends before or after a trip

Children who travel with their parents will learn a broad range of travel behaviors by observation—including waiting in line.

constitutes a type of peer pressure. The social exchange often implies that those returning had a "great time," while those who didn't go did not. Furthermore, the exchange may imply that those left behind should plan a similar trip.

Social Norms

Social norms are guides to behavior within groups and particular cultures. Norms are rules that describe how a person is expected to act in various situations.[5] Once developed, social norms are learned and passed along to each generation.

Outsiders to a community—like tourists—are very noticeable, usually because they are breaking a social norm. Outward signs give the tourist away, such as clothes, speech, ethnicity, or hair style. Beyond this, the tourist may violate social norms in stores, in traffic, at meal times, or at religious services. The tourist may have never been to the destination before nor read about appropriate behaviors. To expect an outsider to go unnoticed is unreasonable.

Social norms are often ignored or broken due to lack of knowledge. This lack of knowledge and inappropriate behavior feed the stereotype that a tourist is someone who knows little about the local people and community. Unfortunately, tourists have little opportunity—and sometimes little inclination—to learn the proper ways of tourism. This especially applies to international travel. Proper behavior is seldom taught to the tourist except by friends and family who may be ill-informed themselves. In the case of legal or safety issues, travel agents or tour guides should point out what should or should not be done in a certain country or culture.

As the world "shrinks" through air travel and as passage between countries opens up and eases, it becomes important for tourists to know proper social behaviors for a diversity of cultures and societies. This is already an established trend among international businesses. Many companies require business travelers to be familiar with the customs and social norms of the countries they are visiting. The standards should be no less for the pleasure traveler around the world.

Even within the United States, social norms differ across subcultures, regions, and states. In such instances, norms are generally beyond the knowledge of newly arrived tourists, unless they have taken the responsibility to learn proper behavior. Consider, for example, the vastly different norms of the Pennsylvania Amish. With respect to social norms, the Amish have many that are not the same as those in the dominant culture. They do not use modern equipment for farming, nor do they use electricity—which means no radios or televisions. Since they dress and live in a manner of the 1800s, the Amish stand out among the residents and tourists. Overly curious or pushy tourists can be offensive to the Amish, who typically avoid excessive contact with visitors. But tourists find the Amish interesting—just as they do Native Americans. As a result, tourist centers have been developed which focus upon the Amish. This provides for cultural and commercial exchange, while still preserving the privacy of the Amish in their homes.

Status and Roles

As a member of a society, a person occupies a position in which certain behaviors are expected. **Status** refers to the position; **role** refers to the behavior within a certain status.[6] Every industrialized society has a multitude of positions such as teacher, farmer, parent, student, neighbor. People occupying such positions are expected to behave as society has prescribed. Through socialization, we all have some idea of how certain roles are to be played. Status and roles are learned and have shared meanings for members of a particular society. This process is part of what we define as culture.

Shared meanings and expected behaviors result in more predictable social interactions among group members. Meanings and expectations can also reduce conflict if members of the culture adhere to role behaviors. For example, bankers acting like doctors or teachers acting like students can be disconcerting and, in some cases, illegal. Of course, the tourist is not without expected role behaviors. The stereotypical tourist is expected to be interested in self-serving pleasures, cheap souvenirs, and places to photograph with little concern for the culture or privacy of the local population. While this is not true in all cases, the stereotype is held by many residents of popular tourism destinations.

One's status in life changes with time and circumstances. Career changes, retirement, and shifts in the family can move a person into another status with new roles. So too for the tourist. Different types of travel demand different roles and behaviors. The manager at a conference plays one role, the family on vacation another. Roles vary according to the circumstances surrounding the tourism event.

All travelers seek tourism experiences, yet very different goals and objectives are sought through many different role behaviors. This occurs because there are different types of tourists. Exhibit 1 notes the roles, behaviors, and impacts of several types of tourists. **Mass tourists**—or those travelers participating in wide-scale travel designed for large numbers of people—generally enjoy accommodations that offer a familiar level of comfort and convenience. Travelers searching for a unique or foreign experience would require more contact with the community, its members, and its way of life. But tourists of this type are fewer in number and, consequently, have less impact on a destination.

Different types of tourists have different impacts on the environment, the culture, the social fabric, and sometimes the political structure of a destination. Each type of traveler can be expected to behave differently while visiting a destination. The photo-taking, souvenir-buying, superficial, short-term visitor is the tourist of humor, resentment, and stereotype. Certain groups can be seen as more exploitive and less sensitive to social and cultural values. Explorers blend into the community, live as local people do, and stay longer—but have contacts with fewer people than members of a charter tour that moves through a community for shopping or sight-seeing.

Groups

Society is composed of individuals that form groups. A **group** is a collection of people who regularly have contact, share structured interactions, have a common feeling of togetherness, and work toward a common set of goals and objectives.[7] The dynamics within and between groups are the mainstay of sociology. As social beings, people use groups to help define who they are and what they may become. It is easy to think of common groups which form around friendships, social functions, religious reasons, neighborhood interests, or parenting needs. Each has a different function with unique goals and objectives. A person could belong to different groups and play very different roles in each one. A lot depends upon how important the group goals are for the person.

Groups are usually informal, and place few rules and demands upon the members. Groups may become more formal as they grow in size or the goals and objectives become more important to the members. Very large groups—such as bureaucracies or formal organizations—may become very formal and controlled.

Social scientists define a range of groups. Four groups particularly relevant to the study of tourism are *reference, peer, primary,* and *secondary*.[8] A reference group refers to a model group. Even though a person is not a member of the reference group—or for that matter, may never be—the reference group still provides standards that guide behavior. A person may imitate the behavior of members of a reference group. In tourism, a common example is the person of lesser means who emulates the rich traveler. Some middle-class travelers—knowing full well they

Exhibit 1   Selected Tourist Roles and Related Impacts

Category	Comments
Explorer	Searching for the new and undiscovered, may blend into or live in the local culture
Impact	* Limited in numbers; often travel alone; little cultural, social, or environmental impacts; willing to accept the local norms and ways of living
Elite	Have been everywhere; have the funds to search out the exotic from the jungle to the mountains
Impact	* Few in numbers; blend into the setting and culture; willing to live as the natives do while on an exclusive, expensive adventure
Off-Beat	Travel to the unusual occasionally to get away from the crowds and the normal fare of tours
Impact	* Limited in numbers in any one location; "put up with" local conditions; do not demand a lot from the local culture or environment; they are noticed by the locals because they appear at unique locations (very remote, unique local cultural events)
Unusual	Searching for unique, but want to do it at a safe distance and with some modern conveniences
Impact	* Larger numbers, take advantage of unusual side trips to remote or unique areas; less adaptable to the local norms, social situation, or environment; demand more and may have more of an impact
Incipient Mass	The modern tourist, large in number, traveling alone or in small groups going to somewhat remote and unique sites
Impact	* Larger numbers; a steady stream of visitors; impacts are noticeable; would prefer Western amenities and the safety of tours and conveniences
Mass	Also modern tourist, large in number, traveling alone or in small groups, attracted in mass to popular "tourist" destinations
Impact	* Increasing numbers; arriving constantly; expecting Western amenities; little concern, adaptation or contact with local culture or social norms; change the nature of the popularized destinations in terms of social and environmental characteristics
Charter	Modern tourists traveling in large chartered groups to popular destinations around the world
Impact	* Large flows of tourists arriving daily; demand Western conveniences; the local community has changed dramatically; tourism dominates the economy and social structure

Based on Valene L. Smith, "Introduction," in *Hosts and Guests: The Anthropology of Tourism,* 2d ed., edited by Valene L. Smith (Phil.: University of Pennsylvania Press, 1989), pp. 11–13.

will never be among the rich and famous—use the elite as a reference group in regard to how and where to travel .

The peer group is a personal membership group. Members of peer groups are similar in age, social status, interests, and values. The peer group is one of the most influential groups in a person's life. What friends or peers in a work or social

Fun-filled adventures at amusement parks are often shared among members of peer or primary groups—or groups that consist of family and friends. (Courtesy of the Wisconsin Dells Visitor & Convention Bureau)

situation think and say about a person is important and can set the standard for one's behavior.

Groups vary along a continuum from primary to secondary groups. A primary group consists of people who know each other well, have very frequent face-to-face contact, and have concern for each other over the long-term. The family unit is an example of a primary group. Unlike a peer group, the ages, interests, and goals of a primary group are more diverse. Plus, the members of primary groups are generally closer to each other than members of peer groups. Tourism is a social experience that is usually shared among primary group members. When you ask people who they travel with, the most common answer will be family and friends. Friendship travel groups may be primary or peer groups, such as a group of co-workers.

At the other end of the continuum are secondary groups. Relationships within these groups are less intimate than in primary groups. Face-to-face interactions are more infrequent, and the bonds between members are weaker. A possible example of a secondary group could be conference delegates who have been assigned to a committee. Such a group will meet, form, and achieve goals, and possibly disband at the end of the conference. The members of this group may hardly know each other, yet work for a time toward a common goal.

The decisions of individual group members are strongly influenced by conformity. **Conformity** is the correspondence of a person's behavior to the norms and expectations of the group. In group travel, individuals develop expectations and behavior consistent with the group. Unfortunately, the behavior of the traveling tourist group can be crude, boisterous, or inappropriate. Many group members—who might otherwise know better—indulge in such behavior just to conform to group expectations. In the case of a family group traveling together, the parents have the ability to control and lead family members through the travel experience.

Group pressures can have positive effects as well. The cohesiveness or unity of a group can lead to effective and efficient activity that helps meet group goals. Groups act in unison as a result of leadership, cohesiveness, and conformity. A large tour group is manageable due to the pressures of conformity, the resultant cohesiveness, and the ability of the tour guide or leader. These pressures keep the group together and, over time, build bonds between the members. Imagine the chaos if everyone in a 100-person tour group decided to go their own way in the middle of downtown London.

Conformity also popularizes some destinations for millions of tourists. The psychocentric tourist who visits the popular destination is, in fact, conforming to the behavior of a larger segment of the traveling public.

Social Stratification

Society is stratified by income, education, and opportunity. **Social stratification** refers to the different segments of the population that exist in a society. Some people live lives of luxury; most people do not. The layers—or groupings—of people between two extremes—one example being wealth and poverty—are the strata of society; better opportunities are generally available to people toward the top.

The elements that differentiate social strata are wealth, income, prestige, and power. The amount and combination of elements that a person has places that person in a particular stratum. Some people are born into wealth, others into lesser means. Some earn their place in society, others inherit their positions. *Income* refers to money earned, while *wealth* refers to property owned that is of some assessed value. Both income and wealth can be measured; having plenty of either one increases the odds of being in a higher social stratum or social class. But neither ensures prestige or power. Sometimes *prestige* comes by birth; in other cases, by deeds and actions. *Power* refers to mobilizing others to accomplish a goal—setting policies for others to follow. Power can be gained through vested authority or influence.[10]

Exhibit 2 provides a breakdown of income in the United States. When you break down the population by fifths, it can be seen that the upper brackets control most of the income. The poorest control only 5% of the income, while those in the highest income bracket control nearly half (43%). This relationship has not changed over the last three decades.[11]

Socioeconomic characteristics such as education, income, and wealth are used to define different social classes. The lines between classes are sometimes blurred. Like income, the population is not evenly distributed among social classes. As shown in Exhibit 3, a very small percent of the population is considered upper class (2%). As a result, this group is often not the target of mass marketing appeals. The largest groups are the lower-middle and upper-lower classes—36% and 38% respectively. This is a huge market. The U.S. Bureau of the Census projects these

Exhibit 2   Income Distributions in the United States

U.S. Population	Income Percentage		
	1950	1983	1985
Top fifth	43%	43%	43%
Second fifth	23	24	24
Third fifth	17	18	17
Fourth fifth	12	11	11
Bottom fifth	5	5	5

Based on Judson R. Landis, *Sociology: Concepts and Characteristics*, 6th ed. (Belmont, Calif.: Wadsworth, 1986), p. 133; and U.S. Bureau of the Census, *Statistical Abstracts of the United States* (Washington, D.C.: U.S. Bureau of the Census, 1987), p. 437.

Exhibit 3   Social Class Distribution in the United States

Class Title	% Population	Comments
Upper	2%	Old wealth, some new wealth, live the luxurious life
Upper Middle	11%	Professionals, business owners, successful, concerned with quality, future-oriented for self and family
Lower Middle	36%	White collar, hard working, conforming to society, home, family and future-oriented
Upper Lower	38%	Includes factory workers, skilled workers, blue collar, good incomes, less future-oriented
Lower Lower	13%	Unskilled workers, moderate to low incomes, oriented to the present, play it "safe" in life decisions

Source: E. Jerome McCarthy and William D. Perreault, Jr., *Basic Marketing: A Managerial Approach*, 9th ed. (Homewood, Ill.: Irwin, 1987), pp. 181–183.

segments to constitute nearly 185 million people in the early 1990s—or nearly three-quarters of the U.S. population.[12]

Family Life Cycles

As might be expected, the various social classes have different travel patterns. The very rich visit luxurious and unique destinations that are often difficult to access and restrictive in terms of membership or costs. The middle class comprises the bulk of travelers the world over. A profile of the U.S. pleasure traveler is a person approaching 40, married, with some college education, a median income approaching $30,000, with no children in the household.[13] The typical traveler is likely to be from a professional, managerial, or sales-oriented occupation. Nearly half come from dual income families.

The problem is that "typical" travelers rarely exist. Rather, travelers come in all types; few are truly representative of the mean. It is sometimes better to think of travelers in broad categories described as stages of the **family life cycle**. Variables used to determine family life cycle stages are age, marital status, and presence and age of children.[14]

Common stages in the family life cycle include young adult singles, divorced or separated, married with no children, full nest I (small children), full nest II (children over five), full nest III (older children), empty nest, sole survivor (still working), senior couples (retired), and senior survivor (retired).[15] These stages reflect the realities and changes of life. Working singles or couples without children have modest incomes that permit travel to be an important part of their lives. In contrast, young families with young children have limitations in terms of time and money. As the family matures, incomes usually increase, generating travel opportunities for the whole family. Travel may increase dramatically for an empty-nest couple, provided that college education costs are not overwhelming. In retirement, two types evolve: (1) those with good retirement allowances that permit tourism; and (2) those who experience a sizable drop in income which dramatically reduces their expenditures for travel and other luxury items.

The social demographics within the family life cycle directly affect the tourism industry. Each stage of the life cycle offers the family a different set of challenges that may influence travel decisions. Trends toward mini-vacations and longer weekends may be related to the new life cycle stage of baby boomers. A large proportion of baby boomers are approaching their mid-forties and moving into the full-nest III stage—which means they have more income and older children. This group, too, may now have time for a mini-vacation, but not for a two- or three-week vacation away from work or from their children's school. Yet, many members of this market group still want to get away—with or without the children. In either case, the trip will be short in duration. Parents will not want to be gone too long if the kids stay behind; and if the kids come along, the trip could be short because of school schedules, work demands, and expense.

Club Med and Hilton Hotels have developed packages to accommodate baby boomers. To meet the needs of busy working couples with children, Hilton developed the BounceBack Weekend. This is a package deal for the family in which kids can stay at the property for free.[16] The Bounceback Weekend is designed to get people out of the house and to a place where they can truly have a relaxing weekend. The package includes low room rates and continental breakfasts for all guests; children of any age stay free if they stay in the same room as their parents. The low rates are available into the next week if the family wants to extend its stay.

Club Med, facing some of the same demographic changes, repositioned its vacation products away from the singles-only vacation to one that could easily include children, married couples, and families. Child care facilities were added to Club Med resorts, and advertising changed to get the message out that Club Med was more than the vacation of choice for singles.[17]

Both the Hilton and Club Med packages represent responses to demographic changes and life cycle patterns. Travel decision-making, travel preferences, and travel patterns *do* change over the course of the family life cycle. For example, the influence of wife and husband in the decision-making process shifts over the course of a marriage. Wives generally dominate in families nearing the later stages of the family life cycle.[18] Priorities change as well. In the earlier stages of the family life cycle, the amount of money spent on a trip is third on the list of issues. As the family approaches retirement, costs and accommodation types take a higher priority.[19]

Understanding family life cycles can be useful for understanding recreation-related tourism. The patterns in recreation and tourism correspond to those observed in other sectors of consumer behavior. Family incomes tend to peak as children age and approach leaving home. The purse strings on funds are more likely to loosen for discretionary activities and products—including tourism. A profile of campers using private campgrounds in Michigan revealed several behavioral and travel differences across the life cycle stages. Families in the younger stages took shorter trips and tended to stay at one campground rather than touring. These younger families also took fewer camping trips than full nest III or empty nest families. Besides taking longer trips, the older families tended to have more expensive equipment (such as recreation vehicles) and to spend more.[20]

It is important to note that the traditional family is hard to find in the United States. Ironically, the single wage earner supporting a spouse and child at home is now, more than ever, an "American dream." In today's world of busy dual career families, only 13%—or about 25 million households—of all married families are what could be called traditional.[21] Only 28% of all households consist of married couples with children under 18—down from 40% in 1970.[22]

Social Interactions

Social and cross-cultural interactions are inherent in the travel process. For millions, they are the reason for travel itself. Contact with other people and cultures is a motivation and goal, and subsequently, an effect or outcome. The social and cultural dimensions of tourism involve members of the host community, the traveler, and the providers of travel services, who may or may not be local residents.

The flow of tourists through the destination generates social interaction among family, business, and community members. Social contact includes face-to-face exchanges as well as more indirect interactions that occur on busy streets and sidewalks. The mere presence of strangers as tourists will have some effect on a community—be it social, economic, environmental, or all three. More people in a community means longer lines at the store, more traffic on the road, and larger crowds at recreation and tourism facilities. Tourists, too, will affect the consumption of such utilities as gas and water. Not all interactions are negative. Among tourism's positive benefits are a boost to the economy, exposure to new ideas, and increased interest and activities in the arts.

Social interactions can be purely social, purely business, or a combination. The most frequently studied interaction is between hosts and guests. Guests are the tourists visiting a community while the people in the community are the hosts. Social contacts might consist of business transactions at stores, friendly greetings on the sidewalk or beach, or inquiries at cafes or malls. Each contact leaves an impression—be it positive, negative, or neutral—with each person involved.

Exhibit 4   Social Interactions in Tourism

Social Interactions Directly Involving Tourists

    Hosts and Tourists
    Tourists and Tourists
    Tourists and Potential Tourists
    Tourists and Providers

Interactions in Support of Tourists

    Hosts and Providers
    Providers and Providers
    Hosts and Hosts

Note: *Hosts* are the residents of tourism destinations who have contact with tourists. *Providers* are people in other sectors of the tourism industry who service the needs of the tourist, but are not located within the destination community.

Exhibit 4 outlines a broad range of interactions, including the most common: the tourist and the local resident or host. The interactions listed on the upper half of the exhibit are those which directly involve the tourist. Besides local residents, the tourist encounters other tourists en route or at the destination. Tourists also meet service providers, such as hotel and airline staff. Interactions with these individuals usually occur beyond or en route to the destination.

In the United States, many communities are divided about the role that tourism should play in their local economies. Host-host interactions in some communities can be less than congenial. But down the road, a community may have a very positive outlook on the effect tourism has on the local population. Intra-community feelings have a tendency to spill over into the exchanges with the guest and can leave the guest with positive or negative impressions.

Social Impacts

Contact with other people generates change. The study of such changes is the study of **social impacts**. Impacts can be simple or complex, short-term or enduring. Social impacts can be thought of as changes in the lives of people who live in destination communities which are associated with tourism activity.[23] Although most studies focus on residents, tourists are also affected by the social impacts of travel and tourism. In the end, all parties involved will be influenced. The tourist meets new people and encounters unique social behaviors. The resident experiences a broad range of behaviors as tourists from around the country or even the world venture into their community.

Both the positive and negative impacts of tourism have been an issue throughout the history of tourism. An early example of a negative impact might be the street crowds in ancient Rome as visitors flocked to the games. A modern day example might be the resentment felt by local residents as they cope with summer tourists flooding the beaches and shops of a small resort town. But tourism has its benefits. Tourism has persistently reduced social barriers as different groups of people encounter each other.

At the core of what most people think of as the social impact is the personal contact between tourists, providers, and hosts. What has to be remembered about social encounters is this: *all* encounters are personal. They may not be warm or intimate, but they *do* involve human contact. Every encounter has the potential to be positive, negative, or merely superficial or mundane. The hundreds of social exchanges that occur within a vacation make a significant contribution to the quality of the experience. The negative feelings of being treated rudely can linger for some time and shade the tourist's perceptions of the destination and its people. The reverse holds true as well. Since hospitality is refreshing, it generates strong positive feelings that the traveler will share and remember for a long time.

Limitations Affecting Impacts

Four basic characteristics tend to limit the quality of the interaction between tourists, providers, and hosts. Limitations occur because tourism social interactions are:[24]

1. Transitory
2. Bound by spatial and temporal constraints
3. Lacking in spontaneity
4. Unbalanced, less than equal

Transitory. By definition and design, tourism is short-term, with little time available to the tourist to be in any one place. This means that any contact among guests, providers, or hosts will be brief, and will provide little opportunity to form close relationships. If a friendship does develop, it is more likely to be tourist to tourist rather than tourist to host.

It is even less likely that close relationships will develop between travelers and service providers. Most social exchanges between tourists and providers are extremely brief. Also, business exchanges are expected to be just that: an exchange of services for money. Once the deal is complete, no further interactions are expected, meaning "no strings attached." It would be emotionally crippling for all parties if every social encounter was a strong emotional exchange. Rather, people—particularly those in service industries—protect themselves by various means including the use of superficial greetings and comments. However, friendliness and a strong concern for quality service is required of all staff—and should be emphasized through excellent training.

Spatial and Temporal Constraints. Tourism, too, presents situational barriers for the host, provider, and guest. Even on vacation, tourists can be pressed for time and impatient with delays and problems which would be normal back home. In order to foster a smooth encounter and deal with the growing numbers of tourists, providers and hosts may begin to make tourism experiences predictable and regimented. This offers efficiencies, but reduces the number and types of social exchanges that can occur.

Lack of Spontaneity. The social interactions of tourists and local residents are often constrained and less than spontaneous—if they occur at all. The chance encounter is most often within the confines of the business transaction or at local attractions used by local residents. Even in non-business settings, social exchanges are likely to be rare.

Unequal Relations. The fourth issue is the "unbalanced" nature of the people or parties involved. Tourists, hosts, and providers often have different socioeconomic backgrounds. Social and economic differences, when noticeably large, make social interactions awkward. For hosts, providers, and guests alike, such encounters may actually be negative and are avoided.

Response Models

Researchers have proposed several models to explain the social impacts of tourism. These include the irridex, attitudinal, and adjustment models.

Irridex Model. The **irridex model** can be used to define the social impacts of tourism on the residents of a destination community.[25] This model suggests that in the beginning stage of tourism development and contact, the residents are excited about the influx of visitors, glad to see them, and pleased that they are spending money. In this initial stage called "euphoria," little planning is done. The visitors just show up and are served by the community as it exists.

In the second stage called "apathy," tourists are seen as common and ordinary; the interest and enthusiasm of the euphoria stage is long gone. Now the host-guest relationship is one of commercial enterprise and marketing. Formality has become part of the process of dealing with the multitudes of visitors.

In the third stage, the residents become concerned and irritated by the tourists. This is called the "annoyance" stage. The community is saturated by tourists and residents are becoming "fed up." In this stage, the community may begin to develop tourism services and expand amenities to accommodate the visitors; sometimes the community may even isolate visitors in tourist sections or corridors.

This leads to the last stage—"antagonism"—in which a strong dislike is felt and expressed toward the tourist. Residents now feel very differently toward the tourists that they previously welcomed to their community. In this stage, local residents most typically begin to generate negative stereotypes about tourists and tourism. While feelings are changing among residents, the types of tourists arriving are probably changing as well—much in line with the tourist roles outlined earlier in Exhibit 1.

Attitudinal Model. The **attitudinal model**, shown in Exhibit 5, suggests that community members can have a positive or negative attitude toward tourists that can be expressed in an active or passive manner. This model is more realistic than others since most residents do have divided feelings about the role of tourism within a community. Different residents can have different attitudes. Some people feel hostile toward tourists while others feel congenial.

Attitudes, too, can change over time. People may change their attitudes from positive to negative and may express these attitudes in different ways. The arrows

Exhibit 5   Attitude and Behavioral Response to Tourists

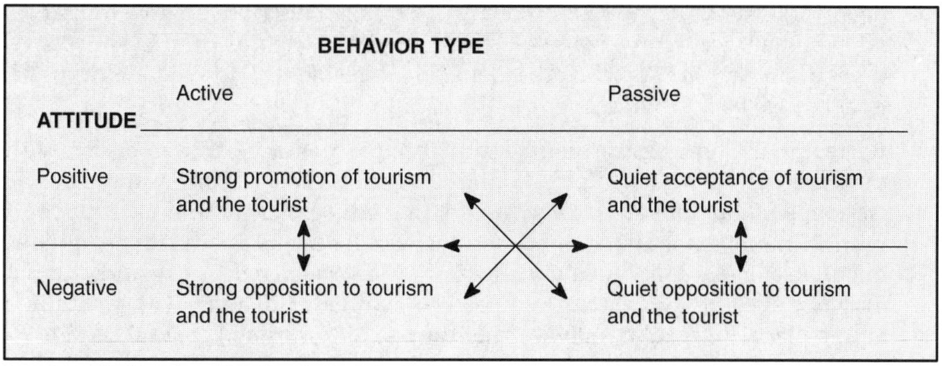

Based on Bjorklund and Philbrick 1972; Butler 1974: as cited and illustrated by Alister Mathieson and Geoffrey Wall, *Tourism: Economic, Physical and Social Impacts* (New York: Longman, 1982), p. 139.

in Exhibit 5 suggest changes in attitudes and modes of expression. As more and more tourists flock to a community, some residents may develop negative attitudes toward tourists and express these feelings openly. This represents a change from previous times when positive attitudes were expressed in a passive way. If a majority of the community becomes negative, then the community may begin to face open conflicts and debate that can damage the hospitality atmosphere. Such divided sentiments can be seen in some parts of the United States. For example, Arizonians often resent "snowbirds" (tourists fleeing the winters of Northern states), and, Oregonians have been known to resist visitors from California. In each case, mild amounts of resentment have been evident, but not so intense as to drastically curtail tourism.

A study of Hawaiian residents' responses to tourism surveys further illustrates how mixed feelings can be held by residents.[26] Residents freely admit that tourists cause problems—for example, 64% said tourism increases prostitution, and 41% cited crowding problems in popular tourist centers. But at the same time, the residents report many positive impacts associated with tourists. Ninety percent felt that meeting tourists from around the world was very educational. Furthermore, a majority of the residents reported that tourism had a more important effect on the economy than other sources of state revenue such as pineapple, sugar, and military bases.

Adjustment Model. An even more complex model—the **adjustment model**—suggests that residents display several types of responses to the tourist, including resistance, retreatism, boundary maintenance, revitalization, and adoption.[27] Some of these responses can be expressed actively, others passively.

- **Resistance**. This response refers to residents taking active, aggressive actions against tourism and sometimes even tourists. Hostility can be expressed in many ways—some overtly, others subtly and indirectly. For example, store-keepers and staff at restaurants and hotels might refuse to help, or to try and speak a guest's language—even when it is known. Resentment can build and, in extreme cases, lead to abuse of tourists or cheating them in business dealings. A review of crime cases in Hawaii reveals that crime against tourists is often higher than crime against residents.[28] Crimes against tourists are sometimes aimed at tourists who are insensitive to residents and who are from different social backgrounds.

• **Retreatism**. Community members may avoid contact or interactions with tourism and the tourist. Retreatism often occurs when a community is tourism-dependent, but still does not accept the industry. In these situations, community members have to embrace the tourist for economic reasons, but maintain a distance and negative feelings on a social level. The visiting tourist may not even be aware that this passive manner of dealing with tourism is taking place. Retreatism may include the use of traditional customs and folkways as community members attempt to isolate themselves from tourists.

• **Boundary maintenance**. This is a common response among subcultures within the United States. As a group, a community may appreciate the tourism business and even the tourists. But through social norms and activities, community members keep a distance between themselves and the tourist. This passive response to tourists is displayed by several religious groups such as the Amish, Hutterites, or Mennonites. Members of these communities may interact with the tourist, but differences in languages, behaviors, and dress are used to maintain a boundary between themselves, their culture, and the tourists.

• **Revitalization**. For some communities, countries, or tourism destinations, the response to tourism has been positive for the social mores and local customs. Local cultural events involving customs, festivals, rituals, or religious ceremonies have become tourist attractions that draw people to the community. Some of these events often survive on their popularity to outsiders. By becoming tourist attractions, historical districts of older American cities—such as Colonial Williamsburg, Virginia—are able to preserve their original architecture and style. Tourist interest and dollars can also assist local communities in restoration efforts. This particular strategy can be active, with efforts to restore customs, festivals, and even buildings being made in an open manner with community support. In other cases, the community may be more passive. Customs and folkways may be rekindled but boundaries maintained—thus keeping social and cultural distances between tourists and residents.

• **Adoption**. In adoption, community members embrace the lifestyle and orientation of the visitor. Many tourist communities in the United States have accepted tourism as part of their social and economic fabric. Such "tourist towns" exist by virtue of the tourist and develop a seasonal pattern shaped by the tourism season. The adoption strategy is an active, positive response to tourism. It usually entails promoting and marketing local resources such as festivals, customs, and local wares to incoming tourists.

Within any one community, various combinations of responses can co-exist and cause conflict. Communities can be divided regarding the role tourism plays within the local customs, economy, and social networks. In each model, the progression and

Two artists from the Great Smoky Arts and Crafts Community in Gatlinburg, Tennessee, put finishing touches on their works. (Courtesy of the Gatlinburg, Tennessee, Chamber of Commerce)

stage of a community is difficult to predict. The models do provide a sense of what changes a community might expect as tourism affects local businesses and citizens to a greater degree. While these models are instructive, it is still not known why some communities respond one way, while others may take an entirely different tack.

Cultural Impacts

Social impacts of tourism focus upon the results of interactions between the tourist and the host or provider. **Cultural impacts** refer to more than the social exchange between people. Cultural impacts can be thought of as the changes in the arts, artifacts, customs, rituals, and architecture of a people that result from tourism activity or development. Arguments persist about the role of tourism in changing the culture of residents and native people. While it is true that changes in a community may occur when tourism development takes place, it is usually not clear whether such changes would take place anyway—even in the absence of tourism. Another industry may have moved in and had the same—if not more dramatic—effect. Culture, too, is dynamic; it changes over time through its own and outside forces. Tourism is but one of the outside forces exerting pressure. For some communities, tourism is the weakest agent affecting culture.

External evidence of a culture includes the art forms, folkways, rituals, and architecture of the residents or native people. A cultural impact occurs to the extent that such skills and artworks are lost or maintained by the influences of tourism. In specific cases around the world, tourism has preserved and nurtured local customs, skills, and rituals. Consider, for one, Native Americans of the Southwestern United States. In the Southwest, the native art is part of the culture sought by tourists. Through the support and interest of tourists, Native Americans have been able to continue their traditions.

On the other hand, the relationship between tourism and culture sometimes exacts a high price. Art may become a trivial commodity designed only for the tourist—as some call it, "airport art." Other costs include the traditions and skills that are lost and no longer practiced because of changes in the community.

Exhibit 6 summarizes the more prevalent social and cultural impacts associated with tourism. Impacts can be direct or indirect. For example, steady tourism growth

Exhibit 6   Summary of Social and Cultural Impacts

SOCIAL INTERACTIONS

Dissolve social barriers
Generate cultural understanding and awareness between societies
Reduce social conflicts between members of other societies
Depersonalize relationships, commercialize relationships
Generate resentment due to social comparison with tourists
Modify the rates of diseases and changes in health
Enhance international understanding and peace

MORALITY AND RELIGIOUS NORMS

Change sexual norms of behavior
Changes in crime rates, prostitution, theft, gambling
Add new norms of behavior to moral codes of community
Shift in importance of traditional religious practices

SOCIAL NORMS

Shift in dress and behavior to reflect that of the tourist
Weaken family structures and shifts in family behaviors
Changes in gender or family role behavior and expectations
Generate conflicts within community
Shifts in response to strangers and outsiders (hospitality)
Generate conflicts between tourists and residents
Development of new social norms of behaviors (e.g., dress)
Sharing national holiday or regional celebrations with tourists
Develop stereotypes of tourists—positive, negative, inaccurate

CULTURAL WAYS AND ACTIVITIES

Increase awareness of cultural history and customs
Increase appreciation of cultural artifacts and architecture
Breakdown of traditional cultural activities and customs
Change in role of traditional foods and languages among residents
Opportunities for cultural and educational exchanges
Change in the role of handicrafts and folkways within the community

DAY-TO-DAY ACTIVITIES

Increase in the pace of life
Experience rapid change within the community
Activity patterns determined by tourist flows
Project positive impressions of destination to outsiders
Awareness by community that they are part of a larger world
Increased congestion and crowding
Competition for local resources—beaches, restaurants, museums
Changes in entertainment opportunities within the community
Shifts in work patterns and methods (farming, service, etc.)

Sources: This table was compiled from a number of sources, including the following reviews and research articles: J. R. Brent Ritchie and Michel Zins, "Culture as Determinant of the Attractiveness of a Tourism Region," *Annals of Tourism Research* 5 (1978): p. 262; Juanita C. Liu, Pauline J. Sheldon and Turgut Var, "Resident Perception of the Environmental Impacts of Tourism," *Annals of Tourism Research* 14 (1987): pp. 23–34; Jafar Jafari, "On Domestic Tourism," *Journal of Travel Research* 25 (1987): pp. 36–38; Alister Mathieson and Geoffrey Wall, *Tourism: Economic, Physical and Social Impacts* (New York: Longman, 1982), pp. 133–176; Maureen McDonough, "Social Impacts of Tourism," paper presented at Michigan State University, Cooperative Extension Service, Fall Training Program, Tawas, Michigan, September, 1989.

is frequently accompanied by new and improved transportation systems. These new roads may directly affect the local farmer by improving that farmer's mobility. Even though this same farmer never comes face-to-face with a tourist, the price of that farmer's produce may be directly tied to the food sold to tourists at local hotels. In this sense, the new roads represent a long-term impact.

As a second example, consider the effect of mass tourism on a festival or event. If mass tourism requires the local festival to expand and move to another community to accommodate crowds, then it is safe to say that the community has experienced direct, social, and cultural impacts of tourism. This was illustrated in a negative way with the expansion of the *Alarde*—an event in Fuenterrabia, Spain, that recreates the 1638 Spanish victory over the French. As the ritual and festival grew in popularity with tourists, it lost the small, intimate atmosphere that it originally had. This change concerned the residents and eventually changed the tenor of the event for the long term.[29] The *Alarde* became a commodity rather than a local community celebration, and lost its charm for the local people.

Tourism is a change agent. As communities and countries embrace tourism, change will occur. Social contact between residents and tourists can be exciting and refreshing. But as the crowds increase, the resident feels the pressure of too many tourists coming too rapidly and too often.

In all communities, some people benefit directly from tourism and come to depend on tourism for their livelihood. At the same time, their neighbors may grow tired of the tourists, the crowding, the traffic congestion, and the long lines at the stores. For many communities, tourism becomes a matter of balance. With proper control, planning, and determination, a community can maintain social and cultural values while adjusting to the demands and economic benefits of tourism.

Endnotes

1. Judson R. Landis, *Sociology: Concepts and Characteristics,* 6th ed. (Belmont, Calif.: Wadsworth, 1986), p. 75.
2. Landis, p. 75.
3. Deirdre Evans-Pritchard, "How 'They' see 'Us', Native American Images of Tourists," *Annals of Tourism Research* 16 (1989): p. 92.
4. Donald A. Hobbs and Stuart J. Blank, *Sociology and the Human Experience* (New York: Wiley, 1982), pp. 43–45.
5. Landis, p. 65.
6. Landis, p. 71.
7. Donald Light, Jr., and Suzanne Keller, *Sociology,* 3d ed. (New York: Knopf, 1982), p. 182.
8. Landis, pp. 95–97.
9. Landis, p. 128.
10. Much of this discussion is based on Donald Light, Jr., and Suzanne Keller, *Sociology,* 3d ed. (New York: Knopf, 1982), pp. 269–274.
11. Landis, p. 133.
12. Judith Waldrop, "2010," *American Demographics,* February 1989, p. 20.
13. U.S. Travel Data Center, *1987 Survey of Business Travelers* (Washington, D.C.: U.S. Travel Data Center, 1988), p. 13.

14. E. Jerome McCarthy and William D. Perreault, Jr., *Basic Marketing: A Managerial Approach*, 9th ed. (Homewood, Ill.: Irwin, 1987), pp. 162–163.

15. McCarthy and Perreault, p. 163.

16. Joan Castonguay, "Research as a Catalyst for Program Development," paper presented at the Annual TTRA Conference, Honolulu, Hawaii, June, 1989.

17. Alastair Morrison, *Hospitality and Travel Marketing* (Albany, N.Y.: Delmar Publishers Inc., 1989), pp. 249–251.

18. Robert M. Cosenza and Duane L. Davis, "Family Vacation Decision Making over the Family Life Cycle: A Decision and Influence Structure Analysis," *Journal of Travel Research* 20 (Fall 1981): p. 21.

19. Cosenza and Davis, p. 21.

20. Daniel J. Stynes and Edward M. Mahoney, "1984 Michigan Commercial Campground Marketing Study," Unpublished Report (East Lansing, Mich.: Department of Park and Recreation Resources, Michigan State University, 1986), p. 32.

21. "Not Traditional," in Status column of *American Demographics*, March 1987, p. 14.

22. Thomas G. Exter, "Where the Money Is," *American Demographics*, March 1987, p. 32.

23. Alister Mathieson and Geoffrey Wall, *Tourism: Economic, Physical and Social Impacts* (New York: Longman, 1982), p. 24.

24. Mathieson and Wall, p. 135.

25. G. V. Doxey, "A causation theory of visitor-resident irritants, methodology, and research inferences," in *The Impact of Tourism*, Sixth Annual Conference Proceedings of the Travel Research Association, San Diego, pp. 195–198. As reported in Peter E. Murphy, *Tourism: A Community Approach* (New York: Methuen, 1985), p. 124.

26. Juanita C. Liu, Pauline J. Sheldon and Turgut Var, "Resident Perception of the Environmental Impacts of Tourism," *Annuals of Tourism Research* 14 (1987): pp. 24–25.

27. Hasan Zafer Dogan, "Forms of Adjustment: Sociocultural Impacts of Tourism," *Annals of Tourism Research* 16 (1989): p. 221.

28. Meda Chesney-Lind and Ian Y. Lind, "Visitors as Victims: Crimes against the Tourists in Hawaii," *Annals of Tourism Research* 13 (1986): p. 173.

29. Greenwood, pp. 178–180.

Key Terms

adjustment model	mass tourists
attitudinal model	role
conformity	social impacts
cultural impact	social norms
cultural tourism	social stratification
culture	socialization
family life cycle	society
group	sociology
irridex model	status

Discussion Questions

1. What is the difference between a society and a culture?

2. What is cultural tourism? What are some common examples?

3. How does the concept of socialization apply to tourism?

4. What four groups are particularly relevant to the study of tourism? What are the basic characteristics of each?

5. What is social stratification? What elements differentiate social strata?

6. How do the stages of the family life cycle affect travel decisions?

7. What are common social interactions that are inherent in the travel process?

8. What four characteristics limit the quality of social interaction?

9. What three responses have been used to explain the social impacts of tourism? What is the basic premise behind each?

10. How do cultural impacts differ from social impacts?

REVIEW QUIZ

When you feel you have covered all of the material in this chapter, answer these questions. Choose the *best* answer. Check your answers with the correct ones found on the Review Quiz Answer Key at the end of this book.

True (T) or False (F)

T   F   1. Society refers to an organized, independent, continuing number of people living in a specific area.

T   F   2. Tourism is *not* subject to the same socialization process that guides behavior within and between groups.

T   F   3. Social norms are often ignored or broken due to a lack of knowledge.

T   F   4. A tourist's ignorance and inappropriate behavior do little to feed the stereotype that a tourist is someone who knows little about the local people and community.

T   F   5. A primary group consists of people who know each other well and have concern for each other over the long term.

T   F   6. The layers, or groupings, of people between two extremes are the strata of society.

T   F   7. Money earned is referred to as wealth.

T   F   8. It only stands to reason that the upper class is the biggest target for mass marketing tourism appeals.

T   F   9. Travel decision making, travel preferences, and travel patterns stay consistent over the course of the family life cycle.

T   F   10. It would be emotionally helpful for all parties if every social encounter were a strong emotional exchange.

Alternate/Multiple Choice

11. Culture is a complex set of:

   a. learned beliefs and customs.
   b. skills and habits.
   c. traditions and knowledge.
   d. all of the above.

12. Which of the following is *not* an example of cultural tourism?

   a. Festivals of Germany
   b. History of Rome
   c. Train trips through the Andes
   d. Ceremonies of an African bush tribe

13.   Which of the following refers to the position a person occupies in society?

    a. role
    b. status

14.   A collection of people who regularly have contact, share structured interactions, and have a common feeling of togetherness is called:

    a. dynamic mainstreaming.
    b. a group.

15.   The changes in the arts, artifacts, customs, rituals, and architecture of a people that result from tourism activity or development are called:

    a. cultural impacts.
    b. social networks.
    c. dynamic effects.
    d. dramatic effects.

Chapter Outline

Learning Objectives

1. Define international tourism within the context of domestic tourism.

2. Explain why international tourism is considered one of the largest industries in the world.

3. Describe the interrelationship between travel flows, popular destinations, and travel receipts and expenditures.

4. Describe the typical international traveler from the United States.

5. Describe the typical foreign visitor to the United States.

6. Outline some of the characteristics and primary activities of Europe's international travelers.

7. Analyze why Japan is emerging as an important force in the international travel market.

8. Compare Japanese travelers with travelers from Europe and North America.

9. Explain why some professionals regard tourism as a peace industry.

5

International Dimensions

THE TOURIST WHO SEES remote parts of another country from the back of a mule or through the windows of a safari van has definitely gotten away from the routines of home and work. Through international travel, a person can see exotic places, experience new cultures, and sample diverse accommodations, cuisine, and methods of travel. One of the most exciting aspects of modern international tourism is the ability of millions of tourists to travel most anywhere in the world promptly, efficiently, and safely. International travel statistics reveal that millions of people want to see the rest of the world. Around the world, popular destinations are packed, and new attractions are sought out by tourists each year.

Defining International Tourism

Different people will define international tourism in different ways. One way to look at international tourism is in the context of domestic tourism. In the simplest sense, **domestic tourism** refers to people traveling within their own country. In contrast, **international tourism** refers to people traveling outside their own country. But international tourism is much more than simply traveling beyond the borders of one's own country. International tourism encompasses all the services required for the tourist—including those in the country of origin, the destination, and any stops made en route. Companies other than airlines or cruise lines are involved. International tourism integrates many public, private, and government agencies including airport authorities, border and customs agencies, harbors and ports, and public transportation systems. In addition, both public and private attractions—including lodging operations—have a stake in satisfying the volume and demand of international tourism. It is not enough to think just of the tourist when defining international tourism. Both sides of the equation—the consumers and the suppliers—must be considered.

From a business perspective, it is easy to think of the businesses connected to international tourism, such as airlines and hotels. Yet, the business of airlines and hotels is not exclusively tourism-related. Airlines carry freight as well as travelers. It is difficult to assess which businesses are fully involved in tourism compared to those which are only partially involved.

Comparing two types of destinations can be enlightening. The Bahamas are an international travel destination, a strong percentage of whose visitors are tourists. The guests staying at Bahamian hotels are usually people on a holiday, in for a conference, or simply traveling for pleasure. Compare this mix to the mix of people staying at hotels in the Chicago business district. On a typical weekday, a strong percentage of the rooms are occupied by business travelers—not tourists. In fact,

Consumers + suppliers

101

Harbors and ports are just one part of a vast international tourism network. (Courtesy of the San Francisco Convention & Visitors Bureau)

managers of such hotels would most likely say that tourism represents only a small portion of their business. Now add the international dimension. Because of the number of international tourists, the Bahamian hotels are definitely in the international tourism business. The managers of the Chicago hotels could rightly claim they service domestic travelers, primarily the business-type.

The Importance of International Tourism

In 1989, global, international, and domestic tourism accounted for more than $2 trillion in expenditures—or about 10% of the world's gross national product.[1] In the United States, estimates are that tourism accounts for 6.7% of the gross national product. If travel conditions remain stable, the industry can be expected to grow in the years ahead.

Many experts view international tourism as one of the largest industries in the world. Tourism creates employment, enhances a nation's tax base, and generates a source of foreign revenue. Countries that have many internationally known attractions may come to rely on tourism for jobs, taxes, and foreign currencies. If their residents travel infrequently to other countries, the country may experience a **travel surplus** which benefits the local businesses along with the general economy.

In 1989, approximately 39 million foreign visitors to the United States spent about $44 billion dollars.[2] American citizens, too, are avid travelers and spend

Exhibit 1   Growth of International Receipts

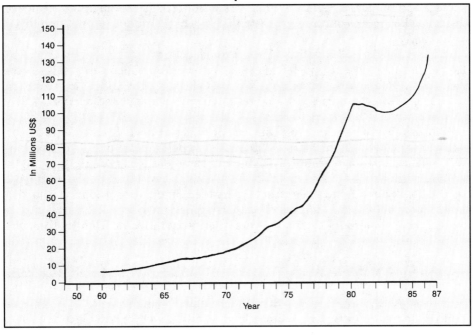

billions overseas. Until 1989, foreign guests in the United States had never out-spent Americans going abroad. In that year, incoming tourists spent $43.8 billion, while U.S. travelers spent $42.6 billion outside the country. This travel surplus of $1.2 billion is projected to grow to $1.5 billion in 1990.[3] Compare this figure to a 1987 deficit of some $9.9 billion.[4] Such dramatic change is taking place because foreign travel to the United States is growing at two times the rate of U.S. travel to foreign nations.[5]

As shown in Exhibit 1, the growth of **receipts**—or money spent by interna-tional travelers—has been fairly steady in the last 40 years. In 1950, more than $2 million was generated by international travelers; by 1960, that amount had tripled to $6.8 million. By then, most of the recovery after World War II had been com-pleted; post-war families were settled, prosperous, and taking vacations. Around this same time—1958—international jet travel was initiated. Advances in avi-ation—plus economy class rates—fostered a steady growth in mass travel. But the growth ended in 1979. In that year, the fuel crisis hit, followed by a worldwide re-cession in the early 1980s. Once again, tourism professionals were reminded that travel is not impervious to world events, especially dramatic economic downturns.

As mentioned earlier, international tourism provides employment for millions of people around the world. As tourism expands on a global scale, so too will the number of people employed in tourism-related businesses. In the United States, tourism is one of the three largest employers. Tourism accounts for more than 6 million jobs with a payroll or more than $70 billion dollars. Simply stated, travel services directly generate more jobs than any other industry in the United States except health services.[6] Travel dominates other countries as a source and creator of jobs. Some European countries estimate that 15% of their population is employed in tourism.[7]

International travel benefits nations through cultural, social, and economic exchange. Such contacts also foster the exchange of ideas which can result in economic activity and diversification. This is especially the case when tourism introduces new technologies, encourages foreign investment, and results in selective relocation of businesspersons.

All things considered, tourism is not without cost. It can degrade the environment as well as dislocate or disrupt societies and cultures. The development of facilities, transportation systems, and amenities to service tourists can be very destructive to the environment. Scenic views and wonders can be destroyed, and the quality of air and water can be degraded. International tourism can also disrupt local norms and cultures by importing new manners of dress, codes of conduct, and social interactions that are often very different from those of the native culture.

Travel Flows

It makes sense that most of the trips individuals or families take in a year are within their own country. Approximately 90% of all travel worldwide is domestic. Yet, the world is full of people who love to travel to other countries. In 1987, nearly 4.3 billion international and domestic arrivals occurred worldwide.[8] Travelers are estimated to have made more than 400 million international trips in 1989.[9]

Exhibit 2 shows the growth in international travel volume over a 40-year period. Like the international tourism receipts shown in Exhibit 1, travel volume has enjoyed substantial and continuous growth. In 1950, slightly more than 25 million international arrivals occurred around the world. By 1960, this number had jumped to nearly 70 million—again, spurred by the dramatic changes in air transportation and fare prices. During the fuel crisis and recession of the early 1980s, international arrivals slowed but did not decline; international receipts, however, did decline. Apparently, tourists and business travelers were still willing to travel—but in reduced numbers and on reduced budgets.

North America and Europe dominate international travel volume, with 18% and 67% of the total, respectively.[10] In Europe, the geography itself accounts for the high volume of international traffic. Europe consists of many different countries within a condensed region—all with relatively free transit across borders. In both Europe and North America, the essentials for international travel are in place: a large population, increasing personal discretionary funds, increased leisure time, and relative political stability. South America, Asia, Africa, and Oceania represent less than 20% of the international tourist traffic.[11]

Most international traffic is intra-regional. This means that international travelers are more likely to travel to other countries within their own region. For example, Europeans travel most often to other European countries while North Americans travel most often to other North American countries.

Exhibit 2   Growth of International Arrivals

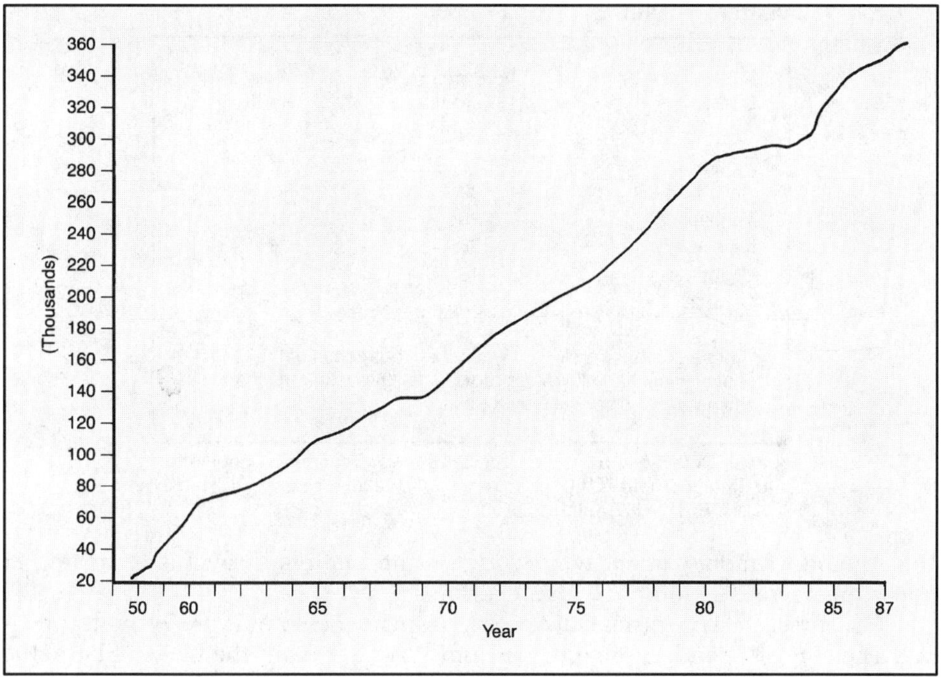

Popular Destinations

Lack of reliable statistical data and different methods for counting tourists make it difficult to pinpoint the world's most popular destinations. In many countries, all people visiting—no matter how long they stay—are counted as foreign arrivals and usually called visitors or excursionists. In other countries, only visitors who stay overnight, a few nights, or longer are counted. Regardless of counting techniques, the countries at the top of most lists can be identified. Within Europe, the strong leaders are Spain, Italy, and France. The United States dominates the Americas as both a point of origin and a destination for international travelers.[12] Exhibit 3 provides figures for the top seven countries receiving the most foreign visitors.

Another important travel pattern to note is that popular destination countries are not always strong sources of international travelers. For example, while countries like Spain and Italy are strong destinations, they are not among the top generators of tourists who visit other countries. This is partly because the standard of living in these nations allows only limited resources for international travel.

Travel Receipts and Expenditures

A slightly different picture emerges when tourism receipts are compared to general travel volume. It is one thing for a country to have large numbers of tourists. It is another to have them spend large amounts of money during their stay. Today,

Exhibit 3   Countries Receiving the Most Foreign Visitors—1988

Country	Volume in Millions	Rank
Spain*	58	1
France	38	2
United States	32	3
Yugoslavia*	30	4
Italy	26	5
United Kingdom*	16	6
Canada	16	7

*These countries include **all** visitors—regardless of the length of stay. Counting all visitors provides larger estimates than estimates which count only tourists.

Source: Developed from the Organization for Economic Cooperation and Development (OECD), *Tourism Policy and International Tourism* (Paris: OECD, 1989), Table 1, p. 90.

the amount of money spent worldwide on international travel is estimated at approximately $200 billion, excluding airfares.[13]

Of course, most countries want people to spend their money freely while traveling. The biggest spenders are tourists from West Germany, the United States, the United Kingdom, Japan, and France.[14] Each of these countries has a standard of living which allows travel and expenditures on hotels, food, tours, and shopping. Even if the number of tourists arriving from these countries is small, the amount they spend often equals that spent by larger numbers of tourists from other countries.

Looking at different countries, it is clear that more people are traveling more often and are spending more in the process. Exhibit 4 provides a sense of how fast and dramatic the changes have been in spending by international tourists. Between 1983 and 1987, West Germany, Japan, and the United Kingdom experienced significant growth in tourist expenditures. During the same period, Japan displayed the most dramatic growth—with spending up nearly 50%.

International travel is subject to another important variable: currency exchange rates. As exchange rates fluctuate, so does the cost of travel—and the feelings of travelers. In recent years, exchange rates have experienced significant swings. This has focused attention on the sensitivity of the tourist to rate fluctuations. An analysis of the number of U.S. arrivals from Japan, West Germany, and the United Kingdom since 1980 reveals that as the dollar dropped against other currencies, the numbers of arrivals from each of these countries increased.[15]

The International Tourist

Being an international tourist requires time, money, health, and an interest in travel, especially in terms of exploring other countries. In addition, a number of other things must be in place. The policy and procedures of both the home and destination country also influence the international travel scene. Tourists need passports;

Exhibit 4   Percent Change in Spending on International Travel

Country	Years 1983–85	1985–87
West Germany	−1.8	26.0
Japan	12.2	49.3
United Kingdom	1.6	35.8
United States	10.4	13.0

Source: I. Iversen and S. Hewin, "Prospects for European, Japanese and U.S. International Travel," in *Travel & Leisure's World Travel Overview—1988/1989* (New York: American Express Publishing Corp., 1988), p. 57. (Based upon data from the respective National Travel Offices.)

exit and entry visas; an exchangeable currency; permission to take currency out of the country; and safe, reasonably priced transportation. These conditions are not always present for millions of potential tourists around the world. Travel is restricted, difficult, or impossible—as was the case for millions of people in Communist-bloc nations prior to 1989.

Even without data, it is possible to paint a composite picture of the international traveler. You could assume that someone interested in going to another country would have the time and money to do so. Next, you might speculate that our traveler would be a bit older than the national average, since it generally takes many years to accumulate money and vacation time. The next section will add to this composite by taking a closer look at the international traveler.

The U.S. International Traveler

Americans like to travel outside their country. On a yearly basis, some 41 million travelers depart from the United States. A recent survey suggests that about 71% of all Americans over 18 have been beyond U.S. borders.[16] The countries visited most often by Americans are their neighbors: Canada (49%) and Mexico (34%). Twenty-six percent of people surveyed report having been to Europe, while 19% report visits to the Caribbean.

In the United States, international travel experiences correspond to education, income, age, and gender. Among Americans, 86% of college graduates have visited another country compared to 62% of Americans with high school diplomas or less. A related finding shows that the higher the income, the higher the likelihood that the person has visited a foreign country. Eighty-four percent of adults with incomes of $50,000 or more have traveled abroad, while only 59% of those with incomes of less than $10,000 have traveled abroad.

Older Americans are more likely to have visited another country at some point in their lives, because discretionary income generally increases with age. Among those over 60 years of age, 78% have been to a foreign country, compared to only 57% of persons 18 to 24 years of age. Finally, men (75%) are more likely to have been to another country than women (68%). This is somewhat due to the military travel that men, more often than women, have experienced over the years. These figures represent a snapshot of the international travel experiences of U.S. adults. Exhibit 5 provides a general profile of U.S travelers to foreign countries other than Mexico or Canada.

The majority of U.S. international travelers take trips for personal reasons such as visiting friends (11%) or family (21%) or simply to vacation (61%). Only 3% traveled abroad for study, while 28% traveled for business; 4% report traveling to attend conventions. These percentages add up to more than 100% because people travel for several reasons at the same time. Finally, it is interesting to note that only 10% of international travelers are going overseas for the first time. For the most part, foreign travel appears to be a familiar activity.

Europe—particularly the United Kingdom—attracts the majority of U.S. overseas travelers. The Caribbean is next in popularity, followed by the Far East. Seventy-five percent of U.S. international tourists travel on economy tourist tickets. Most U.S. tourists stay in hotels and visit only one or two countries. Most U.S. tourists bound for overseas arrange air travel through travel agents. These agents, along with family and friends, are prime sources of information about travel destinations.

Travel groups are generally small in size—a statistical average of 1.6 people. Most people travel alone or as part of a family. About 13% mix business with a family trip, but as noted in the table, young children are usually not included. International—like domestic—travelers are primarily career-oriented professionals and executives whose status and level of income can support travel costs. In this profile, the average income of the U.S. overseas traveler is more than $50,000. The median length of stay is 11 days. The typical overseas traveler spends about $1,000 during the course of a trip.

Foreign Arrivals to the United States

In many ways, foreign travelers to the United States resemble their American counterparts (compare Exhibits 5 and 6). The majority are taking a holiday or visiting family and friends. About the same percentage of foreign travelers are in the United States on business or to study. Foreign travelers appear to be a bit more adventurous than Americans since a larger percentage are first-time visitors. Like U.S. travelers, foreign guests rely on a travel agent for air travel arrangements, hotel accommodations, and general travel information. This suggests that travel agents play a very strong role in providing travel services around the world. Foreign arrivals fly predominantly on economy-priced tickets and in small parties.

As shown in Exhibit 6, the incomes of foreign travelers appear to be a bit lower (under $50,000) than those of their American counterparts. In addition, a larger percentage of foreign travelers (62%) are, compared to U.S. overseas travelers (55%), adult males. Other social and demographic characteristics are similar to those of the U.S. overseas traveler.

While in the United States, the foreign traveler uses a range of transportation modes. About half use domestic airlines; a third arrive in New York City. Among these visitors, only about a third visit three or more states and most—47%—visit only one state. The median number of nights a foreign guest stays in the United

Exhibit 5   Profile of U.S. Residents Traveling Overseas

	1985 Percent	1986 Percent	1987 Percent
Residence			
New York	15	18	12
New York City	11	13	8
California	15	15	16
Los Angeles	5	5	5
San Francisco	3	3	4
Texas	6	6	8
New Jersey	5	6	6
Illinois	6	5	4
Florida	7	5	11
Pennsylvania	4	3	3
Massachusetts	5	3	4
Washington	*	3	3
Puropose of Trip[1]			
Business	28	34	28
Attend convention	5	5	4
Vacation, holiday	62	57	61
Visit friends	10	10	11
Visit relatives	20	20	21
Study	3	2	3
Foreign Trip Experience			
First-time visitors	12	9	10
Repeat visitors	88	91	90
Means of Booking Air Trip[1]			
Travel agent	75	73	71
Self	12	13	14
Company travel department	8	9	8
Other	6	6	5
Information Sources[1]			
Airline	19	21	20
Travel agency	66	64	63
Government sources	7	7	6
Company travel dept.	NA	11	10
Friends, relatives	29	26	27
Newspapers, magazines	11	11	11
Published sources	13	16	14
Type of Airline Ticket			
First class	7	8	7
Executive, business	12	15	15
Economy, tourist	77	74	75
Other	4	4	3
Use of Pre-Paid Package Inclusive Tour			
Yes	27	23	24
No (Independent)	73	77	76
Type and Size of Travel Party			
Traveling alone	40	36	35
Family group	41	44	47
Business group	7	9	8
Mixed business, family, other	13	12	13
Average party size (persons)	1.6	1.6	1.6
Median party size (persons)	1.0	1.0	1.0
Sex and Age of Visitors			
Children under 18	5	4	5
Male adults	55	57	55
Female adults	40	38	41
Average age of male adults (years)	45.1	44.5	43.7
Average age of female adults (years)	43.2	42.5	41.7

(continued)

Exhibit 5   *(continued)*

	1985 Percent	1986 Percent	1987 Percent
Occupation of Visitors			
Manager, executive	26	28	25
Professional, technical	32	33	34
Clerical, sales	7	6	7
Craftsman, mechanic	3	3	3
Government, military	4	4	4
Homemaker	10	10	9
Student	6	5	7
Retired	10	9	8
Airline employee	2	2	NA
Annual Family Income			
Average	$54,549	$55,519	$54,204
Median	$52,881	$57,496	$55,138
Type of Accommodations[1]			
Hotel, motel	78	77	74
Private home	32	34	35
Other	9	9	7
Number of Countries Visited			
One country	62	68	71
Two countries	19	18	18
Three or more countries	19	14	12
Average (countries)	1.7	1.6	1.5
Median (countries)	1.0	1.0	1.0
Main Overseas Destinations Visited[1]			
Western Europe	53	49	44
France	15	12	8
Germany—West	14	12	12
Italy	11	7	7
Switzerland	7	5	4
United Kingdom	25	24	19
Eastern Europe	2	1	2
Caribbean	21	21	24
South America	5	6	6
Central America	3	3	2
Oceania	4	5	7
Australia	*	3	5
Far East	14	18	18
Hong Kong	5	7	6
Japan	6	7	7
Middle East	5	2	3
Africa	2	2	2
Nights Outside the U.S.			
Average	20.6	20.6	20.9
Median	13.0	12.0	11.0
Average Non-U.S. Expenditures			
Per traveler	$ 969	$ 1,022	$ 971
Per traveler per day	$ 47	$ 49	$ 46

[1] Multiple responses tabulated.

Source: *In-Flight Survey of International Air Travelers*, January–December 1985, 1986 and 1987, U.S. Travel and Tourism Administration, and *Travel & Leisure's World Travel Overview*.

States is 11. The most popular destinations are: California, New York, Florida, Hawaii, and Washington, D.C. Foreign visitors can be expected to spend about $1,300 per visitor, or an average of $63 per visitor per day.

Exhibit 6   Profile of Overseas Visitors to the United States

	1985 Percent	1986 Percent	1987 Percent
Residence			
Western Europe	38	43	44
France	5	5	6
Germany—West	7	9	9
Italy	3	3	3
Scandinavia	3	3	3
United Kingdom	12	13	13
Eastern Europe	1	1	1
Caribbean	8	6	9
South America	11	10	8
Central America	4	4	3
Africa	2	3	2
Oceania	5	5	4
Far East	26	26	27
Japan	18	19	19
Middle East	5	3	4
Purpose of Trip[1]			
Business	38	36	37
Attend convention	6	10	8
Vacation, holiday	44	46	48
Visit friends	12	15	16
Visit relatives	20	21	20
Study	5	6	5
U.S. Trip Experience			
First-time visitors	22	25	22
Repeat visitors	78	75	78
Means of Booking Air Trip[1]			
Travel agent	70	72	71
Self	15	14	14
Company travel department	11	10	10
Other	5	5	3
Means of Booking Lodging[1]			
Travel agent	48	51	51
Self	17	15	15
Company travel department	22	20	20
Friends and relatives	10	13	12
Other	12	13	9
Information Sources[1]			
Airline	17	16	17
Travel agency	64	63	62
Government sources	3	2	3
Friends, relatives	18	19	20
Newspapers, magazines	5	6	6
Published sources	9	11	11
Company travel dept.	10	12	12
Other	11	2	3
Type of Airline Ticket			
First class	7	6	6
Executive business	20	17	19
Economy, tourist	70	74	72
Other	3	3	3

(continued)

Exhibit 6 *(continued)*

	1985 Percent	1986 Percent	1987 Percent
Advance Trip Decision Time			
Mean (days)	NA	NA	48.7
Median (days)	NA	NA	32.0
Type and Size of Traveling Party			
Traveling alone	52	47	48
Family group	30	35	34
Business group	9	9	8
Mixed business, family, other	9	9	11
Average party size (persons)	1.4	1.5	1.4
Median party size (persons)	1.0	1.0	1.0
Sex and Age of Visitors			
Children under 18	6	5	5
Male adults	64	64	62
Female adults	30	31	33
Average age of male adults (years)	40.5	40.1	40.7
Average age of female adults (years)	34.0	36.9	37.0
Occupation of Visitors			
Manager, executive	31	29	30
Professional, technical	26	27	27
Clerical, sales	9	10	10
Craftsman, mechanic	3	4	3
Government, military	5	5	7
Homemaker	10	10	9
Student	8	8	8
Retired	4	4	4
Airline employee	3	3	3
Annual Family Income			
Average	$38,705	$42,038	$46,820
Median	$31,572	$36,940	$43,113
Nights Away From Home			
Average (nights)	27.7	26.3	25.6
Median (nights)	14.0	14.0	14.0
Nights Spent in the U.S.			
Average (nights)	22.8	21.6	21.9
Median (nights)	10.0	10.0	11.0
U.S. Port of Entry			
New York City	32	29	29
Miami	14	13	11
Honolulu	12	12	9
Los Angeles	11	12	13
Chicago	5	7	8
Atlanta	NA	5	6
Dallas/Ft. Worth	NA	5	4
San Francisco	6	4	7
Boston	4	4	4
Seattle	3	4	3
Other ports	13	5	NA
Type of Accommodations[1]			
Hotel, motel	80	81	77
Private home	40	40	42
Campsite	2	2	3
Other	5	5	5

Exhibit 6   *(continued)*

	1985 Percent	1986 Percent	1987 Percent
Transportation in the U.S.[1]			
Domestic airline	49	52	50
Inter-city train	8	7	7
Inter-city bus	19	18	18
City bus or subway	25	23	22
Rented auto	37	36	38
Private auto	36	35	36
Other	36	41	38
Number of States Visited			
One state	50	45	47
Two states	23	25	24
Three or more states	27	30	30
Average (states)	2.0	2.1	2.1
Median (states)	2.1	2.0	2.0
Main U.S. Destinations Visited[1]			
California	34	35	37
Los Angeles	20	22	22
San Francisco	17	16	20
New York	31	30	28
New York City	28	28	26
Florida	19	21	20
Miami	10	10	9
Orlando	7	10	9
Hawaii	14	16	14
Washington, D.C.	9	10	10
Texas	7	9	8
Illinois	9	8	7
Chicago	8	7	7
Massachusetts	8	8	8
Nevada	6	7	7
Arizona	6	7	8
Pennsylvania	5	4	4
Washington	4	5	4
New Jersey	4	4	4
Expenditures in the USA			
Per visitor	$1,219	$1,358	$1,384
Per visitor/day	$ 44	$ 51	$ 63

NA = Not available
[1]Multiple responses tabulated.

Source: *In-Flight Survey of International Air Travelers*, January–December 1985, 1986 and 1987, U.S. Travel and Tourism Administration, and *Travel and Leisure's World Travel Overview*.

The European International Traveler

The profound changes in Eastern Europe that began in 1989 make it clear how strong the desire to travel to other countries has become. The removal of travel bans between nations unleashed a pent-up demand. The most powerful expression of this demand was evidenced by the millions who crossed through the Berlin Wall—some for a short visit, others for a day, and some, to move permanently.

Across a range of countries—Netherlands, Spain, Portugal, Hungary, and France—the proportion of citizens who take holidays increases with the level of

The rich history and architecture of Washington, D.C., draws visitors from around the world. Pictured clockwise are the U.S. Supreme Court building, the Jefferson Memorial, and the White House. (Photos courtesy of the Washington Convention & Visitors Association)

Exhibit 7   The Western European Tourist Market—Selected Countries

Country	Population	Travel (%) Incidence		Market Size	Avg. # Trips	Market Volume
		1986	1989			
United Kingdom	41.3M	5%	11%	4.5M	1.3	5.9M
West Germany	48.1M	9%	24%	11.5M	1.0	11.5M
France	40.5M	7%	14%	5.7M	1.1	6.3M
Italy	42.4M	11%	—	4.7M	1.1	5.2M
Switzerland	5.1M	23%	—	1.2M	1.5	1.8M

Note: These figures are based on interviews with individuals 18 years of age or older who had traveled by plane on an overseas vacation and stayed overnight for a minimum of four nights at least once in the last three years. The figures also include those persons who planned to take such a trip within the next two years. In the case of Italy, the criteria meant a trip outside of the Mediterranean. Travel incidence refers to the percent of the population that meets the criteria. The 1989 estimates are based upon the figures supplied in the two reports referenced in the source line. The calculations assume that the population stayed about the same and that the average number of trips was the same in 1986 and 1989.

Source: *Pleasure Travel Markets to North America: Italy, Australia, Brazil, and Mexico—Highlights Report* (Washington, D.C.: U.S. Travel and Tourism Administration, 1989), pp. 3–4. *Pleasure Travel Markets to North America: United Kingdom, France, West Germany, Japan—1989 Highlights Report* (Ottawa, Ontario, Canada: Tourism Canada, 1989), p. 3.

occupation and income, and diminishes with age. These characteristics are similar to those reported for the U.S. population. Some studies reveal that Europeans from large urban areas tend to travel more than their rural counterparts.[17] It could be that rural populations are older or have less income—both barriers to holiday tourism. Language is also an important variable to consider when examining international tourism. For instance, the frequency of reciprocal travel between the United Kingdom, the United States, and Canada no doubt reflects the tourist's preference for visiting countries where his/her own language predominates.

Recent studies suggest that European travelers are becoming more willing to travel to countries outside of Europe. One study of five European countries, conducted in 1986, indicated that many Europeans have the desire and resources for long-distance travel and would consider a trip to the United States and Canada. The study, conducted a second time in 1989 for just three European countries—the United Kingdom, West Germany, and France—showed changes over several years. Exhibit 7 and the following paragraphs outline several key results from these studies:

1. In 1986, only 5% of those surveyed from the United Kingdom and 23% of the Swiss had participated in or desired to take a long-distance trip. By 1989, the percentage of people with such experiences or desires had increased dramatically. Although the second study did not include Italy or Switzerland, it can be assumed that their percentages increased as well. In any case, these figures reveal that the potential market for Canada and the United States is growing.

2. Within the long-distance travel market, European tourists have made or are able to make more than one such trip over a three-year period. For all the countries in Exhibit 7 (except West Germany), the average number of trips is more than one.

3. Europeans are avid travelers. The market for shorter, cross-the-border trips in and throughout Europe is quite large—larger than that reported for long-distance trips.

4. Finally, being able to make a long-distance trip to the United States and actually doing it may be entirely different things. While not shown in the exhibit, these same studies reveal that a sizable percentage of Europeans had visited Canada and the United States within the previous three years. Specifically, 48% of those from the United Kingdom most recently visited the United States, while 16% visited Canada. Forty-two percent of West Germans traveled to the United States, while only 7% visited Canada. Only about 28% of the French visited the United States while 14% traveled to Canada. (Travel from France to Canada is no doubt encouraged by the prevalence of the French language in many parts of Canada—particularly Quebec.) A reported 30% of Italians traveled to the United States while 9% visited Canada. Data for Switzerland was not available.

Across Europe, a sizable number of people take vacations. Exhibit 8 shows the percentage of European residents who take vacations of four days or more. Northern Europeans are more likely to travel than Southern Europeans. This is particularly true for international travel. As noted earlier, even though countries in Southern Europe are among the top international destinations, they generate a modest number of travelers. Spain and Italy, in particular, are among the top five destinations; they attract millions of tourists, but send few abroad.

A closer review of the United Kingdom, West Germany, and France reveals unique differences among these international tourists. Exhibit 9 shows differences in terms of length and type of trip, favored activities, and preferred features. Since some countries did not report the same types of activities or preferences, dashes appear in several columns. Also, information about the Japanese traveler is included as a point of comparison since Japan is one of the fastest growing travel markets in the world.

According to the study, a preference between resort vacations and touring vacations varies among travelers. The Japanese have a strong preference for touring; compared to tourists from France and the United Kingdom, West German tourists are less likely to tour and more likely to visit a resort. Nearly half the tourists from the United Kingdom traveled for the purpose of visiting family and friends—a much higher percentage than tourists from France and West Germany. A small percentage of all European travelers mixed business with vacations, with French travelers predominating.

On average, the length of a trip for Europeans ranged from 25 to 27 days, compared to an 11-night stay for the Japanese. Trips by Europeans were also about five to six days longer than overseas trips taken by U.S. travelers (see Exhibit 5).

Exhibit 8   Vacations and Holidays by European Residents—1985

Country	Percent Taking Vacations	Percent Abroad
Holland	65	42
Denmark	64	28
Britain	61	21
West Germany	60	36
France	58	9
Luxembourg	58	55
Italy	57	7
Greece	46	3
Spain	44	4
Belgium	41	23
Ireland	39	20
Portugal	31	2

Note: These findings apply to European residents 15 years and older who took one or more vacations of at least four days to any destination away from home.

Source: Developed from Somerset Waters, *Travel Industry World Yearbook: The Big Picture—1988* (New York: Child and Waters Inc., 1988), table on p. 91, based upon data from the *Directorate General for Transport (Tourism Service) of the Commission of European Communities.*

It is interesting to note what different nationalities listed as their top ten preferred activities. Travelers from the United Kingdom ranked shopping as their top activity. For residents of all countries, dining out, sampling the local food, taking pictures, touring, and sight-seeing were important pastimes. Among Europeans, the desire to visit museums while abroad was not among the top ten. This seems to make sense since the United Kingdom, France, and West Germany maintain some of the best museums in the world. The Japanese, however, do visit museums. Amusement parks and guided tours were not prime activities for Europeans either. Apparently, these independent travelers have little need to visit amusement parks—which also makes sense, because so few travel with children. Finally, all four countries mention contact with nature and the outdoors as top-ten activities while traveling abroad. This is an important finding for countries such as the United States and Canada which have many beautiful wilderness areas and numerous national parks.

Activity preferences are complemented by the features that overseas travelers rate as important. Climate, friendly people, value for the money, personal safety, and hygiene were all rated high by the international traveler. Marketers must consider such features and benefits when promoting an overseas destination.

Exhibit 9   International Tourists: Japan, United Kingdom, West Germany, France

Characteristic	Japan	U.K.	W. Germany	France
Trip length (mean nights)	10.6	27.9	26.6	25.7
Percent couples	40%	50%	33%	—
Type of Last Trip (%)				
Touring	42%	23%	2%	33%
Resort	18	10	38	—
Friends/Relatives	6	52	28	30
Business/Pleasure	8	8	14	23
City	8	4	10	3
Study	5	—	—	—
Honeymoon	4	—	—	—
Theme Park	3	3	2	—
Cruise	—	—	2	3
Outdoors	—	—	4	7
Top 10 Activities (Ranked)				
Sightseeing in cities	1	4	3	4
Shopping	2	1	6	5
Dining out	3	3	1	2
Guided tours	4	—	—	—
Visiting scenic landmarks	5	6	7	8
Taking pictures	6	2	4	3
Sunbathing/beach activity	7	10	—	—
Visiting amusement parks	8	—	—	—
Swimming	9	—	9	—
Visiting museums	10	—	—	—
Sampling local foods	—	5	2	1
Touring countryside	—	7	10	10
Visiting friends/family	—	8	—	—
Visiting historic places	—	9	—	—
Visiting the seaside	—	—	8	7
Contacting local people	—	—	5	6
Visiting wilderness areas	—	—	—	9
Most Desired Feature (Top 3 to 4)				
Outstanding scenery	1			4
Value for the money	2	1		
Hygiene & cleanliness	3			
Sunny climate		2	1	
Hygiene and cleanliness		3		
Personal safety		4		
Friendly local people			2	2
Warm welcome for tourist				3
Opportunities to learn				1

Source: *Pleasure Travel Markets to North America: Japan, United Kingdom, West Germany, France—Highlights Report* (Washington, D.C.: U.S. Travel and Tourism Administration, 1987).

Travelers of the Far East

The residents of the Far East are known to enjoy international travel and exploration. Like other tourists, citizens from Japan, South Korea, Taiwan, Hong Kong, Singapore, Thailand, and Indonesia travel primarily within their own region. However, to a growing extent, people of the Far East are now traveling worldwide. Far East travelers represent about 26% of the foreign arrivals (excluding Mexico and Canada) in the United States each year.[18]

As a destination, the Far East offers exotic vacation opportunities that range from the lush and lavish to the rugged and rural. From time to time, the instability of the region seriously affects travel patterns and flows. Consider how the unrest in China and the change of government in the Philippines caused tourism to fall in these two countries in the late 1980s.

Japan: An Emerging Market

Japan is a dynamic force in the international travel market. Historically, the Japanese market has grown at a rapid and steady pace. Over the last 20 years, Japan's volume of international travel has swelled. From the mid-1960s to about 1981, the number of Japanese traveling overseas grew from approximately 100,000 to more than 4 million.[19] Since then, the number has reached 8.4 million in 1988 and could exceed 10 million in the 1990s.[20]

The purposes for international travel by the Japanese have also changed. As the Japanese economy blossomed throughout the 1960s, travel was primarily for business. From the mid-1960s through the early 1970s, travel for both business and pleasure grew dramatically then tapered off in the late 1970s.[21] During this time of expansion, travel for pleasure increased in relation to travel for business. In 1964, tourism represented only 19% of all international travel. By 1981, tourism had increased 83%, a percentage which remains just as high today.[22] This evolution of travel patterns is common in many markets as business travelers open the way for the pleasure market.

Destination preferences have also shifted. From the early 1970s to the early 1980s, the number of Japanese traveling to other Asian countries decreased while travel to North America and Oceania increased. Within Asia, the share of Japanese travelers to Hong Kong dropped from 32% in the early 1970s to 20% by the end of the decade.[23] In 1988, North America accounted for 35% of Japanese overseas travel, while Asian destinations accounted for 49%.[24]

The Japanese market should continue to grow in the years ahead. Ninety percent of the Japanese people view themselves as middle class. Individuals in this country of 120-plus million still manage to be aggressive savers—which means they have the financial resources for travel.[25] And people want to travel. A recent poll clearly demonstrates that demand: Of those sampled, less than 1% had recently been overseas, yet 28% expressed a desire to do so.[26]

To manage and encourage the demand for international travel, the Ministry of Transport in Japan developed the **Ten Million Program**—an administrative program designed to promote overseas travel by Japanese residents.[27] The goal of the program is to have 10 million travelers go abroad by the year 1991; in 1988, 8.4 million went abroad. While this may seem like a large number, relatively few Japanese, when compared to other countries, actually travel abroad. For example, while 5% to 7% of Japanese citizens traveled abroad, 48%, 43%, and 17% of citizens from Great Britain, West Germany, and the United States had traveled abroad.

The Ten Million Program encourages Japanese to stay longer and enjoy their international travel. The program also works with the governments of other countries to help make travel to those countries easier and more enjoyable. Promotional campaigns are well coordinated for each target destination; services

The hotels and resorts of Hawaii are popular destinations for international travelers.
(Photo of the Hyatt Regency Waikiki at Hemmeter Center courtesy of Wimberly, Whisenand, Allison, Tong and Goo Associates)

at all destinations are specifically tailored for Japanese tours. The Japanese government invites foreign tourism officials and interested parties from the private sector to Japan for special seminars designed to facilitate international understanding and tourism.

In sum, the Japanese model for international tourism goes beyond the personal motivations of the residents. The government and private sector interests have a large stake in promoting the volume of international travel among Japanese residents. This program attempts to offset trade imbalances between Japan and other Western nations, to expose residents to other cultures, and to promote a better lifestyle among residents.

The Japanese Traveler. In 1989 alone, the three million Japanese visitors to the United States represented the third largest group—behind Canada and Mexico.[28] Japanese travel to the United States has grown dramatically over the last four years—up approximately 100% since 1985. Furthermore, the Japanese spend more than other visitors, some $6 billion in 1990 alone. This figure represents more than 17% of the total spending by international visitors; it is also larger than that of any other nationality despite the fact that Japanese visitors spend fewer days in the

United States compared to other visitors—on average about 11 nights as opposed to 26 nights.[29]

Cultural differences can usually explain the travel spending patterns of the Japanese. Among the Japanese, the tradition of "omiyagi" dictates that gifts be purchased for family and friends while abroad.[30] This means that a significant amount of time and money is devoted to shopping. On average, the Japanese spend about $1,608 each, or about $129 per visitor per day. Compare this to $1,384 per visit—or $63 per visitor per day—for other overseas visitors to the United States.[31]

In addition to their preference for shopping, the Japanese also like to sample the food, see the sights, and take photographs. Urban areas, with their amusement parks and museums, often attract the Japanese. They also like to visit the national parks, not so much to hike and camp as to view the scenic beauty. Few Japanese (19%), compared to other overseas visitors (36%), come to the United States to visit friends or relatives.[32]

As do some Europeans, the Japanese like to tour and experience resort vacations in the United States. Nearly half the arrivals from Japan are based in Hawaii, which limits the boundaries of their tours and resort experiences. The potential exists for expanding the range of tours as more direct flights become available between Japan and U.S. cities.[33] Yet, the ability of the continental United States to manage and address the Japanese and other foreign markets still requires cross-cultural training and preparation.

International Tourism and Peace

Since the times of the Grand Tour, goal-oriented tourists have had many opportunities to learn about the world and its people while traveling. For hundreds of years, arguments have been posed that tourism played a significant role in terms of economic development and human understanding. But tourism requires peace and political stability. Terrorism and other violent political events of the 1980s made it clear that such violence not only devastates human life and values, but also causes the collapse of tourism in the targeted region.

In 1986, terrorism struck the world hard, especially in Europe and the Mediterranean. By the time the summer tourism season came, fears were high and travel was down. Comparison between the summers of 1986 and 1985 showed that travel to Greece was off as much as 66% for the month of June; by August, volume was still off by 57%. These downward trends were also apparent in other countries across Europe[34] while in Asia, the tragedy of Tiananmen Square in 1989 shocked the world and virtually halted tourist travel to China. Hotel occupancy dropped dramatically and tours were canceled.

Some professionals suggest that tourism is a peace industry. Some argue that tourism provides the opportunity to appreciate the diversity of the people in the world. The interactions and the learning which results from tourism can help reduce tension and correct misunderstandings among people. As one researcher notes:

> As we travel and communicate in ever-increasing numbers, we are discovering that most people, regardless of their political or religious orientation, race or

Current Events Shaping Travel and Tourism

Eastern Europe

The world changed in 1989. The "fall of the wall" reshaped world politics and will have a lasting effect on international tourism. As barriers break down between East and West political blocs, opportunities for tourism will open up in Eastern Europe and the Soviet Union.

The ability of East Germans to visit and move to the West started a flow of people across borders that has not occurred in decades. Many people flocked to see or participate in the dismantling of the Berlin Wall. Soon after, Europeans were clamoring to see Europe's "other half," and advertisements and promotions for exclusive tours appeared.

The tourism industry must wait and see how these changes in Eastern Europe will alter travel patterns around the world. Certainly, some travelers from the West will rush to see these countries that had been hidden for so long behind the "Iron Curtain." But like all new destinations, Eastern Europe will probably attract modest numbers of people compared to the numbers now attracted to more established, mass tourism destinations.

It remains to be seen how and when Eastern European countries, resorts, and cities will respond to such levels of attention and opportunity. Changing passport requirements and customs regulations are just first steps. Problems leftover from centrally-planned economies plague the general business climate—and tourism. From currency value and exchange difficulties to lack of a trained, service-oriented work force, Eastern Europe faces massive problems and challenges in terms of tourism.

Becoming a destination and attraction is only one half of the issue; the other is becoming a *source* of tourists. Many Eastern European countries and their residents lack the financial resources either to host world travelers or to embark on tours themselves. Such conditions show few signs of improvement in the immediate future. The transition to market economies and democratic societies for the nations—and for their residents—will take some time. The opening of Eastern Europe provides many new destinations for tourists. However, it will take awhile for tourism to develop and succeed in these areas.

Europe 1992

Western Europe is moving rapidly toward becoming a single European market by the end of 1992. Financial, physical, and social constraints should lift in 1993 as industries are deregulated and trade barriers fall. Western Europe faces innumerable challenges as it moves toward the end of 1992—with tourism being just one. One analyst notes that the European commission charged with creating a unified market has done little to develop a tourism policy.[1] To date, a few changes are in process, including: a European passport, increases in duty-free allowances, easier currency transactions, and more freedom to cross borders.[2] The competition among European destinations and accommodations stands to increase as such changes occur, keeping a unified Europe competitive in the world tourism market.

Energy Issues

When Iraq invaded Kuwait in August 1990, international tensions escalated among Arab countries, and between Iraq and other nations. U.S. troops were sent to

(continued)

Saudi Arabia to protect that nation from invasion and to safeguard Western oil interests. The Persian Gulf conflict illustrates how vulnerable the world—and tourism—is to disruptions of the oil supply. Many people, faced with increased prices at airline ticket counters and at gasoline pumps, took a second look at their vacation plans. Since energy prices, availability, and economic well-being go hand-in-hand in much of the Western world, conflicts in the Persian Gulf stand to shake tourism in the years ahead.

1. Peter Akerhielm, Chekitan S. Dev, and Malcolm A. Noden, "Europe 1992: Neglecting the Tourism Opportunity," *The Cornell Hotel and Restaurant Administration Quarterly*, May 1990, p. 104.
2. Akerhielm, et al., p. 106.

BERRY'S WORLD

© 1988 by NEA, Inc

Cartoons often reflect public sentiment—here the traveler's fear of political terrorism. (Courtesy of United Media, New York, New York)

socioeconomic status, want a peaceful world in which all are fed, sheltered, productive, and fulfilled.[35]

In October 1988, the "First Global Conference: Tourism—A Vital Force for Peace" was held in Vancouver, Canada. The goal of the conference was to explore and discuss how the international tourism industry can facilitate and contribute further to the goal of peace through tourism.[36] The conference was structured around four sub-themes: peoples (social, cultural, and economic dimensions); habitats (natural, built, and technological); bridges (communication, education, and exchanges); and actions (policy, marketing, and development). Within each of these sub-themes, papers were solicited to address the relationship between tourism and peace. Over the course of the conference, 73 sessions were held with hundreds of speakers from across the globe. Concerns about tourism exploitation, environmental degradation, and prejudice were explored. Philosophical and technological concerns with respect to tourism and peace were discussed. The conference represented a large-scale effort to act upon and confirm the assumption that tourism can be the source of understanding between different cultures and orientations. Tourism, in other words, can help lead the way toward world peace.

The connection between peace, travel, and human freedom was demonstrated to the entire world in 1989 as the Berlin Wall fell and people rushed to visit the "forbidden," the "other," and friends and family. Peace and understanding among people seemed to be a little closer and clearer. Tourism professionals have the potential to move the industry in just such positive ways in the years ahead. But the tourist must also act responsibly. Such responsibilities and commitment may have been best expressed by the *Credo of the Peaceful Traveler,* developed at the Vancouver peace conference:

> Grateful for the opportunity to travel and to experience the world, and because peace begins with the individual, I affirm my personal responsibility and commitment to journey with an open mind and gentle heart; accept with grace and gratitude the diversity I encounter; revere and protect the natural environment which sustains all life; appreciate all cultures I discover; respect and thank my hosts for their welcome; offer my hand in friendship to everyone I meet; support travel services that share these views and act upon them, by my spirit, words and actions; and encourage others to travel the world in peace.[37]

Endnotes

1. David L. Edgell, Sr., *Charting a Course for International Tourism in the Nineties: An Agenda for Managers and Executives* (Washington, D.C.: U.S. Department of Commerce, 1990), p. 9.

2. Phone interview with the U.S. Travel and Tourism Administration staff in Washington, D.C., April 27, 1990.

3. "USTTA Predicts Second Record-Breaking Year for Inbound U.S. Tourism," *Hotel & Resort Industry* (April 1990), pp. 8–9.

4. Don Wynegar, "International Travel In Review," in *Second Annual Travel Review Conference Proceedings: The 1987 Experience—A Basis for Planning* (University of Utah, Salt Lake City: Travel and Tourism Research Association, 1988), p. 25.

5. "USTTA Predicts Second Record-Breaking Year for Inbound U.S. Tourism," pp. 8–9.

6. Edgell, p. 14.

7. Allan M. Williams and Gareth Shaw, "Western European Tourism in Perspective," in *Tourism and Economic Development: Western European Experiences,* edited by Allan M. Williams and Gareth Shaw (New York: Belhaven Press, 1988), p. 32.

8. "Worldwide Travel Markets," in *Travel & Leisure's World Travel Overview—1988/1989* (New York: American Express Publishing Corp., 1988), p. 9. (Based upon World Tourism Organization figures).

9. Edgell, p. 9.

10. "Worldwide Travel Markets," p. 10.

11. Douglas Pearce, *Tourism Today: A Geographical Analysis* (New York: Longman in cooperation with Wiley, 1987), p. 39.

12. Somerset Waters, *Travel Industry World Yearbook: The Big Picture—1988* (New York: Child and Waters Inc., 1988), p. 7.

13. Edgell, 1990, p. 9.

14. Waters, p. 7.

15. Wynegar, pp. 30–31.

16. Timothy Q. Rounds, "Where in the World Have You Been?" *American Demographics* 10, no. 5 (May 1988): pp. 30–33.

17. Pearce, p. 26.

18. Waters, p. 66, based upon data from the U.S. Travel and Tourism Administration.

19. Pearce, p. 56.

20. Fumio Tamamura, "How Outbound Japanese Tourism Impacts the International Marketing Scene," in proceedings of *Travel and Tourism Research Association, Twentieth Anniversary Conference* (Salt Lake City, Utah: Bureau of Economic and Business Research, University of Utah, 1989), p. 65.

21. Pearce, pp. 55–56.

22. Pearce, p. 57.

23. Pearce, p. 57.

24. *Tourism in Japan—1989* (Tokyo, Japan: Japan National Tourist Organization, 1989), p. 9.

25. Tamamura, p. 66.

26. Jin Nishino, "Current Leisure and Recreation Research in Japan," *World Leisure and Recreation,* 31, no. 3 (Fall 1989): p. 13.

27. *Tourism in Japan—1989*, pp. 19–25.

28. Don Wynegar, "A Review of 1989 International Travel—U.S. Inbound Travel," paper presented at the Fourth Annual Travel Review Conference, Washington, D.C., February, 1990. (Co-sponsored by Travel & Tourism Research Association, U.S. Travel and Tourism Administration, U.S. Travel Data Center.)

29. Wynegar, data from overheads at the presentation.

30. *Pleasure Travel Markets to North America: Japan, United Kingdom, West Germany, France—Highlights Report* (Washington, D.C.: U.S. Travel and Tourism Administration, 1987), p. 15.

31. "Japanese Travelers to the U.S.," *Reed Travel Market Reports,* July 1989, p. 5. (Based upon U.S. Travel and Tourism Administration's In-Flight Surveys.)

32. "Japanese Travelers to the U.S.," p. 4.

33. Tamamura, p. 66.

34. John Brady and Richard Widdows, "The Impact of World Events on Travel to Europe During the Summer of 1986," *Journal of Travel Research* 26 (1988): p. 10.

35. Louis D'Amore, "Tourism—The World's Peace Industry," *Journal of Travel Research* 27 (1988): p. 39.

36. D'Amore, p. 40.

37. Jafar Jafari, "Tourism and Peace," *Annals of Tourism Research, 1989,* Vol. 16, p. 442. Reprinted as it was quoted in this conference review by Jafar Jafari, p. 442. He attributes the development of the credo primarily to Cynthia Fontayne.

Key Terms

domestic tourism
international tourism
receipts
Ten Million Program
travel surplus

Discussion Questions

1. What is the difference between domestic and international travel?

2. What are some of the companies and agencies that constitute the international tourism system?

3. Why is international tourism considered one of the largest industries in the world?

4. What is meant by the terms travel surplus and receipts?

5. What interrelationships exist between travel flows, popular destinations, travel receipts, and expenditures?

6. How would you describe the typical international traveler from the United States?

7. How would you describe the typical foreign visitor to the United States?

8. What are some of the characteristics and primary activities of the European international traveler?

9. Why is Japan becoming an important force in the international travel market?

10. Why do some professionals regard tourism as a peace industry? How can tourism contribute to world peace?

REVIEW QUIZ

When you feel you have covered all of the material in this chapter, answer these questions. Choose the *best* answer. Check your answers with the correct ones found on the Review Quiz Answer Key at the end of this book.

True (T) or False (F)

T   F   1. The term "international tourism" refers to people traveling outside their own country.

T   F   2. In the United States, tourism is one of the three largest employers.

T   F   3. Popular destination countries are not always strong sources of international travelers.

T   F   4. Seventy-five percent of U.S. international tourists travel on economy tourist tickets.

T   F   5. Foreign travelers to the United States do not resemble their American counterparts.

T   F   6. Northern Europeans are more likely to travel than Southern Europeans.

T   F   7. The Ten Million Program discourages the Japanese from international travel.

T   F   8. The Japanese spend less than other foreign visitors coming to the United States.

T   F   9. Successful tourism requires peace and political stability.

T   F   10. The goal of the First Global Conference was to explore and discuss how the international tourism industry can facilitate and contribute further to the goal of peace.

Alternate/Multiple Choice

11. Foreign travel to the United States is growing at _____ times the rate of U.S. travel to foreign nations.

    a. two
    b. four
    c. six
    d. eight

12. In Europe, _____ accounts for the high volume of international traffic.

    a. geography
    b. population

13.   The average income of the U.S. overseas traveler is more than:

    a. $25,000.
    b. $50,000.
    c. $75,000.
    d. $100,000.

14.   The proportion of European citizens who take holidays increases with the level of occupation and income and:

    a. diminishes with age.
    b. increases with age.

15.   The Japanese have the financial resources to travel because they are:

    a. mostly upper class.
    b. aggressive savers.

Chapter Outline

The Economic Question
Lifelong Ideas
    Idea 1:   Employment and Inflation
    Idea 2:   Voluntary Exchange
    Idea 3:   Comparative Advantage
    Idea 4:   Productivity
    Idea 5:   Relating Sales to Income and Employment
    Idea 6:   Supply and Demand Drive Tourism
    Idea 7:   Externalities
    Idea 8:   Opportunity Cost
    Idea 9:   Marginal Costs
    Idea 10: Rising Service Sector Costs
    Idea 11: Increasing Output Versus Equality
The Tools of Tourism Economics
    Tool 1: Abstraction
    Tool 2: Economic Theory and Tourism
    Tool 3: Economic Models and Tourism
    Tool 4: Demand/Supply Analysis
    Tool 5: Benefit/Cost Analysis and Efficiency
    Tool 6: Economic Impact Analysis

Learning Objectives

1. Identify some basic causes of inflation within the general economy and within the service sector.

2. Describe the nature of productivity and its relation to the equitable distribution of resources.

3. Define the basic economic concepts of voluntary exchange, comparative advantage, externalities, opportunity cost, and marginal cost, and explain how they apply to the tourism industry.

4. Explain the use of abstraction, economic theory, and economic models as basic tools of economists.

5. Outline the fundamentals of supply and demand in a free market system.

6. Describe the nature and goals of benefit/cost analysis.

7. Describe the nature and goals of economic impact analysis.

8. Explain the proper use of multipliers and input-output models.

6

Economic Dimensions

This chapter was written and contributed by Dennis B. Propst, Ph.D.,
Assistant Professor, Department of Park and Recreation Resources,
Michigan State University, East Lansing, Michigan.

Economics is a very broad discipline. It tries to answer many questions by using a wide variety of methods. In one chapter, it would be impossible to cover all the various theories, concepts, and methods of economics as they relate to tourism. Instead, our emphasis will be on the most relevant and most talked about issues, concepts, and tools.

The real benefit of studying economics as it relates to tourism is that it causes us to focus on serious national and international problems and proposes ways to solve those problems. Tourism is a significant global force which will affect you in many ways throughout the rest of your life. As a citizen, consumer, tourist, employee and/or employer, you will be required to make decisions and influence others concerning the form and nature of tourism development. Although the social and environmental effects of tourism development deserve attention, it is the economic effects that often take the forefront in the media and the minds of politicians.

What tourism questions can be addressed through economics? What are the likely consequences of economic decisions about tourism? What are the proper ways to use economic tools in decision-making over tourism? How are economic tools misused in the study of tourism? Although this chapter will certainly not make you an expert in the economics of tourism, it will help you examine tourism issues in a practical manner. And it will help you ask tourism analysts and decision-makers the types of questions that produce practical and useful answers.

The first part of this chapter looks at some of the tourism issues that economics can address. The second part concentrates on the tools that economists may use to try to evaluate tourism issues.

The Economic Question

The fundamental question that economics tries to answer is: How should scarce resources be allocated? There are simply not enough resources to produce everything consumers want. Therefore, individuals, businesses, and governments must make decisions concerning the best uses of existing resources.

The free market system is one mechanism for determining how to allocate resources. Consumers make demands in the marketplace. Businesses respond by supplying what consumers demand as long as these businesses can operate at a profit. If consumers do not value something enough to pay a price that allows business to make a profit, business will apply its resources elsewhere. The resources that might have been used on the first product or service will be used in products or services that consumers value more highly. In this way, market forces allocate resources to those areas where they are most valued.

Individual consumers try to maximize their satisfaction by purchasing what they want at the lowest prices. Individual businesses try to maximize their profits. Governments try to look beyond the concerns of individual consumers and businesses to larger societal needs.

Tourism is a curious mix of public and private goods, all of which contain an element of scarcity. Gasoline and tennis racquets are examples of products which tourists consume. They are produced by the private sector in most capitalist countries. Fuel is a scarce resource due to finite supplies of oil. Another world oil crisis may drastically affect tourism as governments decide how to allocate this resource. Similarly, sports equipment industries cannot produce unlimited supplies of tennis racquets because the raw ingredients needed to produce these products (labor, fuel, materials, and so forth) are limited and are in demand for use in other products and services. Thus, the private sector must constantly wrestle with resource scarcity.

However, in many countries, governments administer natural, cultural, and historic attractions and resources for the collective good of those countries' populations. Such resources and attractions are called **public goods**. The public good component of tourism arises because tourists are drawn to locations with natural, cultural, and historic resources. Governments have decided that these scarce amenities are worthy of protection. Nobel Laureate Paul A. Samuelson's theory of public goods provides the rationale for such government involvement. Simply put, governments must get involved in the provision of certain goods for which there are many *free riders.*

Free riders are those who benefit from a good or service without having to pay for it. For example, governments have decided that national parks should be preserved. Many people who benefit by knowing that national parks still exist or that they or their grandchildren have the option of visiting a national park do not have to pay anything for these benefits. Private businesses are not motivated to produce goods for which there are many free riders because they cannot charge for the full benefits.

Beyond its resource preservation function, government plays a major role in promoting tourism resources to foreign visitors and sometimes supervising their behaviors when they temporarily reside within its borders. For these reasons, the public sector continues to be an important partner in the supply and price of tourism resources.

The Reagan Administration's New Federalism policy of removing government from people's lives and allowing the market mechanism to operate more freely caused governments to reassess their role in the provision of tourism resources and facilities. Public agencies began charging more and higher fees as tax revenues became increasingly unreliable sources of funds to cover operation costs. Increasingly, the private sector was encouraged to provide more tourism services and facilities.

A popular comic strip expresses the irony of charging more and higher fees for the use of public spaces. (Reprinted by permission of NEA, Inc., New York, New York)

Still, the public provision of certain tourism goods and services continues to be a significant policy in the United States. Society must constantly wrestle with the scarce nature and proper balance of both public and private tourism goods and services.

Lifelong Ideas

There are a number of fundamental economic concepts that you will find truly useful in the years to come. The following pages present 11 basic ideas organized into two groups. The first five ideas pertain to **macroeconomics** (the branch of economics dealing with analyzing a whole economy or a large sector of it). The last six ideas pertain to **microeconomics** (the branch of economics dealing with analyzing individual units or markets in an economy).[1]

Idea 1: Employment and Inflation

Increasing employment usually increases inflation as well. If we increase employment in tourism, the prices of goods and services for local residents may rise due to the attempt to extract maximum profit from tourists. Conversely, steps to decrease inflation will likely increase unemployment.

This is a crucial point for both the United States and Third World countries. In the United States, it means that low income groups may no longer be able to live in communities that rely primarily on tourism. For Third World countries, it means that over-reliance on tourism (or, for that matter, any single industry) is dangerous if there is no means of channeling tourism profits into other sectors. That is, the inflation caused by a growth in tourism will hurt local residents if they cannot capture a share of the profits. Countries that rely almost solely on tourism are often disappointed as the profits go to foreign banks and stockholders instead of back into their own economies.[2]

Idea 2: Voluntary Exchange

The concept of voluntary exchange is fundamental to a free market economic system and must not be forgotten in tourism. This concept means that both parties (governments, businesses, or individuals) engaged in a transaction must gain or expect to gain something from the transaction; otherwise they will not do it. America gains by the influx of Japanese tourists because of their spending. Japan gains political strength by showing that it contributes to the worldwide balance of trade and that its citizens, and hence its economy, are prosperous.

Certain laws and government policies sometimes prohibit mutually beneficial exchanges. For example, policies preventing indigenous populations from selling locally produced goods and services at fair market value to tourists restrict the economic system.

Idea 3: Comparative Advantage

Clearly, economies that are not self-sufficient must engage in trade to meet their needs. Surprisingly, however, even self-sufficient economies can improve their standard of living by engaging in trade. This is because all economies are better at producing certain goods than others. One economy may possess abundant oil reserves, while another possesses fertile farmland. The concept of **comparative advantage** states that, if each economy produces what it produces best, trade improves the efficiency of the affected economies.

This concept applies directly to tourism. The assumption that all states should raise their tourism promotion budgets to increase their market share of tourists is misguided. There is a limited pool of tourists from which to draw. States and regions should consider their position within this competitive market.

For example, it could be that State A has the best attractions and services and thus receives the top end (direct effects) of tourist spending. Nonetheless, State B may be better at providing the factors needed to produce tourism goods and services: recreational equipment, boats, labor, supplies, transportation of supplies, and so forth. State B thus receives a large share of tourism spending effects in production rather than in retail and wholesale consumption, at which State A excels. State A is said to have a comparative advantage in the "forward linked" factors of tourism production, while State B has a comparative advantage in the "backward linked" factors.

Like State B, many areas would be better off developing their competitive advantage in the production of tourism goods and services to be exported (that is, backward linked industries), rather than trying to capture more tourists.

Idea 4: Productivity

In the long run, the productivity of labor affects our material well-being and the amounts we can afford to spend on tourism more than any other economic force. It affects how frequently people travel for pleasure and how much they are able to spend. It affects how much governments can invest in tourism promotion and infrastructure development. Thus, policies and laws aimed at improving productivity in general will also benefit those who depend on tourism.

Idea 5: Relating Sales to Income and Employment

More sales does not necessarily mean more income or jobs. *Sales* refers to the total amount of revenues businesses receive from the sale of their products to tourists. *Income,* on the other hand, refers to the amount of money households receive in the form of employee wages, interest on investments, and rent and royalties received from the ownership of property. Income is the amount of earnings claimed on income tax forms each year. Sales and income are *not* the same.

It is not necessarily true that high tourism sales result in high incomes. What counts is the proportion of sales that tourism employers allocate to their employees in the form of wages and where and how those employees spend and invest those wages.

Money spent by tourists begins to leak out of an economy almost immediately. Tourism businesses themselves may spend a large portion of their tourist revenues on products produced in another country, state, or region. Tourist business employees also receive part of tourist revenues as wages, and will likely spend some of their wages in non-local businesses. In addition, the seasonal nature of most tourism businesses requires them to hire part-time employees (for example, students) who may not be residents of the region. The part-time employees who live or go to school outside the region may send portions of their income out of the region. Additional tourist sales escape in the form of dividends and royalties paid to stockholders living outside the region.

Furthermore, some of the jobs in tourism may require little training or skill and consequently pay only minimum wages. Combine this with the seasonal nature of much of tourism employment, and you can see how hard-core unemployment may be hardly affected.

Idea 6: Supply and Demand Drive Tourism

The interaction between supply and demand keeps the free market system going. When a desired good or service is in short supply, the prices rise. When supplies are abundant, prices tend to decrease. This interaction can clearly affect tourism and play an important role in decisions about tourism development. As more tourism resources become available—for example, as the number of cruise ships grows—the prices tend to decrease, all other things being the same.

Idea 7: Externalities

Externalities occur when the voluntary exchange between two parties affects one or more uninvolved third parties. Externalities escape the control of the market system. (Examples of public goods which produce positive externalities include public education, health services, and parks.)

In the case of parks, society has decided, through elected representatives, that these scarce resources yield societal benefits that would not exist if government did not intervene. For example, one of these parks or nature preserves may contain a plant or animal whose genetic composition holds the key for the cure of AIDS. Destruction of the home of this organism may destroy the production of a good which would otherwise benefit all of society. Individual businesses are not usually motivated to produce parks and preserves. The costs and risks are too great. Even if the risks were reduced by knowledge of the exact location of an AIDS-curing species, the cost of a nature preserve might still be too high and many people who benefit (for example, relatives of the afflicted, scientists, nature enthusiasts, city dwellers) could not be forced to pay.

Similar reasoning can be applied to public education and health services. Society has deemed adequate health care a meritorious social good and underwrites the cost of this good for lower income groups. This is because the price private businesses could extract from these groups may not allow them to operate at a profit. Furthermore, if health care reduces the general level of contagion, even people who can afford health insurance will benefit by not getting sick as often.

Examples of negative externalities include pollution, higher taxes, and crowding. If allowed to operate with no intervention, the free market system provides no financial incentive that will motivate the producer of these negative externalities to minimize the damage. Government intervention can help control some negative externalities. For example, governments can force polluters to pay the costs of cleaning up the pollution they create. Thus, polluters will have an incentive to cut down on the amount of pollution they generate. In addition, since the cost of pollution control will drive up the polluters' costs, the products they sell will become more expensive. This means that the consumers buying those products will share more equitably in paying the true costs associated with the products.

Tourism has both positive and negative externalities. Positive externalities may include economic growth, additional recreational and cultural opportunities for local citizens, social interaction and exchange of new ideas between people from different regions, and the preservation of natural and cultural attractions. Negative externalities may include unwanted changes in the character and appearance of communities, environmental degradation from overdevelopment or poorly planned development, and crowding—which results in increased costs for roads, sanitation, police activity, and fire protection. It remains to be seen how charging for negative externalities might be applied to tourism.

Idea 8: Opportunity Cost

Resources are scarce and we must make choices. What are the costs of our choices? To an accountant, cost means how much is directly spent to obtain something, like a new car or a college education. To an economist, cost means **opportunity cost** or the value of the next best alternative you have to give up for something else. For example, the amount you would earn working instead of going to college is one

Pristine coastal areas are often threatened by industrial and agricultural uses of water that cause pollution. (Courtesy of the Washington State Tourism Division)

measure of the value of a college education, not the actual tuition and room and board costs.

In much of the world, water is a scarce resource. Clean water is even scarcer. Tourism and clean water go hand in hand. Clean water provides scenery, clean beaches, clean places to swim, and a viable sport fishing industry. What is the cost of clean water to, for example, America's Great Lakes states? The fact that portions of the Great Lakes are polluted is a demand factor that the Great Lakes states must resolve in order to increase tourism.

More fundamentally, the Great Lakes states must decide among alternative resource uses. Simply put, the governments of these states must choose between economies that emphasize, on the one hand, clean water for tourism or, on the other, industrial and agricultural uses of water that may lead to further pollution. Economists argue that the relevant cost of cleaning up the Great Lakes for tourism is not how much is spent on tourism development, but the opportunity cost of giving up jobs and income from certain industrial developments and agricultural practices.

Idea 9: Marginal Costs

There are two components of the free market: consumers and producers. Both consumers and producers continually make decisions about which goods and services to buy and which to sell. To economists, consumer purchase decisions are based to a large degree on the concept of *utility*, or how much satisfaction consumers receive from a good or service. Utility is measured by how much money the consumer is willing to give up in exchange for goods and services. On the other hand, producers' decisions are influenced by production costs, or how much of certain inputs are required to produce various outputs.

Marginal costs should guide seller decisions. Marginal cost refers to the change in total costs associated with producing one more unit of output—for example, an additional weekend package at a tourist resort. Marginal cost analysis allows a business to determine if it can increase its profit by offering discounts on a selective basis.

Suppose a tourist resort charges $1,000 for a family weekend package. On weekends that the resort does not expect to sell out, can the resort increase its profits by reducing its price to $800 for certain categories of consumer—for example, senior citizens? The likely answer is "yes."

This is because the resort must pay most of the cost of providing weekend packages regardless of how many rooms are used. Full costs include costs of maintenance, insurance, property taxes, and so on. Thus, the full costs are largely irrelevant. The relevant costs in deciding whether to reduce the weekend package rate are the extra, or marginal, costs. These include registering the additional guests, the food and beverages these guests consume, the additional linens and utilities required, and so on. The marginal costs are probably quite small in this case. A guest who pays the resort more than its marginal cost will contribute to the resort's profits. It is probably more profitable to sell some weekend packages for $800 than it is to leave the rooms empty.

Idea 10: Rising Service Sector Costs

The costs of certain services (for example, education) are rising, but what we receive is less (more crowded classrooms, fewer good teachers). These costs are rising faster than inflation because of increased productivity in manufacturing. Technological advances in manufacturing increase productivity and push wages upward. The resulting inflation brought about by higher wages in manufacturing leads service sector employees to demand and receive higher wages. However, it is more difficult to increase technology in service sectors than in manufacturing. Because it still requires one garbage collector to drive a truck or one night clerk to register hotel guests, the cost of such services is forced to increase. Thus, tourism costs rise while productivity remains the same.

Increasingly, tourism businesses are searching for technological ways to improve productivity by employing labor-saving devices. A recent example in the hotel industry is the use of automatic check-out systems. Furthermore, tourism businesses may continue to reduce labor costs by employing part-time workers (students, retirees, and so forth) or by importing cheaper foreign labor.

Idea 11: Increasing Output Versus Equality

There is often a trade-off between the size of a country's output and the equity with which that output is distributed. For example, tax cuts are generally thought to increase productivity and output by providing greater rewards for working, saving, and investing. However, tax cuts also appear to widen the gap between the winners and losers in an economy. This is because tax cuts put relatively few resources back in the hands of the poor. If the tax cuts come at the expense of social programs, the poor may even come out behind. In contrast, lowering taxes places proportionately more money in the hands of the upper classes and businesses that already have the initiative, training, and financial resources to succeed. These sectors are typically more economically efficient with their additional resources—so output increases. Some social critics see this as the rich getting richer.

Conversely, tax-funded programs for the economically disadvantaged—such as food stamps and aid to families with dependent children—may lessen productivity by channeling some resources to households that may not be as economically efficient as others. In essence, equality must be "purchased" with the greater output that a more efficient, but perhaps less equitable, use of resources would provide.

Since people have different value judgments about the importance of equality, there will always be disagreements about how much equity to purchase. The market can do well at promoting efficiency, but poorly at promoting equality.

In tourism, the equity issue arises in deciding how much to charge for the use of public resources and attractions, such as national and state parks, museums, and zoos. Raising fees for the use of such attractions may discriminate against the poor. Raising taxes is one alternative to raising fees, but it is not popular in this era of taxpayer revolt. As we have seen, cutting taxes may not be the answer to achieving equity either. The question then becomes: should we adopt a policy of lower taxes for the economically disadvantaged, while maintaining the same level of fees for public tourism resources, or even increasing them? If so, would lower income groups be motivated, with the extra income in tax savings, to be more productive as well as to spend some of their income on tourism? Or, should the government continue to subsidize *public* tourism resources, while allowing market forces (which extract the maximum price consumers are willing to pay) to operate freely? Policymakers must constantly wrestle with these trade-offs.

The Tools of Tourism Economics

Now that we have looked at several important economic concepts, let's turn our attention to the various tools that economists use. A quick glance through an economics textbook suggests that the primary tools of economists are mathematics and statistics. However, economics is much more. Economists also use historical inquiry and policy analysis to evaluate certain problems that affect all society. Most of these problems are illustrated in the 11 ideas just discussed.

Tool 1: Abstraction

Because the world is so overwhelmingly complex, it is often necessary to abstract from reality in order to understand anything. Abstraction means ignoring incidental details in order to focus on the most important aspects of a problem.

Economists are not the only ones to make abstractions from the real world. We all do in everyday life. Tourists make abstractions when they travel. They have images of places that may or may not match reality. Right now, you can probably imagine the Sahara Desert, even though it is likely that you have never been there. Such images affect tourist demand for travel destinations.

People often form images of exotic destinations which may or may not reflect the reality of the actual place or situation. (Courtesy of the Texas Department of Commerce, Tourism Division)

The artful aspect of any discipline, including economics, is maintaining a balance between abstraction and reality. This is a difficult task because the "correct" degree of abstraction depends on the problem being studied. It also requires a great deal of tourism experience.

Let's look at two examples of abstraction in tourism economics. The first example is at the microeconomic level. Suppose you want to know who gains and who loses from tourism development in a community. Because of time and funding limitations, you would probably not study all aspects of the problem. You may divide community residents into high, medium, and low income groupings and then evaluate which of these groupings would benefit most and least. However, you probably would not consider residents' height, weight, and hair color. You might examine which age groups receive the most and least benefits, but you would probably not consider length of residency or family size. Each time you make one of these decisions, you are abstracting from the real world in an attempt to make the best decision possible.

The second example is at the macroeconomic level. Suppose you want to know what will happen to the total output of a large, economically diverse region if it decides to invest more money in tourism development. How many and what types of jobs will be affected? How will income levels change in various sectors of the economy? This is a complex problem involving countless decisions by government officials, businesses, and consumers. It would be impossible in such a case to examine the effects of the investment on each individual business. Many abstractions must be made.

For example, decisions must be made about which businesses are related to tourism, both directly and indirectly. Then it is necessary to decide how to group similar businesses into larger economic sectors (for example, all hotels/motels/ bed and breakfasts into a lodging sector). However, too much abstraction may cause you to lose essential information. For example, the public sector also provides lodging in the form of campgrounds, cabins, and cottages. Since the effects of the public sector in terms of a region's output are different from the effects of the private sector, you may decide to define both a public and a private lodging sector.

Three ingredients can assist in deciding the optimal level of abstraction. First, knowledge of the tourism industry is required. Second, commonly used economic principles (the 11 ideas) should be applied. Third, appropriate economic tools (theories and models) should be employed.

Tool 2: Economic Theory and Tourism

The lay person has a tendency to think of theory as irrelevant. Nothing could be further from the truth. The noted social psychologist Kurt Lewin argued that "nothing is as practical as a good theory." By this, Lewin meant that theories help us understand the real world.

A theory is a deliberate abstraction which attempts to explain how observed relationships work. Thus, theories help predict what might happen in the future under other conditions. Chemists' theories, based on real world observations, explain what happens when two molecules are combined at various temperatures or under different levels of pressure. An entire chemical industry applies these theories to develop products which society demands.

Theories and hypotheses are often confused. It is a hypothesis to suggest that, in a given community, more investment in golf courses will increase the household incomes of lower socioeconomic classes in that community. However, a theory of how economic prosperity is determined by government or private sector actions might be used to explain *why*, in the face of increasing golf course investment, the proportion of lower income classes is increasing or decreasing.

Theories do more than describe the world. They explain and predict. Without theory to guide policy decisions, the economics of tourism becomes a mere exercise in description. This is dangerous because statistics alone can be misleading. Merely observing that increased investment in golf courses has increased output, but had little effect on lower income residents, does not explain the relationship. It is likely that some factor common to both variables—golf course sales and income effects— is creating the observed relationship.

Economic theories explain the observed relationship by exposing the underlying force: **linkage**. These theories explain that if the linkage between sectors that produce a round of golf and those that affect lower class incomes is minimal, then no matter how great the total sales, the effect on lower class incomes will still be minimal. Thus, to maximize the effects of golf course sales on lower class incomes,

---

Tourism Economics: Discussion Topic #1

A resort in one of the Great Lakes states is considering hiring summer employees from a foreign country to perform routine housekeeping and maintenance chores. The resort owners claim that foreign workers are more willing and more reliable in performing so-called "menial" tasks than their American counterparts. The local community is up in arms, claiming that the jobs should go to local residents first and that to obtain high quality American labor, the resort should pay higher wages and benefits. Suppose that you are a member of the Board of County Commissioners for the county in which this resort is located. What would be your arguments for or against a proposed ordinance that would restrict tourism business hiring to local residents only? Would you be in favor of or against providing tourism businesses with tax incentives to hire only local labor? Why? (It might help you to refer to Ideas 1, 5, and 10 discussed earlier in this chapter.)

---

the government might adopt a policy which gives incentives to golf course developers for hiring more local labor, especially from the region's lower income classes.

Furthermore, in a community considering more golf course development, theories help predict what might happen to lower class incomes if policies are or are not enacted to encourage the hiring of local labor. Because of sound and useful theories, the same type of reasoning can be used to understand the effects of other types of tourism developments.

Tool 3: Economic Models and Tourism

Economic models are another class of tools that economists use to describe relationships. An economic model refers to a simplified, small-scale version of some aspect of the economy. Engineers often use physical models as abstractions of the real world. For example, the U.S. Army Corps of Engineers uses a scale-size model of the entire Mississippi River to predict the effects of water flow if the positions of dams and levees are altered. The results of this particular model are very accurate. However, models are not always as accurate; for example, stock market models did not accurately predict the "Black Monday" stock market crash in October of 1987.

Clearly, there is some uncertainty in the use of models. Their accuracy is gauged in terms of how often they can predict what happens in the real world— not by whether they are always correct. Economists' models are mostly expressed in the form of graphs, equations, and words.

When we say that tourists travel to those destinations and buy those products that maximize their satisfaction, we are stating an economic model of tourist behavior. Likewise, with computers and with data supplied by the U.S. Department of Commerce, it is possible to develop a model of the entire economy of any region in the United States—without even going there. We can then provide the model with various levels of tourist spending and allow the model to help us predict what will be the effects on jobs and income. These are fairly simplified abstractions of the real world, but they are useful roadmaps for decision-makers.

Theories and models do not provide all the answers. In tourism, the facts and information needed to build good economic theories and models are often lacking. For example, one basic piece of information essential to estimating either tourist demand or the economic impacts of tourist spending is a reliable estimate of the number of tourists visiting an area. Many regions and states within the United States and other countries have poor estimates of the number of visitors. There are other important information gaps as well.

The point is that we will never have all the information we need to construct perfect theories or models. Thus, value judgments in the face of uncertainty will always play a role in policy decisions affecting tourism development. Even when there is a theory or model, not all tourism experts will agree about its usefulness or accuracy. Nonetheless, to properly evaluate and contribute to economic decisions affecting tourism, you need to realize when policy decisions are based on value judgments, disputed facts, accepted theories or models, or a combination of these elements.

Tool 4: Demand/Supply Analysis

Demand and supply analysis is the fundamental investigative tool of economists. **Supply** and **demand curves** are graphs that relate price to quantity. In economics, it is very important to distinguish between a change in demand or supply and a change in quantity demanded or supplied.

Exhibit 1 shows this difference for demand. The slope of the demand curve *D* reflects the fact that, as the price of a good or service falls, the amount that consumers are willing to purchase (in other words, the quantity demanded) increases. Movement along a fixed demand curve—that is, *a change in quantity demanded*—occurs when *only* the price of a good or service changes. All other factors are assumed to remain constant. These other factors include the prices of all related goods, consumer income, consumer tastes, expectations about the future, and the number of buyers. If any of these five factors changes, the demand curve itself *shifts* to the right or left—for example, to D_1 or D_2 in Exhibit 1. This is *a change in demand*, in contrast to a change in quantity demanded.

Exhibit 2 shows a similar situation for the supply curve. The upward slope of the supply curve *S* reflects the fact that, as the price of a good or service goes up, the amount that suppliers are willing to produce (in other words, the quantity supplied) increases. Movement along a fixed supply curve—that is, *a change in quantity supplied*—occurs when *only* the price of a good or service changes. All other factors are assumed to remain constant. With regard to supply, these other factors are the prices of resources and other factors of production, technology, the prices of other goods and services, the number of suppliers, and the suppliers' expectations. If any of these five factors changes, the supply curve itself *shifts* to the right or left—for example, to S_1 or S_2 in Exhibit 2. This is called *a change in supply*, in contrast to a change in quantity supplied.

When we combine supply and demand curves (see Exhibit 3), the point at which they cross is called the **equilibrium price and quantity.** Equilibrium indicates the point where the quantity of a good or service that buyers demand and purchase is just equal to the quantity that sellers supply and sell. In equilibrium,

Exhibit 1   The Demand Curve

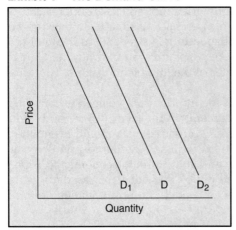

Exhibit 2   The Supply Curve

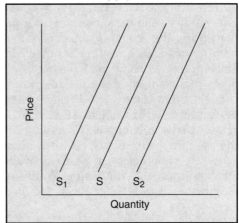

Exhibit 3   The Market Supply and Demand Curves

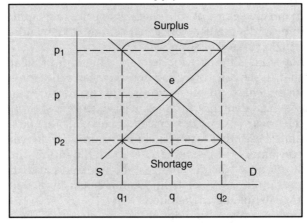

there is no tendency for price and quantity to change. When the market price is above or below the equilibrium price, market adjustment occurs because free market forces move naturally toward equilibrium.

For example, at price p_1 (above equilibrium) in Exhibit 3, buyers will demand quantity q_1, but suppliers will supply quantity q_2. This will create a surplus. In order to sell this surplus, suppliers will begin to undercut one another's prices. As the price falls, consumers will buy more and suppliers will supply less, until the equilibrium price p and quantity q are achieved.

Conversely, at price p_2 (below equilibrium), buyers will demand quantity q_2, but suppliers will only supply quantity q_1. This will result in a shortage. In this situation, buyers will bid up the price in an effort to get the undersupplied good or service. As the price goes up, suppliers will supply more. This will continue until the equilibrium price p and quantity q are achieved.

Exhibit 4 **Supply and Demand for Nights at Private Campgrounds**

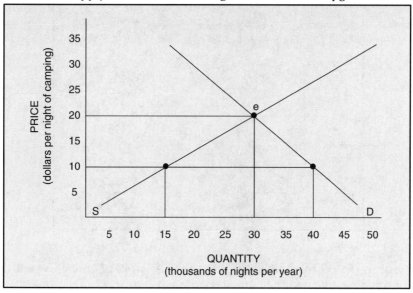

A price above or below equilibrium will not persist in a free market system for any extended time. Sometimes, however, buyers call on governments to interfere with the free market system by creating **price ceilings** below the equilibrium price. That is, the government tells suppliers that they cannot charge more than a set maximum amount. Similarly, sellers sometimes ask governments to create **price supports** above the equilibrium price. That is, the government guarantees suppliers a price above equilibrium. While the political pressure to impose ceilings or supports can be intense, the consequences of doing so can be significant. By setting a price below equilibrium, price ceilings create shortages. Conversely, price supports create surpluses.

Let's apply these concepts directly to tourism. Exhibit 4 is a supply and demand graph for nights of camping in private campgrounds. The downward slope of the demand curve shows that, as the price of a night of private camping decreases, the number of nights demanded increases. Movement along this demand curve occurs when only price changes—that is, there is a change in quantity demanded. The demand curve itself could shift if other factors change—for example, the price of camping in public campgrounds, the cost of tents and other camping implements, public awareness and wariness of Lyme disease.

The upward slope of the supply curve in Exhibit 4 demonstrates that at higher prices, private campground operators will supply more nights of private camping—that is, they will increase the quantity supplied by building more campsites. When *current* private campground operators increase their supply due solely to price increases, there is a change in quantity supplied. If *new* private campground operators enter the business because of its attractive profitability, the supply curve itself shifts to the right and there is a change in supply. Other factors that could

Exhibit 5   Supply and Demand for Three-Day Cruises

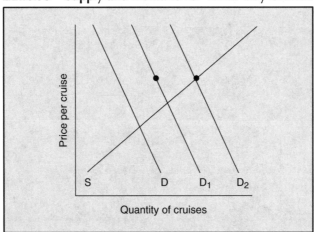

shift the supply curve might include a change in the price of lumber (wooded land used for camping may become more valuable as a source of timber) or a change in land values (perhaps due to nearby development).

Point *e* in Exhibit 4 shows that equilibrium is 30,000 nights per year at $20 per night. If the price is below $20, suppliers will supply fewer camping nights than campers wish to purchase, and frustrated campers will bid the price up. If the price is above $20, the quantity supplied will exceed the quantity demanded. This situation will force campground operators to undercut their competitors by reducing their price in order to sell their desired quantities of camping nights. This undercutting will continue as long as supply exceeds demand.

As another tourism example, recent developments in the cruise line industry illustrate demand and supply interactions. The demand for cruises grew dramatically throughout the 1980s—that is, the demand curve shifted to the right. (This is graphed as the movement from D to D_1 in Exhibit 5.) The number of passengers and resulting earnings in the cruise line industry rose sharply. In response to this rising demand, the cruise line industry increased its supply of ships. In fact, it produced so many ships such that supply now (temporarily) exceeds demand. If the cruise line industry cannot somehow increase the demand for its product (that is, shift the demand curve from D_1 to D_2), it will have to reduce prices to move along the supply curve to equilibrium. In actuality, cruise lines have been slashing fares and discounting up to 60% of the cost of a cruise since the mid-1980s in order to increase demand. They have also been spending money to promote the image that cruises are no more expensive than other forms of vacationing. We will return to this example in the following section.

Tool 5: Benefit/Cost Analysis and Efficiency

Economic benefit/cost analysis and **economic impact analysis** are two of the most basic tools economists use, including those who study tourism. **Economic benefits**

and costs are microeconomic issues reflecting how consumers make decisions about what to buy and how firms can remain profitable. **Economic impacts** are macroeconomic concerns about the aggregate number of jobs and amount of income a region can expect from economic development of various industries like tourism. Although they are often confused, *benefits and impacts have separate and distinct meanings.* Since they are such fundamental measures and the ones you will likely encounter in tourism, the rest of this chapter is devoted to explaining what they mean and how they should be applied to tourism issues. We will look first at economic benefits and costs.

Individual firms can examine the benefits and costs of supplying a certain product which consumers demand and then decide whether the enterprise will be profitable. Governments can assess the benefits and costs of a government-subsidized project like public housing and decide whether the project will be efficient. In economics, **efficiency** is defined as the absence of waste of resources like labor and equipment. Efficiency is said to be achieved at the government level when the benefits to consumers and society exceed government costs.

Let's return to the cruise line example. Is the cruise line industry's decision to cut prices and increase promotion an efficient one? The industry is trying to avoid wasting its excess capacity of ships. To do so, it will have to weigh the benefits and costs of its decision to slash prices and change its promotion strategy.

Consider Exhibit 6. Cutting prices from $500 per three-day cruise to $300 for the same cruise will result in more consumption of three-day cruises. A lowering in price results in a movement along the demand curve. At $500 per three-day cruise, benefits were area AHIB, or $1,500,000 ($500 × 3,000). At $300, benefits can be estimated as area AEFC ($1,650,000) or $300 times 5,500.

If demand is stimulated by a new promotion strategy which emphasizes the comparability of prices to other forms of leisure travel, then there is a shift in the demand curve. In this case, the demand curve shifts to the right and, at $300 per cruise, benefits increase from area AEFC to area AEGD. Recall from earlier in the chapter that factors which shift the demand curve are population size, consumer incomes, consumer tastes, expectations about the future, and prices and availability of related products. By changing its promotion strategy, the cruise line industry hopes to affect consumer tastes—one of the demand shifters.

Now the industry must consider the costs of its decision. Costs include the direct costs of additional advertising as well as the opportunity costs of the decision to lower prices. In this case, the opportunity cost of lowering prices is the cost of the next best alternative, leaving prices where they are. The industry may fear that slashing prices too much will be detrimental in the long run by training consumers to believe that prices will only go down. If consumers expect prices to fall even farther, the current demand curve may shift to the left, making things even worse for the cruise industry. Given this possibility, the industry may decide to leave prices at or near their current levels, and to concentrate on one of the demand shifters.

Benefit/cost analysis based on the laws of supply and demand can extend beyond the level of the firm to entire tourism regions. At the regional or national level, the question becomes broader and more complex. For example, at the regional or national level, unemployment represents a wasted resource. To use tourism as an

Exhibit 6   Three-Day Cruises: Demand and Demand Shifters

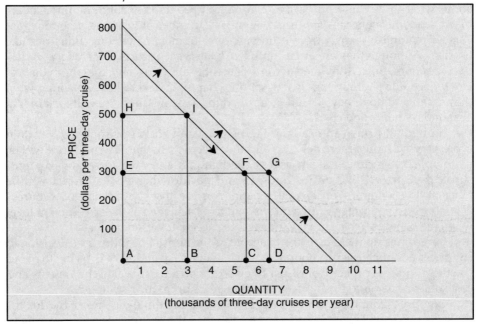

example, the issue centers on the relative benefits and costs of stimulating more employment in tourism versus doing so in manufacturing or agriculture.[3]

Tool 6: Economic Impact Analysis

Benefit/cost analysis is used to measure the efficiency of business decisions or government projects. Economic impact analysis (**EIA**) is used to take a snapshot of an entire existing economy and determine the effects of tourist spending on employment and income in that economy.

Let's suppose that you travel to your favorite spring break destination and upon arrival you spend $20 at a gasoline station. As a tourist, you have spent $20 in the destination community. That amount is counted as sales to the gasoline station. We could sum the sales receipts from all gasoline stations in the community and multiply by the percentage of sales to tourists to find out the gasoline sector's total amount of sales to tourists. Remember, however, that there is a difference between sales and income (see Idea 5). In an economic impact analysis, the focus is not on the amount of sales as such, but rather on the *impact* of those sales on income and employment.

There are three elements that contribute to the total impact of a given amount of sales. These are:

- **Direct impact:** the first-round effect of tourist spending (for example, how much gasoline stations spend on goods and pay their employees per dollar of tourist spending)

- **Indirect impact:** the ripple effect of additional rounds of recirculating the initial tourist dollars (for example, purchases of additional goods and services by other firms in other sectors)

- **Induced impact:** further ripple effects caused by employees in affected firms spending some of their wages in other businesses (for example, gasoline station employees spend part of the wages in local firms, whose owners and employees also spend additional money in a given area)

The total impact equals the direct plus indirect plus induced effects.

To continue the example, the gasoline station owner must take part of the $20 you spent and buy more gasoline from a wholesale distributor. If the distributor is located some distance from the gasoline station, the owner may also have to pay substantial transportation fees. In addition to gasoline, most gasoline stations sell other items like oil, food, beverages, and repair services. Therefore, the owner must take another part of your $20 and purchase more of these additional items, as well as pay wages and benefits to employees.

Clearly, the spending of your initial expenditure goes through numerous rounds. In the first round of spending (direct impacts), the gasoline owner buys more gasoline and (let's say) bakery items. The owner also pays wages to employees. In the second round, the wholesale gasoline distributor and the baker buy additional items and pay wages to their employees (indirect impacts)—all with part of your $20. Furthermore, the gasoline station employees spend part of their salaries on groceries, rent, automobiles and so on (induced impacts). In the third round, employees of the bakery and the gasoline distributor spend part of their salaries (more induced impacts) and the grocery stores, landlords, and automobile dealers purchase goods and pay wages (more indirect and induced). Like the ripples resulting from a stone hitting a pool of water, the initial amount of tourist spending reverberates throughout the economy.

To calculate impacts properly, you must first determine the region of impact. Is the affected region the community, the county, several counties, the state, parts of several states, or the entire nation? This is a critical question because at each round of spending, some **leakage** occurs. The amount of leakage is smaller in large, relatively self-sufficient economies than it is in small economies with little diversity.

To illustrate, assume that the region of interest is a community popular with students on spring break. Further assume that all wholesale gasoline distributors are located outside the community and that all bakeries are located within the community. The amount of your $20 that the gasoline station owner pays to the distributor immediately leaks out of the community and has no further impact. However, the amount paid to bakeries stays in the community, at least initially, and can be properly counted as economic impact in the form of goods purchased locally and wages paid to local employees. In terms of employee income, there is further leakage. The gasoline station and bakery employees will spend part of their incomes on purchases made outside the community. Employees may also save part of their incomes and pay non-local taxes—two actions which further reduce the amount that may be circulated locally.

Tourism is often desirable because it injects "new" dollars into a region. New dollars, or **injections**, are defined as money spent in a region by non-residents of the region. (Other types of injections include exports, firms borrowing money from banks, and government expenditures). An injection of new dollars can properly be subjected to economic impact analysis. Resident spending on locally produced tourism goods and services, while desirable, does not represent the circulation of new money and is generally not counted as new dollars or direct impact. To determine what to include as the injection of new money, the boundaries of the study region must be carefully set.

Multipliers. Once the region is defined, how are the effects of the recirculation of new dollars expressed? EIA uses a specific measurement device called the **multiplier**. Above, we illustrated how tourist expenditures can ripple, or multiply, as new money circulates throughout a region's economy. The size of the multiplier reflects the impact of the various rounds of recirculation before the new dollars leak entirely from the region.

A multiplier expresses the impact of a given investment in terms of change in employment, income, or output (sales) in a region. The key word is "change." Multipliers may be used to guide investment decision-making by demonstrating the income and employment changes resulting from alternative tourism development scenarios.

The size and complexity of the local region affect the size of the multiplier. In general, the more interdependent the sectors in a region are, the larger the multiplier effect of a given investment will be. This implies that multiplier effects are greater in larger or more diverse regions than in smaller regions or in communities where economic diversity is low. As community self-sufficiency in providing tourist goods and services rises, the need to import will decrease. The dollars remaining in the community to be reused by residents before disappearing to non-local purchases and savings will increase.

To continue our example, the spring break community will receive more of the multiplier effect of tourist spending if it includes both wholesale gasoline distributors and bakeries instead of just bakeries.

Multiplier Measurement. It is very important to realize that there is no one tourism multiplier which will apply to all situations in all regions. There are actually many different types of tourism multipliers.[4] If the wrong multiplier is used, the resulting economic impact analysis can be in error by millions of dollars in income and hundreds of jobs even for a relatively small region. Unfortunately, multipliers are often applied incorrectly. For example, **income** and **sales multipliers** are very different, but since they are both measured in dollars, they are often confused. When considering the accuracy of an economic impact analysis, you must always ask: What type of multiplier was used, and was it used correctly?

In tourism economic impact analysis, the components of the following general equation must be determined:

$$TEI = G \times S \times K$$

where *TEI* = total economic impact (income or jobs, usually)

    G = total number of tourists in each group of tourists with similar spending patterns (cruise line vacationers, campers, people just visiting for the day, overnight visitors, festival attendees)

    S = average spending by each tourist in these groups

    K = a multiplier expressing the change in the amount of employment or income

Keynesian-type multipliers, which are income multipliers named after the economist John Maynard Keynes, are the appropriate types of multipliers to use for *K* in the above equation. The income multiplier is commonly used in tourism because it most clearly demonstrates the economic impact on destination region residents. In general, Keynes' original formulation of the income multiplier was:

$$K = \frac{\Delta Y}{\Delta J}$$

where *K* is the multiplier
ΔY is the change in income that arises from an additional economic stimulus, like tourism
ΔJ is the injection, or change in tourist spending that brought about the additional income

Economists calculate Keynesian-type multipliers "by hand" or through the use of input-output models. Either approach requires the skills of an expert and a great deal of information. Estimating multipliers can be costly and time-consuming. The general formula for calculating multipliers by hand is:[5]

$$K = A \times \frac{1}{1 - BC}$$

where *A* = percentage of tourist spending remaining in the region after subtracting leakages

    B = percentage of income spent by residents on locally produced goods and services

    C = percentage of resident spending remaining as local income after subtracting leakages

Thus, if 50% of tourist spending remains after leakages, 60% of resident income is spent locally, and 40% remains as local income, the income multiplier is:

$$K = .5 \times \frac{1}{1 - (0.6 \times 0.4)} = 0.66$$

In other words, for every dollar of tourist spending, 66 cents in local income is generated. In tourism, the amount of income generated is typically less than the amount tourists spend because of leakages. Thus, *K* is usually less than 1 for tourism unless the study region is very large and diverse.

We stated earlier that it is a common mistake to confuse sales and income multipliers. Sales multipliers are also called output or transaction multipliers. Whatever they are called, *sales multipliers alone are virtually useless as tourism planning tools* unless they are translated into income and employment effects.

Sales multipliers tend to be quite large (in the range of 1.5 to 3.0 for counties in the United States) compared with income multipliers (in the range of 0.20 to 0.80). For this reason, they tend to be attractive political tools used to justify additional tourism development. However, high sales multipliers give false impressions of the true impacts of tourist spending. This is because sectors showing the greatest increases in tourist sales are not necessarily those where the highest income and employment effects are generated. It is misleading and valueless to multiply total tourist sales by a sales multiplier and refer to the product as an economic impact of tourism (TEI). Idea 5 and Tourism Economics: Discussion Topic #2 provide examples of the incorrect application of a sales multiplier and the resulting errors.

Another common mistake is to use a **ratio multiplier** for *K* in determining total economic impact. A ratio multiplier for tourism is the sum of direct plus indirect plus induced effects divided by direct effects:

$$M = \frac{\text{direct} + \text{indirect} + \text{induced}}{\text{direct}}$$

Ratio multipliers therefore divide sales by sales, income by income, or employment by employment. The units in the numerator and denominator are the same. In contrast, the Keynesian-type multiplier shows income divided by sales. It is essential to understand the difference because available input-output analysis computer software produces both Keynesian-type and ratio multipliers.

Ratio multipliers *can* be used as indicators of a region's economic self-sufficiency. Assume that community A has a ratio sales multiplier for tourism of 2.5, while the same multiplier for community B is 1.5. This means that one tourist dollar spent in community A generates an additional 2.5 dollars in *sales* in various rounds of spending. The same dollar would generate an additional 1.5 dollars in sales in community B. In terms of tourism, community A is more self-sufficient than community B. However, this conclusion does not tell how much of tourist revenues escape from each economic sector during each round of spending. Furthermore, it is mathematically and theoretically incorrect to multiply tourist sales by a ratio multiplier as a measure of total economic impact.[6]

Input-Output Models. Input-output models provide the second means of calculating Keynesian-type multipliers. Such models are powerful economic tools and their use is proliferating with the availability of high speed, high storage personal computers. They not only automate the calculation of multipliers; they also show how industries, households, and governments interact with one another and the rest of the world. Thus, unlike hand-calculated multipliers, input-output models derive employment and income multipliers for specific sectors of the economy instead of just the aggregate effects on the whole destination region. This

Tourism Economics: Discussion Topic #2

Suppose that a county in Wisconsin holds the Wisconsin Cheese Making Festival each year. The costs of holding this festival include additional police and fire protection, water and sewage costs, traffic congestion, and local business losses (local retailers complain that they lose much money during the week-long festival because it is difficult to find parking near their businesses and their usual customers spend their money elsewhere). Because these costs increase each year, the county has hired three economists to determine the benefits of the festival.

During the festival, trained interviewers query a random sample of festival-goers each day. From these interviews, the three economists learn that 49% of the festival participants are county residents. They also learn that county residents spent $300,000 during the week, whereas out-of-county visitors spent $700,000 (total spending of $1,000,000). Using the same input-output model, the three economists make the following estimates:

$$\text{direct income per dollar spent by festival-goers} = \$0.40$$

$$\text{indirect + induced income per dollar spent} = \$0.20$$

The Keynesian income multiplier $(\Delta Y/\Delta J)$ is 0.60 per dollar spent (0.40 + 0.20/1.0). In addition, the three economists know that the sales multiplier for the entire state is 2.0. In computing the benefits, the three economists derived the following results:

Economist 1: TEI = $700,000 × 0.60   = $ 420,000;

Economist 2: TEI = $700,000 × 2.0   = $1,400,000;

Economist 3: TEI = $1,000,000 × 2.0 = $2,000,000.

Clearly, there are big difference between the estimates of these economists. Who's right?

Economist 3 has erred by including all spending. The $1,000,000 figure includes both resident and non-resident spending, yet, in economic impact analysis, the focus is on the injection of new dollars into a region. Resident spending does not add new dollars to the county and thus should not be counted.

If $700,000 is the correct spending figure, what is the correct multiplier? Unless two regions are nearly the same in size, population, and economic structure, it is incorrect to apply a multiplier developed for one region to the other region. For example, a state's tourism multiplier should not be used in one of its counties. In addition, 2.0 is a sales multiplier and does not show the effects of $700,000 in tourist spending on employment and income. Thus, the estimate of the second economist can be eliminated. Does this mean Economist 1 is correct?

When measuring *impacts*, Economist 1 made the correct interpretation. The $700,000 in non-resident spending resulted in $420,000 in additional income to the households of the host county.

However, none of the economists did what they were hired to do: measure *benefits*. To provide a benefit/cost analysis, the economist would have to examine the costs of those added services like extra police and fire protection, plus the costs of developing the festival (promotion, labor), plus the opportunity costs of the next best alternative. The economist would also examine the benefits which, in this case, include total festival spending ($1,000,000) by residents and non-residents.

is because input-output models group various types of businesses into industrial sectors and arrange them in a matrix. This matrix shows the total value of all sales made by each sector to each other in an economy. It also shows the purchases made by each sector from each other sector.

For example, the input-output matrix would group all gasoline stations into one sector called "gasoline and oil." It would then show how much the gasoline and oil sector sells to all other sectors, such as households, as well as how much this sector buys from other sectors, like wholesale distributors, utilities, and households in the form of labor. Using matrix algebra, the model then takes tourist spending for gasoline plus all other tourist spending and shows how this spending affects what the gasoline and other sectors buy from and sell to each other. Thus, an input-output model calculates the direct, indirect, and induced effects of tourist spending. Think of it as an elaborate accounting system that keeps track of the transactions and flows of new money throughout an economy.

The power of an input-output model is in its ability to show employment and income effects on a sector-by-sector basis. In this way, a picture of who gains and who loses by tourism spending can be painted. Knowledge of such demand/supply interactions permits the government to make enlightened decisions about whether to encourage more tourism investment, and, if so, the specific types of sectors and businesses to entice.

Input-output models show the flow of tourist spending throughout a given economy for a fixed period, usually one year. One criticism of input-output models is that they are used long after they have become outdated. Because new models are so difficult, costly, and time-consuming to develop, old models are sometimes used and reused. However, if there have been major changes in an economy since the year for which the model was developed, the model must be updated. If there were only minor changes, the original model may produce estimates that are within a reasonable range of accuracy.

Endnotes

1. I owe the organizational structure of this part of this chapter and the 11 "ideas" to William J. Baumol and Alan S. Blinder, *Economics: Principles and Policies,* 3d ed. (San Diego: Harcourt Brace Jovanovich, 1985).

2. For a discussion of this topic, see A. Mathieson and G. Wall, *Tourism: Economic, Physical and Social Impacts* (Harlow: Longman, 1982).

3. For a discussion of what is the most efficient mix of employment in agriculture, manufacturing, and tourism—the mix where waste is minimized—see "Tourism USA: Guidelines for Tourism Development," available from the U.S. Department of Commerce's Economic Development Administration. It presents an excellent illustration of how such a question may be answered using benefit/cost analysis, as well as many other useful examples of the issues and tools discussed in this chapter.

4. For a discussion of at least 14 different types of multipliers and their mathematical formulae and interpretations, see Harry W. Richardson, "Input-Output and Economic Base Multipliers: Looking Backward and Forward," *Journal of Regional Science* 25, no. 4 (1985): pp. 607–661.

5. This formula for the income multiplier is algebraically equivalent to $K = \Delta Y / \Delta J$.

6. For more information, see Brian H. Archer, "Economic Impact: Misleading Multiplier," *Annals of Tourism Research*, (1984): pp. 517–518.

Key Terms

comparative advantage
demand curve
direct impact
economic benefit/cost
economic benefit/cost analysis
economic impact
economic impact analysis
economic models
efficiency
equilibrium price and quantity
externalities
income multiplier
indirect impact
induced impact
injection

input-output models
leakage
linkage
macroeconomics
marginal cost
microeconomics
multiplier
opportunity cost
price ceiling
price support
public goods
ratio multiplier
sales multiplier
supply curve

Discussion Questions

1. How do free market forces work to allocate scarce resources efficiently?

2. How does specialization according to comparative advantage increase output? Why should a self-sufficient economy engage in trade?

3. Why are externalities beyond the control of the market system?

4. In general, what are the opportunity costs that must be weighed when a region is deciding whether to invest more money in tourism development?

5. How is economic theory useful? What does theory allow us to do that mere description does not?

6. What is the difference between a change in demand and a change in quantity demanded? between a change in supply and a change in quantity supplied? What factors might cause a change in supply or demand for luxury resorts?

7. What are price ceilings and supports? What types of consequences tend to occur when governments interfere with the free market system?

8. How are economic benefits and costs different from economic impacts?

9. Why must the boundaries of an economic region be carefully determined before the impact of tourist spending on that region can be calculated?

10. How are multipliers sometimes used improperly for political purposes? What happens when a sales multiplier is used to estimate total economic impacts?

REVIEW QUIZ

When you feel you have covered all of the material in this chapter, answer these questions. Choose the *best* answer. Check your answers with the correct ones found on the Review Quiz Answer Key at the end of this book.

True (T) or False (F)

T   F   1. As more tourism resources become available—for example, as the number of cruise ships grows—the prices tend to increase.

T   F   2. Opportunity cost means the value of the next best alternative you would have to give up for something else.

T   F   3. A theory is a deliberate abstraction which attempts to explain how observed relationships work.

T   F   4. In tourism, the facts and information needed to build good economic theories and models are plentiful.

T   F   5. A change in demand occurs when factors of production change.

T   F   6. In equilibrium, there is a tendency for price and quantity to change.

T   F   7. When the government guarantees suppliers a price above equilibrium, it is called a price support.

T   F   8. Benefit/cost analysis is used to measure the fluidity of business decisions or government projects.

T   F   9. Economic injections are defined as money spent in a region by non-residents.

T   F   10. Sales multipliers alone are virtually useless as tourism planning tools unless they are translated into income and employment effects.

Alternate/Multiple Choice

11.   The interaction between supply and demand:

   a. hinders the free market system.
   b. keeps the free market system going.

12.   Negative externalities may include:

   a. unwanted changes in the character and appearance of communities.
   b. economic growth.
   c. social interaction.
   d. preservation of natural attractions.

13.   Lowering taxes places proportionately _____ in the hands of the upper classes.

   a. more money.
   b. less money.

14.   A simplified, small-scale version of some aspect of the economy is called a:

   a. linking.
   b. theory.
   c. hypothesis.
   d. model.

15.   Price supports create:

   a. surpluses.
   b. shortages.

Chapter Outline

Environment: Definitions
Environment and Tourism Behavior
    Behavioral Settings
    Authenticity
Environmental Perception
    Cognitive Maps
The Geography of Tourism
Environment as an Attraction
    Ecotourism
    Urban Natural Attractions
The Tourism-Environment Connection
    Environmental Impacts
    Environmental Quality and Tourism
The "Greening" of Tourism
    Alternative Tourism
A Tourism Ethic

Learning Objectives

1. Define environment, behavioral setting, and program.

2. Describe the role of environment in various forms of authenticity.

3. State what is meant by the concept of environmental perception.

4. Describe cognitive maps and their uses.

5. Point out the significance of landmarks and images.

6. Explain the increasing importance of geography to tourism.

7. Contrast three forms of ecotourism.

8. Recognize the relationship between tourism and the quality of the environment.

9. Examine the implications of the Green Movement.

10. Compare alternative and mass tourism.

11. Recognize the importance of a tourism ethic.

Environmental Dimensions

7

Everyday activities take place in all types of settings: the home, the workplace, the grocery store, or a city street. Vacations, too, unfold in many environments: parks, resorts, hotels, pools, beaches, mountain trails, restaurants, and family cabins. As varied as they are, environments share one attribute: they are critical to the success of tourism. It is simplistic but true that the environment surrounds us. Yet, by taking this fact for granted, the influence of the environment is sometimes ignored or overlooked.

A destination implies an environment. With respect to tourism, one assumes that the tourist prefers a particular type of environment. Tourists think of the environment in terms of the feature that caught their eye as they searched travel agency brochures for a vacation spot. The beach, the ocean, and the sunset were among the initial environmental images that attracted the tourist's attention. Tourists seek out a specific environment for the activities it supports—such as mountain climbing or hiking—or as a backdrop to other activities—such as golfing or tanning by the seaside. The tourist could perform many of these activities elsewhere, but golfing at the local club or tanning in the backyard is just not the same as doing these things in an exotic location.

Whether as a backdrop or as a main attraction, the environment is important to the success of a tourism destination. Ironically, the popularity of a setting can be its undoing. The abuse of the environment can destroy the very elements that brought the tourist to the destination in the first place. The tourism industry has a vested interest in maintaining and preserving the environment—if not for altruistic reasons, then certainly for the well-being of the tourism industry and the success of individual tourism businesses.

Environment: Definitions

A common view of the environment is that it includes everything beyond one's body, such as the air, the water, the land, and buildings. This broad view is not particularly helpful in reviewing the varied aspects of tourism.

Different types of tourist experiences are related to very different types of environments. For example, the natural resources of a national park provide a tourism environment considerably different than that of a resort. Instead of "roughing it" in a tent and hiking to rocky beaches, resort tourists might find themselves strolling from an amenity-laden room to the poolside.

For the purposes of this chapter, the term **environment** refers to both the social and physical characteristics surrounding an individual. The physical characteristics of a resort might be the pools and ocean beaches; staff, patrons, and other

157

tourists provide the social characteristics. The importance of each characteristic may vary within different types of environments. For example, a remote wilderness area will have fewer social characteristics than a ski resort. Together, these characteristics give environments an ambience—or an atmosphere—that people sense through **social** and **environmental perception.** Tourists, staff, and visitors contribute to that ambience by their very presence. Ambience is a dynamic condition affected by the people moving in and out of an environment.

Environments can be large or small, immediate or distant, private or public, natural or urban. The Midwest is a large-scale environment, as is New York City. The rain forest in South America is a large, natural ecological environment, as are the great deserts of Africa and the United States. At the other end of the continuum, a person's bedroom is an environment that is smaller, more personal, and observable.

Environment and Tourism Behavior

People adjust, adapt, and respond to the environment. Knowing about an environment can provide a good deal of information about the people who interact with it. Take the hotel pool setting on a sunny, warm day—you could predict a number of behaviors and interactions with some certainty. You could predict, for instance, that people will be sitting by the poolside in swim wear, lathered in suntan or sunscreen lotion, and sipping refreshments. You could stretch your predictions further and say that these people will occasionally get up from their lawn chairs and take a swim in the pool. Knowing the environment that people are in gives you—the observer—a lot of predictive power. You could also predict with some certainty that these same poolside behaviors will *not* occur in church services on Sunday!

Behavioral Settings

While international airlines fly across the world and bring people to different types of vacation and business environments, most of the social, cultural, and business aspects of tourism occur within small or limited settings. The *immediate environment* can be referred to as the **behavioral setting**—or simply the **setting**.[1] This means that a setting is a smaller subset of the environment that regularly surrounds the person—usually a familiar situation. The physical and social characteristics of the setting generally provide continual feedback. In addition, a behavioral setting implies people; it needs to be occupied. Although a mountain range is an ecological environment, it is *not* a behavioral setting until tourists or others use it for some activity or purpose.

Settings have **programs.** This means that settings are designed for orderly, planned behaviors. The hotel lobby is an example. The physical design of the setting fosters the program: guest registration, certain guest services, and guest checkout. In turn, this program is supported and acted out by the people within the setting. The objects in the setting—such as a computer reservation system or an information desk—help execute the program. When the physical, social, and action components of a setting work well together, the setting is said to have a "good fit."

A city street becomes a behavioral setting—rather than an environment of concrete, steel, and glass—only when people are present. (Photo by Ann M. Halm)

Settings have several characteristics.[2] First, settings require a minimum number of people to carry out the program. Hotel lobbies need people, staff, and guests. Second, settings have time and place boundaries. For example, a hotel lobby may be open 24 hours a day and may be bounded by a hallway, elevator, or city street. Third, settings are active. They require or demand action from the people entering the setting and from people carrying out the program. Four, settings are self-regulating— they draw essential people and objects to them and reject or eliminate disruptive activities, people, or elements. For instance, people looking for a place to eat are directed from the lobby to the dining room where the program is designed for food service. Finally, the setting is modified by the people or objects within it. If, for instance, the lobby is extremely busy, extra personnel may be called in to help.

For a setting to have a "good fit," the tourist must know how to get there and how to behave once he/she arrives. Tourists who have a hard time assessing the setting may behave poorly or misuse the setting. The programs of some settings may not work because people do not understand them. For example, the introduction of computer technology to a property using an "old-fashioned" reservations system or an amusement park using "primitive" ticket counters may cause temporary upheavals; newly trained personnel may experience difficulties with the systems and unintentionally disrupt the programs as they try to adjust to new procedures. Another common instance of misunderstanding involves foreign guests who enter a setting but are unable to read or interpret its visual signs, or the intentions and behaviors of other people. In such situations, guests can become frustrated in their attempts to be active participants in the setting.

Authenticity

Another interesting dimension of settings is **authenticity**. Authenticity means *really* seeing and experiencing what a place, its people, and attractions are like. This desire to see the real, to live as the natives do, and to get behind the scenes is a significant factor in modern tourism.[3] Authenticity also encompasses the desire of tourists to not only see and experience, but buy the authentic artifacts of a culture. Advertisements often target tourists' desire for authenticity by suggesting that they will be able to experience a community's customs and environment much as the locals do.

Authenticity may mean historical artifacts that fascinate the tourist—such as the Liberty Bell; or, authenticity can refer to artifacts of other cultures which travelers may seek out, explore, and purchase. For example, travelers to America's Southwest can both see and purchase the handicrafts and art of that region's Native Americans. Some of this art is very old, as well as authentic. Some of it, however, is very recently produced and is just as beautiful and authentic in its own right. The list goes on, from art of the locals in Southern Portugal to the handiwork of the Amish in Mid-America. Modern artifacts and cultural activities that try to replicate historic or older artifacts may in time become authentic. This is referred to as **emerging authenticity**.[4] Given time, local crafts may actually become authentic artifacts of the community.

The environment plays a distinct role in authenticity. Often, the *real* can only be observed by going to the destination itself. The real "feel and flavor" of a European city can only be truly experienced by visiting or living there. The authenticity of famous cities, hotels, and natural attractions like the Grand Canyon can only be fully appreciated by an actual visit. Some authentic artifacts, novelty items, or certain works of art can only be seen or purchased within the context and location of their origin. There is also added psychological and social significance if a person can say, "I purchased this vase while visiting China. The evening markets are great places to shop, and I saw this unique vase on display the last evening we were there."

A recent and famous display of culture, social traits, and regional artifacts was the Van Gogh art collection in Amsterdam in 1990. That the artist's works were collected and presented in his home country lent the art show special significance. In this way, the environment enhanced a grand display of art. People from around the globe came to see the exhibition in the summer of 1990.

With **staged authenticity**,[5] the environment is used to enhance or support the authentic or to give the appearance of authenticity. Settings, although they may be imitations or re-enactments, are arranged to suggest the real thing. Such settings

Tourists can step back into the "Old West" by observing the re-creation of a frontier village at such museums as the Old Cowtown in Wichita, Kansas. (Courtesy of the Wichita Convention and Visitors Bureau, Wichita, Kansas)

are fine, provided that the tourist is aware of the situation. For historical events, there is no choice but re-enactment and, typically, the "way" the event is interpreted and re-enacted is often controversial. For the most part, the environment must support the display or interpretation of the event. Take, for example, a historical festival. The location, props, the clothing, and the actions of the participants may be orchestrated to develop a feel of authenticity. Some tourists may see it for what it is—a show or reproduction—and be disappointed. Others may appreciate the opportunity to view an event that provides a glimpse of the past.

A hotel develops a mood or atmosphere for a restaurant or lounge by designing the environmental characteristics of light, sound, color, and fabric to achieve the desired effect. The same requirements apply to the staging of an authentic display for tourists. For instance, displaying the Crown Jewels of Great Britain under heavy guard in the historic London Tower leaves little doubt in the tourist's mind that the jewels are genuine. For another example, picture a Hawaiian luau. This traditional feast features native food and entertainment, both of which will be enhanced by the authenticity of the physical surroundings.

Tourists vary in terms of their desire to experience the authentic.[6] For some, a re-creation is fine; others will go out of their way to experience a genuine event, meal, or festival. This concern for the authentic is also becoming a significant marketing and advertising theme. As the number of tourists seeking unique and authentic experiences continues to increase, so too will the promotions that address this market segment. Destinations will claim to provide such experiences, either by staging or by presenting actual opportunities. Some communities will stretch their physical and social limits to maintain, display, and preserve their authenticity. Adventure tours now make it possible for the tourist to "become a local" in many different environments, allowing vital interaction with people from remote parts of the world.

Environmental Perception

The perception of the environment stands apart from other types of perception. In environmental perception, the task for the observer involves perceiving a large, complex, multi-dimensional target. Perceiving an environment draws on all the senses, unlike perceiving a painting, for example, wherein vision is the primary sense being used.

To perceive something large-scale, such as a tourist environment, perception must be comprehensive. You must be able to perceive what is in back, front, above, and below; in other words, what surrounds you. Since the entire environment cannot be perceived simultaneously, memory is required. This is especially true for large tourism environments such as ski resorts or famous cities. Perceptions are built on a collection of images that become memories as the tourist moves through the large environment. Contrast this with viewing one painting in one particular museum.

Besides requiring more time and the use of more senses, environmental perception requires the observer to move around within the environment. Consider how the members of a family on tour will set out to explore a hotel, resort, or motel complex—even before their bags are unpacked. Perception of the environment requires this type of active exploration—both within and between different settings.

Perceptual processes are important to the marketing of tourism. People's perceptions of a destination will undoubtedly influence their inclination to visit it. Perceptions of distance, ease of access, difficulty of travel, and the level of comfort associated with the accommodations will make a difference in the decision-making process.

Cognitive Maps

Movement from one environment to another is an important part of tourism. Fortunately, the tourism industry makes modern travel easy through various modes of transportation—despite flight delays or traffic jams. In the United States, the predominant modes of transportation are automobiles and airlines. All tourists need some sense of geography to orient themselves within an environment or while en route. Without this sense, traveling can be very unnerving.

A sense of sights, sounds, and excitement are part of the cognitive map which helps guide an individual through the crowds of a beach or amusement area. (Courtesy of the Greater Fort Lauderdale Convention & Visitors Bureau, Fort Lauderdale, Florida)

One way all travelers—including tourists—orient themselves to the world is by using **cognitive maps**. A cognitive map is a mental representation of the world. Cognitive maps refer to a collection of information that one uses to orient one's self within an environment or setting. A cognitive map of an amusement park, for instance, would contain much more than a physical representation of pathways and rides. Such a cognitive map might include the screams of joy and excitement of roller coaster riders; emotions and feelings are an important part of a cognitive map. Such a cognitive map might also feature the feel of the crowd at a particular ride, the smell of popcorn, the taste of cotton candy, or the sound of a barker's spiel.

Knowing tourists' cognitive maps can shed light on how they perceive a destination. For example, in a study of tourists visiting Michigan, certain parts of the state were perceived as better for tourism and recreation than others.[7] Travelers were given a road map and asked to circle those areas of the state that they thought were good for tourism and recreation. The areas they circled were based more on the perceptions of the traveler than on those of government officials or tourism professionals.

The cognitive maps of tourists frequently do not coincide with the physical or social boundaries charted by tourism and community officials. When making their marketing plans, tourism officials should recognize that tourists do not always adhere to city boundary lines. Rather, they tend to enjoy the beach and the scenic sights as they occur, with little notice that Monday's picnic occurred at one city beach and that Tuesday's swimming occurred at yet another beach. Since tourists do not typically differentiate between various adjoining communities, tourism officials might consider cooperative efforts which market such communities as a single destination.

Landmarks. One of the important features of cognitive maps are **landmarks**: distinguishing features that provide a reference point. Landmarks provide information about direction and distance. A tourist's directions will often include landmarks: "Go three blocks west until you reach the large, old *church* on your left."

Research suggests that landmarks are perceived as bolder and larger than they really are.[8] Landmarks are remembered easily, and are recalled as very distinctive. In addition, when asked about landmarks within a certain environment, people tend to recall landmarks as visually in sight of each other. In reality, sometimes they are not. As the name implies, landmarks are remembered as guides along the way, but may actually be farther apart than people remember.

Images. Images sometimes result from cognitive maps. The concept refers to the perceptions a person has of some thing, place, or event that is not directly before the observer. Think of your car in the garage, or your parked bicycle. Even though the bike or car is not in front of you, you can see it in your mind. In other words, you are experiencing an image. An image is a very real mental process and product—just like a cognitive map.

To address the environmental perception processes, tourism advertising tries to create the best environmental images possible for the destination. Brochures show beautiful pictures of the beach from a hotel window; television ads show people having fun under a pristine waterfall; and radio ads feature the laughter of a family running along the beach. Environmental imagery is a powerful force within the industry. Tourists make decisions based on images; they have to live with the results of those decisions—be they good or bad.

Images of a destination may be developed in two ways. *Organic images* are developed by experience and exposure to a particular site through pictures, words from friends, television shows, and through the strongest experience of all—an actual visit. *Induced images* are generated by planned promotions and advertisements. Advertisements create an induced image in the hopes of attracting tourists to the site.[9]

Studies of tourism destination images have revealed that people have specific images of a destination, often based on very little information. A good share of what is exciting about tourism is visiting new places, believing that they will be beautiful, exciting, different, and engaging. In our electronic age, the scope and accuracy of induced images is extensive and varied. Nature shows, travel shows, and coffee table picture books all provide explicit images of environments, people, and activities. In fact, a curious traveler can dash out to the local video store and rent a video focusing on island-hopping in Hawaii, fishing in Alaska, cruising in Scandinavia, and scuba diving in the Caribbean. One can almost feel the ocean mist or experience the charm of an old inn. This modern version of an induced environmental image is powerful, immediate, far-reaching, and of high visual and audio quality.

Imagery sets up expectations. The destination that does not meet such expectations will decline. Satisfaction is based on the destination meeting or surpassing the tourist's expectations; to do less is to dramatically shorten that destination's business life cycle.

The power of environmental images is illustrated by international market studies of tourists from France, Japan, West Germany, and the United Kingdom conducted in 1989 by the United States and Canada. In these studies, tourists reported outstanding scenery—along with beautiful national parks and forests—as strong and positive environmental images associated with both the United States and Canada.[10] Tourism businesses can productively use such information when designing marketing efforts aimed at these international markets.

The Geography of Tourism

Geographical elements of tourism include the movement of people, the location of tourism destinations, and the routing of vacations. The skilled tourist knows where famous attractions are located. The tourist uses geography daily to follow road maps and to find attractions. The tourism executive also needs a keen sense of geography to fully appreciate the vastness of the tourism industry stretching around the globe.

Gilbert Grosvenor, President and Chair of the National Geographic Society, illustrates the importance of geography to tourism. He collects stories from travel agents about the confusion that people may have over where places are. Among his cast of characters is the couple who wanted to take a cruise to Las Vegas, and the man who wanted to go to Illinois—to visit Cleveland.[11]

Although humorous, these examples typify people's ignorance of geography. Grosvenor goes on to note that among Americans, about 14% cannot find the United States on a world map; 25% cannot find the Pacific Ocean, and about 20% cannot identify a single country in Europe.[12] Such lack of knowledge can be problematic in today's world. As Grosvenor comments:

> The United States cannot afford geographic ignorance in the age of global travel, intercontinental ballistic missiles, satellite TV, terrorism, Third World debt, and computerized money transfers. *Not* in the age of ozone holes, and greenhouse effects and nuclear accidents, such as that in Chernobyl.

> The U.S. is part of a global village—we must know that village. We do not understand the world at a time when there are pressing economic, environmental, and political reasons that should compel us to understand the world.[13]

Geographical knowledge is not what it should be in the United States—and that costs the tourism industry. If people do not know where a place is, it is difficult for them to include it among their range of potential destinations. In 1989, the oil spill in Alaska resulted in loss to the state of tourist dollars. Many people canceled vacations to Alaska because they thought the oil spill would affect the part of the state they were going to visit—even though that vacation site might be more than 700 miles away from the spill.[14]

The geography of tourism also includes the flows and patterns of tourists from one country to another. The routes and linkages between various countries illustrate the important relationship between geography and tourism.

The strange and unusual beauty of the South Dakota Badlands can be easily viewed from a car window—making them part of a scenic drive to beat all scenic drives. (Courtesy of South Dakota Tourism)

Environment as an Attraction

As stated earlier, the environment is, itself, an important tourist attraction. For centuries, people have sought out unique scenery. Sight-seeing has been an enjoyable pastime decade after decade. For many years, it was the number-one recreational pursuit among American families. The Sunday afternoon drive, the summer camping trip, or the trip to the local park have long been customary for millions of Americans.

In the mid-1800s, American tourists considered the first national parks in the United States as "homes" of abnormal, peculiar sights, to be visited because they were weird, grotesque, and unusual. Only in time did the stagecoach and rail traveler of the late-1800s come to appreciate the peaks, valleys, and other natural wonders of national parks.

At first, the lands comprising some of our oldest national parks were considered by many to be of little economic value. These lands were distant from cities, and their timber and water were plentiful elsewhere. However, early nature writers and explorers informed the American public that these lands were exquisite and worth saving for future generations. By 1872, land for the first national park, Yellowstone, was set aside. It was not until 1916 that a permanent U.S. government agency—the U.S. National Park Service—was established to care for and manage park lands.

Ecotourism

The natural environment has always been an attraction, but the reasons for seeking it out have changed. Throughout the nineteenth century, many writers and artists influenced by the Romanticists viewed nature as the handiwork of God. Trips to awe-inspiring natural environments were considered worthy adventures that could bring a person closer to God. Over time, more secular joys inspired people to see and to be in nature.

Around the world, parks, nature reserves, and natural settings are becoming increasingly popular tourist destinations. The U.S. National Park System of the United States attracted 9 million foreign visitors in 1989—or more than 20% of the total foreign visitors to the country.[15] This type of environmentally oriented tourism—in which tourists from around the globe seek out natural wonders—is called **ecotourism**.

Since World War II, the number of national parks worldwide has grown dramatically. Estimates are that about 1,164 national parks are spread across the continents. An additional 3,297 nature preservation areas also attract international visitors and scientists.[16]

In the United States, the National Park System includes 80 million acres and 355 areas; 50 of these areas are national parks. The U.S. National Park System is considered one of the best in the world. The Grand Canyon National Park hosted more than 3.9 million visitors in 1989, while total visits to the National Park System numbered nearly 300 million.[17]

Parks and preserves offer the camera-carrying tourist or scientist the chance to view wildlife and grand vistas. These areas also present unique settings for river rafting, kayaking, camping, and mountain climbing; and opportunities for biological study and observation.

Adventure tourism constitutes a growing portion of nature-based tourism. Adventure tourism frequently tests the tourist's skills and places him/her in an unusual, remote, and exciting environment or culture—one very different from what the tourist is used to. There are three categories of adventure tourism.[18] The first is *high-risk adventure tourism*. Here, the tourist might test his/her skills in mountain climbing, river rafting, or some other type of high-risk activity demanding top physical conditioning. This type of adventure tourism relies extensively on the environment.

The second type is sometimes called *soft adventure tourism*—tourists are not challenged as extensively; the demands of the environment are less than those made in the high-risk category. Tourists are less likely to be camping out; most will stay at modest accommodations. Here again, the natural environment plays a central role in shaping the character of travel and provides the resource for the activity.

When tourists seek out unique cultures to visit they are participating in the third category: *cultural adventure tourism*. These types of tourists are keenly interested in the accommodations and customs of the local residents; the natural environment plays a lesser role. Risks and challenges are more likely to be related to cultural and language differences. The tourist appreciates these differences because the social environment provides the primary source of interest.

Another subgroup of ecotourism is **science tourism**, in which scientists and students travel to national parks and preserves for scientific purposes.[19] A recent trend in the travel industry is the working vacation—tourists pay not only to accompany scientific expeditions, but to work on them. Archaeological "digs" are the most frequently requested type of science tourism.

High-risk adventure tourism demands that tourists be in peak physical condition to undertake such strenuous activities as white-water rafting. (Courtesy of Four Corners Expeditions, Buena Vista, Colorado)

Urban Natural Attractions

Even within cities, natural or landscaped places are among nature-oriented tourism attractions. Frequently appearing on tourist itineraries are the famous gardens of Europe, Asia, and U.S. cities. Gardens developed for royalty attract millions, as do the unique parks and estates of the rich. Locations of note include the palace and gardens at Versailles, the Summer Palace in Beijing, China, the estates of American presidents, and unique and magnificent urban parks like Central Park in New York City.

In the United States, the National Park Service maintains impressive attractions in or near urban areas. These facilities offer tourists the opportunity to be near nature without traveling long distances. Facilities such as the Golden Gate National Recreation Area in California attracted 16.7 million visitors in 1989.[20]

The Tourism-Environment Connection

Tourism is often the cause of **environmental degradation**; a particular destination suffers because too many tourists use it. Residents may feel that tourists do not really care about the environment; they may feel that tourists simply come to use it, abuse it, and then move on.

On the other hand, tourism does not have to be destructive. It can be argued that tourism is a positive environmental force since it fosters the preservation of wildlands and wildlife, or historic buildings and structures. Communities can

Exhibit 1   Selected Impacts of Tourism on the Environment

Positive	Negative
Historic preservation	Loss of historic sites
Biological preservation	Loss of habitat
Improved road systems	Littering, vandalism
Improved infrastructure	Degradation of parks and preserves
Creation or preservation of parks, nature preserves	Loss of parks and open space to tourism development
Development of public spaces	Wear and tear on infrastructure; extensive resource consumption
Improved level of development	Extensive development
Better use of marginal lands	Negative changes in land use
Improved waste management	Excessive waste generation
Generated concern for the environment	Water and air pollution

grow and prosper through tourism attractions such as nature areas or historic buildings. City centers, too, can become attractions when environmental features are saved for future generations to enjoy.

Environmental Impacts

Environmental impacts are usually measured by degree. To the extent that tourism generates revenue to develop better roads and sewer systems, it is positive. But to the extent that tourism causes roads to fall into disrepair, or strains the waste management system beyond capacity and threatens public health, tourism is negative. Just as increased tourism may result in increased litter and vandalism, it may also generate the kind of community pride and concern that can eliminate or reduce litter and vandalism. Exhibit 1 lists various positive and negative consequences tourism can have for the environment.

National parks and preserves attract tourists who spend money in the surrounding communities. Here, the effects of tourism are indirect. Animals do not heed park and preserve boundaries, nor do poachers. Originally, the lands for parks or preserves may have been "saved" for ecological purposes, and as a source of tourism revenue. In poor rural countries, however, parks and preserves deprive residents of desperately needed resources.[21] This creates a conflict between the tourists, managing agencies, and residents—a conflict which can be destructive and even life-threatening. Consider the case of managers patrolling preserved lands against poachers. In certain parks—particularly in Africa—rangers face dangerous, armed conflicts on a regular basis.

In most third world countries, tourism is not the primary cause of the environmental degradation. Rather, the ecological balance is strained by the activities of poachers and by the legitimate, survival needs of residents. Conservation of resources may have been the initial reason a park was established. Over time, however, tourist expenditures become important to the government and to the surrounding communities. A classic dilemma ensues between the residents who need the resources within the park to survive and the need of the government to preserve the resources of the park to continue to attract tourists. Throughout the world, conflicts continue to arise between government policy and the needs of various groups. Many of these conflicts have not been fully mediated or resolved.

The most significant positive effects related to tourism occur when local citizens are better able to care for their own community and environment. In urban areas around the world, much of the preservation of historical inner cities, waterfronts, and buildings lies in their value as tourist attractions. For example, most of the ancient dwellings in Beijing, China were systematically destroyed to make room for high-rise housing. Now, rehabilitation and conservation techniques are being used to preserve selected old city dwellings—in part, because of their tourism value. In the United States, Boston Harbor and Baltimore are examples where historical waterfronts have been preserved or rehabilitated. In such situations, tourism can be a positive force for change, conservation, and preservation.

Environmental Quality and Tourism

It is too simplistic to think only in terms of how tourism influences the environment; environmental quality also influences tourism. It is difficult to specify exactly what makes an environment a high quality one. Most people consider an environment is in "top notch" condition when the biological elements—such as plants and animals—are healthy and the water and air are clean and unpolluted. Clearly, there are two levels of analysis: the perceptual and the technical. Perceptually, an environment may look clean and healthy, but when measured technologically, this may not be the case at all. Certain lakes in Canada and in the northern United States may appear clear and blue, but may be biologically dead from acid rain. Tourism will be influenced by both types of environmental quality.

While tourism sometimes causes environmental problems, other industries can and do damage the environment—and tourism—in the process. The complex inter-relationship between tourism and the environment involves many who are not directly involved in tourism. Other major influences on the environment include industry, regulatory agencies, and the citizenry. The actions of these diverse groups can affect the quality and appearance of the environment and, in turn, influence the decisions of tourists. Tourists will stay away from a destination when it is contaminated or despoiled.

The pollution of East Coast beaches with medical waste had serious economic consequences for coastal communities and for tourism. Medical waste and other garbage drifted ashore in the summer of 1988. Beaches were closed up and down the New Jersey coast and parts of New York. For the rest of that summer, tourists stayed away from the coast. The next year, tourists were slow to return, even when the pollution was cleaned up and safely removed.

European tourism was hampered by the Chernobyl nuclear accident in the Soviet Union in 1986. In the spring, after the accident had spread radiation over parts of Northern Europe, tourists began to change their summer travel plans. By summer, tourism to Europe was reduced. As a final example, consider how tourism in Alaska dropped off after the 1989 oil spill. Here again, an episode of environmental degradation directly influenced travel plans. Tourists went elsewhere if they felt that oil was going to be polluting their destination.

The "Greening" of Tourism

Across North America and Europe, citizens are searching for other ways to conduct activities which affect the environment—including tourism. Polls reveal how strong environmental concerns are becoming in the United States. A recent headline read: "83% Fear for the Environment"; within this group, 67% reported being most concerned about hazardous waste, 57% about water pollution, and 51% about the wilderness.[22]

A poll conducted by the National Wildlife Federation also showed that the American public is very concerned about the future of the environment; 50% of those polled thought that the environment would be worse in five years, while only 11% thought that the environment would be better, and 39% that the condition of the environment would be about the same in five years.[23] What these polls demonstrate is that Americans are taking the environment seriously. They expect their political representatives and the business community—including tourism— to do the same.

The tourism industry should be concerned with the environment for two reasons: First, whether perceived or real, fears about the contamination of a particular environment will ultimately devalue that environment as a tourist attraction. Second, many environmental issues are linked to transportation. Any major shifts in transportation patterns due to unacceptable levels of toxic auto emissions, for instance, will have serious consequences for the tourism industry—especially for areas without access to convenient and efficient public transportation. Increasing levels of air pollution, as well as future energy shortages, will certainly force many industrialized countries to re-evaluate their transportation policies.

Environmental activists who promote less destructive methods in agriculture, community development, rural development, and tourism are often considered members of the **Green Movement**. **Greens** represent a distinct, political segment of the environmental movement; the Green Party is, in fact, an established political party in several European countries. Throughout the 1980s, Greens organized against acid rain, nuclear weapons, and wasteful agricultural practices, among other environmental concerns. Today, the Green Party is a rapidly growing force in European politics. In 1989, a growing number of Green Party members joined the European Parliament—an advisory parliament to the European Economic Community.[24] Like Americans, the Europeans consider the environment a top priority.

Environmental attitudes and activities are related to tourism in several direct ways. As noted earlier, tourists stay away from environments perceived to be degraded. But also, those concerned with environmental issues have noted the often negative environmental impacts of tourism construction and development. In Great Britain, residents protested the *Eurotunnel*—the subterranean rail system which connects Great Britain with the European continent via the English Channel. It transports freight and people faster than boats and cheaper than airplanes. For tourism, it means that travelers can move more quickly between the United

Kingdom and Europe. The Eurotunnel will have important implications for tourism as Europe unites politically as well as economically.

This is just one in thousands of events occurring each year in which the goals of tourism conflict with the well-being of the environment. Such tourism facilities as resorts, golf courses, and access roads into public forests, airports, and amusement parks often create conflict. As the tourism industry continues to grow, industry professionals must be sensitive to the noise and air pollution, loss of wildlife habitat, and simply the loss of open space caused by tourism development.

Alternative Tourism

Concerns about the serious negative consequences associated with tourism have encouraged the exploration of better ways to manage mass tourism and tourism development. Proponents of **alternative tourism** (sometimes called *responsible* or *green* tourism) argue that tourism should be conducted on a smaller scale in terms of the number of tourists and the dimensions of tourism development. Alternative tourism proposes more respect for the resources, the local people, and the environment. This respect should be evident in the design and nature of the attractions, and in the attitudes and behaviors of the residents and tourists.

The reconciliation of the environment and tourism begins with the local community. Tourists will have little reason to respect the environmental resources of a community if the community itself does not respect these valuable resources. Alternative tourism is proposed as a way to soften the impact of travel on social, cultural, and environmental resources. It provides a means to maintain a long-term flow of tourism without the downward spiral of degradation, community resentment, and eventual loss of business.

Exhibit 2 outlines the characteristics of mass and alternative (green) tourism. The perspectives are presented for each side of the issue, but the phrasing favors the views of alternative tourism. Note that the terms characterizing mass tourism imply negative effects. In mass tourism, the environment is overrun with tourists, and the community does not share in the economic benefits. On the other hand, green tourism is smaller scale; it is designed to have less of an impact on the environment and on the social fabric of the community. Or so it is claimed. While green tourism seems to make sense, the consequences of tourism for the environment and the community may still be less than positive.[25] Any change associated with tourism is hard to contain. The changes brought about by contact with tourists—in small numbers or large—is difficult to manage, much less prevent. It is not just the numbers of tourists, or the size of the development, that creates negative or positive impacts. The structure and pattern of tourism within the community must be monitored to assess the impacts of tourism. The point is that even on a small-scale, tourism has consequences—sometimes more than anticipated.

Exhibit 3 compares a few of the impacts associated with mass and alternative tourism.[26] The upper portion of the exhibit shows that different types of tourism bring different types of change to a community. For one, the number of tourists varies from large to small. Within a mass tourism framework, the number of tourists can grow to be quite large over the long term. Mass tourists are often contained within tourism enclaves; particular routes may be outlined for transport

Exhibit 2 Comparison of Mass and Green Tourism

MASS TOURISM	GREEN TOURISM
Large-scale	Small-scale
Uncontrolled	Controlled
Unplanned	Planned
Short-term	Long-term
Absent owners	Local owners
Price-conscious	Value-conscious
Growth-oriented	Managed, controlled development
Large groups of tourists	Moderate to small tourist groups
Rapid means of transport	Appropriate transport, may be slow
Imported lifestyles	Local lifestyles
Loud tourist image	Quiet tourist image
Poor labor education	Education for laborers
Scattered development	Concentrated planning and development
Developed by outsiders	Local developers
Build to peak capacity	More moderate development plans
Loss of the historic	Preserve the historic

Based on R. W. Butler, "Alternative Tourism: Pious Hope or Trojan Horse?" *Journal of Travel Research* 28, no. 3 (1990), p. 42.

Exhibit 3 Change and Implications Associated with Tourism

CHANGE

	Mass Tourism			Alternative Tourism	
	Duration				
	Short-Term	Long-Term		Short-Term	Long-Term
Tourist					
Numbers	Modest	Large		Few	Small
Location	Limited	Resorts		Community	Widespread
Resource					
Capacity	Problem	Problem		Minor	Problem

IMPLICATIONS

	Mass Tourism			Alternative Tourism		
	Social	Environmental	Economic	Social	Environmental	Economic
Tourist						
Numbers	negative	negative	positive	positive	positive	negative
Location	neutral	negative	positive	negative	negative	negative
Resource						
Capacity	negative	negative	negative	neutral	positive	neutral

Based on R. W. Butler, "Alternative Tourism: Pious Hope or Trojan Horse?" *Journal of Travel Research* 28, no. 3 (1990), p. 43 and author's analysis.

or tours. In the long run, mass tourism can exceed the capacity of the community and cause environmental degradation.

Even a continual stream of a small number of tourists to a wide range of areas can negatively affect the host region. Although alternative tourists may be fewer in number, they will travel beyond the enclaves of the mass tourist and come in direct contact with many local people. In this case, the social consequences could become negative, where they are only neutral for mass tourism—assuming, of course, that mass tourists remain isolated in tourism enclaves.

The lower portion of Exhibit 3 further spells out the implications of tourism in social, environmental, and economic areas. While the effects of mass tourism are primarily negative, some economic effects are positive. The classic dichotomy is between a large number of tourists degrading the environment and, at the same time, enriching the local economy through increased taxes and sales of products and services.

Alternative tourists will affect a region—particularly in the long run. The well-prepared tourist may not spend that much money, especially in the remote sections of the host region; the uncertainty of whether supplies are available may cause tourists to purchase items outside the area. If the number of tourists remains small, the capacity of the region is less likely to be exceeded by alternative tourism, although it can happen. Long-term financial benefits are likely to be minimal as well, which, in turn, can create tremendous pressure to expand facilities to bring in more tourists and tourism dollars.

Both types of tourism create an impact of some sort. Mass tourism is not likely to fade away. Many tourism communities cannot afford to phase out this form of tourism—nor do they want to. But like mass tourism, the consequences of alternative tourism must be examined carefully. Further discussion of alternative tourism reveals the following points.[27]

1. As the name implies, alternative tourism provides a complementary form of tourism. It represents a different type of activity with more opportunities for the tourist to meet the local people and see more of the destination.

2. Alternative tourism can remedy some of the problems caused by mass tourism, but cannot, in all probability, replace it. The result would be too costly and undesirable for tourists and destinations dependent on mass tourism.

3. Alternative tourism can satisfy particular types of tourists in particular types of settings. For example, alternative tourism works within rural communities which offer the tourist the opportunity to visit or stay at a farm as part of a farm vacation.

4. Alternative tourism can be an early step in the tourism development process. Tourism planning is required to keep a development small and the numbers of visitors at reasonable levels. The process is one-way. It may be possible to control the level of tourism activity and thereby prevent the development of mass tourism. But it is almost impossible to go the other direction and convert a mass tourism destination into a site for small-scale alternative tourism.

A Tourism Ethic

In the end, it is up to residents to plan for the type of tourism that best fits the community. Tourism rarely occurs by accident; people want it, foster it, or tolerate it.

Communities need to take control and shape the type of tourism that fits their lifestyle, their community, and does not destroy their surroundings.

Residents need to adopt and use a tourism ethic. This means that when planning for tourism, residents must consider the social, cultural, and environmental consequences of tourism. Just the fact that alternative tourism is being discussed within the industry acknowledges that mass tourism has contributed to the destruction of resources around the world and is becoming cause for concern. Change is required—and that change begins with the host community.

Tourists, too, must adopt a tourism ethic—they must consider the social, cultural, and environmental consequences of their actions. This requires knowledge and tourism education. Most tourists do not realize what it means when they litter "just a little bit." They also might not understand what it means to purchase banned products that may be contributing to the destruction of a species (ivory from elephant trunks) or a special environment (destroying coral in the ocean). Tourism education is necessary for the tourist and resident alike. Both need to become more sensitive to each other's needs and culture—and to the consequences of being insensitive and unaware.

Tourism professionals and educators have a stake in developing a tourism ethic. The long-term future of tourism is more secure to the extent that such an ethic conserves resources, smooths relations between hosts and guests, and assists with the management of tourism. Like environmental ethics, it will take a long time to develop a tourism ethic. The task—although large and time-consuming—should not be shunned. In the long run, tourism may not be able to absorb the costs of doing otherwise.

Endnotes

1. Allan W. Wicker, *An Introduction to Ecological Psychology* (Monterey, Calif.: Brooks/ Cole Publishing, 1979), pp. 8–12.

2. Wicker, pp. 8–12.

3. Dean MacCannell, *The Tourist* (New York: Schocken Books, 1976), pp. 96–97.

4. Erik Cohen, "Authenticity and Commoditization in Tourism," *Annals of Tourism Research* 15, no. 3 (1988): p. 379.

5. MacCannell, p. 98.

6. Cohen, p. 377.

7. Joseph D. Fridgen, "Use of Cognitive Maps to Determine Perceived Tourism Regions," *Leisure Sciences* 9 (1987): p. 110.

8. This discussion on landmarks is based on Stephen Kaplan and Rachel Kaplan, *Cognition and Environment* (New York: Praeger, 1982), p. 47.

9. Clare Gunn, *Vacationscape: Designing Tourist Regions*, 2d ed. (New York: Van Nostrand Reinhold, 1988), p. 24.

10. *Pleasure Travel Markets to North America: United Kingdom, France, West Germany, and Japan—Highlights Report* (Washington, D.C.: U.S. Travel and Tourism Administration, 1989), pp. 6, 20, 31, 41.

11. Gilbert M. Grosvenor, "Keynote Address," presented February 5, 1990 at the Fourth Annual Travel Review Conference, Washington, D.C., Proceedings—*1989: A Reflection*

of the Past, An Image of the Future (Salt Lake City, Utah: Travel and Tourism Research Association, 1990), p. 1.

12. Grosvenor, p. 1.

13. Grosvenor, p. 1.

14. Grosvenor, p. 1.

15. James M. Ridenour, "The Nation's Parks—Resource Issues for the 1990s," Keynote address presented March 29, 1990 at the *Outdoor Recreation Trends Symposium III*, Indianapolis, Indiana.

16. Jeffrey A. McNeely, "The Future of National Parks," *Environment* 32, no. 1 (January/February 1990): p. 37.

17. Ridenour, Director of the NPS, "Natural Resource Attractions," in the Fourth Annual Travel Review Conference Proceedings—*1989: A Reflection of the Past, An Image of the Future* (Salt Lake City, Utah: Travel and Tourism Research Association, 1990), p. 71.

18. Karen Ida Peterson, "What Was Hot in Adventure Travel—1988?" in the *Third Annual Travel Review Conference Proceedings: The 1988 Experience—A Basis for Planning* (Salt Lake City, Utah: Travel and Tourism Research Association, 1989), pp. 95–96.

19. Jan G. Laarman and Richard R. Purdue, "Science Tourism in Costa Rica," *Annals of Tourism Research* 16 (1989): p. 213.

20. Ridenour, p. 72.

21. McNeely, pp. 20, 36.

22. Denise Kalette, "Poll: 83% Fear for the Environment," *USA Today*, April 13–15, 1990, p. 1A.

23. Marcy Eckroth Mullins, "The Future of our Environment," in the "USA Snapshots" section of *USA Today*, March 31, 1988, p. 1A. Source of the data: National Wildlife Federation.

24. Tom Burke, "The Year of the Greens: Britain's Cultural Revolution," *Environment* 31, no. 9 (1989): pp. 20, 41.

25. R. W. Butler, "Alternative Tourism: Pious Hope or Trojan Horse?" *Journal of Travel Research* 28, no. 3 (1990).

26. Much of the analysis on mass versus alternative tourism is drawn from Butler.

27. "Alternative Tourism:," pp. 44–45.

Key Terms

adventure tourism	environmental perception
alternative tourism	geography
ambience	Green movement
authenticity	Greens
behavioral setting	image
cognitive map	landmarks
ecotourism	program
emerging authenticity	science tourism
environment	social perception
environmental degradation	staged authenticity

Discussion Questions

1. What is meant by the term environment? by behavioral setting? by program?

2. What role does the environment play in different types of authenticity?

3. What sets environmental perception apart from other forms of perception?

4. How would a typical traveler use a cognitive map?

5. What is the significance of landmarks and images?

6. Why is geography becoming increasingly important to tourism?

7. What is ecotourism? What are its various forms?

8. What connections can be drawn between tourism and the quality of the environment?

9. What is the Green Movement?

10. How does alternative tourism differ from mass tourism?

11. Why will a tourism ethic be important in the future?

REVIEW QUIZ

When you feel you have covered all of the material in this chapter, answer these questions. Choose the *best* answer. Check your answers with the correct ones found on the Review Quiz Answer Key at the end of this book.

True (T) or False (F)

T   F   1. Knowing the environment that tourists are in gives the researcher a lot of predictive power.

T   F   2. Environmental perception requires the use of memory.

T   F   3. A mental representation of the world is called a cognitive map.

T   F   4. Images that are developed by experience and exposure to a particular site through pictures, word from friends, television shows, or an actual visit are called induced images.

T   F   5. Cultural adventure tourism frequently involves testing a tourist's skills through such physically demanding activities as mountain climbing or river rafting.

T   F   6. Few, if any, environmental issues are linked to transportation.

T   F   7. Those concerned with environmental issues frequently ignore the negative environmental impacts of tourism construction and development.

T   F   8. Alternative tourism is sometimes called irresponsible tourism.

T   F   9. With mass tourism, the environment is overrun with tourists, but the community shares in the economic benefits.

T   F   10. With appropriate direction, a mass tourism destination can be converted into a site for small-scale alternative tourism.

Alternative/Multiple Choice

11.   The term "ambience" means:

   a. environmental perception.
   b. atmosphere.

12.   Which of the following is *not* a characteristic of setting?

   a. a requirement of people
   b. time and place boundaries
   c. static inactivity
   d. self regulating

13.   Distinguishing features that provide reference points for the tourist are called:

   a. cognitive maps.
   b. landmarks.

14. Environmentally oriented tourism—in which tourists from around the globe seek out natural wonders—is called:

    a. ecotourism.
    b. geographical knowledge.
    c. adventure tourism.
    d. cultural tourism.

15. Environmental activists who promote less destructive methods in agriculture, community development, rural development, and tourism are often considered members of:

    a. the Green Movement.
    b. Parliament.
    c. Congress.
    d. the Agrarian Party.

Part II

Chapter Outline

Basic Components of Travel Services
    The People
    The Government
    The Infrastructure and Superstructure
    The Businesses
Attractions and Resources
Accommodations
    Accommodation Volume and Use
Transportation
    Airlines
    Rail Service
    Cruise Lines
    Motor Coach Travel

Learning Objectives

1. Describe the basic role that governments play in tourism.

2. Distinguish between the tourism infrastructure and superstructure by naming basic elements of each.

3. Describe the general nature of business strategies and arrangements in the tourism marketplace.

4. Describe the range and nature of tourist attractions.

5. Identify general forms of accommodations available to international travelers.

6. Analyze how deregulation and liberalization have affected the airline industry in the United States and Europe.

7. Describe the nature of modern rail service.

8. Identify some common features of the modern cruise.

9. Point out several issues and trends that may influence the cruise industry.

10. Predict the future of motor coach travel.

8

Services for the Traveler

WHILE THE TOURIST is enjoying the trip, the sights, the fine food, and the lovely view from the hotel room, thousands of people are working in a broad range of industries that support tourism—both domestically and abroad. People ranging from airline pilots to taxi drivers to hotel staff to ticket-takers all contribute to the tourist's experiences.

Through contact with other people, the tourist comes to know about services in the tourism industry. The fact that so many people can provide so many services with such proficiency is partly due to the related businesses, services, and government policies which support tourism. This chapter will describe the montage of services related to both domestic and international tourism. Discussion will focus on the nature and provision of services, and their place within a larger economic, social, and cultural system.

Basic Components of Travel Services

Businesses that provide quality service in a warm and efficient manner are those most likely to be competitive and long-term. Ironically, the quality of service is not fully appreciated until something goes wrong. Until such time, supportive efforts are often overlooked or taken for granted. Unfortunately, negative reactions to poor service can have lingering effects on the customer and can translate into lost business. Tourism businesses around the world care about tourist needs and desires; most address these needs and desires through personal services.

The People

You cannot talk about service without talking about people. It takes thousands of people to move one tourist around the world—including those in direct contact with the traveler, such as flight attendants, and those behind the scenes, such as baggage handlers and aircraft mechanics. The flight attendant on the aircraft offers friendly assistance to the tourist, but so do the "invisible" service providers such as baggage handlers and aircraft mechanics. Even seemingly small things—like making sure that the magazines in a hotel lobby are current—involve people.

The first contact a tourist has with the tourism industry is most likely to be through a person: a representative of a tourism enterprise. In this first encounter, the way the service is provided does make a difference, since it sets the tone for the character and quality of the trip.

TRAVEL AGENT.

181

The Government

All governments have a role to play in tourism. Even in countries where tourism is nearly non-existent, governments may forbid the entry of visitors or the exit of residents. Fortunately, most governments have a positive attitude toward tourism, viewing it as a source of revenue and a boost to the national economy.

Governments which support tourism through policy or promotion provide a service to tourists and the tourism industry. Supportive services result from agreements between governments on matters of trade and exchange. In the realm of tourism, agreements can focus on travel documentation, passports, visas, and air travel opportunities.[1]

Governments provide services to tourists in other ways. Nations around the world offer tourism information services to international tourists through **national tourism offices (NTO)**. Information can include maps, tour books, hotel information, key phone numbers, and guidebooks to landmarks and tourist attractions within the home country. An NTO is usually located in a major city that appeals to incoming tourists, and whose population also enjoys traveling.

The Infrastructure and Superstructure

Hotels require roads and streets, while airports require runways. The downtown hotel also needs to be connected to the city water, sewer, and utility systems. Such supporting systems are called the **infrastructure**. The hotels, convention centers, and other such facilities are called the **superstructure**.

Generally, the infrastructure includes all forms of construction on and below ground which are required for human activity and communication. In contrast, the superstructure refers to forms of construction above ground such as hotels, shopping malls, restaurants, and tourism attractions.[2] A resort complex situated along a beach represents a tourism superstructure. This superstructure—a building and facility above ground—is supported by the infrastructure—the "invisible" water, sewage, and utility systems.

All such facilities and developments must be paid for. In the case of the infrastructure, the government covers most of the expense. National and local governments assist with the development of the road system, the water supply system, the sewer hookups, and utilities. Systems are planned, built, and developed to support further development—be it housing or a combination hotel and conference center. The services provided by the infrastructure will serve the local residents as well as guests. The infrastructure must always be in place before other facilities can be developed. A hotel with no roads to reach it would be a failure, while a restaurant without water would be a health hazard and a disaster. In general, modern tourism needs a developed infrastructure. But like every rule, there are exceptions. With tourism, the exception might be the remote, primitive setting that attracts explorer types willing and able to live as the natives do.

In many countries, the government is a key player in the development of the tourism superstructure. The government may be the sole owner of an attraction such as a national park, a historic park or building, or an entertainment facility. In other cases, the government may be a partner. In the United States, the government

A sports attraction such as the Indianapolis Hoosier Dome depends on a complex infrastructure of roads and utility systems to keep it running. (Courtesy of McGuire Studio, Inc., Indianapolis, Indiana)

may provide tax incentives to a private tourism business to develop a hotel or an attraction. In other countries, such as China, many of the hotels are joint ventures between the government and foreign private or national investors. Governments may also own and manage public lands as another tourism service. National parks are a good example. The tourist's access to natural resources is usually based upon an infrastructure of roads, water, and utility systems. Few superstructures are built within a national park. If any, they are often placed there by private businesses with a lease from the government.

The Businesses

Private businesses are other major contributors to tourism development and services. So many travel and tourism companies are involved in tourism nowadays that it is difficult to trace all the connections. Companies may own other companies. Businesses, too, may own portions of other companies or merely have an agreed upon working relationship with an allied firm. Sometimes, an international firm will own one type of business in one country and an entirely different type in another.

Diversification is a long-term, common, and often successful corporate strategy in the tourism marketplace. Nowhere was diversification more quickly displayed than in Eastern Europe in late 1989 and 1990. Europe's fast-changing political world presented many new opportunities for businesses from other parts of the globe. In early 1990, Lufthansa—an airline 51% owned by the West German government—expressed its intent to purchase a portion of Interflug—the state-owned airline of East Germany. Like diversification efforts undertaken by private airlines and hotels, the package assembled by these two state-dominated airlines included catering, a flight training center, and a computer system.[3]

Hotels can be owned by a diverse set of parent companies, including other hotels, banks, insurance companies, and brewers. Many airlines own hotels. In these situations, the movement of tourists can be complemented by accommodating the tourists at their final destination. Some airlines also own and manage computerized airline reservations systems, freight companies, catering services for their hotels and planes, and feeder airlines. Feeder airlines are smaller, regional airlines which meet commuter needs in less populated areas by connecting these regions with larger airline hubs or centers.

The international investment in tourism-related enterprises is a two-way street. American and European companies are the dominant players in the international hotel industry. Well-known U.S. hotels have foreign parent companies. For example, Hilton International has headquarters in the United States, but its parent company is in the United Kingdom. This is also the case for Travelodge and Holiday Inns International.

There are many such **multinational corporations** in the tourism industry. These large corporations hold many advantages over individual tourism businesses competing in the international arena. For one, corporations bring brand-name recognition to a product. Other advantages may include greater or easier access to funds, development and planning techniques and programs, accurate and timely information about international markets, and sophisticated and expensive technology (such as inter-linked reservations systems).[4]

Companies with facilities in several countries also have the advantage of knowing the local labor markets and cultural differences. They can also build standards of quality into their operations that are recognized across international boundaries. For example, international hotel chains can develop and offer a consistent look and line of services at every one of their properties—no matter where a facility is located.

Many broad-based multinational companies serve the international traveler. Exhibit 1 provides a selective list of the more prominent service and manufacturing businesses associated with tourism. A majority of these businesses have international linkages or partnerships. Many, too, are diversified in various tourism-related entities. It would be unrealistic to ignore the roles that "indirect industries" have played in domestic and international tourism. For example, consider the changes brought to tourism by automobile and airplane manufacturing. Domestic tourism boomed as automobiles became less expensive and available to more people. In a similar way, the advent of cheap international airfares made international travel affordable to more people.

Attractions and Resources

Attractions power the tourism industry. People travel to see and do things associated with attractions. Tourists are always searching for more interesting and

Exhibit 1   Tourism Businesses, Services, and Indirect Enterprises

Direct	Indirect
Hotels and motels	The construction industry Food service Cleaning services
Restaurants	Food production and transportation
Airlines	Aircraft manufacturing Computer reservations systems Food catering Airport terminals/centers
Car rentals	Auto manufacturing
Travel agencies	Computer systems Publishing companies Advertising companies
Cruise ship industry	Water ports Shipbuilding
Amusement parks	Equipment manufacturers Food service Advertising industry
National parks/reserves	Natural resource management systems
Urban and rural parks	Park management systems Food and entertainment companies
Tour operators	Motor coach manufacturing Advertising industry Air and rail transport companies Rail and mass transit stations
Auto tourism	Auto manufacturing Road construction Auto services
Tourism attractions	Community services Shopping malls Museums
Tourism promotion	State/National tourism offices General advertising businesses Media enterprises

Note: It is easy to think of tourism in terms of the obvious transportation or accommodation industries—such as airlines and hotels—while overlooking many of the indirect or allied businesses. In the table, the more apparent tourism industries are listed on the left, while the indirect are listed on the right. Many companies—such as hotel and airlines—also have international interests and involvements. They may own part of another similar company or an allied business in another country. An airline may own a smaller regional or feeder airline, hotels in several destination countries, and computer reservations system.

exciting places to visit. Activities associated with attractions are as varied as the tastes of the consumer. The range is immense: from gambling to sight-seeing, from relaxing on the beach to intense mountain climbing, from learning at a museum to

Exhibit 2   Tourism Attractions

Natural Resources	Commercial	Historical	Social/Cultural
National parks	Resorts	Monuments	Festival
State parks	Amusement parks	Historic homes	Crafts
Shorelines, lakes, and oceans	Casinos	Museums	Ethnic events
Mountains	Convention centers	Battlefields	Art museums
Unusual landscapes	Retail centers	Landmarks	Unique culture

art appreciation. Exhibit 2 provides a small list of attractions ranging from the natural to the urban or commercial facility.

Attractions are owned by private or public entities or a mixture of the two. For example, national parks in most countries are public lands. Local retail outlets which sell souvenirs are private, while the local museum may be owned and run by a non-profit historical society. Some attractions—such as national parks—are extremely natural-resource dependent. And some of the most beautiful resorts—typically privately owned—are natural-resource-dependent by virtue of being located in gorgeous natural settings.

Major tourism attractions within a country can lure both domestic and international travelers. The ruins of Rome are an important heritage for Italians, but are also a primary destination for travelers from around the world. The Great Wall of China, the Pyramids of Egypt, the Grand Canyon National Park in the United States, and Stonehenge in the United Kingdom all represent attractions on an international scale.

Attractions—commercial or natural—bring in tourists—domestic or foreign. Disney World and Disneyland are very popular the world over. The development and success of the Disney operation in Japan attests to the appeal of theme-oriented amusement parks. Natural attractions and resources are also a big part of the international tourism business. Wilderness areas, parks, beautiful scenery, and landscapes are important activities when traveling overseas. In some countries, national parks and reserves form the bedrock of the tourism industry. This is especially true for Africa with its numerous game preserves. The artistically manicured parks and gardens of Europe represent some of the most beautiful landscapes in the world and attract millions of international guests.

Accommodations

People seeking out attractions need to have places to eat, sleep, and purchase supplies. In contrast to the trading posts and inns of old, accommodations today are very sophisticated, extensive, and diverse. The tourist can choose from accommodations that range from a luxury hotel and resort to a primitive wilderness campsite in the backcountry of a national park.

Accommodations can be categorized in a number of ways: by price, by location, by type of visitor, and by type of facility. Luxury hotels are at one end of the scale while budget hotels are at the other. Some properties are located within the city limits while others are within the suburbs. One facility may target business travelers while another may cater to families on vacation.

It is difficult to put international lodging accommodations into strict, mutually exclusive categories. **The Organization for Economic Cooperation and Development (OECD)** reports 11 different types of accommodations plus two "other" categories in their reports of travel and tourism activity across Europe, the United States, Japan, Australia, and New Zealand. (The OECD is an association of 25 countries promoting economic development and cooperation among nations.) The "other" categories refer to other "hotels and similar establishments" and "supplementary means of accommodation." Such accommodations vary by country or by reporting agency and might include bungalow hotels, rented farms, houseboats, or rented camper-vans.

Accommodations available to the international traveler can be grouped according to these categories: hotels, motels, inns, bed and breakfasts, paradors, timeshare and resort condominiums, camps, youth hostels, and health spas.

Hotels. Hotels dominate the accommodations sector of the tourism industry across the world. The hotel has been the centerpiece of many major cities in the United States and Europe for years. Traditionally an urban facility, hotel settings range from the largest downtowns to the most remote islands. The following discussion presents several useful and general classifications of hotels.[5]

Commercial. Commercial hotels cater primarily to business travelers although individual tourists, tour groups, and small conference groups may be among the clientele. Amenities may include free morning newspapers and coffee, guestroom computer terminals, and services such as laundry and valet, concierge, and gift shops. These hotels usually have room service, a coffee shop, and a formal dining area. Swimming pools, saunas, and health clubs are sometimes part of the facility. Commercial hotels are often located in the downtown or business districts of many cities and smaller communities.

Airport hotels. As the name suggests, these hotels are strategically located near airports. These facilities are designed to provide convenience for travelers. Services may include parking and shuttle service to and from the airport terminal. Airport hotels vary in their level of service. Markets include business travelers; airline passengers with short layovers or cancelled flights; and meeting, conference, and convention groups.

Conference centers. Although many hotels provide meeting space, these hotels are specifically designed to provide all the services and equipment necessary for successful meetings. Most full-service conference centers offer lodging accommodations as well as meeting facilities.

Economy hotels. Economy class hotels offer little beyond clean rooms. Amenities are few and service is limited. Food service is generally not provided—or if it is, on a very limited basis. These properties target the cost-conscious traveler. Markets include vacationing families, tour groups, businesspeople, and conventioneers.

Suite hotels. Accommodations at suite hotels are more than just a single room and bath. Hotel suites often include a living room, a separate bedroom, and in some cases, a kitchenette. The suite has definite advantages for many travelers. Business travelers find suites appealing since they offer a place to conduct a small meeting or to entertain in an area separate from the bedroom. The extra room offers a degree of privacy not available in a typical hotel room. Suites also serve as temporary quarters for families relocating between homes.

Residential hotels. Guests of residential hotels stay much longer than guests at other hotels since the hotel, in essence, becomes a home. Marriott's Residence Inns represent a modern version of the residential hotel, but with limited service. The facilities within the unit—such as the kitchen, fireplace, and separate bedroom—are, in a sense, the amenities. Residential hotels usually offer housekeeping services, a dining room, room meal service, and sometimes a cocktail lounge. Food and beverage divisions are generally small and exist more as a convenience to travelers than as a revenue center to the property. Residential hotels range from single rooms for individuals to full suites for families.

Casino hotels. As the name implies, these hotels house gambling facilities. The amenities, services, and attractions are designed for, and marketed to, the gambling guest. These properties can be quite luxurious. To attract gaming revenues, casino hotels frequently offer top-name entertainment, extravagant shows, specialty restaurants, and charter flights.

Resort hotels. Here again, the hotel caters to a special guest—the tourist on vacation. But unlike some other properties, the resort hotel is the guest's planned destination. Resorts are located in particularly scenic areas such as the seashore or mountains—generally away from the clamor of large cities. Resorts, too, might offer spa and health club facilities. Most resorts today are four-season operations, full-service, and enriched with amenities. Resorts also provide special activities for guests such as dancing, golf, tennis, horseback riding, nature hikes, skiing, swimming, and so forth.

Motels. Like hotels, motels can be full-service, amenity-laden, and expensive. Motels can also be economical. Most motels are located along major highways or toll roads to take advantage of automobile traffic. Parking is usually free and accessible.

Inns. Inns have a long tradition in Europe as a place where weary travelers can rest. Many inns have only a few rooms. Inns generally have limited food service that is offered through a set menu. Inns seem more personal to the business or pleasure traveler because they are small and often conveniently located in major cities.

A variation of the inns is the pension. A pension is a large home converted into a guest house for travelers. The name "pension" is used most often in European countries. In the United States, such establishments might be called inns.

Bed and Breakfasts. Bed and breakfasts—or B&Bs—derive their name from the fact that they provide overnight accommodations and breakfast to guests. These properties can range in size from a few guestrooms in a private home to a small building with 20 to 30 rooms. The owner usually lives on the premises and is responsible for serving breakfast. B&Bs have long been popular in England. Recently, the B&B gained popularity in other parts of the world—including the

The fireplace, tapestries, and furnishings in this guestroom reflect the personal touches which have made inns and B&Bs popular options for many travelers. ©1986 Stephen J. Pyle from *Michigan's Town and Country Inns* (University of Michigan Press, 3rd edition)

United States, Europe, and Australia. As the number of rooms increases within a B&B, it becomes difficult to differentiate it from an owner-occupied inn or a very small hotel.

Paradors. Old, historical buildings converted to lodging establishments by the government or by regional or national tourism offices are sometimes called paradors. The term and concept originated in Spain and appears infrequently in the United States. Paradors could be compared to historical buildings which have been converted to lodging establishments and offered through the U.S. National Park Service or by selected state park systems.

Timeshare and Resort Condominiums. The tourist has a unique range of options for resort vacation lodging through the timeshare or condominium concepts. In the case of the condominium, a tourist owns a suite or room within a hotel or condominium complex and uses it as needed. This same unit can also be rented to other travelers. Usually, the owned condominiums are contained within a complex of rooms or suites that are rented as regular hotel or resort rooms. Most guests cannot tell the difference between an owned and a rental unit.

Timesharing is a modification of condominium ownership. Units are owned, but not completely. The timeshare owner may own one-tenth of a unit and, as a result, shares the unit's use and costs. In some cases, the owner may only purchase a certain set of weeks to use the unit; in others, actual deeds to the property may be jointly owned by a group of investors. The timeshare title implies that the unit is shared with others throughout the year. Today, timeshare owners have the option of trading the use of their units with others. This gives owners a unique opportunity to vacation at comparable prices at destinations around the globe. Several companies are available to help timeshare owners locate other timeshare owners interested in swapping units.

Camps. Camping has a long history in most countries, including the United States. Camping refers to setting up sleeping arrangements on physical sites (called camps) made available for the purpose. Millions upon millions of campsites are available to the modern tourist. Just as astounding are the range and types of amenities offered at the modern camp. Travelers can set up a tent, park a recreation vehicle, or sleep under the stars in a sleeping bag. Campsites may be provided through a private enterprise or through government resources such as parks and forests. Many organizations offer group campsites to their members. These include boys and girls clubs, labor organizations, or religious groups.

Youth Hostels. Around the turn of the century, the economical hostel system began in Europe and spread to the United States. Estimates are that some 5,000 youth hostels exist around the world today, with some 254 in the United States.[6] The youth hostel offers overnight lodging, limited amenities and services, and sometimes, food services in the form of kitchen facilities.

Health Spas. Health spas are specialized accommodations designed to foster good health and good spirit. In several countries—including Germany, England, and the United States—health spas and baths represent some of the earliest lodging accommodations available to the health-conscious leisure traveler. In Europe, the services and amenities have grown in sophistication—with the primary focus on healing and health promotion. In the United States, the emphasis on slimness has fostered the development of luxurious and specialized spas for those needing help with weight control.

Accommodation Volume and Use

The number of rooms within lodging facilities that are available to the traveling public varies dramatically from country to country. Within a country, most properties will be located where the demand is most pressing: near tourist attractions—created or natural. Exhibit 3 shows a listing of the top hotel chains in the world.

The tourist has many options for lodging aside from the large established chains. In Spain, for example, an array of lodging accommodations are available other than traditional hotels. These include extensive "undeclared" lodging opportunities—estimated in excess of 9 million lodging beds—in private villas, apartments, and second homes. Among the declared beds available, hotels represent approximately 60%, camps 23%, and declared apartments 17%.[7]

Exhibit 3   Largest Hotel Chains Worldwide

Company/Location	No. of Rooms	No. of Hotels
Holiday, USA	360,958	1,868
Best Western Intl., USA	255,217	3,306
Sheraton, USA	135,000	465
Ramada, USA	130,932	769
Marriott, USA	118,000	450
Quality Intl., USA	112,810	978
Days Inns, USA	104,625	775
Hilton Hotels, USA	95,862	271
Trusthouse Forte, UK	89,546	893
Accor, France	80,034	700
Logis et Auberges, France	77,985	4,658
Prime Motor Inns, USA*	66,245	519
Club Mediterranee, France	61,860	249
Balkantourist	56,250	386
Motel 6, USA	51,572	452
Hyatt Hotels, USA	50,797	92
Radisson Hotels, Intl., USA	46,600	191
Ladbroke, UK	45,630	139
Bass, UK**	45,099	253
Saison, Japan	38,921	99
Econo Lodges of America	37,984	467
Super 8 Motels, USA	35,991	574
Sol, Spain	35,944	140
Aircoa, USA	35,116	154

   * Prime Motor includes Howard Johnson Franchise Systems, Inc., with
     54,757 rooms.
  ** Company is also listed as a corporate chain with its own listing.

Source: "300 Hotel Companies," *Hotel & Restaurants International* (July 1989): p. 44.

Estimates are that there are about 10 million rooms available to tourists around the world—with about 50% of those in Europe. The United States and Canada account for approximately 29% of the world's rooms, numbering more than 2.8 million.[8] The average worldwide hotel occupancy rate is approximately 70%. In 1988, Europe had an occupancy rate of 70%, while the United States and Canada reported rates of 66% and 70%, respectively. The highest occupancy rate for a region is 77% for the Pacific Basin; among this group of countries, Thailand reports a remarkable 90% occupancy rate.[9]

The international network of hotels and motels attracts both leisure and business travelers. On average, rooms are occupied by approximately 50% domestic travelers and 50% international travelers. While this is the world average, most countries fill their hotels with a larger proportion of foreign guests than domestic visitors. The exception is the North American market of Canada and the United States where 85% of guests are domestic travelers. Europe is 53% foreign, while the African and Middle Eastern market is 75%.[10]

These figures tell us that, on the domestic scene, many residents cannot afford to travel, much less stay in hotels. Lower-end lodging options such as camping, budget motels, and inns are more likely to cater to domestic markets. Nearly a quarter of all guests at hotels worldwide are individual tourists; added to this is another 14% who are touring as part of a group tour package.[11] Nearly 40% of the hotel guests worldwide are taking part in the international accommodations system.

Transportation

Transportation is essential to the success of all tourism—domestic or international. As in other countries, the primary mode of domestic tourism and travel in the United States is private automobiles. Recent figures estimate that private vehicles accounted for 78% of the person-trips in the United States in 1989. In contrast, air service constitutes approximately 18% of all person-trips in the United States.[12] The remainder of person-trips are taken by bus, train, or other means such as a boat or bicycle. Across Europe, rails account for approximately 5% to 10% of all ground transport and 15% of the tourism-related traffic.[13]

Mass tourism—as it is known internationally—could not exist without inexpensive and accessible transportation. All destinations on the globe—including remote resorts, islands, and the far reaches of the Pacific Rim—rely on efficient means of transportation being available to tourists. For international tourism, airlines constitute the most prominent sector of the transportation industry.

Airlines

Accessible air service is a hallmark of international tourism. In fewer than 50 years, air travel has shifted from the mode of choice for the rich, strong of heart, and adventurous to the mode of convenience for most international travelers.

Airlines truly symbolize international travel and international business. Like international hotels, the giant airlines have business interests in many nations and frequently, in many tourism-related and allied industries. International air travel mushroomed in the last 20 or so years after dynamic beginnings in post-war Europe and America. Airlines have fostered innovations in tourism marketing, promoted new airplane designs, struggled through the first stages of airline deregulation, and shared in the blossoming of mass tourism on a grand international scale.

Today, changes in air transportation are constant, rapid, and sometimes unpredictable. Terrorism bred new concerns over the safety of airports and the need for airline security. Air accidents have called attention to aging fleets and air traffic control safety. And finally, the changes in Eastern Europe will require airlines and other international tourism businesses to carve out niches and business arrangements in new, unfamiliar markets.

Exhibit 4   Market Share for International Scheduled Air Traffic

Region	1983	1984	Years 1985 Percent	1986	1987
Europe	32.6	31.9	31.3	30.2	30.1
Africa	2.9	2.8	2.7	2.4	2.2
Middle East	3.2	3.2	3.1	3.0	2.8
Asia/Pacific	16.0	16.3	16.3	16.3	17.0
North America	40.3	40.7	41.6	42.9	43.1
Latin America/ Caribbean	5.1	5.0	5.0	5.2	4.7

Note: These figures exclude chartered traffic, which is more prevalent in Europe than North America. The figures may not add up to exactly 100% due to a rounding error.

Source: "Travel and Tourism Analyst Database," in *Travel and Tourism Analyst*, no. 4, (London: The Economist Intelligence Unit, 1989), pp. 101–102, after Table 3. Based upon data provided by the International Civil Aviation Organization (ICAO), 1988.

Amidst all these changes, air traffic grew about 7.5% per year between 1972 and 1988.[14] In 1988, the number of paying passengers carried one kilometer—or about six-tenths of a mile—was 1,551.8 billion. The majority of this traffic consisted of *scheduled flights* in various countries around the world. Scheduled flights are those made available on a regular basis by the airlines—or those commonly reserved by the traveling public flying from one destination to the other. Scheduled flights represented about 91% of all traffic in 1987. *Unscheduled flights* are usually prearranged chartered flights. These flights travel to a destination and back with most of the same people. Most unscheduled flights are international and resort-based in nature, and are often taken around holidays.

Air travel is a very competitive business, operating on profit margins of 2% to 3% over the last 10 years. Years of fare wars and discount battles between airlines have yielded reasonable air travel prices for consumers. In 1988, 91% of all paying passengers used some type of discount. The average discount was 61% off full fare.[15] U.S. airline profits are further complicated by load factors—or the percent of available seats that are occupied as each plane departs. Sixty percent of seats are occupied by paying customers; this means that millions of seats are empty throughout the year.

Among the various markets, the United States is still a dominant player. However, U.S. airlines are losing their market share. From 1972 to 1988, the U.S. market share dropped from 54.8% to 43%—including chartered flights.[16] On the other hand, when chartered flights are excluded, North America generally increases its share while Europe loses a point or two. Exhibit 4 provides market share percentages for six regions from 1983 to 1987. In light of the rapid political and economic changes facing Europe, it is unlikely that these small changes reflect a growing trend. However, it is likely that competition from other carriers will increase in Europe in the years ahead.

The Asian/Pacific market is also expanding, reflecting the growth of travel in and out of Japan, Taiwan, Thailand, and Australia. In fact, the growth of these travel routes is expected to continue. These nations will be generating even more tourism and business travel as they become increasingly popular tourism destinations for international travelers.

Deregulation and Liberalization. In 1978, the United States deregulated the airline industry, making it possible for airlines to set their own rates and routes. The idea was to introduce competition into the system, remove government intervention as much as possible, and subsequently lower prices. **Deregulation** turned out to be a very controversial decision by the Carter administration; the debate about its value rages even today.

Since 1978, air traffic has grown in the United States and around the world. But this growth has not occurred without questions about the effect deregulation has had upon prices and service. Some of the changes and concerns associated with deregulation include:[17]

- Limited financial success

- Mergers and airline bankruptcies (some 214 carriers have disappeared since deregulation)

- Increased international competition and international investment by foreign and U.S. companies

- Increased pressure on the few remaining small airlines

Even among major airlines, few have been truly financially successful since 1978. Average net profits are well below the U.S. average for industrial manufacturers.[18]

The mergers created larger companies which control the majority of the U.S. market. In the first ten years of deregulation, the largest eight airlines gained 10% more of the market—thus harnessing 92% of the entire market.[19] In 1989, for the first time, the top three airlines—American, United, and Delta—carried more than half of the domestic passengers.

The size and number of airlines have changed dramatically since deregulation. A noticeable consequence of deregulation has been the growth of regional or feeder airlines and hub airports. The growth of such subsidiaries has resulted in what one analyst calls "mega carriers." These carriers control regional or feeder airlines and computer reservations systems, and have partnerships with hotels and auto rental companies.[20] In other words, these giant airlines essentially build and control an entire system that provides transportation and services to customers.

The final vote is still out on the success of deregulation. In Europe, a similar process is under way—all with an eye on the mixed results achieved in the United States. Some have argued that **liberalization**—or full deregulation—in Europe is not desirable since the industry and route systems are not as large as those in the United States. Other differences from the U.S. airline industries include the strong role of government, the shorter distances flown by the European airlines on average, competition between different types of transportation, the strong roles of charter flights, and independent computer reservations systems. Coupled with Europe's protectionist tendencies, these differences suggest that the government may keep its hand in air travel in the new Europe of the 1990s—even with liberalization.[21]

To whatever extent it is taken, liberalization will restructure the European airline industry. The volume of traffic will continue to grow and place even more pressure upon world airports and airport services. The results of all these changes may lead to competitive prices if not to more congested air travel. The tourists of the 1990s will have much different air travel experiences than the typical air traveler of the 1970s.

Computer Reservations Systems. The large computerized reservations systems owned by the world's major airlines are interesting components of international travel. Systems have been in place in the United States for some time. But in Europe, most systems are no more than four or five years into the planning stages with some only recently coming on line. The five major U.S systems and their owners are: Sabre (American Airlines), Pars (Northwest, TWA), Covia (United), System One (Texas Air), and Datas II (Delta). Canada has Gemini (Air Canada, CAI); Japan has Jalcom (JAL) and Fantasia (JAL, All Nippon Airways, Qantas); and Australia has Qantam (Qantas). Abacus is a system owned by several airlines and serves various countries in the Far East. In Europe, there are two major systems owned by a variety of airlines across Europe—Galileo and Amadeus.

Exhibit 5 shows that these systems are linked with other systems in other countries. Computer reservations systems have become major marketing vehicles for the airline industry. They provide travel agents with immediate access to the fares and flights of airlines that are part of the system.

Rail Service

Trains were once the backbone of tourism development. Trains replaced horses, foot travel, stagecoaches, and river boats with efficiency and speed. Trains dominated Europe and the United States for most of the late 1800s. But with the development of automobiles and better roads, rail service deteriorated. Its demise took place in a matter of years—from the turn of the century to the end of World War II.

Today's transportation market is very different from that of a hundred years ago. Rail service competes not just with automobile travel, but with motor coach and airplane travel as well. Rail service constitutes only 5% to 10% of the surface travel market in Europe[22] and a similar small percentage in the United States.[23] In contrast, rail service commands a significant percentage of the market in other countries or regions. Japan, the Soviet Union, and India top the list of countries with the largest numbers of passengers transported by rail.[24]

The volume of tourist travel by rail varies from country to country. For example, transportation by air and sea is more prevalent in island countries. In the United Kingdom, nearly 34% of visitors arrived by sea and 66% by air in 1987. Contrast these figures with Spain where 60% of visitors arrived via road systems and 33% arrived by air in 1987. Rail brought in fewer than 10% of arriving tourists in most European countries.[25]

In Europe, the shorter distances between countries make the private car the primary vehicle for international travel. The volume of European international

Exhibit 5 Airline Computer Reservations Systems

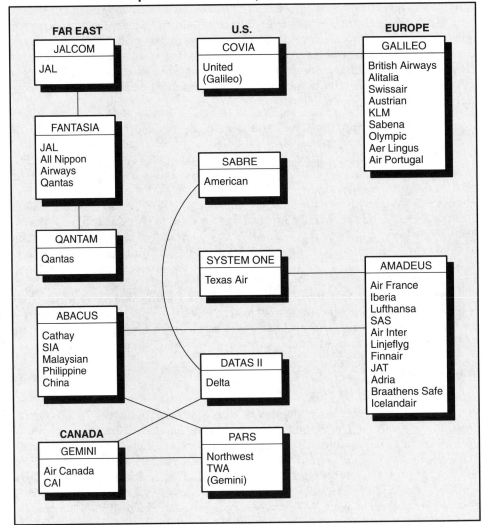

Source: *International Air Transport Association (IATA) Review,* January 1989.

traffic by train has declined since the mid-1980s. Part of this may be due to the complexities of fares and passports across national borders. The decline, too, may be caused by the general reduction of quality and competitiveness between the rail systems of various European countries. It is notable that, although rail traffic across borders has decreased, the use of the train within a country's border has increased.[26]

The issue of how much the government should subsidize the rail system is a matter of controversy in many countries. **Amtrak**—the acronym stands for American travel by track—is subsidized in part by federal funds appropriated yearly by Congress and administered through the Department of Transportation. Congress established Amtrak in 1970 to take over intercity passenger operation from railroads that desired to drop passenger service. Projections are that it will be sometime near the year 2000 before Amtrak is self-supporting. This projection is based on a number of changes that will influence U.S. rail service. These include better service and additional routes, newer equipment and cars, Amtrak's entry into the airline computer reservations system, and a three-fold increase in travel agencies authorized to sell Amtrak tickets. Agency tickets now represent about 40% of total ticket sales.[27] In addition, there is the continued push to use mass transit to help alleviate congestion problems on city routes and major highways.

In Europe, government funding of rail systems will probably diminish as the unification of Europe becomes more of a reality. For the most part, subsidies do not always generate more market share. More often, the success of these rail systems is determined by the types of services offered, the cost, the speed, and the routes available to the business and pleasure traveler. In France, the number of people traveling by rail is expected to increase with the opening of the Eurotunnel between England and France. The importance of rail in transporting people around Central Europe also increased with the opening of the Euro Disney project in 1992. The Disney project is located near Paris; the supporting rail system is expected to carry some 10 million visitors a year.[28]

Looking ahead, several things will have to change if rail wishes to compete: customer service, the speed of transport, and the types and costs of tickets. In the United States, the process of purchasing and reserving tickets has improved since Amtrak linked up with the airline reservations system. In Europe, similar efforts are underway with the new and emerging computer reservations systems. As one travel analyst notes:

> It is clear that in the field of sales distribution lies one of the railways' biggest and most urgent challenges in the future. The public is becoming increasingly accustomed to, and used to expecting, trouble-free purchase of services, especially in the travel field. The techniques exist and are increasingly being employed by the railways' competitors to facilitate trouble-free sales and route planning through computer reservations systems. Unless a passenger is able to obtain, either directly or through his travel agent, easy and reliable access to all the needs of his rail journey, he will turn to another means of transport that can fulfill these needs.[29]

To meet the inevitable changes, the European Conference of the Ministers of Transport adopted a "Resolution on Railways" in 1988. This resolution suggests that railways improve quality of services, develop high-speed rail networks, conduct structural improvements, and modify management practices in order to compete in the liberalized transportation world of a unified Europe. In addition, the resolution urges European governments to grant independence to the railways, assist with reducing the debt held by the railways, eliminate distorted competition, and remove barriers at border crossings as much as possible.[30] All these measures imply a reduction in government subsidies, an increase in competition, and, hopefully, an increase in quality services to the public.

The German Maglev train promises to carry travelers to their destinations at speeds up to hundreds of miles per hour. (Courtesy of Transrapid International, Munich, Germany)

The fast-train European rail system now under construction could be considered one of the most far-reaching transportation projects ever attempted. When completed, the system will stretch from Scotland, across Northern Europe and Central Europe, down to Greece on one side, and into Spain and Portugal in the west. This system will cover some 19,000 miles, with costs approaching $100 billion. Train speeds are expected to reach 185 miles per hour on portions of the system. Again, these efforts anticipate the new, unified Europe of the 1990s. The system, too, will address the growing need to remove pressure from the airline system and an overcrowded road system.

Cruise Lines

Before the rail and road systems of modern society, water transportation was the means of choice. But in the passenger ship industry, change was harsh and rapid—especially in North Atlantic routes. Between 1953 and 1969, trans-atlantic jets took their toll; the market share for ships fell from more than half to less than 10%.[31]

Before discussing cruise ships, it is important to remember that ferries still move millions of people across waterways for business and pleasure. Ferries serve as a connection between families and friends, workers and employers, and travelers and destinations across rivers, bays, and harbors. Prominent waterways with ferry crossings include the English Channel, coastal waterways of the United

Ferries still take travelers from "point A to point B" in many parts of the world. (Courtesy of the Alaska Division of Tourism, Juneau, Alaska)

States, the seas between Caribbean islands, the Great Lakes, and waterways of Southeast Asia and South America.

The cruise represents an exciting alternative vacation package. Modern cruise lines offer the finest in entertainment, cuisine, sight-seeing, and all-around luxury. Cruise passengers can combine romance and fine dining with excitement and shoreside shopping. Or, the passenger can simply stay on board to enjoy features such as gambling casinos, broadway shows, or evening walks on deck. Some feel that the cruise ship is no longer just a means of travel to exotic destinations but an attraction in its own right.

The cruise ship of the future will continue to add amenities and unique activities to the roster—bigger and better shows, more activities for the health-conscious, and unique itineraries. Such amenities and features are already becoming cruise industry staples because of a trend to build larger ships for the cruise market. Ships carrying 1,000 passengers or fewer were once the standard. Now, newer vessels can house up to several thousand. Ships are in the blueprint stage which could accommodate 5,000 passengers. In some respects, these larger crafts become self-contained floating attractions.

The cruise industry has been booming in recent years. More ships and berths are available than ever before. Both the capacity of and demand for cruise lines is growing around the world. For example, the capacity of the North American region is projected to grow 8% to 10% into the first part of the 1990s; growth over the

Exhibit 6   World Cruise Market Shares: 1987

Country	Passengers	Market Share
United States	2,500,000	72.5%
United Kingdom	125,000	3.6%
West Germany	150,000	4.3%
Italy/France	120,000	3.5%
Canada	50,000	1.5%
Rest of World	500,000	14.5%
Total	3,445,000	100.0%

Source: Tony Peisley, "New Developments in World Cruising," *Travel and Tourism Analyst*, no. 3 (1988): pp. 6–7.

last few years has been 6% to 9% a year.[32] Estimates suggest that approximately 3.5 million people were passengers on cruise lines in 1987. With the growth of the last few years, worldwide cruising could reach 4 million passengers a year.

One way to look at the cruise ship market is in terms of the passengers' country of origin. As can be seen in Exhibit 6, the United States dominates the cruise market (72.5%), followed by West Germany (4.3%) and the United Kingdom (3.6%). The cruise industry is truly international. First, passengers come from a variety of countries and the ships themselves may stop at a number of international ports of call. Second, passengers may actually fly to another country to begin their cruise, taking part in a trend called **flycruising.** For example, in 1987, 25% of cruise passengers from the United Kingdom flew to the Caribbean for their cruise as part of a flycruise package.[33] Third, while the United States dominates the passenger market, ship owners come from a variety of countries. Most ship owners are headquartered in Europe. In addition, various cruise lines have ships built in any number of countries across Europe.

In terms of activity, the Caribbean receives approximately 2.5 million or more visitors a year.[34] Second to the Caribbean is the Mediterranean, garnering 15% of the overall cruise market.[35] Other popular cruise destinations include Hawaii, the West Coast of the United States up along Canada to Alaska, the St. Lawrence Seaway between Eastern Canada and the United States, the canals and rivers of Europe and the northern fjords of Scandinavia, the Amazon of South America, and the Nile of Africa. River cruises are being developed on interior river basins in China. While the Chinese market is small and very regional, it has the potential to grow by attracting those who seek a unique way to see the rural side of this huge country.

The list of possible destinations could go on and on to reflect the growing popularity and potential of the cruise sector. In the largest market—the United States—less than 5% of the public has ever taken a cruise. The cruise industry itself only accounted for 2% of the pleasure trips of three or more days taken in 1988.[36] About a third of the U.S. cruise market consists of 18- to 34-year-olds.[37] As this market matures and gains leisure time and financial security, so too might the cruise industry blossom and grow.

The following paragraphs present other issues and trends that may influence the cruise industry. While these represent challenges, the cruise industry appears well-positioned to address the needs of world travelers for years to come.

Expansion. As cruise fleets expand, so too must the ports of embarkation and ports of call. If such ports do not expand, the size and number of new ships threaten to put these ports under severe strain. As noted earlier, some newer ships may have capacities of up to 5,000 passengers. If and when such enormous ships are used, cruise lines must be sensitive to the effect that 5,000 disembarking passengers will have on a port. In fact, cruise planners must know whether any ports can even handle such "mega ships." Today, very few actually can; this limits the number of stopovers that a ship of such size could make during a cruise.

Expanding capacity also demands that the number of consumers increase at the same level. While only a small percentage of American tourists have taken a cruise, it is not clear if their interest will grow in tandem with the industry. A challenge facing the cruise industry today is to create a genuine desire or need to take a cruise. Potential exists in some of the biggest tourism-generating nations of the world such as the United States, West Germany, Britain, and Japan. It is a matter of strategically marketing the cruise concept so that the actual number of tourists matches the projected capacity.

This is no easy task. The North American market shows signs of becoming soft because of a slowdown in passenger cruise growth rates and the tremendous increase in building more cruise ships. Simply put:

> Saddled with too many boats and too few bookings, cruise-line operators in Florida and travel agents across the country are scrambling for passengers.[38]

It is still too early to know if this is a trend. But the discounts offered by the cruise industry may become a standard for some time, much like the discounts that have come and stayed in the auto and airline industries. The cruise market has potential, but the implied potential has yet to be realized.

Size. Mega ships are not the only type of vessel being built for the cruise industry. Smaller, luxury-oriented, or theme-oriented ships are increasingly being constructed to fill special cruise market niches. Practically speaking, the smaller ships can call on a wide range of ports and sail into river basins. Smaller size passenger loads also make the trip more intimate. One drawback to smaller ships is that many are not capable of crossing the open ocean. This means that, unlike larger ships, they cannot be easily moved into expanding markets or away from faltering markets because they cannot be quickly sailed across the ocean to another market.[39]

Cruise Length. The length of cruise preferred by tourists is changing. The fastest growing cruise length is three to five days. Today, 88% of all cruising is for eight days or fewer. Only 12% of the market enjoys a cruise vacation of more than a week.[40]

Mergers. Mergers are the game of the day in the cruise industry. Larger firms are buying out smaller or specialty lines to penetrate unique markets. The consequences of cruise line mergers—like those of airline mergers—are disputed. As cruise lines expand in size and increase in efficiency, they may continue to bring bargains to the public, while the actual number of cruise line owners shrinks. The fewer but larger firms will be more capable of stimulating consumer interests which, in turn, will augment expansion. As these forces work together, the industry will be in a strong position to offer stable, low-cost, quality cruises. On the darker side, mergers could mean fewer options, more price control, and less innovation. In the end, it remains to be seen whether mergers will mean higher prices for the average consumer taking the average cruise.

Security. Tourism is based upon safety and security. The implications for the cruise industry were very apparent when the cruise ship Achille Lauro fell victim to terrorism in 1985. The number of Americans cruising in the Mediterranean dropped to nearly zero in the next season. Several lines were severely affected, while some failed entirely. Taking advantage of its inherent flexibility, the industry responded by moving ships out of the region. Just like all other sectors of the tourism industry, the cruise industry is concerned with maintaining the safety and security of its ships and passengers.

Economics. The cruise industry is based upon cooperation between the ship lines and ports of call. It is imperative that the residents and officials of destinations perceive the call as beneficial.

Economic impact is a complex matter. The new larger ships may make fewer calls at ports, while smaller, more mobile ships may call on the traditional cruise industry ports.[41] The result is that the passengers on the larger ships will spend more time on board—meaning that they will spend less money on shore. Smaller ships would still disembark passengers, but not in the volume of larger vessels. The overall effect can be both positive and negative depending upon which ports are involved. In addition, some cruise lines are buying their own small islands for the exclusive use of the ship's passengers. This means that the economic impacts on surrounding communities are minimal at best because the ship may not call on a community port at all. In these instances, the whole cruise and its passengers is self-contained.

From an economic perspective, the short-term visits of the passengers represent a challenge to the cruise lines and local communities alike. The cruise lines expect that a community will be able to accommodate the visitors it brings into port. This means that a quality tourism superstructure must be in place. Shops, events, and historical attractions must be developed and ready to provide service to the visitors.

To meet the demands of the cruise market, a community must be willing to invest considerable sums of money. This is generally acceptable when the economic benefits equal or exceed the expenditures. But in some communities, the costs may be larger than what passengers actually spend while on land, even when the gains acquired through docking agreements are included. The cruise industry represents approximately 10% of the Caribbean's tourism business[42]—a figure that may not inspire the type of cooperation required between the cruise lines and the local governments. In the case of the U.S. Virgin Islands, the expenditures of the cruise ship passenger do not typically equal that of other tourists. One estimate is that one air tourist spends 6.6 times the amount spent by an excursionist.[43] (The

Buses—or motor coaches—have long been favorite vehicles for urban sightseers. (Photo by Ann M. Halm)

term excursionist refers to a person visiting the Islands only briefly by water—generally a cruise ship passenger.) What concerns the Islands is that trends point toward more cruise visitors, while the number of visitors arriving by air is not expanding nearly as fast.

In summary, the cruise line industry has grown rapidly and may be reaching a plateau. The costs, social impacts, and overcapacity may slow down the industry if new marketing efforts are not productive.

Motor Coach Travel

In the United States, motor coaches—or buses—log some 8 billion passenger miles each year. Although the industry experienced severe declines in ridership during the 1980s, this figure represents growth.[44] Motor coach transportation offers those with limited budgets an inexpensive way to see the country or to travel to another region. In the United States, Greyhound was hit by a major labor strike in 1990 which hampered the industry for several months. The results of this labor dispute will not be fully known for some time.

Tours and motor coaches go together and have done so for a long time. Motor coach tours take tourists to just about every kind of attraction imaginable: the mountains, the ocean, a flower festival in Michigan, a play festival in Canada, and the religious plays of Germany. One after another, buses traverse the countryside to popular attractions and regions.

The typical motor coach tourist is an older woman who is more than likely pleased that the tour operator takes care of the details.[45] The motor coach itself has undergone many improvements in recent years. This is especially the case in Europe. The vehicles used today by more upscale operators are miles ahead of what used to be called a bus. The packages available to the tourist are not only varied but are structured differently. More leisure time is planned into the excursion, the times are more manageable, and the tours are better matched with the interests of the tourists. The bus trip as an endurance test is a thing of the past. Theme tours, tours with a range of activities, and those just for sight-seeing are now all available at a reasonable price. Those wanting to travel in style and luxury may be subject to more heady prices.

In Europe, unification will definitely affect motor coach travel. Deregulation of the industry in England suggests that some loss of service has occurred. However, the number of motor coach operators has increased, generating competition and innovations.[46] In the United States, deregulation of the industry in 1982 also created losses in service for rural parts of the country—especially towns and villages. Within a five-year period, some 4,500 communities across the nation lost all or part of their bus service; 900 others, however, gained service.[47]

Motor coach tours should continue to do well as populations in the Western world mature—given that the industry can modify its image as a tour option for the elderly and as an inexpensive tour with little value. In fact, motor coach tour operators may have a competitive advantage as they position their service as one of convenience within a very crowded and busy transportation system.

This chapter has examined some of the services available to international and domestic travelers as they embark upon and enjoy their journeys. Even though the nature of service can vary across countries, the intent is usually the same: to satisfy the tourist. As mass tourism begins to touch more and more points on the globe, the image, practice, and expectation of service becomes increasingly uniform across societies and cultures.

Endnotes

1. Chuck Y. Gee, James C. Makens and Dexter J. L. Choy, *The Travel Industry*, 2d ed. (New York: Van Nostrand Reinhold, 1989), pp. 75–79.

2. A. J. Burkart and S. Medlik, *Tourism: Past, Present, and Future* (London: Heinemann, 1974), p. 229.

3. Susan Carey, "Lufthansa Signs Pact to Purchase Stake in Interflug," *The Wall Street Journal,* 8 March 1990, p. A-11.

4. Matthew McQueen, "Multinationals in Tourism," in *Tourism Marketing and Management Handbook,* edited by Stephen F. Witt and Luiz Moutinho (New York: Prentice-Hall, 1989) pp. 286–287.

5. Gerald W. Lattin, *The Lodging and Food Service Industry,* 3d ed. (East Lansing, Mich.: Educational Institute of the American Hotel & Motel Association, 1993), pp. 114–120.

6. Gee, et al., p. 316.

7. Manuel Valenzuela, "Spain: the Phenomenon of Mass Tourism," in *Tourism and Economic Development: Western European Experiences,* edited by Allan M. Williams and Gareth Shaw (New York: Belhaven Press, 1988), p. 46.

8. Somerset R. Waters, *Travel Industry World Yearbook—The Big Picture—1988* (New York: Child and Waters, Inc., 1988), p. 125. Based upon World Tourism Organization data.

9. Pannell Kerr Forster, Report—*Trends in the Hotel Industry, International Edition* (Houston, Texas: Pannell Kerr Forster, 1989), pp. 78; 88.

10. Jeanne V. Beekhuis, "Overview of Travel Worldwide," in *Travel and Leisure's World Travel Overview 1988/1989* (New York: American Express Publishing Corporation, 1988), p. 40. Based upon *Worldwide Hotel Industry, 1988,* Horwath and Horwath International, p. 54.

11. Beekhuis, p. 54.

12. Suzanne Cook, "1989 Domestic Travel in Review," paper presented at the *Fourth Annual Travel Review Conference,* Washington, D.C., February 1990, p. 14.

13. David Williams, "European Rail Travel," *Travel and Tourism Analyst,* no. 5 (1988): pp. 8–9.

14. "Travel and Tourism Analyst Database," in *Travel and Tourism Analyst,* no. 4, (London: The Economist Intelligence Unit, 1989), p. 98.

15. Charles J. Kreinar, "1988 U.S. Domestic Scheduled Airline Review," in *Third Annual Travel Review Conference Proceedings,* February 1989, (Salt Lake City, Utah: Travel and Tourism Research Association, 1989), pp. 53–54.

16. "Travel and Tourism Analyst Database," p. 98.

17. George W. James, "Financial Performance and Future Prospects of U.S. Major Airlines," *Travel and Tourism Analyst,* no. 2, (1989): pp. 5–16.

18. James, p. 10.

19. Doug Carroll, "Higher Fares, Better Service Are Forecast," *USA Today,* 4 October 1988, p. 2-B.

20. Claxton E. Lovin, "Commuter/Regional Airlines: Changes to Carriers Since Code Sharing and Future Impact," in *Tourism Research: Globalization—The Pacific Rim and Beyond,* Proceedings of the Twentieth Annual Conference of the Travel and Tourism Research Association, June, 1989 (University of Utah, Salt Lake City, Utah: Travel and Tourism Research Association, 1989), p. 273.

21. Richard Pryke, "European Air Transport Liberalization," *Travel and Tourism Analyst,* no. 6 (1988): pp. 13–18.

22. Williams, p. 7.

23. Gee, et al., p. 246.

24. Gee, et al., p. 251.

25. *Tourism Policy and International Tourism in OECD Member Countries,* p. 214, Table 20.

26. *Tourism Policy and International Tourism in OECD Member Countries,* p. 118.

27. Collen Bush, "1990 Outlook for Rail Travel," in *1990 Outlook for Travel and Tourism— Proceedings of the Fifteenth Annual Travel Outlook Forum* (Washington, D.C.: U.S. Travel Data Center, 1989), p. 123.

28. "Transport," in *Tourism Policy and International Tourism in OECD Member Countries,* pp. 118–119.

29. Williams, p. 14.

30. "Transport," in *Tourism Policy and International Tourism in OECD Member Countries,* pp. 117–118.

31. L. J. Lawton and R. W. Butler, "Cruise Ship Industry—Patterns in the Caribbean 1880-1986," *Tourism Management* 8, no. 4 (December 1987): p. 336.

32. Robert H. Dickinson, "1990 Outlook for the Cruise Industry," in *1990 Outlook for Travel and Tourism—Proceedings of the Fifteenth Annual Travel Outlook Forum,* (Washington, D.C.: U.S. Travel Data Center, 1989), p. 125.; Gee, et al., p. 228.

33. Tony Peisley, "New Developments in World Cruising," *Travel and Tourism Analyst,* no. 3 (1988): p. 10.

34. Beekhuis, p. 31.

35. OECD, 1989, p. 122.

36. Dickinson, p. 125.

37. Peisley, p. 8.

38. Rick Christie, "Cruise Operators Hope Marketing Push Will Put the Wind Back in Their Sales," *Wall Street Journal,* 3 April 1990, p. B-1.

39. Peisley, p. 15.

40. Dickinson, p. 125.

41. Peisley, p. 15.

42. Peisley, p. 16.

43. Mary Fish and Jean D. Gibbons, "U.S. Virgin Islands' International Tourism: An Industry at the Crossroads," *International Journal of Hospitality Management* 6, no. 1 (1987): p. 13.

44. Gary J. Graley, "1990 Outlook for Greyhound Intercity Bus Travel," in *1990 Outlook for Travel and Tourism—Proceedings of the Fifteenth Annual Travel Outlook Forum* (Washington, D.C.: U.S. Travel Data Center, 1989), p. 127.

45. Robert Whitey, "The Domestic Market for Package Tours," in *Third Annual Travel Review Conference Proceedings,* February 1989 (Salt Lake City, Utah: Travel and Tourism Research Association, 1989), p. 77.

46. OECD, 1989, p. 121.

47. *The Bottom Line: A Summary of Surface Transportation Investment Requirements 1988-2020* (Washington, D.C.: American Association of State Highway and Transportation Officials), p. 39.

Key Terms

Amtrak

deregulation

diversification

feeder airline

flycruising

infrastructure

liberalization

multinational corporation

national tourism office (NTO)

OECD

superstructure

Discussion Questions

1. What basic role do governments play in tourism?

2. What is the difference between the infrastructure and the superstructure? Name some basic elements of each.

3. What is meant by the term diversification? What forms of diversification are common in tourism-related businesses?

4. How would you describe the range and nature of tourist attractions?

5. What are some general forms of accommodations available to international travelers?

6. How has deregulation affected the airline industry in the United States? in Europe?

7. What is the nature of rail service today?

8. What are some of the features of the modern cruise?

9. What trends might influence the cruise industry?

10. What seems to be the future of motor coach travel?

REVIEW QUIZ

When you feel you have covered all of the material in this chapter, answer these questions. Choose the *best* answer. Check your answers with the correct ones found on the Review Quiz Answer Key at the end of this book.

True (T) or False (F)

T   F   1. Most governments have a negative attitude toward tourism.

T   F   2. Hotels, convention centers, and other such facilities are called the super-structure.

T   F   3. Diversification is a short-term corporate strategy in the tourism market-place.

T   F   4. Natural attractions and resources are a big part of the international tourism business.

T   F   5. Airline deregulation has been a booming success.

T   F   6. One of the major problems with the new "mega ships" is that few ports can handle them.

T   F   7. Expanding the capacity of cruise fleets demands that the number of consumers increase at the same level.

T   F   8. Today, 88% of all cruises are for two weeks or longer.

T   F   9. Passengers on smaller cruise ships spend more money on shore than passengers on the larger ships.

T   F   10. Motor coach transportation offers those with limited budgets an inexpensive way to see the country or to travel to another region.

Alternate/Multiple Choice

11. The accommodations sector of the tourism industry across the world is dominated by:

    a. hotels.
    b. motels.

12. Hotels that are specifically designed to provide all the services and equipment necessary for meetings are called:

    a. commercial hotels.
    b. airport hotels.
    c. conference centers.
    d. suite hotels.

13. In Spain, a historic building converted into a guest house for travelers is called a:

    a. pension.
    b. parador.

14.   In 1978, the United States made it possible for airlines to set their own rates and routes. This political decision was called:

    a. deregulation.
    b. liberalization.
    c. capitalism.
    d. competition.

15.   In Europe, the shorter distances between countries make the _____ the primary vehicle for international travel.

    a. private car
    b. train
    c. plane
    d. ship

Chapter Outline

Tourism Planning
    The Need for Public Participation
    The Tourism Planning Process
    Government Planning
    Private Sector Planning
Tourism Development
    Benefits
    Costs
    Concerns in the Third World
The Tourism Development Life Cycle
Examples from Selected Countries
    Canada
    China
    France
    Spain
    Portugal

Learning Objectives

1. Relate tourism planning to tourism development.

2. Point out the importance of community and resident involvement in tourism planning.

3. List the ten basic steps in the U.S. model for tourism planning.

4. Identify the salient features of the Canadian model for tourism planning.

5. Describe the general role of the federal government in tourism planning.

6. Describe the basics of tourism planning at the state, regional, and local levels.

7. Distinguish between private sector planning and government planning.

8. List the general costs and benefits of tourism development.

9. Identify concerns associated with tourism development in the Third World.

10. Identify the four life cycle stages associated with tourism development.

11. Apply basic knowledge gained through this chapter by discussing the consequences of the tourism planning and development efforts undertaken by the French government.

12. Describe tourism enclaves within the context of the tourism planning and development efforts in Spain.

9

Tourism Planning and Development

TOURISM PLANNING is the process of preparing for **tourism development.** It is also a tool for addressing the choices associated with tourism development. Planning fosters the achievement of tourism goals and objectives and the assessment of tourism benefits and costs.

Tourism development comprises the planning, building, and management of tourism attractions, accommodations, transportation, services, and facilities. It is the long-term process of readying a destination for tourists or improving a destination's attractiveness to tourists.

This chapter examines tourism planning processes that initiate and control development and gives examples of how various countries have addressed important tourism development issues.

Tourism Planning

In general, planning refers to methods and means used in making decisions about the future. One researcher notes that planning is predicting—and that predicting requires some estimated perception of the future.[1] The developers of a suburban mall, for example, start with an idea. They picture a mall of a certain size and type, with specific stores, located in a specific place. Such an image of the future is the beginning of a plan. Of course, planning is much more than this. All the activities and efforts that make the image a reality are steps in the planning process.

The tourism planning process involves creating a future that is acceptable to the community and to others. Since tourism involves hospitality, the planning, design, and building of tourism facilities must be sensitive to guest needs. To meet guest needs and to be competitive, tourism developments must be unique, friendly in appearance, and accessible to the tourist.

Planning not only guides future actions but also assists in problem-solving. Planning is dynamic, ongoing, and should be done continuously to address specific problems and needs. It helps developers and communities adapt to the unexpected and avoid undesirable consequences.

Since tourism relies heavily upon the goodwill of the local residents, tourism planning must carefully consider the desires and preferences of the local community. Overall, planning for tourism development should result in improving the community.[2]

The Need for Public Participation

Planning for tourism requires the creativity of the entire community to remain vital and attractive. Through the tourism planning process, the community can collectively assess its own potential and that of the surrounding area for tourism.

Local citizens have both the right and the obligation to become involved in the planning processes that will shape the future of their community and their lives. They will have to live daily with the consequences of tourism development, including increased numbers of people, increased use of roads, and various economic and employment-based effects. Tourism that depends upon attractions and services also depends upon the hospitality of the local people. The success of a project is threatened to the extent that the development is planned and constructed without the knowledge and support of the local residents. Anger, apathy, or mistrust will ultimately be conveyed to the tourists. For the most part, tourists are reluctant to visit places where they feel unwelcome.

The Tourism Planning Process

A host of planning models and frameworks are available in planning literature and within professional journals. Most planning efforts share some common procedures and elements—at least among the industrialized nations of North America and Europe. Centrally planned economies—such as those in the Communist bloc before the Berlin Wall came down in 1989—have very different planning models. Most of the decision-making in bloc nations occurred at centralized governmental units or within the Communist Party.

In the United States and Canada, tourism planning is seen as a local or regional effort that involves community residents. Because planning has sometimes been neglected or done poorly due to lack of time, funding, desire, or expertise, both the United States and Canada have started extensive programs designed to foster systematic tourism planning. Some programs at the federal, state, or provincial level make planning *a requirement* before allocating government funds for tourism development or marketing.

What follows are two simple models offered to communities by the U.S. Travel and Tourism Administration (USTTA) and the province of Alberta, Canada. All the complexities of planning cannot be explored in this brief outline. But what readers can gain is a general impression of the steps and procedures involved in tourism planning.

A U.S. Model. Exhibit 1 presents a circular model of a planning process developed by the USTTA for U.S. communities. The model is included in USTTA's *Tourism USA* publication, which is available to communities and states throughout the country.[3] The exhibit is much less detailed than the following discussion, but is presented to help readers visualize the interrelated steps in the planning process. The steps are:[4]

1. Develop tourism leadership within the community.

    This initial planning stage requires the identification of leaders within the community who will rally community members, businesspeople, and other

(handwritten in left margin: TOURISM ENCLAVES)

Exhibit 1   The Planning Process: U.S. Model

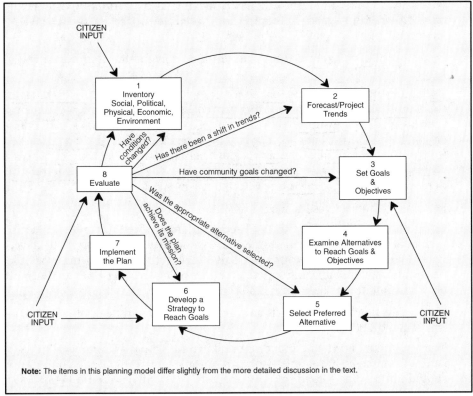

Note: The items in this planning model differ slightly from the more detailed discussion in the text.

Source: Deirdre K. Hirner, Glenn Weaver, Craig W. Colton, Glenn A. Gillespie, and Bruce T. Cox, University of Missouri, Columbia, *Tourism USA—Guidelines for Tourism Development* (Washington, D.C.: U.S. Travel and Tourism Administration, Department of Commerce, 1986), p. 20.

civic leaders around the issue of tourism. This leadership will stimulate the formation of tourism planning committees and tourism-related organizations.

2. Develop tourism organizations to implement planning.

   In the second stage, leaders form the needed organizations to promote public awareness and acceptance of tourism. These could include a tourism planning committee, a tourism council, or a subcommittee of the local Chamber of Commerce. These organizations will undertake appropriate and related activities, and eventually coordinate promotional efforts, seek external funding, and assist with implementing the plan.

3. Inventory and describe community or regional assets, tourism resources, and liabilities; assess the social, political, physical, and economic conditions of the community or region.

   To understand the strengths and weaknesses of a community or region, an inventory of assets, resources, and liabilities needs to be undertaken. The gathered information will be used to identify current tourism opportunities as well as what tourism opportunities are lacking. The information can also be used to pinpoint what the community needs in order for tourism to be successful.

4. Project what assets and resources are likely to come to the community in the future.

   Projections need to be made for economic growth, for the availability of labor, for markets, and for future building and construction. These projections provide insight into how the community might change in important social, political, and economic ways. Of course, projections would also be made for tourism. The community should look at whether the present tourism activity will be enhanced by new tourism development. The community should also determine where and how large future tourism markets will be.

5. Set goals and objectives for the tourism plan.

   Goals and objectives need to be discussed and worked out by community members in terms of what the community wants to achieve through the development and promotion of tourism. Goals and objectives set for tourism should be modest, obtainable, and workable. It does no good to set goals that cannot be reached; it dooms the tourism plan before the process actually begins.

6. Investigate alternative methods and means of obtaining the established tourism goals and objectives.

   There are many ways to achieve goals—including those associated with tourism development. In the initial phases of tourism planning, the community should not become locked into one method. Alternatives should be assessed and evaluated, and the pros and cons examined before decisions are made. Excellent approaches may be identified, but they may be too costly, inappropriate, or infeasible.

7. Select an approach and use it as a guide for the tourism plan and development strategies.

   After evaluating alternative methods, one approach should be selected and used to guide further planning. The community must remember that the approach is a guide—not a concrete formula. Changes, adaptations, and modifications will naturally occur as the planning process unfolds.

8. Prepare and put in place an implementation strategy.

   At this point, the community should be ready to specify the methods to carry out the plan and to assign responsibilities. The persons who are going to be involved should be identified—as well as the extent, nature, and time of their involvement. Activities should be outlined; details should be given on who will do them at what time. The plan should spell out what will be needed from the community and existing tourism businesses, and what will be needed from outside experts such as additional planners, developers, and financial partners.

9. Execute the plan.

This straightforward step needs to be taken once the plan is complete. Since no plan is ever static, situations that occur as the plan is implemented may require alteration of the plan. Good planning helps a community anticipate the future and respond creatively to the unexpected.

10. Reassess and evaluate the plan.

All plans and developments are subject to evaluation and assessment. At all times, the community should be asking if the plan is working and moving toward meeting the stated goals and objectives. If not, the plan should be modified, continued, and re-evaluated at a later date.

The details of how the foregoing steps are carried out vary with the community or region. In some communities, the Chamber of Commerce may have professional planners available to lead the effort. In others, local tourism businesspeople and residents take it upon themselves to work out the details. Most important is this simple point: planning for tourism is critical and increases the probability of success. The planning effort itself may be more important than the particulars of how a task is done.

A Canadian Model. The province of Alberta, Canada, offers a unique *Community Tourism Action Plan.*[5] Communities receive detailed planning manuals, complete with step-by-step instructions. Exhibit 2 lists the 24 steps in the model, which is more detailed than the U.S. model. For discussion purposes, the planning process is abbreviated in the following list and offered as a comparison to the U.S. model. The Alberta planning process assumes that community leadership has already been established, that a planning organization has been developed, and that discussions are under way regarding the value of tourism to the community. The steps in the abbreviated model are:

1. List, describe, and rank present tourism market profiles—those persons presently using the community as tourists. Secure the help of local tourism businesses in this process.

2. List and evaluate the community tourism assets—resources as well as concerns.

3. List and evaluate potential tourism markets. Ask who would visit the community in the future that is not doing so now.

4. In light of the projected markets, reassess assets and concerns about tourism development within the community.

5. Develop goals and objectives for tourism within the community.

6. Rank tourism objectives and develop actions and strategies for meeting each objective.

7. Formulate a draft of the tourism action plan; seek approval from the sponsoring organization; revise as necessary.

8. Solicit input from tourism business leaders and the general public; revise accordingly.

Exhibit 2 The Planning Process: Canadian Model

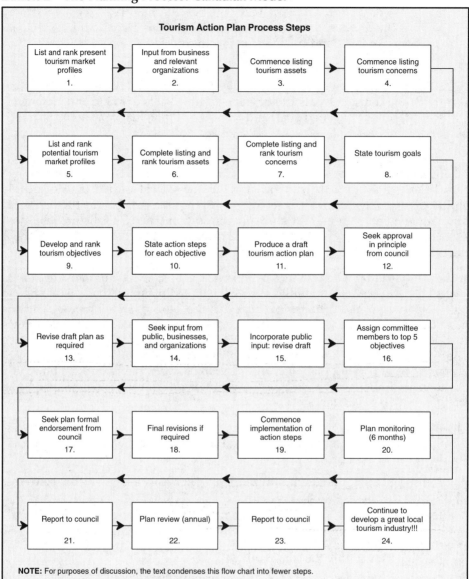

Source: *Community Tourism Action Plan*, revised, Process Book 3 (Edmonton, Alberta, Canada: Alberta Tourism, 1988), inside cover.

9. Within the planning committee or council, assign members to complete the revisions of the strategies for each of the objectives. With the revisions completed, seek final approval from the total planning group.

10. Implement the plan and its action steps.

11. Monitor and evaluate the plan as it is implemented.

12. Report on the success and failures of the plan to the appropriate governing and funding units. Frequently review the plan and its implementation; revise as necessary.

The Alberta planning package has other components as well. Workbooks provide a detailed, sample tourism plan—complete with worksheets, goals and objectives, and flow charts. The first workbooks civic leaders receive outline the costs of tourism; additional workbooks discuss organization of planning and action committees. Exhibit 3 shows a progress chart from one of the CTAP workbooks. This chart is designed to help the community planning committee stay on track. The Alberta program is discussed later in the chapter to show its effectiveness in tourism development.

Government Planning

Planning can be as simple or complex as the law, the planners, and citizens will allow. As a process, tourism planning varies across regions and countries. In the case of centrally planned economies, most tourism planning occurs at the national or federal level. In the United States, tourism planning is more likely to be conducted at state, regional, and local levels.

Federal Level. In the United States, the federal government's tourism efforts are directed toward transportation, financing, safety and health, and attracting international tourists to the United States. Air traffic control services, for example, are a function of federal agencies, as are safety inspections of airplanes and airport security. Roads are critical to domestic tourism, and the federal government plays a key role in building and maintaining them. A freeway in and through a region can mean life or death to tourism destinations and businesses, depending on how the freeway is routed. Policies related to visas are examples of government activity affecting domestic and international tourism.

The USTTA, a federal government agency, provides the planning model described earlier. Educational, planning, and research materials to foster the development of both domestic and international tourism are among other resources sponsored or produced by the USTTA.

One particular USTTA effort demonstrates the type of assistance that the federal government can provide in domestic tourism. In 1989, the USTTA sponsored research and workshops designed to foster tourism in rural America—an area suffering severe economic decline.

Other federal agencies may plan for tourism to the extent that they operate or manage tourism attractions. The National Park Service within the Department of Interior manages millions of acres of park lands, historical sites, and monuments that attract millions of tourists. The management, promotion, and services provided must be planned; this usually occurs at the park level with approval given at higher administrative levels.

State, Regional, and Local Levels. Most tourism planning in the United States occurs on regional and local levels with support from the state, depending on where

Exhibit 3 Worksheet for the 24 Community Tourism Planning Steps

TOURISM ACTION PLAN PROGRESS CHART		
STEP	**DATE COMPLETED**	**COMMENTS**
1. List and Rank Present Tourism Market Profiles		
2. Input from Businesses and Relevant Organizations		
3. Commence Listing Tourism Assets		
4. Commence Listing Tourism Concerns		
5. List and Rank Potential Tourism Market Profiles		
6. Complete Listing and Rank Tourism Assets		
7. Complete Listing and Rank Tourism Concerns		
8. State Tourism Goals		
9. Develop and Rank Tourism Objectives		
10. State Action Steps for Each Objective		
11. Produce a Draft Tourism Action Plan		
12. Seek Approval in Principle from Council		
13. Revise Draft Plan as Required		
14. Seek Input from Public, Businesses, and Organizations		
15. Incorporate Public Input; Revise Draft		
16. Assign Committee Members and Time Lines to Action Steps on Top 5 Priority Objectives		
17. Seek Plan Formal Endorsement from Council		
18. Final Revisions, if Required		
19. Commence Implementation of Action Steps		
20. Plan Monitoring (6 Months)		

Exhibit 3 *(continued)*

STEP	DATE COMPLETED	COMMENTS
21. Report to Council		
22. Plan Review (Annual)		
23. Report to Council		
24. Continue to Develop a Great Local Tourism Industry		

Source: *Community Tourism Action Plan,* revised, Worksheets (Edmonton, Alberta, Canada: Alberta Tourism, 1988), p. 1.

Buildings such as the Mission San Antonio de Valero—a site of siege during the battle of the Alamo—have become today's historic tourist attractions. (Courtesy of the Texas Department of Commerce, Tourism Division)

a destination is to be developed. Some states work with regional and local authorities and the private sector to develop statewide tourism plans. Unfortunately, only 65% of the states report having a travel development plan or policy statement to guide their work.[6] The nature of comprehensive planning at the state level is still emerging. State offices continue to grapple with such responsibilities as public relations, marketing, and acting as conduits for funding state and local tourism advertising.

Very few states are actively involved in capital development of tourism attractions or facilities. However, state or local governments may be active partners in planning such facilities. This can occur through regulatory processes such as issuing construction permits or selling land to developers who plan to build a tourism attraction.

Generally speaking, state-level tourism planning is more likely to be associated with tourism attractions and accommodations that are owned and managed by the state or the state transportation department. Common examples include parks and museums.

Transportation is an important factor in state and community tourism planning. Tourism planning and development hinge upon easy access; planning for transportation must be part of any tourism plan. Local tourism planners must consider the state transportation office as a resource—if not a full partner—in any tourism development plan.

In Michigan, the Department of Transportation offers technical assistance to communities and is sometimes a funding partner with communities in tourism development. Each year, the Department of Transportation partially funds road-building projects that foster tourism and subsequent economic development. Such funding is in cooperation with communities that have submitted tourism project proposals whose success depends upon roads being built or expanded.

At the local level, tourism planning may occur within a number of organizational structures such as Chambers of Commerce or Visitor and Convention Bureaus. These groups will often create tourism subcommittees to coordinate planning, development, or marketing functions. In some communities, separate tourism councils, associations, or tourism planning groups may be formed to coordinate a community-wide effort in developing tourism as part of the community's economic base.

Private Sector Planning

In most industrial nations today, tourism planning at the private business level is very specific, particularly to the business involved, and carried out by specialized consultants or in-house staff. In the case of attractions such as franchised amusement parks, consultants and in-house planners may plan and develop the park complex to the specifications of a parent company.

Hotels, restaurants, motels, and other attractions are often built to conform to both tourism development plans and facility plans. Consider how the location, size, orientation, and potential target market of a hotel may be part of a community-wide plan for tourism development. Once the plan is decided upon, the community may approach hotel builders or chains in seeking particular facility plans that fit the community-wide tourism effort. Some large hotel, restaurant, and amusement park chains maintain planning and development units within their corporate structures to plan and build specific facilities on specific sites.

Representatives of tourism businesses should address productive business activity and assess the available services, accommodations, attractions, and transportation linkages. Other businesspeople should examine commerce and how new tourism businesses will influence existing ones.

Fort Delaware State Park appeals to Civil War buffs, dungeon fans, and ghost hunters. The fortress was finished in 1859 and housed Confederate prisoners of war in the early 1860s. (Courtesy of the Delaware Tourism Office)

Even a manufacturing company that produces parts for companies outside the community should become involved. One reason for such involvement might be the company's location. In many instances, manufacturing plants are located on the edge of town and may be the first facilities that tourists see as they enter the community. As such, they should be clean and well-maintained. Attractive landscaping and fencing and signs to welcome visitors are among features a plant might provide.

In these and other ways, seemingly unrelated businesses play a direct role in tourism development within a community. If their involvement is missing or misunderstood in the planning process, tourism development may never reach its full potential.

Tourism Development

Tourism development is the long-term process of preparing for the arrival of tourists. It entails planning, building, and managing the attractions, transportation, accommodations, services, and facilities that serve the tourist.

Worldwide, many countries, regions, communities, and even neighborhoods encourage tourism development. The reasons behind tourism development are usually quite simple. Like other industries, tourism is seen as a business that provides economic assistance to a community.

Benefits

The following list cites some of the benefits that might be derived from tourism development:

- Increase in employment
- Stimulation of business activity
- Increase in business diversity
- Increase in taxes collected
- Increase in sales of goods and services
- Increase in community pride and concern for community history, culture, attractions, and artifacts
- Enhancement of community appearances
- Conservation or restoration of historic sites or attractions
- Conservation of natural resources as a tourist attraction

Costs

As the saying goes, "There's no such thing as a free lunch." Various costs are associated with tourism activity and development; the following are examples:

- Increase in the use of sewer and water systems, requiring further development of the community infrastructure
- Increase in the costs of maintenance and repairs of the community infrastructure
- Increase in number of people and vehicles, resulting in congestion
- Shifts in the pace of the community's cultural and social life, as well as the community's structure
- Damage to the environment
- New or increased expenses related to promotions, advertising, and marketing
- New or increased investment costs incurred by the community

Planners and developers at the destination usually change the landscape, the environment, and even the arrangement of businesses within the community to accommodate tourists. For example, consider the community with one hotel which for many years sufficiently met the needs of occasional business and pleasure travelers. As tourism developed, two or more additional hotels were needed and were built. The increased number of visitors also placed a demand on the community to develop more restaurants and shopping facilities. At the same time, the addition of these shops and malls dislocated smaller local businesses, parks, and other features that had satisfied residents for many years—that is, before tourism development began to affect the community.

Clearly, tourism development requires community members to make choices. Trade-offs have to be made between the benefits and costs of tourism. There is no simple way for a community to proceed with tourism development without setting priorities. Determinations must be made about how the development will look, as well as who will benefit the most, who will benefit the least, and who and what will have to change.

Concerns in the Third World   High Risk Investment

Tourism development is further complicated in Third World countries by the influence of foreign investors and multinational tourism companies. Besides sharing power with foreign investors and multinationals, Third World communities courting tourism face many challenges. Some of the challenges are as follows.[7]

1. Many of the forces which shape tourism in the Third World are at work in the country where tourists originate—not in the destination country. For example, the promotions that spark interest in the destination appear in the brochures, newspapers, and other media of the country of origin. Residents of the destination have little—if any—involvement in creating the image that is portrayed to potential tourists.

2. Tourist demands for certain amenities and a particular level of development may be beyond the ability or desire of the Third World community to deliver—even though the destination needs the business, jobs, and currency.

3. Since control of tourism is jointly—but often unequally—shared with foreign investors or companies, Third World nations have a difficult time controlling the flow of currency and products. For example, decisions about menus and interior designs of restaurants and hotels may be decided in a corporate boardroom in Europe; and products and design materials may be imported—rather than local. This results in leakage. Leakage occurs when a country or region pays for imported goods from another nation—thus drawing monies from the local economy and funneling them into profits for the exporting nation.

4. Investment risks are higher for Third World communities or governments than for foreign companies. Frequently, the local community takes out loans for developing the infrastructure that will be needed to support accommodations and attractions. The community may also offer tax breaks to the investing tourism business. Unfortunately, if the business fails, the community suffers the loss.

5. Tourism development in the Third World favors mass tourism. Tourism attractions and accommodations are standardized to meet the expectations of the Western tourist; profits are based on tourist volume. The combination of these two features—plus the price-sensitive nature of most Western tourists—means that tourism activity may be volatile. All might go well for a while, but a change in price may shift tourism traffic to another very similar destination. The results are downturns in both business and profit for the original destination.

From the Third World perspective, any tourism development plans that target the international tourist come with a handful of serious concerns. Benefits can be substantial, but before moving ahead at full speed with development plans, all residents, communities, and governments must weigh the costs.

Industrialized nations, too, will suffer costs and setbacks if they do not properly plan for tourism. It is doubtful that any tourism developer wants to see his/ her efforts turn into scattered strips of fast-food places, hotels, and unsightly attractions. Communities, tourism planners, and developers often overlook what has been created in the name of tourism. They may also overlook what it is that tourists would truly like to see and experience. One researcher calls such oversights "tourism myopia" and writes:[8]

> The present unrelated and often bizarre mass of development has a very simple and logical explanation but little excuse. It is the result of independent decision making based on a myopic view of tourists by the many developers of land, public and private. Tourists are seen to be simply fried chicken eaters; boat, camera, lot, and RV buyers; and myriad other specific product consumers. The scattering of private and public land development reflects the fragmentation of this view. And it thus fails to represent an understanding of the tourist as a whole person, one whose actions and needs are consistent throughout his period of travel who seeks some continuity over the course of the experience. The multiplicity of development is not integrated to form a total personal environment from home to destination and back.[9]

The Tourism Development Life Cycle

Like consumer products, tourism developments go through **life cycles**.[10] Tourism developments may start slowly with a few tourists, but will continue to expand as the destination grows in popularity. This typifies the first two stages of the cycle: a *start-up stage* followed by a *growth period*. Growth is rarely without end. Tourist numbers do level off and leave the development in a plateau stage—or a stage that economists and planners call *maturation*. Eventually, the number of tourists may begin to drop off, and the tourism development may go through a *decline stage*. Ultimately, if something is not done about the problem, the development may go bankrupt and dissolve.

Fortunately, the latter stages of this cycle can be averted through effective planning and marketing. New attractions can be added, remodeling can take place, and entirely new groups of tourists can be persuaded to visit. Such innovations occur all the time. Disney World, for example, added the Epcot Center in Florida to attract different or changing markets in the United States and abroad. Epcot is an example of a new attraction within an existing development that is designed to bring back loyal tourists and recruit new visitors.

The point is that a tourism development does not go on forever. Quality long-range planning should include strategies that address the decline stage. The long-range plan should offer guidance on how to systematically improve, change, remodel, and add to the development to head off its potential demise.

Examples from Selected Countries

Tourism planning and development varies around the world. The following sections discuss different approaches to tourism planning and development taken by several different countries.

Canada

Canada, much like the United States, strives for cooperation and coordination between the different levels of government. At the federal and provincial levels, both technical planning and financial assistance have been provided to provinces, private enterprise, and local communities. In the 1970s, the Canadian government entered into tourism agreements with the provinces, offering to assist them in uniting a fragmented tourism industry and focusing resources on regions where there appeared to be a potential for economic development and growth.[11] These agreements included planning for tourism at the regional level, and development through grants and loans.

In Ontario, these agreements meant that the province could focus tourism development in strategic locations.[12] Specific "tourism development zones" were identified. These zones represented regional locations where tourism was seen as the most profitable and beneficial venture to the province. The province was an active planning partner with the regions and communities. The province called for or assisted with inventories of tourism attractions and resources, economic analyses, assessments of opportunities, and market analyses; it also assisted in planning goals, objectives, strategies, and action plans. In the mid-1980s, these planning efforts resulted in funding for project proposals, historic site renovation, infrastructure development, and services. The planning and technical assistance provided by the province and federal government focused communities upon their own potential, and led to tourism development that might not have occurred under other circumstances.

Alberta, along with Ontario and the other provinces, received funds for the development and marketing of tourism through the Canada/Alberta Subsidiary Agreement on Tourism Development. The agreement brought in some $56.3 million in Canadian dollars for development and marketing efforts between 1985 and 1990.[13] In addition, the province developed an intensive tourism planning program, discussed earlier in this chapter in the planning section.

The *Community Tourism Action Program (CTAP)* provides financial assistance on a matching basis to communities interested in developing and promoting tourism as a viable economic industry. A total of $30 million in Canadian dollars is available to communities over the operating period of 1988 to 1993.[14] Communities interested in participating must prepare a Tourism Action Plan. This plan must be developed and approved before funding assistance can be received; application forms for funding are contained in the CTAP package. Any proposed facilities must be outlined within the community's Tourism Action Plan. This ensures that any funded development at the community level would not be initiated until the planning had been completed.

In effect, the province and the federal government stimulated tourism planning and development through grants and matching funds (the community provides a certain proportion of funds and the remainder is provided by the province). Important to this whole process is Alberta's systematic planning program, designed to ensure that communities do their homework and look carefully at their potential for tourism development.

Drawing from the same funding source, the *Team Tourism* program was developed for Alberta communities. Similar to CTAP, the program allots $20 million over a five-year period (1986 to 1993) to fund marketing efforts identified in tourism marketing plans.

China

In China, tourism developments are mainly planned and controlled by the government. Recent policies within China have made it possible for foreign investors to function as tourism businesses, usually in cooperation with a Chinese partner. For example, many of the hotels operating in Beijing are partly or wholly owned by the Chinese government. The government also partly or wholly owns travel agencies and airlines. Tourism planning occurs in government offices; the results influence the daily businesses of the government-owned attractions and accommodations. Change and movement toward a diversity of ownership occur to the extent that the government permits outside investors.

France

France is noted for its summer vacation resorts along Mediterranean beaches, winter holidays at ski resorts, and historical and cultural opportunities in Paris. But the summer congestion along the southern coast has been a long-term problem and shows little sign of abatement. In the early 1960s, the government decided to expand the coastal resorts to lessen the congestion and stem the tide of currency being taken out of the country by French tourists. France invested some six billion francs in the Languedoc-Roussillon region. Today, this region offers an additional 180 kilometers [112 miles] of coastal resort area. Seven resort complexes now stand where swamp and marsh lands previously stood. Estimates are that only 500,000 visitors came to the area in 1964. Recently, this number grew to more than 3.5 million.[15]

The expansion of the Languedoc-Roussillon region represents a strong planning initiative on the part of government to develop lands for tourism. This massive effort provided incentives for investors, brought new visitors to the region, and took some pressure off other tourism areas suffering from congestion, high prices, and air and water pollution.

Arguments continue about the impact of the resort development in the Languedoc-Roussillon region. Certainly, marsh lands and wildlife breeding grounds were lost. Planning and development were hasty. Little attention was paid to the value of the lands, marshes, and coastal areas as the project was initiated.[16] The development brought more auto traffic into southern France. Congestion intensified along major north-south routes through France and spread into northern Europe. From an economic perspective, this new region was seen as successful. Estimates are that 30,000 new jobs resulted from the region's tourism and commercial activity

Exhibit 4 Map of France

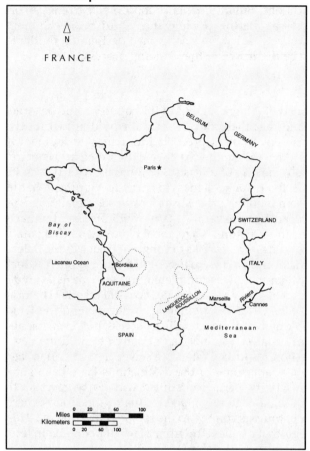

from 1965 to 1980. During a recent summer, tourists reportedly spent an estimated 3 billion francs in the resorts.[17]

Better planning took place in developing the second major oceanside resort in the Aquitaine.[18] The goals of the project included preserving the natural value of the coast and nurturing the area's economy. These efforts stood in contrast to the development-at-all-costs attitude in the Languedoc-Roussillon region. But even so, citizens criticized and attempted to block development efforts. The project has been moving at a slower pace, partly due to the economic downturns of the early 1980s and the resistance the project has faced over the years.[19] Exhibit 4 provides a map of France showing the tourism regions developed under the initiative of the French government.

The foregoing cases illustrate the positive and negative aspects of tourism planning and development at the regional and national levels. Local citizens, if not involved in the process, may feel left out of the plan and may resist the project.

Tourism development along the sensitive coastal zone of *any* country has serious ecological implications. Environmentally concerned citizens can bring such issues to a boil in protest—as was the case in France. Tourism development brings change and visitors—two factors that have concerned destination residents for ages. Such concerns should be addressed in the planning process.

Spain

Spain also reasoned that large regions of the country could be targeted for tourism development—and that these developments would attract tourists. In the early 1960s, the Spanish government promoted tourism development through several national policies. Areas along the coast were identified and construction began.

Unfortunately, the lure of tourists and foreign currency was stronger than the desire to plan effectively for such mass tourism development. In the early stages of development, Spain paid the price for its lack of solid planning. Tourism development was accompanied by several negative environmental impacts and a serious deficiency in the infrastructure. No regional planning mechanisms were in place—even in areas with considerable risks of congestion such as the Balearic Islands. Forests and rich agricultural land were lost—in addition to other valuable resources.[20]

After the development was completed, success was measured by the growing numbers of tours that appeared in the new coastal resorts. The price was right for the tourist. Inexpensive tours originating in Europe and the United States were available to people of modest means. Such success, however, had its consequences. Road and airport capacity was not large enough to hold the new influx of tourists—and congestion resulted. Water and sewer capacity often lagged behind demand.[21] In recent years, some of the destinations have been subject to negative types of tourism activity. Large tours filled with party-goers let their revelry get out of hand, creating a negative image for the region. Today, there is speculation that the number of tourists coming to the region is leveling off. This example illustrates the problems that can develop from a lack of planning. In this case, problems took fewer than 20 years to develop.

In its quest for the mass tourism market, Spain has also pushed the development of **tourism enclaves**. These enclaves are self-contained resort complexes that cater to all the needs of tourists arriving as part of a tour or other type of package. Spain has a series of such tourist enclaves designed to accommodate millions of visitors on tour each year. Reservations and billings are managed through computer systems. Restaurants, entertainment, recreational facilities, and activities are all on-site—catering to the convenience-seeking tourist with little interest in the community, its residents, the countryside, or local and regional culture.

Basically, these resorts were meant to appeal to the tourist looking for a good deal in an all-inclusive setting with tourists of similar backgrounds. Many tourists from Europe and North America select destinations with such factors in mind. Certain nationalities are more likely to vacation in one resort, while other nationalities may visit another.

Such regionalization of visitor patterns is evident in Spain's Canary Islands in the Mediterranean Sea. For example, one study revealed that 41% of the tourists on one of the Canary Islands were from the United Kingdom, while on another island,

The beaches, desert views, activities, and unique accommodations have made the Club Med village in Sonora, Mexico a popular tourism enclave for American tourists. (Courtesy of Club Med, New York, New York)

45% were from West Germany.[22] Such regionalization is even more pronounced at particular resorts. In some cases, most of the guests may be from just one country. Of course, the popularity of the package tour, language, and the desire for comfortable customs and mannerisms all contribute to visitor homogeneity.

Today, Spain is still one of the top three destinations in the world in terms of tourist volume. Even though the country has had difficulties with its tourism planning and development efforts, it still has the climate and resources to be popular with tourists from around the world. To a great degree, the success of tourism in southern Spain hinges on the resolution of the infrastructure and development problems that evolved over the last 15 years.

Portugal

The government of Portugal moved into tourism planning and development in a big way, focusing upon the area bordered by Lisbon on the northern coast and the Algrave on the southern coast.

Portugal took a slightly different approach than Spain. The tourism enclaves developed in southern Portugal are designed to attract the upscale tourists—those with more discretionary funds and time than the typical mass tourist. The accommodations available to the tourist at the planned tourism enclaves created this shift in targeted clientele. As one researcher notes:

> By 1984 over 90 per cent of foreign tourists stayed in three-star (or superior) hotels, compared to only 48 per cent of the domestic tourists. Together with the expansion of second homes, apartments, motels, tourist villages and camping, this led to considerable change in the types of accommodation being provided in response to a growing market segmentation.[23]

While most of the investments for developing these tourist areas were from private sources, the government offered financial assistance, incentives, permits, and permissions. The government also sponsored international promotions to spark interest in Portugal as an international tourism destination. Until recently, the pace of upgrading the infrastructure may have fallen behind the pace of building and development in some areas. Since Portugal's recent entry into the European Economic Community, funds have been more available from European lending institutions and programs to improve the infrastructure.[24]

A noticeable result of the planning and development efforts in these selected nations is this: development is more likely to occur in specific target locations. The result of such efforts will be tourist villages or enclaves where a high concentration of tourists play, sun, and relax—often without any contact with the local people or landscape. The same pattern of development has occurred in such islands as Jamaica in the Caribbean and in such peninsular areas as Mexico's Cancun. Tourism development in the United States is more scattered and fragmented—except for fully inclusive resorts. The visiting tourist has little choice but to meet and interact with local residents in their shops and community facilities.

What should be remembered from all these examples is that planning—centralized or local—is important to the long-term success of tourism, tourism businesses, and the quality of life for the local residents.

Endnotes

1. Clare Gunn, *Tourism Planning,* 2d ed. (New York: Taylor and Francis, 1988), p. 15.
2. Deirdre K. Hirner, Glenn Weaver, Craig W. Colton, Glenn A. Gillespie, and Bruce T. Cox, University of Missouri, Columbia, *Tourism USA—Guidelines for Tourism Development* (Washington, D.C.: U.S. Travel and Tourism Administration, Department of Commerce, 1986), p. 28.

3. Hirner, et al.

4. Hirner, et al., pp. 19–40.

5. *Community Tourism Action Plan,* revised, Process Book 3 (Edmonton, Alberta, Canada: Alberta Tourism, 1988).

6. *Survey of State Travel Offices 1989-1990* (Washington, D.C.: U.S. Travel Data Center, 1990), pp. 80–86.

7. John Lea, *Tourism and Development in the Third World* (New York: Routledge, 1988), pp. 6-7; 12-13.

8. Clare Gunn, *Vacationscape: Designing Tourist Regions,* 2d ed. (New York: Van Nostrand Reinhold, 1988), pp. 7–9.

9. Gunn, *Vacationscape,* p. 8.

10. Peter E. Murphy, *Tourism: A Community Approach* (New York: Methuen, 1985), p. 86.

11. Georgina Montgomery and Peter E. Murphy, "Government Involvement in Tourism and Development: A Case Study of TIDSA Implementation in British Columbia," in *Tourism in Canada: Selected Issues and Options,* edited by Peter E. Murphy (Victoria, British Columbia, Canada: University of Victoria, 1983), p. 184.

12. S. Gordon Phillips, "Organizing a Tourism System: The Ontario Example," in Robert Christie Mill and Alastair M. Morrison's *The Tourism System* (Englewood Cliffs, N.J.: Prentice-Hall, 1985), pp. 348–351.

13. *Community Tourism Action Program Guidelines* (Edmonton, Alberta, Canada: Alberta Tourism, 1988).

14. *CTAP Guidelines.*

15. John Tuppen, "France: the changing character of a key industry," in *Tourism and Economic Development: Western European Experiences,* edited by Allan M. Williams and Gareth Shaw (New York: Belhaven Press, 1988), p. 190.

16. Fred P. Bosselman, *In the Wake of the Tourist: Managing Special Places in Eight Countries* (Washington, D.C.: The Conservation Foundation, 1978), p. 62.

17. Tuppen, p. 190.

18. Bosselman, p. 63.

19. John Tuppen, *The Economic Geography of France* (Totowa, N.J.: Barnes & Noble Books, 1983), p. 341.

20. Manuel Valenzuela, "Spain: the phenomenon of mass tourism," in *Tourism and Economic Development: Western European Experiences,* edited by Allan M. Williams and Gareth Shaw (New York: Belhaven Press, 1988), p. 46.

21. Valenzuela, p. 46.

22. Valenzuela, p. 44.

23. Jim Lewis and Allan M. Williams, "Portugal: Market Segmentation and Regional Specialization," in *Tourism and Economic Development: Western European Experiences,* edited by Allan M. Williams and Gareth Shaw (New York: Belhaven Press, 1988), p. 102.

24. Lewis and Williams, p. 120.

Key Terms

leakage

life cycle

tourism development

tourism enclaves

tourism planning

Discussion Questions

1. What is the relationship of tourism planning to tourism development?

2. Why is it important for a community and its residents to be involved in tourism planning?

3. What are the ten basic steps in the tourism planning process presented by the USTTA?

4. How does the Canadian tourism planning model differ from the U.S. model? What are some of the basic steps?

5. What is the general role of the federal government in tourism planning?

6. What type of tourism planning occurs on the state, regional, and local levels?

7. What distinguishes private sector planning from government planning?

8. What are the general benefits of tourism development? What are the costs?

9. What challenges face the Third World in terms of tourism development?

10. What are the four life cycle stages associated with tourism development?

REVIEW QUIZ

When you feel you have covered all of the material in this chapter, answer these questions. Choose the *best* answer. Check your answers with the correct ones found on the Review Quiz Answer Key at the end of this book.

True (T) or False (F)

T   F   1. The process of preparing for tourism development is called tourism planning.

T   F   2. After evaluating alternative methods of meeting tourism goals and objectives, several approaches should be selected and used to guide further planning.

T   F   3. Most tourism planning occurs at the national or federal levels in centrally planned economies.

T   F   4. In some states, the Department of Transportation offers technical assistance to communities and is sometimes a funding partner.

T   F   5. Manufacturing plants located on the edge of town need not be considered in tourism planning and development.

T   F   6. Even though a Third World destination needs the business, jobs, and currency, certain amenities and a particular level of development may be beyond the ability of the community to deliver.

T   F   7. Investment risks are higher for Third World communities or governments than for foreign companies.

T   F   8. Tourism development in the Third World favors mass tourism.

T   F   9. If a tourism attraction is developed properly, it goes on forever.

T   F   10. Quality long-range planning should include strategies that address the decline stage.

Alternate/Multiple Choice

11. The success of a tourism project is threatened to the extent that the development is planned and constructed:

   a. without the support of the local residents.
   b. with the support of the local residents.

12. One thing that will doom a tourism plan is:

   a. asset and resource projection.
   b. unobtainable goals and objectives.
   c. labor availability studies.
   d. community asset and resource inventories.

13.   Most tourism planning in the United States occurs at the:

   a. local and regional level.
   b. state level.
   c. national level.
   d. multi-regional level.

14.   One of the benefits of tourism development might be:

   a. the increase in taxes collected.
   b. a decrease in taxes collected.

15.   When a country or region pays for imported goods—thus drawing monies from the local economy and funneling them into profits for the exporting nation—it is called:

   a. economic disparagement.
   b. leakage.

Marketing Plan is Simply a part of a Business Plan.

Marketing
↓
Sales.

Chapter Outline

The Evolution of Marketing
Business Perspectives
    Production Orientation
    Sales Orientation
    Marketing Orientation
    Societal Orientation
Product Life Cycles
    Introduction Stage
    Growth Stage
    Maturity Stage
    Decline Stage
Planning for Marketing
Marketing Plans
    Business Objectives
    Analyzing Marketing Conditions
    Analyzing the Competition
    Identifying Target Markets
    Developing a Marketing Strategy
    Budget Allocation
    Implementation and Evaluation

Learning Objectives

1. Trace the evolution of marketing in modern business and in tourism.

2. Identify and compare four business perspectives.

3. Characterize the four stages of the product life cycle.

4. Describe the importance, benefits, and seven elements of a quality tourism marketing plan.

5. Outline six elements marketing planners should consider when analyzing market conditions.

6. Recognize the importance of analyzing the competition and identifying target markets.

7. Identify variables involved in market segmentation and the criteria for evaluating various segments.

8. Indicate the purpose of developing a marketing strategy and objectives.

9. Define positioning and its five "Ds".

10. Specify the points that marketing planners should remember when implementing and evaluating a marketing plan.

10

Marketing Perspectives and Planning

MARKETING IS MORE THAN SELLING a product—like toothpaste—or even a service—like dry cleaning. In the tourism industry, marketing "sells" experiences. But marketing means more than just selling. It is, in fact, so central to tourism that all too often marketing overshadows other business activities in the complex picture of what tourism is all about.

Successful marketing influences the bottom line in all businesses. But in tourism, much like other service industries, marketing can contribute directly to tourist satisfaction and enjoyment. Satisfied customers generate more customers by spreading the good word and returning—all behaviors that eventually contribute to the bottom line. This is the reinforcing behavioral and business cycle that results from successful tourism marketing.

This chapter will briefly explore the development of marketing within the context of other business perspectives. It will also deal at some length with marketing planning issues and the development of a marketing plan.

The Evolution of Marketing

Traditionally, **marketing** was seen as a process of selling a product or service to people who may or may not have needed that particular product or service. Industrial heritage in many countries has shaped the way people have come to view business activities. Industrialization permitted Western societies to produce a range of consumer products efficiently and in mass. Once developed, these products had to be sold, delivered, and consumed—making selling an important business function. Marketing has evolved dramatically from its early beginning—as simply support for sales—to a business function which attempts to first identify, then satisfy, human needs and desires. This human side of marketing is especially important to tourism.

Marketing and its role in modern business have changed dramatically over the years. At first, marketing meant selling and was considered just one of the many functions of a business. Over time, as competition increased and the consumer became more sophisticated, marketing grew as a business function; customers' needs and desires began to be investigated and assessed. This evolution has led some to speculate that marketing is the major function of a company and should play a central role in all business activity.

233

Effective marketing involves everyone in a hospitality operation, from the general manager, to supervisors, to servers.

Marketing has undergone similar transformations in the tourism industry. At one time, advertising and promotion were enough to stimulate business. Now, the public and increasing competition demand more. In response, aggressive tourism companies have made marketing a pervasive process with the expectation that all members of the organization cooperate.

Marketing in the tourism industry is a continuous process in which management plans, researches, implements, controls, and evaluates activities designed to satisfy both the needs and wants of the customer and the objectives of the organization. To be most effective, marketing requires the efforts of everyone in an organization. Effectiveness, too, can be enhanced by the actions of complementary organizations.[1]

Successful marketing requires that tourism business management interact with both potential and actual tourists. This interaction may include promotions, advertising, sales, and the actual delivery of service. The basic task of marketing is to bring consumers and suppliers together by first learning who the consumers are and then seeing the business through their eyes.[2] It is important to know what the customer *wants* as opposed to simply selling what the organization has to sell. This differentiation reflects how marketing has evolved into a process that is responsive to people and their needs.

Business Perspectives

Marketing is a business perspective and an orientation—a mental set or approach to doing business. Several business perspectives apply to how a business should create and distribute a product or service.[3] These include production, sales, marketing, and societal orientations.

Production Orientation

The major function of a business with a **production orientation** is to produce goods and services as efficiently as possible; the needs of customers play only a small role. Production-oriented companies sometimes overlook the needs of the customer in the interest of furthering the production process. For example, a production-oriented tour company might overlook the comfort of its customers by making time schedules too tight. The number of tourists rushed through a tour operation (production) becomes the goal—instead of customer satisfaction.

Production-oriented tourism enterprises are often short-sighted when it comes to understanding customer needs and desires. For example, an amusement park may offer attractions based on their best guess of what customers want. When attendance at one or more of those attractions declines, park management may attempt to bolster sagging sales by increased promotion rather than eliminating or changing the attractions.

Sales Orientation

Businesses with a **sales orientation** try to market a product or service over time by trying to improve the sales effort. More salespersons may be hired, more ads taken out, and more sales training conducted, but little may be done to modify the product or service to satisfy the customer. In tourism, competition can change dramatically and quickly. A hotel may offer an acceptable product or service, but as tastes change, hotel management may respond by hiring more salespersons, and paying for more advertisements instead of changing with the trends. As a result, that hotel will miss opportunities afforded by the changing market. While a sales orientation may provide short-term improvements, it will not solve the fundamental reality of changing trends.

Marketing Orientation

A **marketing orientation** is a comprehensive approach that requires the business to be in touch with the marketplace—the shifting tastes and preferences of consumers. A business that is marketing-oriented is customer-oriented. A true marketing orientation requires that all employees be sensitive not only to the goals of the organization, but to the importance of the customer. Customer satisfaction is all-important. A marketing orientation seeks to discover the customer's likes, dislikes,

Exhibit 1   Comparison of Marketing and Production Perspectives for a Resort

| | Orientation | |
Issue	Marketing	Production
Attitude toward the tourist	Happy tourists with satisfied needs are critical to the resort	Keep the tourists coming, the more the better, keep them moving through
"Product"	Hospitality services and accommodations are designed to satisfy the tourist and modified as tourist needs change	What you see is what you get, no special effort to offer novel desirable amenities
Customer service	Critical, besides the accommodations; extra services are provided with a smile	The room is clean and available, no need to pay attention to other tourist needs while on site
Advertising	Aimed at tourist need satisfaction and benefits	Aimed at showing what a great facility the resort is, little attention to tourist satisfaction
Sales force	Help the tourist find the right vacation amenities at the resort	Bring in the tourists, little attention to fit between type of tourist and resort

Source: E. Jerome McCarthy and William Perreault, Jr., *Basic Marketing: A Managerial Approach*, 9th ed. (Homewood, Ill.: Irwin, 1987), p. 31.

and desires. Once these things are known, products and services can be created or modified accordingly.

Change is a given in the competitive tourism industry. Tourists are always searching for new experiences—and tourism businesses must be quick to provide them. In short, a marketing orientation is a must for all tourism businesses.

A marketing orientation has the potential to alter the thinking of everyone in a tourism business. Exhibit 1 shows the implications of different business orientations for a resort. The exhibit shows how management and employees would respond to a tourist depending on their business orientation.

When a marketing perspective prevails, the whole organization is prepared to meet the demands of the visitor. All employees—from the CEO to the janitor—are vitally concerned with customer satisfaction. For example, the marketing-oriented resort wants satisfied tourists who will truly enjoy their stay. The production-oriented company, however, may only care that so many persons were booked that day and pay little attention to whether tourists and accommodations fit. Such a production-oriented resort might not have the foresight to avoid booking a seclusion-seeking couple in the same section as a large group of college students on spring break.

Societal Orientation

A more recent and sometimes controversial perspective is the **societal orientation**. Like the marketing orientation, the societal orientation operates on the premise that consumer wants and needs are very important. However, this perspective goes beyond individual wants and desires and addresses longer-term social and community needs and interests. A societal orientation suggests that certain types of products or services may not be in the best interest of either the consumer or society.

Over the last 20 years, businesses have faced this dilemma: What should be done when a product, however popular, is known to have a negative impact upon either the customer or society? The auto industry presently faces this dilemma in terms of customers' desire for large cars and the increased energy consumption and pollution attributed to larger cars. Similarly, tobacco industry profits come from a product that is labeled as dangerous to personal and public health. These are difficult issues for such companies. But as one researcher speculates: "To the extent societal marketing appears profitable, companies can be expected to give it serious consideration."[4]

Within the tourism industry, societal marketing has, to some extent, been in fashion for a number of years. Spas and resorts offer health treatments and relaxation—activities that are good for the consumer and, arguably, good for society.

Societal orientation continues to play a role in tourism today. First, a sensitivity to social values and the well-being of tourists provides new products and services to the traveling public and, to an increasing extent, protects environments. New products may develop simply because they are seen as healthful and important to the tourist. For example, many hotels now offer no-smoking rooms to guests who desire them. This recent marketing development is customer-oriented and has positive societal attributes. Finally, the open courtyard design of some new hotels is not only attractive, but offers visual safety and a strong sense of security to the person traveling alone.

The true business and social values of the societal marketing perspective have yet to be fully understood. What is clear is this: tourism businesses that use such an approach in good faith will gain public favor and correspondingly increased business. As the public becomes more sensitive to health, the environment, and other social issues, businesses that ignore the societal values held by the traveling public do so at the peril of losing market share and profits.

Product Life Cycles

Products and services go through changes over time. This process of change has predictable patterns and is referred to as the **product life cycle**. For example, think of how a tourism business starts out. Basically, the business is established and begins to offer services. If the services are popular, the business will flourish. In this growth period, the business expands and may even offer new services or variations on the original services. At some point, the business may stabilize and begin to taper off. For many, this means a business decline, and, sometimes, the end of the business. The four stages which make up the product life cycle are: *introduction, growth, maturity,* and *decline*.[5]

Introduction Stage

In the introduction stage, the product or service is developed and made available. In this stage, customers see or hear about the product or service for the first time.

Jogging trails are part of the fitness packages offered by some hotels in an attempt to attract and retain the health-conscious traveler. (Courtesy of Camel View—A Radisson Resort, Scottsdale, Arizona)

New products and services usually need a lot of promotion in order to get the word out that the product exists and to describe its features and attributes.

In recent years, new tourism products and services have included all-suite hotels, "frequent flyer" and "frequent stay" programs offered by major airlines and hotel chains, an "underwater" hotel in Florida, timesharing, and such unique activities as swimming with dolphins, baseball training with professional ballplayers, and cruises with theme programs and shows. New packages aimed at changing customer tastes are a constant component of the tourism industry.

In the introduction stage, the competition may just be starting to copy or improve upon the service or product. In the tourism industry, it does not take long for a new product to be copied and for the competition to become very keen. For example, a new airfare package can often be duplicated within days.

Growth Stage

As the name implies, the growth stage features growth in the volume of sales and profits. Growth may continue indefinitely, but that is rarely the case. Companies that have consistently grown over the years have consistently and quickly adapted to new market and economic forces. Plus, they have added to their service or product lines. Marketing and consumption are not static processes; a service or product that is static will surely fail in the long term. Recent tourism services and products in the growth stage are golf resorts and adventure travel packages.

During the growth stage, competition increases and improvements are made to the product or service by both the original business and by competitors.[6] Advertising promotion intensifies, and there is a rush to meet the growing demand by all competitors. At some point, prices may be reduced to maintain customer loyalty.[7] For many businesses, profits tend to flatten in the latter part of the growth stage.

Maturity Stage

In the maturity stage, growth rates decline and sales level off. Today, many tourism businesses are in the maturity stage. These include some older motel and hotel chains, some traditional tourism destinations, a few rental car companies, and certain airlines. While these companies are currently large and successful, they stand to enter the next stage of the life cycle if they do not continually change and modify their marketing approaches. The repeated airfare wars of recent years represent one strategy used by maturing tourism businesses that are striving to expand growth.

To maintain profits and sales during the maturity stage, several approaches are possible.[8] Products and services can be modified, enhanced, or changed and the "new and improved version" placed on the market. A different market niche can be discovered or expanded. Through advertising and promotion, customers can be encouraged to increase their use of a product or service—or even to find new uses for an old product or service. Prices can be reduced at the same time that advertising is increased. Means of distribution or of informing the customer about the product can be changed.

Companies facing this stage of the product life cycle must consider all such strategies for stimulating sales and profits. Refurbished airplanes, hotels with gyms and spas, and mobile phones in rental cars are other examples of such strategies.

Decline Stage

Many mature businesses seem to be larger than ever, never seeming to fall into decline. Consider, for instance, IBM, certain major airlines, or McDonald's. The long-term success of these companies lies in several strategies—strategies that require solid marketing research, planning, and implementation. Marketing is a process; if done well, it increases the chance of success and permits a business to avoid the last stage of the product life cycle.

Other businesses are too slow in adapting to changing tastes and economic forces and thus face eventual decline or even failure. Witness the tremendous decline in rail use over the past 50 years. As Theodore Levitt observed:

> They let others take customers away from them because they assumed themselves to be in the railroad business rather than in the transportation business. The reason they defined their industry wrong was because they were railroad-oriented instead of transportation-oriented; they were product-oriented instead of customer-oriented.[9]

In short, avoiding decline means knowing what business one is in and being prepared to frequently redefine it. This is not a new theme or concern. Since Levitt's observation years ago, many have called for a strong customer orientation and the need to understand that service is paramount to the success of tourism businesses. Put succinctly and dramatically: "Service is not *a* competitive edge, it is *the* competitive edge."[10] It is important not to lose sight of this point in the planning and execution of a tourism marketing plan.

Planning for Marketing

Today, business success requires planning. Facilities, human resources, and marketing all require major planning efforts if a modern tourism business is to succeed. All planning implies a concern for the future. Businesses need to consider *alternative* futures and plan for each in order to increase the probability that planning goals will be achieved.

New businesses, especially, require a **business plan**. If for no other reason, new businesses need a plan to provide documentation on a business's potential for success—documentation required by lending institutions. Such business plans will invariably include extensive information about the market conditions: competition, potential demand, and the like. For established businesses, the **marketing plan** is usually part of a larger, longer-term, general business plan or corporate strategy. While the marketing plan focuses on potential markets and methods to reach them, its objectives have to mesh with those of the business as a whole. For example, it would be inappropriate for a resort to propose a marketing objective to increase its market share of novice underwater divers if expanding the capacity of the training pool and dive charter boat were not part of the overall business plan.

The marketing plan should be a written document. With a written plan to refer to, management and staff can avoid misunderstanding, distractions, and diversions. A written plan can also reveal new opportunities. Listed below are other benefits of marketing plans:[11]

1. **Point of reference.** A marketing plan provides a reference point for all members of the organization. The plan lays out the required activities to be completed and often, by whom. The plan orients organization members, consultants, and other service vendors employed by the organization.

2. **Key market focus.** The marketing plan targets key markets so the organization can avoid expending effort on markets that offer less potential.

3. **Integration of objectives and priorities.** A good marketing plan clarifies how much and what kind of attention should be given to the various target markets. It establishes priorities for promotion, budgets, and management and staff activities.

4. **Criteria for success.** Through the statement of objectives, the marketing plan creates criteria by which to measure success. These goals and objectives can be compared to actual achievements in sales, market share, net profits, or other measures of success.

5. **Continuity.** The marketing plan offers the organization continuity. Staff and management may come and go, but the plan will provide a blueprint for activity over time for both new and old members.

Marketing plans vary in detail, content, and scope; all should provide a road map on how to proceed which will inform and guide the efforts of all members of the organization.

Marketing Plans

Marketing plans vary in structure and process. This section offers a synthesis of two types of plans, one drawn from hospitality[12] and one from recreation.[13] Important elements of a quality tourism marketing plan include:

- A set of business objectives
- An analysis of current and projected market conditions
- An analysis of the competition
- An identification of target markets—or the **market mix**
- Development of a marketing strategy—or the **marketing mix**
- Budget allocation
- Implementation and evaluation

Business Objectives

The first step in developing a marketing plan is to decide on the business objectives. For a tourism business, objectives would include making a profit and hopefully satisfying customers. A state travel office's objectives would not include "making a profit," but rather "satisfying customers (visitors)" and, possibly, increasing the total number of visitors to the state during a given time frame. A restaurant association might establish a primary objective of increasing membership. This, in turn, could fulfill a secondary objective of generating increased operating revenue through increased membership fees.

Objectives should provide guidance for operations and key management decisions. Objectives, too, should constitute a standard by which effectiveness can be measured. This means that objectives should be measurable or quantifiable in some way, and doable within a given time frame. Objectives should be reviewed regularly and modified if conditions or circumstances change radically.

A simple set of objectives for a resort could be as follows:

Over the next three years the hotel located within the resort complex will increase occupancy rates by 2% and revenues by 3%. At the end of the three-year period, management will be able to measure performance and determine if the objectives set forth in the marketing plan were actually met and if not met, what is needed for improvement.

Objectives should be simple and realistic. Achievable objectives are better than "pie in the sky" objectives which only lead to failure. Also, objectives for different parts of the organization should not conflict. In the preceding example, the objectives for the hotel within the resort complex suggest growth. However, managers of the pool, spa, and restaurant might think growth unrealistic because their particular facilities are too small and understaffed. A marketing plan with clearly outlined objectives would detect such apparent conflicts and resolve them before developing the rest of the marketing plan. A successful marketing plan integrates the objectives of entities within the organization as well as the developmental and economic goals of the region.

Analyzing Marketing Conditions

All marketing efforts require a comprehensive analysis of the context in which a product or service is to be sold. Planning to market a service should not take place without understanding the social, political, and economic circumstances, and trends which may influence the satisfaction of customers, sales, and profits. The term **marketing conditions** refers to the social and economic context within which a tourism service or product is exchanged. In traditional marketing approaches, analyzing these conditions is often referred to as "environmental scanning."[14] Analyzing or assessing market conditions would appear to be a common sense component of marketing plans. Unfortunately, planners often neglect this important component. Many may avoid dealing with business, social, and cultural circumstances because they can do so little about them. In the marketing plan, these circumstances are sometimes called external factors. While they may be beyond the control of the management, external factors must be recognized, their potential effects on marketing analyzed, and marketing strategies implemented which will either ameliorate or capitalize on those effects. For example, smart tourism businesses are closely monitoring the travel tastes of the "baby boom" generation as this potent market segment matures in age and in earnings—both factors which free up discretionary time and income for travel.

In today's world, change is constant and rapid; change is so rapid that marketing plans made today are likely to be outdated by the time they are implemented. The frequently used example is the company that continued to make buggy whips at the time automobiles were replacing horses as a means of transportation. Technological innovations were about to revolutionize transportation and travel behavior. Businesses who saw change coming had time to prepare and provide products and services that fit the market conditions of a new and changing travel period. Those that did not look ahead lost profits—and sometimes their businesses.

Successful tourism businesses must analyze societal changes and trends and prepare for their ramifications. Several market conditions must be analyzed and treated in the context of the marketing plan: demographics, culture, technology, economics, politics and policy, and the natural environment.

Demographics. **Demographics** is the study of groups of people, particularly the characteristics and trends of various groups *within* a population or *compared to* other population groups. For example, the population of the world is increasing dramatically each year. Growth, however, is occurring primarily in less-developed countries; growth in Western nations has slowed considerably, with a consequent "aging" of their populations. Related to population growth are population shifts due to migration within countries or to immigration. Such demographic factors will have profound implications for tourism and travel in the years ahead. Another demographic factor compares age groups within a population. The maturation of the U.S. population—especially the baby boom generation—will continue to alter the nature of tourism for years to come. As this predominant age group matures, tourism businesses will likely increase those activities which appeal to older travelers. For example, the increasing popularity of golfing may be partly due to the maturation of the American and European populations. As J.W. Marriott, Jr., recently stated, resort complexes of the future will not be built without an accompanying golf course.[15]

The swelling populations of developing countries will have to be considered as new markets for tourism products and travel services. As segments of these large populations become economically successful, they will begin to represent a growing share of the tourism market—much like the expansion of the Japanese travel market that accompanied Japan's economic success and stability.

Migration is another demographic trend worth watching. In the United States, migration to the sunbelt over the last 10 to 15 years created many economic opportunities for tourism and travel. Airport development in the Southwest and West reflects population growth. Phoenix, Arizona, for example, is experiencing rapid population growth and has become a popular resort destination. This upturn has spurred resort development, airport expansion, and the growth of affiliated travel businesses, such as car rental agencies.

Migration also affects those areas that people have left behind. In the early 1980s, the Midwest experienced a decline in population. On the positive side, resorts and tourist destinations may be less crowded and experience less development pressure. The downside is that there may not be enough people left in the region to keep tourism going. The image of a region suffering economic difficulties fosters economic downturns. In sum, demographic trends—be they birth rate, migration, or aging—all significantly influence tourism, and must be taken into account by an effective marketing plan.

Social and Cultural Conditions. Effective marketing must take cultural and social conditions and trends into account. In the modern global marketplace, social and cultural shifts will become more and more complex and will occur more rapidly. This poses increasing challenges for tourism marketing—especially to international travelers.

Marketing planning must be informed about the traditional values associated with a nation's dominant culture, as well as cultural norms of various subcultures. The manner of dress around the pool in one country can be different from that of another. The traditional siesta of Latin American cultures reflects time use patterns that are different from those practiced in the United States. A lack of cultural understanding can lead to cultural conflicts in marketing efforts.

The relationship between culture and tourism can be viewed from a number of different perspectives. First, culture can be seen as the *motivation* for travel. A family may vacation in Ireland specifically to experience the culture, local customs, and folkways. Culture can also be seen as a *precondition* for travel. In other words, people of certain cultures may be more inclined or able to travel than those of other cultures. Within the marketing context, cultural factors must be reviewed to determine if they support or hinder travel. In a recent presentation, the President of Fuji Tours of Japan noted that in Japan, the social and cultural norm seems to be that newlyweds—if they can afford it—travel abroad for their honeymoon.[16]

The United States is a society which contains several subcultures such as Hispanic, Jewish, and African-American. Each has characteristics of the dominant American culture, but also possesses and maintains unique customs, beliefs, attitudes, or norms. The organization of culture and society is relevant to a marketing plan because the various social groups have different preferences and predispositions for tourism and travel. For many years, tourism businesses courted only the dominant culture. More insightful businesses began to incorporate minority cultural preferences into their marketing strategies and profited greatly from this untapped potential.

Family lifestyle changes, health consciousness, concern for diet and food quality, and the practice of saving money constitute other social and cultural norms for tourism decision-makers to consider. Take, for example, different cultural attitudes toward saving. The Japanese, encouraged by both culture and government, are avid savers. As a result, many have the funds to travel and have become, aside from the West Germans, one of the dominant travel markets in the world.

The "good old days" are no longer. People, society, and the world have changed—and so have lifestyles. The American dream of owning a home is still alive, but that home may be smaller and loaded with technological devices to make life more enjoyable. The "average" household may no longer include "2.5" children. Work patterns have changed; many people now work on flexible schedules which allow more discretionary time for leisure, recreation, and tourism.

While tourism is associated with leisure time, trends in work patterns and changing attitudes toward work must be recognized. Many Americans are becoming more sensitive to self-fulfillment; they are providing their own definitions of success, their own ideas about what constitutes quality of life. For most, work is still very important, but there appears to be less belief in the philosophy that hard work is going to serve one well through a lifetime. Most likely, travel will continue to be an important part of one's lifestyle and may eventually be perceived as a right as well as a privilege.

Technology. Electronic technology has made it possible to turn one's home into a recreation and leisure center. Looking ahead, tourism professionals have to be concerned about the extent that high-technology homes will cut into the travel market. As an example, a recent study of affluent Americans (income $50,000-plus) indicates that 72% prefer to spend their leisure time at home rather than find entertainment about town.[17] Such a finding clearly has implications for the hospitality industry—particularly for restaurants and entertainment facilities.

However, technological innovation can and does provide new opportunities for the tourism industry. New technologies have reduced the cost of travel (more efficient planes and automobiles), contributed to new types of tourism destinations ("hi-tech" attractions at amusement parks), and produced innovations in reservations, profit management, and demand forecasting (new computer reservations systems and analysis software programs). The marketing plan must consider unfolding changes in technology that may offer competitive advantages, create new customer expectations, or alter the destination itself. A clear example of technology reshaping tourism destinations can be seen at attractions such as Disneyland and Disney World.

Unquestionably, the computer ranks foremost among the changes wrought by technology. The computer is changing the character of the home, the workplace, *and* the tourism industry. Computers pervade the industry—from the terminals at the hotel front desk to the in-room, guest-operated devices in fully automated properties. Such systems vary in design and affect the manner in which guests check in and check out. Some use in-room computer terminals or guestroom telephones to access and display information on a guestroom television screen—much like the on-screen programming featured on many of today's VCRs. Business travelers can be seen toting lightweight portable computers to use while in-flight, during layovers, and in hotel rooms. A hotel that caters to such a trend, through room design and auxiliary attachments such as rental printing machines, could have an edge in attracting business travelers.[18]

Advances in video technology have brought tourism adventure and travel excitement into our homes. It is now possible to rent a video on travel in Germany, and use the information for future travel decisions. Potential buyers in the leisure timeshare market can borrow a video of a potential timeshare site; they can then review the video in their own home without actually traveling to the site and talking to salespersons. If the prospective timeshare were in Hawaii, that video could save more than a few dollars!

Other technological developments which could influence tourism include new materials research, biotechnology, health research, communications, transportation, artificial intelligence, and fiber optics. Breakthroughs in any of these areas could change our understanding of tourism and the process of travel. *Total Recall*, an Arnold Schwarzenegger movie released in the summer of 1990, featured a travel agency providing a new twist on "armchair" travel—clients were strapped into a chair while customized memories of a complete vacation were electronically planted in their brain cells! Whether or not "memory" travel is one of the technological marvels awaiting the tourism industry, marketing plans must keep abreast of new technology or risk early obsolescence.

Economic Conditions. The most obvious marketing condition monitored by market managers is the economy. The general state of the economy is basic to all marketing plans. Important, too, is the health of the economy in particular regions or countries where target markets reside. High unemployment, inflation, and increasing interest rates are economic conditions that can inhibit travel and tourism. In inflationary times, money does not buy as much—meaning that buying power is diminished. The discretionary dollar is stretched and the potential tourist may have fewer funds available for tourism. Mass tourism is sensitive to recession with its unemployment, layoffs, and reduced credit.

Travel volume decreased during the recession of the early 1980s. Travel did not really fully recover until 1987. Then, volume surpassed the previous high in 1981—just before the recession got underway.[19] Business travel is also sensitive to the health of the general economy. Hotels, motels, and rental car agencies feel the effect immediately when economic conditions weaken as travel activity falls off.

International tourism is sensitive to currency exchange rates which are the product of a nation's economic health. Foreign arrivals to the United States accelerated in the mid- to late-1980s as the dollar weakened against the currencies of Japan, England, and Germany. Although Americans are also sensitive to exchange rates, overseas travel has remained relatively strong for U.S. travelers—despite the decline of the dollar.[20]

Other economic factors should be accounted for in the marketing plan. A few select indices and their effect on tourism include:

- Durable goods purchases (may compete with tourism for discretionary dollars)

- Interest rates (increased costs to borrow vacation money)

- Energy costs (may increase airline fares and the costs of auto trips)

- Availability of discretionary and disposable income after taxes (money available for travel and other purchases)

Marketers should also observe the business cycle. Whether the economy is moving in or out of a recession will definitely affect tourism.

Politics and Policy. As an industry, tourism is very vulnerable to the shifting winds of politics, governmental policy, and national and regional security. Before packing their bags, tourists must feel that they will be safe when visiting another country. Furthermore, certain governmental policies may foster or hinder travel abroad or even within regions. Monetary policies that restrict how much currency tourists may take abroad can influence travel flow patterns. Visa, passport, and length of stay policies can also have a positive or negative effect on tourism. Deregulation of the airline industry is another example of a political decision which affected tourism.

Even today—as throughout history—political calm and security within destination countries is essential to fostering tourism. Terrorism through the 1980s had a profound influence on travelers' perceptions of certain countries and, consequently, on their travel plans. The student protests and killings in China in June of 1989 had an immediate impact. Cruise line visits, general travel, and packaged tours from around the world were halted immediately after this tragedy. It will take years before travel to China returns to normal.

Natural Environment. The environment has always been a decisive variable for travelers around the world. Trips to exotic locations have been an attraction for travelers for centuries. Mountain retreats, beautiful beaches, and exotic islands are primary destinations for millions of people.

Today, the quality of the natural and physical environment has become a criterion on which travel decisions are based. Overdevelopment, air pollution, beach pollution, water quality, and sanitary conditions are growing concerns for the tourist and the tourism industry. It is difficult to package an oceanfront vacation tour for tourists who know or even think the beach is polluted and littered. It is foolhardy for the marketing manager to ignore environmental and natural resource issues when making marketing decisions. Given economic and political stability, the long-term health of a particular destination's environment is the next most important consideration for marketing managers.

Analyzing the Competition

The success of any business partially rests in understanding the competition. Since change in tourism is so constant and rapid, competition must also be monitored. Changes in business practices, in attractions, and destination offerings can have immediate consequences for a business.

Monitoring starts with simple questions such as: Who are the competition? Where are they located? What do they offer that is different? What do they have that is similar or better? Simple techniques can help answer these questions. For example, one could use the phone book to count the number of direct competitors located in the immediate area. One might also observe competitors' business practices and levels of business activity. One might consider personally sampling the service and facilities of a competitor. This is a good way to learn about the competition and about new ways of doing things. Monitoring the literature in the appropriate trade magazines, publications, newsletters, and through affiliated associations may prove useful. In some cases, a business might hire consultants to assist in monitoring the competition, and in assessing one's own weaknesses and strengths relative to the competition.

Competition in the tourism industry includes similar and dissimilar businesses, and a host of events, attractions, and potential uses of the traveler's time and discretionary income. As an example, the hotel trying to position itself as a weekend getaway not only competes with other hotels, but with a host of home-based events ranging from the Saturday night barbecue at the park to the showing of the new movie release on the family VCR.

Identifying Target Markets

Two of the central questions of a modern marketing plan will be "Who buys our product or service and who else could we sell to?" In today's marketplace the answer is far from simple. In tourism as in other industries, there is too much competition and too many expensive ways to reach every potential customer. Modern marketing plans, through market research, seek to identify **target markets**. Target markets are distinctly defined groupings of potential buyers at which sellers aim or "target" their marketing efforts. The more that is known about the target markets, the more efficiently marketing efforts can be designed to reach and persuade them.

For a hotel, the most obvious "targets" are business travelers and pleasure travelers. Traditionally, hotels have a higher percentage of occupancy during *weekends* due to the pleasure traveler, or tourist. While weekend occupancy is near capacity during the summer season, it is considerably lower during other seasons. To obtain higher overall occupancy, hotel management will seek to increase *weekday* occupancy—an objective best served by courting the business traveler. Sales trips, conventions, conferences, and other business activities tend to take place during weekdays. This combination of different markets targeted by one supplier is known as the market mix. If the hotel in our example has enough business and pleasure travelers to assure an overall occupancy of, say, 90% or more, it could be said to have an ideal market mix.

However, hotel management may wish to further break down the broad target markets into smaller segments to more efficiently focus its marketing efforts on a more distinctly defined target market. Remember, the more you know about a target market, the more you are able to attract and serve it. This process of breaking down a market into more clearly identifiable segments is called **market segmentation**. Let's go back to our hotel to see, in simplified terms, how market segmentation might work.

First, we segment our business traveler target since it's too cumbersome a target to serve efficiently. Accordingly, many hotels further break this target into smaller segments—most prominent of which is the *corporate* business traveler. The corporate traveler is often considered a more desirable target market because it is perceived to provide a higher and more consistent volume of occupancy. Therefore, our hotel will seek to increase corporate business while maintaining the level of general business occupancy. Also, since large corporations are relatively few in number, our hotel can now concentrate its marketing efforts (and budget) more concisely.

This does not mean that our hotel will neglect its pleasure traveler. Our hotel may segment its potential pleasure market into categories. These targets could be:

- Single guests, ages 21–35

- Couples, ages 25–45, without children or who want a weekend away from the children

- Families

Some hotels establish a long-term reputation by targeting families—offering family weekend specials and emphasizing activities for the children. Others—depending on the appropriateness of their facilities—will target families for one part of the off-season, and singles or married couples without children for another part of the season. If our hotel were to try to appeal to all the above segments at the same time, it would likely fail. Couples seeking the romantic would certainly clash with a bunch of boisterous, fun-loving kids—an inappropriate market mix, to say the least.

Market Segmentation. As our hotel example illustrates, there are many ways to segment a market. Segments can be developed based on a number of variables[21] including:

1. **Geography**—counties, regions, countries, city size, market area, travel distance

2. **Demographics**—age, sex, family size, family life cycle, income, occupation, household size, second-home ownership

3. **Products and Services**—benefits sought, equipment type (RV, scuba, etc.), loyalty, user status (first time, heavy user, etc.), purchase behavior (frequent flyer members)

Business travelers enjoy the many amenities and services afforded by hotel marketing strategies. (Courtesy of the Radisson Mart Plaza Hotel, Miami, Florida)

4. **Psychographics**—lifestyle, personality, attitudes, interests, opinions, motivations

Depending on the specific tourism business, one or more of these variables could be useful in the marketing process. In the case of a restaurant, a geographic segmentation—defining a target segment close to the establishment—might be most appropriate. In addition, the geographic segment might be further divided by income to target those families in the middle- to upper-income levels. Choosing which segments to target is not easy, but it is an important part of the market plan. A review of market analyses for similar businesses may be a useful starting point. Personal knowledge of the business may also suggest useful variables for consideration.

Several criteria can be used to evaluate the usefulness of various segmentations. Market segments should be:

1. **Substantial**—They must be large enough to be worthy of the marketing effort.

2. **Exploitable**—They must be uniquely defined according to needs and preferences, so much so that a segment can be readily exploited by responding to its

needs and preferences. An analysis of how well a new product or service meets the preferences of a targeted segment in relation to the existing competition is sometimes called the **competitive criteria**.[22]

3. **Identifiable and Accessible**—The characteristics of a segment should permit it to be identified and located; to be reachable by advertising or other forms of promotion; and once reached, accessible to the service or the product offered.

4. **Durable**—A potential market segment should be lasting or durable.[23] For instance, a fast-food chain considers locating a new outlet in a geographic area which is changing from a family-oriented population to a retirement community. The teenage segment might be worth targeting for a year or two but, in the long term, unprofitable. The marketer must be convinced that the segment pursued has the duration required to yield a profit.

As we have seen, potential or target markets are identified by market segmentation. Sometimes, further study reveals that a market segment is too small, too difficult to reach, or uses the service or product too infrequently. The marketing plan must provide a careful evaluation of market segments to ensure that those segments chosen as target markets are worth pursuing or *targeting*.

Developing a Marketing Strategy

Once the appropriate targets are identified and analyzed, the marketing plan will develop a strategy to profitably exploit them. The marketing strategy attempts to reach and persuade the target markets through a wide range of tactics and tools—chiefly, advertising and promotion. Furthermore, it will "prioritize" and "customize" tactics and tools to each target market in order to obtain the optimal use of the human and financial resources available.

The overall mixture of marketing tactics and tools employed to capture all of the target markets is called the marketing mix. (To avoid confusion, remember the "market" in "market mix" is a noun—market mix refers to the combination of markets targeted by the marketing plan. "Market*ing*," on the other hand, is a verb; it implies action. So, "market*ing* mix" refers to all the *actions* suggested by the marketing strategy.)

Establishing Target Market Objectives. Like the business objectives discussed earlier, the objectives for each target market should be simple, specific, and quantifiable. An objective for a Florida resort might be as follows:

> Increase guest nights by five percent among tourists from three Midwest city markets (Chicago, Detroit, and Minneapolis) during the winter months over the next three years.

This is clear, to the point, and identifies the segments which will be targeted. Like objectives for the business as a whole, objectives for each target market limit and focus the marketing activity. Objectives help clarify how to spend the marketing budget and provide criteria to be evaluated later.

Positioning. Positioning—in its marketing context—is a potent concept. It is a marketing strategy which attempts to "position" a product or service favorably in

The Grand Hotel has established a secure spot in the resort marketplace. (Courtesy of the Grand Hotel, Mackinac Island, Michigan)

comparison with the competition or "position" it to better serve particular market segments. Well before a product or service enters the marketplace, market research should reveal how well it can be expected to appeal to various market segments and how well it compares with the existing or potential competition. The product or service can be *positioned* to reach target markets not reached or ill-served by the competition, or it can be positioned by virtue of its design or conceptual superiority to the competition.

Positioning—especially as a component of a marketing strategy—offers yet another tactic: *image.* If you can't re-design your product or service or favorably position it to capture different markets, you may be able to change consumers' perceptions of it. Is baking soda perceived by consumers as a product for baking? Is it a product that fights nasty refrigerator smells? Or is it a toothpaste targeting upscale, health-conscious "yuppies"? Take your pick—or, more accurately, *position* it.

To further clarify positioning, one researcher offers the following *five "Ds" of positioning:*[24]

1. **Document**—Identify (document) the benefits that are most important to the tourists expected to use the service or product.

2. **Decide**—Decide what image you want to project to the selected markets.

3. **Differentiate**—Identify the competition and determine how your product or service differs from that of the competition.

4. **Design**—Build these differences into the product or service; use the marketing mix to convey these differences to the target markets.

5. **Deliver**—Provide the consumer what was promised.

Two things should also be noted about positioning. First, although positioning includes perception, it is not *merely* perception. Second, the product or service must meet the expectations established by positioning.

Budget Allocation

Once the marketing strategy has been detailed, it is time to determine how much money must be budgeted in order to implement each component of the strategy. Presumably, many possible marketing strategies will have already been eliminated as too costly, or—and this is most often the case—management will have already imposed a ceiling for spending on marketing efforts. Given such a limit on spending, the marketing plan must allocate a limited amount of money available to implement each activity proposed by the marketing strategy.

Budget allocation should be relatively easy if the marketing strategy has been carefully constructed—that is, if the target markets are clearly identified according to their potential profitability and each element of the marketing mix rated according to its potential impact. Budget allocation adheres to a hierarchy of priorities. The target market with the greatest potential for profit will be allocated the biggest piece of the budget pie.

As the marketing plan is implemented, it may become apparent that money is needed for further market research, or for a type of advertising not envisioned by the marketing mix, or for a variety of unforeseen factors. The marketing plan budget should anticipate and provide for these contingencies insofar as possible.

Implementation and Evaluation

It has often been said about affairs of the heart that "timing is everything." Timing is also crucial to the implementation of the marketing plan. For example, if the marketing plan calls for a "saturation" advertising campaign, a series of radio spots must be timed to coincide with, closely precede, or follow other media placements. Marketing plans should include a tightly reasoned, detailed implementation schedule. For large tourism businesses, the implementation schedule may not only be exceptionally detailed, but include the assignment of specific managers to oversee each element and provide systematic progress reports for top management.

Having forecast the desired results of each component of the marketing strategy, the marketing plan should help a tourism business prepare for the results of implementation. If a restaurant marketing plan, for instance, projects a heavy influx of Sunday traffic as a result of setting in motion a particular marketing strategy, the restaurant manager had better hire sufficient staff. It would be far better to pay for over-staffing than to be understaffed and disappoint the new customers that the property worked so hard to obtain.

Finally, to paraphrase the poet—"The best laid plans often get lost in the shuffle." The plan looks good, management implements a few activities, business increases, management keeps busy with the new business—but fails to implement

other elements of the plan. This scenario is particularly apt for small businesses where "management" is one person—the owner. However, the increased business in this scenario may be no more than a "blip" on the marketing radar screen—the neglected elements of the plan may turn out to be more important for long-term success. If the marketing plan is well-conceived, every part of it is worth implementing and may, in fact, be crucial to a business's success or failure.

Success or failure (or something in between) is the question raised by the evaluation of the marketing plan. After each element of the plan has been implemented (or, sometimes, *while* it is being implemented), its effectiveness should be evaluated. As we learned earlier in this chapter, business objectives and our target market objectives should be stated in such a way as to provide a clear standard by which to measure their achievement (or lack of achievement).

Effective evaluation, however, requires more than a standard for measurement; it requires accurate and informative measuring techniques. In addition, various accounting procedures, financial analyses (including software programs), and other evaluation processes will help determine just how effective your marketing plan has been. Substantial upturn in volume or improved profitability may seem to be enough to validate a marketing plan's success. And it is—to a certain extent. However, precisely identifying those elements of the plan which were most effective will provide invaluable information for future marketing efforts. Conversely, detailed and specific evaluation will reveal those elements which didn't work or didn't work very well—again, valuable knowledge for the future.

Endnotes

1. Alastair M. Morrison, *Hospitality and Travel Marketing* (Albany, N.Y.: Delmar, 1989), p. 4.
2. Christopher W. L. Hart and David A. Troy, *Strategic Hotel/Motel Marketing,* rev. ed. (East Lansing, Mich.: Educational Institute of the American Hotel & Motel Association, 1986), pp. 3–4.
3. Philip Kotler, *Marketing for Nonprofit Organizations,* 2d ed. (Englewood Cliffs, N.J.: Prentice-Hall, 1982), pp. 21–23.
4. Philip Kotler, *Marketing Management: Analysis, Planning, and Control,* 4th ed. (Englewood Cliffs, N.J.: Prentice-Hall, 1980), p. 36.
5. William M. Pride and O. C. Farrell, *Marketing: Basic Concepts and Decisions,* 3d ed. (Boston: Houghton Mifflin, 1983), p. 149.
6. Pride and Farrell, p. 195.
7. E. Jerome McCarthy and William D. Perreault, Jr., *Basic Marketing: A Managerial Approach,* 9th ed. (Homewood, Ill.: Irwin, 1987), p. 260.
8. Kotler, 1980, pp. 296–298.
9. Theodore Levitt, "Marketing Myopia," *Harvard Business Review,* September/October 1975. As reprinted in Hart and Troy, pp. 15–16.
10. Karl Albrecht and Ron Zemke, *Service America! Doing Business in the New Economy* (Homewood, Ill.: Dow Jones-Irwin, 1985), p. 16.
11. Morrison, p. 202.
12. Morrison, p. 204.

13. Edward M. Mahoney, "Recreation Marketing: The Need for a New Approach," *Visions in Leisure and Business* 5 (Winter 1987): p. 70.

14. Kotler, 1980, p. 98.

15. J. W. Marriott, Jr., presentation given at the Michigan Governor's Tourism Conference, April, 1989, Grand Traverse Resort, Traverse City, Michigan.

16. Fumio Tamamura, "How Outbound Japanese Tourism Impacts the International Marketing Scene," in *Tourism Research: Globalization—the Pacific Rim and Beyond,* Travel and Tourism Research Association (TTRA and Bureau of Economic and Business Research, University of Utah, 1989), p. 65.

17. Knapp Communications Corp. study, 1988, as reported in *Lansing State Journal,* March 1, 1989, p. 1D.

18. For further information regarding computer use in the hospitality industry, see Michael L. Kasavana and John J. Cahill, *Managing Computers in the Hospitality Industry,* 2d ed. (East Lansing, Mich.: Educational Institute of the American Hotel & Motel Association, 1992).

19. *1989 Domestic Travel: A Historical Perspective,* Special Studies in Travel Economics and Marketing (Washington, D.C.: U.S. Travel Data Center, 1990), p. 9.

20. Harvey Shields, "America Seeks Out the World—Part II," in *Third Annual Travel Review Conference Proceedings* (Salt Lake City, Utah: Travel and Tourism Research Association and Bureau of Economic and Business Research, University of Utah, 1989), p. 35.

21. Daniel Stynes, "Marketing Tourism," *Journal of Physical Education, Recreation and Dance* 54 (April 1983): p. 43.

22. Morrison, p. 144.

23. Morrison, p. 144.

24. Morrison, p. 191.

Key Terms

business plan
competitive criteria
demographics
market mix
market segmentation
marketing
marketing conditions
marketing mix

marketing orientation
marketing plan
positioning
product life cycle
production orientation
sales orientation
societal orientation
target markets

Discussion Questions

1. How has marketing and its role evolved in modern business? in tourism?

2. What are four business perspectives? How do these perspectives differ from each other?

3. What are the four stages of the product life cycle? How would you describe each?

4. Why is a marketing plan important in today's business world?

5. What are five benefits of a marketing plan?

6. What are the basic elements of a tourism marketing plan?

7. What six elements should marketing planners consider when analyzing market conditions? Why?

8. How would you describe the process of market segmentation? What are some of the variables that identify market segments?

9. What is positioning? What are its five "Ds"?

10. What important points should marketing planners remember when implementing and evaluating a marketing plan?

REVIEW QUIZ

When you feel you have covered all of the material in this chapter, answer these questions. Choose the *best* answer. Check your answers with the correct ones found on the Review Quiz Answer Key at the end of this book.

True (T) or False (F)

T   F   1.   Marketing has been seen as a process of selling a product or service to people who may or may not have needed that particular product or service.

T   F   2.   Successful marketing does not require that tourism business management interact with both potential and actual tourists.

T   F   3.   Businesses with a marketing orientation try to market a product or service over time by trying to improve the sales effort.

T   F   4.   In the introduction stage of the product life cycle, customers see or hear about the product or service for the first time.

T   F   5.   Demographic trends—be they birth rate, migration, or aging—do not significantly influence tourism.

T   F   6.   Political calm and security within destination countries have no effect on tourism.

T   F   7.   Since change in tourism is so constant and rapid, competition can be ignored.

T   F   8.   The process of breaking down a market into more clearly identifiable segments is called market segmentation.

T   F   9.   If you cannot redesign your product or service, you cannot change a consumer's perception of it.

T   F   10.   Effective evaluation of a marketing plan requires nothing more than a standard of measurement.

Alternate/Multiple Choice

11.   The major function of a business with a production orientation is to produce goods and services:

     a.   as efficiently as possible.
     b.   as rapidly as possible.

12.   The term _____ refers to the social and economic context within which a tourism service or product is exchanged.

     a.   business objectives
     b.   marketing conditions

13.   The most obvious marketing condition monitored by market managers is:

     a.   technology.
     b.   the economy.

14. The study of groups of people—particularly the characteristics and trends of various groups *within* a population or *compared* to other population groups—is called:

    a. demographics.
    b. population shifts.
    c. population maturation.
    d. extrapolation.

15. Which of the following is *not* one of the five "Ds" of positioning?

    a. document
    b. debate
    c. differentiate
    d. design

Chapter Outline

The P-Mix
    The Product
    Programming
    Packaging
    Partnership
    Place
    Price
    Promotion
Interactive Marketing
    Tourist and Employee Interactions
    Tourist and Tourist Interactions
    Tourist and Setting Interactions
    Tourist and Community Interactions
Internal Marketing
    Customer Service Philosophy
    Employee Training
    Personnel Policy
    Organizational Communication
    Recruitment and Retention of
        Employees
Market Research
Private and Public Tourism Marketing

Learning Objectives

1. State how the traditional four "Ps" of marketing differ from the P-mix for tourism marketing.

2. Differentiate between products and services and how each is marketed.

3. Describe programming, packaging, and marketing partnerships.

4. Examine some of the complexities involved in setting prices for tourism products and services.

5. Describe how promotion can be used as a form of communication.

6. Discuss five promotion techniques used in marketing.

7. Describe the unique features of the interactive marketing mix.

8. Summarize two of four key interactions which compose the interactive marketing mix: tourist-employee and tourist-tourist.

9. Summarize two of four key interactions which compose the interactive marketing mix: tourist-setting and tourist-community.

10. Summarize the salient features of the internal marketing mix.

11. Explain the basic elements of market research.

12. Describe the importance of marketing to both the public and private sector.

11

Marketing Tools and Strategies

IF THIS CHAPTER WERE ABOUT a durable consumer product, then a discussion of traditional **marketing mix** elements would be sufficient. Tourism "products" are different. Since tourism is so experiential and service-oriented, it requires a marketing mix with a more complex set of variables.

This chapter will address the marketing mix for tourism as well as two other forms of marketing: **interactive marketing** and **internal marketing**. Interactive marketing deals with a reality peculiar to the tourism industry: that marketing is essential *after* a tourist arrives at a destination. Internal marketing treats the staffs of tourism businesses as essential targets of specified marketing efforts.[1] Finally, this chapter will introduce some basic market research approaches, and close with a few paragraphs that re-emphasize the importance of marketing in both the private and public sector.

The P-Mix

The traditional mix of marketing activities for manufactured goods includes the four Ps: *product, promotion, place,* and *price*. Stated succinctly, a "typical marketing mix includes some product, offered at a price, with some promotion to tell potential customers about the product, and a way to reach the customer's place."[2] For tourism, the traditional four Ps of marketing are combined with four additional Ps—programming, packaging, partnership, and publicity (including public relations). We call this the **P-mix**.[3]

Marketing the tourism product—an experience—is far more complex than marketing a consumer product. This section will discuss the various tools that can assist with the marketing process.

The Product

In a traditional sense, a product is usually something tangible that is manufactured and made available for sale to the public. The product is priced to cover costs, to generate a profit, and to be competitive in the marketplace. It is promoted chiefly by advertising and is distributed to the consumer at some location, such as a retail outlet. A manufactured product may also include accessories, warranties, instructions, and installation services. It will usually carry a brand name and be sold as a discrete package.

Clearly, marketing a tourism "product" requires a considerably different approach than marketing a manufactured product. First of all, tourism businesses are service-oriented—and service-oriented businesses are different from product-oriented ones. Services are usually intangible, at least in the physical sense. As such,

Tourists "consume" the atmosphere—as well as the service—of a hotel. (Courtesy of the Opryland Hotel, Nashville, Tennessee)

they are difficult for the customer to recognize immediately. The customer usually comes to the place the service is offered, but instead of taking a product home, the customer interacts with those providing the service. Tax preparation services, for instance, require the customer to provide financial information and interact with the professional staff to create the "product." In this case, the product is documentation which will be delivered to the appropriate governmental tax agency. In the tourism industry, those on a vacation must travel to the destination and "consume" the service, the amenities, and the atmosphere. The production and consumption of the service occur at the same place and at the same time.

Products Versus Services. For a more concrete perspective on the differences between products and services, compare the services offered by an island resort and those associated with a manufactured product—a stereo system.

A stereo system has *tangible features* that can be measured and specifications which can be easily shared with the customer. In contrast, services offered by the resort are more abstract. While the resort's environment can be observed, the services, the "feel" of the rooms, or the friendliness of the staff cannot be observed nor evaluated in detail before an actual trip. Travel literature may create an image of the resort, but will lack certain details. Will the room, for instance, feel small or spacious? Both products and services have tangible and intangible characteristics, but tourism services are much closer to the intangible end of the spectrum.

Several other characteristics distinguish the stereo system from our island resort. The stereo system is a distinct physical object which implies *ownership*—it can be taken home, observed, and used. Such is not the case with our island resort—we can't take it home with us. All we can "own" are a few souvenirs and, perhaps, some memories captured on film. In the tourism industry, the primary "product" is experience. In a marketing context, resorts do not sell occupancy; they sell experiences: activities, memories, and the opportunity to learn, socialize, challenge one's self, or, simply, to be alone.

Another difference between the stereo system and the resort is *participation*. The stereo system is developed independently of the consumer; the manufacturer has little or no actual contact with the customer. In contrast, the resort experience can only be created with the tourist being present and participating in its creation. The tourist has to travel to the site, check into the resort, order the food, and participate in the activities. The employees participate, too. They check the tourist in, prepare and serve the food, organize the activities, maintain the facilities, and seek payment for their role in creating the tourism experience. Stated another way:

> In a service business, you find that you're dealing with something that is primarily delivered by people—to people. Your people are as much … your product in the consumer's mind as any other attribute of that service.[4]

One may purchase an excellent stereo despite poor service and unpleasant surroundings. At the resort, poor service, rude employees, and unpleasant surroundings can destroy the "product."

A stereo system can be returned and re-sold; the tourism experience cannot. A lost room night or a canceled historic tour cannot be replaced—it is gone forever. A tourist can shorten a vacation, change location and plans, but a bad day on vacation is *non-returnable*. This means that the purchase of tourism experiences places the tourist—as a consumer—at risk. The tourist must mitigate this risk by seeking out as much prior information as possible.

Consistency is critical for the success of tourism businesses; tourists have to know that when they visit, they will receive quality treatment, time after time and visit after visit. Consistency of quality requires employee training, a positive marketing attitude, attention to detail, and a strong commitment to tourist satisfaction through service.

Tourism is a *seasonal* product—meaning that certain sites are more popular at certain times of the year than others. Demand during certain seasons—especially summer—is considerably higher than demand during others. Manufactured goods are less seasonal; demand is usually stable throughout the entire year. Resorts, tourist communities, and attractions must plan their business around the peak season while trying to create profitable use of the facilities during the off-season.

As a tourism supplier, an amusement park sells experiences and memories that cannot be returned. (Courtesy of Tacoma Pierce-County Visitor & Convention Bureau, Tacoma, Washington)

Tourism Suppliers. Finally, our comparison of service and product marketing will not be complete without mentioning the "manufacturers" and "distributors" of tourism products. Tourism suppliers can be classified in a number of ways. The following list is not exhaustive, but illustrative. Some overlap exists; the categories are not mutually exclusive. For example, resorts are included under lodging and under attractions, while cruise ships represent a form of transportation with accommodations.

- Transportation—airlines, buses, trains, cruise lines, car rentals

- Lodging—hotels, motels, resorts, camps, park campgrounds

- Attractions—amusement and theme parks, unique natural resources, resorts, selected cities, historic sites, cultural events and places

- **Food and beverage**—restaurants, international food markets, food service facilities

- **Tourism intermediaries**—travel agents, tour brokers, meeting and conference planners, travel managers

- **Tourism marketing organizations**—cities, state travel offices, travel and tourism consultants, convention and visitor bureaus, regional tourism marketing organizations

Each supplier on this list may play a role in creating a tourism experience. During any trip, some—if not all—of these businesses may provide a service that is designed to enhance the tourism experience.

People. In a service-industry such as tourism, the quality of service is determined by the quality of the people who deliver it—the employees. Employees can make or break a tourism business. The following considerations with respect to employees are important ones:

1. **Labor pool**—Tourism enterprises need employees. In these days of tight labor markets, finding available, qualified employees can be problematic.

2. **Training**—This topic will be covered in more detail later in this chapter under internal marketing. Training is important if marketing goals are to be met.

3. **Role**—In any tourism endeavor, the role played by employees—especially those on the "front lines"—in delivering services to the tourist should not be undervalued. The tourist-employee interaction is at the heart of the tourism experience.

Programming

You are staying at a beach resort with your family. You notice a flier—delivered along with the morning paper—which invites you and the kids to attend poolside games in the afternoon. The lifeguard will be on duty. Activities for the children are planned. If parents would like to do so, they can join a snorkel class while the kids are entertained at poolside. All this is free except for a small fee for the snorkeling gear. This is an example of activity programming offered at a tourism destination. Such **programming** makes the resort more than just a beautiful location offering lodging, food, and drink.

Programming can be critical to the success of a tourism experience.[5] Programming enhances the tourism experience and creates greater customer satisfaction; and it may increase guest spending. Programming can take place at almost any tourism destination. Hotels and resorts commonly use programs to enhance the experiences of their guests. Some are theme-oriented. For example, the La Santa Sport resort in the Canary Islands is oriented toward the active, sports-minded traveler and family. Each day is filled with sports opportunities, lessons, and training facilities that range from weight-lifting, tennis, and track to windsurfing in a nearby ocean bay. Club Med is yet another example. Club Med is world-famous for its programming—programming which effectively attracts customers and which includes restaurant/dinner theaters, theme menus, and special recognition activities.

Exhibit 1   Benefits of Packaging Tourism Experiences

Customer	Convenience
	Economy and savings
	Planning and efficiency
	Implied quality
	More complete activity and program
Participant	Attracts off-season business
	Appeals specifically to special groups
	Improved business efficiency
	Uses complementary facilities and businesses in destination region
	Takes advantage of new trends
	May increase repeat business, length of stay, per-visit spending
	May stimulate publicity
	May increase tourist satisfaction

Based on Alastair M. Morrison, *Hospitality and Travel Marketing* (Albany, N.Y.: Delmar, 1989), p. 256.

Natural resource-based destinations such as national and state parks have used programming for decades to attract visitors. Guided nature hikes, posted trails, and nature information centers are examples of such programming which enhances visitors' stays.

Packaging

Closely related to programming is **packaging**—combining a range of services and programs into one package for one price. As a concept, packaging has been around a long time. Some of the first packages—group tours designed by Thomas Cook to attract the English middle class—appeared in Europe before the turn of the twentieth century. Today, package deals for all types of destinations fill the Sunday papers and the walls of your local travel agency. The combinations are endless and include fly-drive packages, cruise line trips with airfare included, and the ever present "three-or-seven-nights-at-the-hotel-of-your-choice-airfare-and-transfer-charges-included" package.

Packaging has become an art and a successful component of any marketing effort. Packaging includes many benefits for the tourist as well as the tourist business; in other words, benefits can be *customer-related* and *participant-related*.[6] Participants might be the tourism and allied businesses that agree to be involved in the package—such as the airline, hotel, and charter fishing service. Exhibit 1 outlines the benefits of packaging for the customer and the participating business.

Partnership

Marketing partnerships are most often formed to develop service and destination packages and to share the costs of promotion. Cruise lines, for example, offer air-included trips and resorts offer off-site secondary trips and tours. Such partnerships have been common for years. The costs of promotion and the changing tastes of the tourist make it cost-effective to pursue partnerships. Plus, it makes sense for related elements of the tourism industry to work together and offer services in a

convenient manner with potential cost savings for the customer. Consider the resort that wants to enlarge a package by offering off-site tours and events to its
guests. The resort makes a deal with a local firm to supply the required transportation at a lower per-person rate than normal. The local firm makes up in volume
what it loses in reduced rates, while the resort can offer a more attractive package
at minimal cost.

Partnerships vary in their degree of integration and connectedness. Partnerships are fully integrated and connected when they offer a single package to the
customer; other partnerships are related only by offering a variety of services as a
promotional benefit. The Delta Airlines-Disney World partnership is one that is
both integrated and connected. The partnership makes sense: travel modes are integrated with a destination and its accommodations. The partners put all the details of the package together. These partners offer flexibility to the traveler by
allowing them a choice of hotels and a rental car agency special.[7] With this kind of
partnership, all the tourist has to do is select a package, make a few location and
price decisions, decide on a date, and take off.

Some partnerships are less integrated; travelers play a more active role in obtaining the benefits. Examples of such partnerships include frequent flyer programs offered by airlines in cooperation with hotels and car rental agencies. The
bonus frequent flyer miles are obtained by staying at certain hotels and renting
cars from selected rental agencies; the tourist, however, makes the connection by
selecting the airline, hotel, or car agency. From the partners' point of view, the
promotional partnership is designed to create more business, encourage repeat
business, and enhance customer loyalty. But it is the customer who, in effect, puts
the "package" together by his/her discrete choices. Some partnerships offer
promotional incentives which are even less integrated than the frequent flyer packages. A number of airlines have formed marketing partnerships with long-distance
phone carriers and credit card companies to enhance and promote each other's services. One example is the partnership between Northwest Airlines and MCI Communications. The rationale for such partnerships is purely promotional: customers
are encouraged to make connections between the two services—increasing profits
for both.

Place

Tourism services and products must be distributed in some manner at specified
locations. Technically, the place of distribution is a holdover from product marketing orientations. However, *where* a tourism service is distributed is just as important as where a manufactured product is distributed. In both cases, distribution
should be designed to facilitate the exchange between suppliers and consumers. If
a person wants to travel by air to Florida, he/she should be able to purchase a
ticket and destination lodging at the same time and at the same place. Developing
or making use of combined distribution channels can be critical to the success of
the marketing plan.

In today's marketplace, tourism services can be purchased from many distribution channels. Marketers create such channels for the purpose of enhancing
the traveler's convenience and thereby increasing sales. Services can be delivered

directly or indirectly through various channels. An airline can sell tickets directly to the tourist or indirectly through a travel agent or other intermediary.[8] Besides the travel agent, distribution channels include tour wholesalers, corporate travel managers, incentive travel officers, and meeting planners.

As can be seen, the number of intermediaries has grown for both the consumer and the tourism supplier. Many large corporations have internal corporate travel offices to assist with travel arrangements, management of travel costs, and travel planning. Tour brokers develop package tours for individuals and groups. Tour packages may have multiple destinations and alternative types of travel modes. Meeting planners act as intermediaries between business travelers and convention or seminar sites. They package the travel, lodging, meeting facilities, and sometimes arrange off-site tours and activities. Incentive travel planners—often a specialty of travel agencies—arrange travel for the corporation that rewards or motivates successful employees or employee groups through travel. Top sales people, for instance, may receive an all-expense-paid trip to Hawaii at the end of the year. These incentives or rewards may be arranged in-house but are often arranged by incentive travel planners.

Depending on the goals and nature of the business, the tourism marketing planner must consider this broad range of travel retailers and distributors. The airlines and rental car agencies generally permit tickets to be sold through most of the available distribution means. The same is generally true for hotel reservations, although special packages or rates may be distributed exclusively through certain agencies, by the hotel itself, or through meeting planners.

As the distribution of travel services has become more complex and varied, it has also become placeless, timeless, and faceless. Travel agencies with free long-distance telephone numbers (commonly known as toll-free or 800 numbers) can be located almost anywhere. Many agencies can now make reservations 24 hours a day without personal, face-to-face contact with customers. Tickets can be paid for by credit card and sent the next day by express delivery. For a small service charge, tickets can even be delivered to a counter at the airport. Nevertheless, many travelers will still desire the counsel and comfort that can only come from direct, face-to-face contact with a "live" travel agent.

Price

Many believe that price is the most important element of the marketing mix—the one element, in fact, which motivates the traveler to purchase service. However, the *perceived value* of the service is just as important as the actual purchase price. Within the context of a marketing plan, the importance of price is mitigated by a number of other factors such as the perceived quality of a supplier's service and the reputation or effectiveness of the supplier's advertising.

Price is complex; it has many meanings for both the consumer and the supplier. If you know the price of a service, you know more than simply what it costs. Price implies value, quality, and sometimes, rarity. If the consumer is not fully knowledgeable about a service, higher price will often translate as better quality. Through association, price confers social image and prestige. Items or services which appeal to social image and prestige often require a premium price.

Setting a price for a tourism service or product requires more than guesswork. General business goals and target market objectives should be considered. All too often, the true costs of producing and delivering the tourism service are not fully considered; they must be examined and included in the pricing decision. Although this seems to be common sense, many smaller tourism enterprises overlook costs when considering the price of their product or service. Overlooking costs can eat up profits and may eventually lead to bankruptcy. In addition to costs, the enterprise must also set a price which appears reasonable to the tourist. In most tourism businesses, there are upper limits beyond which the tourist is not likely to purchase a particular service. However, there are always some markets which may be able and willing to pay higher prices for selected services; others may be more price-sensitive and motivated to purchase only by bargain prices.

Establishing a price for tourism services varies dramatically across the industry. Hotels, resorts, restaurants, and amusement and theme parks all have pricing methods common to their respective services. Public sector attractions such as national and state parks and city-owned museums and attractions have pricing considerations which differ from those of the private sector. As a process, pricing is best understood in relation to basic economic concepts: the extent and nature of the demand must be determined and competitors' prices analyzed. If there are reasonable alternatives to the service, it must be priced accordingly. A review of tourism pricing policy suggests that the following factors and steps should be considered when establishing a price for tourism products and services.[9] *POSITIONING!*

1. **Integrate goals, pricing, and profit.** Prices for selected services should be considered within the context of marketing and business goals. Both short-term profits and increased market share should influence pricing policy. The profit margin should be established within the context of the size of the business, the economic climate in the region, and the nature of the targeted markets.

2. **Consider the key markets.** Market types and price sensitivity must be considered since each target market may respond differently to price. The ability and willingness of key markets to pay should be analyzed.

3. **Analyze demand.** In conjunction with price sensitivity, demand for the service should be analyzed and prices projected for each target market.

4. **Match price with quality.** Quality, to the consumer, is often indicated by price. Make sure the price is set in accordance with that perception.

5. **Calculate costs.** The true costs for producing and delivering tourism services must be calculated and figured into price decisions. Costs include labor, taxes, supplies, and interest, as well as commissions, advertising, and promotional costs. Each business must comprehensively review its financial books to calculate the true costs of doing business—including variable, fixed, and marginal costs.

6. **Consider the competition.** Well-conceived prices position the business favorably in relation to the competition and will affect the competition. The competition may alter its prices in response to the price another business sets.

Nevertheless, prices should not be based solely upon what the competition does.

7. **Consider the marketing mix.** A business should evaluate how the price of any one service will interact with others offered by the firm. The impacts of price on other elements of the marketing mix should be considered as well. High-priced services demand high-quality promotion as well as high-quality performance.

8. **Use a pricing procedure.** The final price should be based on technical analysis, not on hunches, feelings, or a look over your shoulder at the competition. Several techniques are available to assist the market and finance manager in establishing specific prices for various tourism products and services. Hotels, restaurants, amusement parks, museums, airlines, and rental car agencies all have known business pricing practices that can be accessed through associations, consultants, or other financial advisors.

Promotion

Through promotion, a business, organization, or association communicates with potential customers, employees, management, the competition, and various publics. Promotion involves furthering the sale of a service or product through tools such as advertising or personal selling. The primary target for promotion is the potential customer. In tourism, this customer could be the tourist or an intermediate audience that sells directly to the tourist—such as a travel agent or tour operator.

Promotion as Communication. Exhibit 2 shows basic communication elements. In this model, promotion techniques such as advertising or public relations are designed to send a message to the tourism audience. The sender or source can be a tourism business such as a resort, an allied business such as an airline, or a public agency that promotes tourism such as a state travel office. The person who receives the message usually knows the source and associates the sender with an affiliation or group; this will influence how the message is received and interpreted. The promotional materials sent by a state travel office will be seen in one way while an ad sent by a destination considered a "tourist trap" will be seen in quite another. This affiliation process is related to the concept of source credibility. **Credibility** is but one of several characteristics which sources are assumed to possess. Credibility refers to the perception that the source is honest and trustworthy. This process of associating characteristics with a source is called **attribution.** Attribution is the process wherein qualities such as reliability, image, attractiveness, and honesty are attributed to sources. Such attributes influence how a message source is perceived; a message may be less persuasive when a source is perceived as lacking credibility.

The source conceives the message and must then put it into symbols. **Encoding** refers to the process of translating the conceived message into a form—usually language or visual symbols—that can be received by others. You may recall the shape and style of a Holiday Inn sign. Such a symbol represents not only an image, but an identification message encoded for travelers. The traveler decodes the symbol or message, interprets it, and may decide to purchase or not purchase. The decision and resultant action become feedback for the source. In turn, this feedback

Exhibit 2   Communication Model

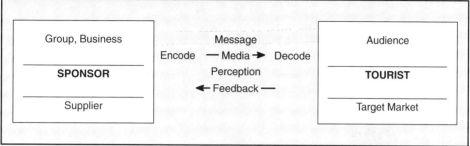

Based on Philip Kotler, *Marketing Management: Analysis, Planning, Implementation, and Control* (Englewood Cliffs, N.J.: Prentice-Hall, 1980), p. 471; and Edwin P. Hollander, *Principles and Methods of Social Psychology*, 2d ed. (New York: Oxford University Press, 1971), p. 212.

may stimulate more messages that explain the service in more detail or cause the product or service to be dropped or modified.

The model in Exhibit 2 assumes that the message will inform, persuade, and stimulate action. The source and the receiver are both assumed to be motivated by a number of wants and desires. These *salient motives* can be obvious or not so obvious.[10] The salient motives of an advertisement booked on Michigan TV stations during the winter by a Florida resort should be fairly obvious. A less obvious—or underlying salient motive—for the resort might include breaking into a new market, increasing market share, and increasing profit. These motives are not stated directly in the advertisement, but may be attributed to the source by the receiver. The receiver in our example may also have salient motives in addition to escaping the Michigan winter. These may include status, power, and "keeping up with the Joneses." Such motives are rarely appealed to directly, but are frequently encoded within the message.

Messages are most often transmitted through the mass media. Each medium—radio, television, print—will be used in some combination within a comprehensive marketing plan. The combination used will be guided by a realization that communication is dynamic, interactive, and influenced by subjective factors like the perceptions, motivations, cultural backgrounds, and socio-economic characteristics of the audience. Understanding the complexities of communication is essential to creating an effective marketing plan.

Five types of promotion techniques are used in marketing. Marketing, advertising, or promotional managers are responsible for mixing and blending these techniques to increase product or service awareness and to facilitate sales. The five techniques are: personal selling, advertising, publicity, public relations, sales promotion, and word of mouth.

Personal Selling. Personal selling refers to face-to-face interactions designed to persuade a customer to buy a product or service. Personal selling takes place at many locations: the counter of an airline or a car rental service, at a hotel front desk, or at a restaurant table. Personal selling relies on the salesperson's communication skills and his/her knowledge of and enthusiasm for the product or service being

Exhibit 3   Travel and Tourism Advertising Expenditures in 1988

Business	Amount Spent in Millions on Advertisements in the U.S. Media
U.S. airlines	$607
Foreign airlines	$ 99
Cruise lines	$167
U.S. domestic destinations	$130
Foreign destinations	$ 99

Note: The total spent in U.S. media was more than $1.1 billion dollars. Among domestic destinations, individual states spent more than $71 million on advertising alone in 1988.

Source: *Trends in Travel and Tourism Advertising Expenditures in United States Measured Media 1984–1988,* A Special Report for Ogilvy and Mather, July 1989, p. I–2.

exchanged. These factors shape the important interaction between the seller and the potential buyer.

Personal selling is an important element in tourism businesses. The travel agent, for instance, must develop a personal relationship with a client in order to be effective. An agent must devise or present a travel package that takes into account the client's lifestyle and preferences. The agent's persuasive powers are also enhanced by having visited the site or used the package he/she is trying to sell. This is why resorts, airlines, and tour packagers frequently offer free or heavily discounted trips to travel agents.

In a sense, every employee in a tourism business is engaged in personal selling. Since tourism is a "people-pleasing" industry that depends on repeat business, the positive attitudes and dispositions of everyone from housekeeper to manager become potent selling tools.

Advertising. At its best, personal selling can reach only a minute fraction of the potential clients available through advertising. Managers use advertising to build a new business, to introduce a new product or service, or to increase the market share of an established business. A travel agency which relies heavily on personal selling is well-advised to attract new clients with a well-placed ad in the newspaper's Sunday travel section or a timely TV spot on a local station.

Various types of advertising are important to a variety of tourism businesses. Tourism businesses buy ads in all media—television, radio, newspapers. In 1988, paid advertising for all travel categories among private travel businesses totaled more than $1 billion.[11] Among the top ten advertisers were a hotel chain, a rental car chain, a cruise line, and six airlines. More than 25% of all travel advertisements from the private sector were placed in magazines. Again, the top advertisers were airlines, car rental chains, hotels, and cruise lines. Included among the top 25 magazine advertisers were five governments: Canada, Mexico, Bermuda, Puerto Rico, and the state of North Carolina.[12] Exhibit 3 looks at media spending in 1988.

In the United States, individual states and even cities promote tourism and travel. Advertisements may be placed locally, regionally, nationally, or in foreign countries. At the federal level, the U.S. Travel and Tourism Administration places advertising in foreign markets to stimulate travel to the United States. In 1986, for example, U.S. advertising in foreign markets amounted to nearly $80 million.[13] A single U.S. airline (United) spent nearly $52 million for advertising in 1987.[14]

For many tourism businesses, direct mail is a cost-effective component of their advertising budgets. Direct mail can target potential clients and attract repeat business more efficiently than mass media advertising. An airline, for instance, can use the list of its own "frequent flyers" to announce new incentives. Direct mail advertising concerns and other firms and associations sell mailing lists. The same airline might purchase a mailing list of the frequent flyers from other airlines to tout its own incentive program.

Advertising, especially in today's changing and competitive international marketplace, is important to the tourism industry. Increasingly, the advertising budget will represent a heftier percentage of operational expenses for successful tourism businesses.

Publicity and Public Relations. Basically, publicity means coverage of a product in the news media. Publicity is often mistakenly called "free advertising." However, the adage applies: "There's no such thing as a free lunch." If the publicity about a product or service is negative, it can cost—and cost dearly. If the publicity is positive, it is often the result of the work of paid public relations specialists. Nevertheless, good publicity can generate positive, sometimes spectacular, payoffs in increased sales.

Good—sometimes even neutral—publicity has several advantages, other than cost, over paid advertising. A product or service mentioned in the news media is often perceived to have more credibility than a paid advertisement. In the midst of an almost overwhelming abundance of competing messages, publicity can often help the claims of a particular tourism business to stand out.

Advertising, however, does have specific advantages over publicity. Through advertising, a firm can control the content and timing of a message, and it can be tailored for a specific audience. Publicity is inherently unpredictable; a travel writer might praise a destination one day and condemn it another.

Public relations, dealing as it does with people's perceptions, is close to the heart of any tourism business. That is why larger firms often have a full-time professional public relations person or staff, supported by a large budget. Smaller firms may often hire public relations consulting firms on a temporary, one-time basis. Even large firms will sometimes hire a public relations firm when their staff is overwhelmed. This can happen when some disaster or negative publicity affects their business.

Sales Promotions. In sales promotions, exposure to or awareness of a service or product is obtained by various incentive or discount programs such as contests, coupon redemption, free samples, or special displays at retail outlets. An incentive is designed to persuade a consumer to try a product or service.

Discounts are another sales promotion method which provide short-term incentives and are capable of quickly stimulating sales. In the tourism business, discount coupons will often appear in a local newspaper ad about a particular destination. Discounts can be used to stimulate sales in general or to bolster sagging sales for a particular market.

In the summer of 1989, regional Seven-Up distributors joined forces with a Michigan amusement park. Together these two non-competitive businesses offered a special amusement park ticket discount for those turning in an empty Seven-Up can at the amusement park gate. The promotion benefited both companies: regular Seven-Up consumers were induced to sample the attractions of the amusement park, while regular amusement park patrons were encouraged to try Seven-Up.

Word of Mouth. Word-of-mouth promotion describes people talking to each other about their experiences as consumers. In the motion picture business, a movie that is performing well at the box office because people are telling their friends about it is said to be "doing good word of mouth." Indeed, good word of mouth is considered crucial to a movie's success, regardless of how many millions are spent on paid advertising.

Word of mouth is just as crucial to success in the travel business, particularly with respect to hotels, resorts, and vacation sites. People—especially satisfied tourists—talk to others—and they talk a lot about their trips and travel experiences. Travelers take more of a risk regarding the quality of their vacation; they usually cannot sample the experience and there are no guarantees. Word of mouth is more persuasive than paid advertising; its credibility is very high. Studies suggest that friends and relatives are sources of information about a trip, destination, or attraction up to 50% of the time for certain types of trips. U.S. tourists traveling overseas report that friends and relatives are information sources 27% of the time. For foreign visitors to the United States, 20% reported using friends and relatives as sources of information.[15] Among tourists traveling to and through the state of Nebraska by auto, 40% to 50% of them reported that friends and relatives provided information about which state attractions to visit.[16] The researchers also found that hotels with good word-of-mouth recommendations have higher retention rates for their guests.[17] Those tourists who first heard favorable recommendations for a hotel by word of mouth were most likely to return.

Word-of-mouth promotion is a two-way street. A traveler with an unsatisfactory experience with an airline, hotel, resort, or vacation site is likely to relate that experience to friends and relatives. The only control a tourism business can exert over the word-of-mouth process is to maintain the highest possible standards for service and facilities.

Interactive Marketing

Beyond the P-mix, the nature of the exchange between the tourist and the destination can be considered part of the marketing mix. Four key interactions influence tourist satisfaction. These are the interaction between tourist and employee, tourist and setting, tourist and other tourists, and tourist and the destination community.

Like the P-mix, interactive marketing mix elements are not considered in isolation from each other or from other elements of the marketing plan.

Interactive marketing mix elements have unique features. First, each involves the tourist, or customer. Second, each involves an interaction—an exchange or encounter. This means that the social and psychological characteristics of the tourist—such as perception, social interaction, and expectations—are operant. Third, the location for the interaction is most often at the destination. Fourth, the tourist is, in most cases, already committed in some way to the destination. In the case of a hotel, a tourist probably already made a reservation. Even a "walk-in" may be expected to have a sense of commitment in that he/she has taken the time to check out the hotel and to ask about availability and price. Interactive marketing should take advantage of such opportunities by converting a potential customer into a satisfied guest or visitor. Fifth, the interactive marketing mix elements are produced and delivered in full view of the tourist. Unlike behind-the-scenes personnel training, the interactive marketing mix elements are up front and on display. The *result* of training influences how the interaction between the tourist and employee unfolds. Much of what supports interactive elements—such as promotion—goes on in the background. The tourist sees and experiences the end result.

Interactive marketing should manage what is referred to in many business circles as "moments of truth."[18] *Moments of truth* are instantaneous emotional responses which may occur anytime a tourist has the opportunity to develop perceptions about the company—whether through ads, contact with employees, or the first sight of the company or destination itself. Interactive marketing, if managed well, fosters positive moments of truth.

Tourist and Employee Interactions

One of the most critical points of contact is between the tourist and the employee. Over the past 15 years, the exchange between customer and staff has been accorded special attention, often under the headings of "service," "service quality," or "service marketing." The importance of service to the tourism industry cannot be overemphasized. Tourist satisfaction drives interactive marketing. Every exchange a tourist has with staff should be designed to enhance the tourist's satisfaction.

The tourist's first contact with a tourism business may begin with an advertisement, followed by a trip to that destination. The first encounter begins what is called the **service cycle**.[19] That encounter and every encounter thereafter is part of the service cycle. Most often, the most crucial contacts are with employees. The employee not only represents the tourism business but is a co-producer of the tourism experience. The fine-dining experience or the relaxing two days at poolside are created in part by the quality of the service offered by employees. Every exchange is a marketing opportunity for the tourism business and should be treated that way in the training and development of employees.[20] Staff members not only need to know the business well, they must also be trained in every conceivable way to serve the tourist's interests. This includes the willingness to offer extra information and guidance to the tourist to help make the most of their stay or visit.

Tourism businesses need to remember that tourists are concerned about their satisfaction, value for the money, and quality. In contrast to customers of other service-oriented businesses, the expectations and goals of tourists are to have a good time and enjoy themselves—in *every* case. Contrast this with the purchase of accounting services. The objectives of an accounting service are clearly different from those of a tourism business. Most people do not hire an accountant expecting good times, relaxation, and enjoyment. Tourists, however, do attribute this expectation to those around them—including the staff.

Sometimes, however, employees who have been serving tourists for weeks, or even years, may have lost their verve for service. Many, at the very least, will show a bit of wear at the end of the day. Well-managed service organizations monitor employees for burnout and exhaustion to avoid negative interactions with customers. Personnel managers should also screen their potential employees for people who truly *like* people; training does have limitations. The tourist-employee interaction is largely a controllable element of the mix, due in part to management's control over personnel training, staff selection and retention, and a management philosophy which states that the customer is "number one." The interactions between guests and employees can be managed by the proper use of the following variables:

1. **Appearance**—Clean uniforms or clean clothing, good grooming, and personal hygiene are essential.

2. **Principles of conduct**—Employees should know how to properly greet customers, deal with complaints, and provide assistance; a customer-oriented attitude is a must.

3. **Awards and incentives**—Recognition and rewards should be given to employees who are most successful in their encounters with tourists.

4. **Knowledge and communication**—To be fully service-oriented, employees must possess knowledge of the business's goals and objectives as well as have a sense of how their activities contribute to these goals and objectives. Management can convey such information to staff verbally or through communication channels such as meetings and newsletters. Communication will be discussed in more detail in the section on internal marketing.

5. **Training**—Training is critical. Employees must be instructed on what to do and how to do it when dealing with tourists. The quality of the tourist-employee interaction heavily depends on training. Ignoring training while concentrating on promotion or product development is a dangerous course for businesses *so* dependent on the service image. The service and quality so appreciated by millions of customers who visit Disney attractions result from extensive training programs for all members of the organization.

Successful interaction has direct implications for tourist satisfaction and, consequently, sales and profits. In the tourism business, neglecting the quality of service delivered at the front lines is tantamount to neglecting the bottom line.

Tourist and Tourist Interactions

While on vacation, at a conference, or on tour, a traveler's experience is influenced by encounters with other travelers, local residents, and employees. The relationship between tourists and other tourists is another interactive marketing mix element that can and should be managed. For some tourists, other tourists can be a bother; to others, they are *the* attraction. Managers must see the interactions of all guests and visitors as a marketing opportunity which can generate positive feelings about the attraction, the hotel, the resort, or the destination.

People are social beings and generally like being around others who are friendly and courteous. There are, however, important exceptions. For example, some tourists are seeking solitude and relaxation. If a tourism business seeks to satisfy this target market, it should be prepared to deliver solitude, relaxation, and adequate separation from more socially oriented guests. It is important for a business to know how it is perceived, what it offers to satisfy guests, and how to manage guest interactions.

Tourist-to-tourist interactions can be managed in a number of ways. Managers must above all ensure that targeted markets are compatible. For example, a resort should not target the mature market and the college market for the same season. Marketing should focus on complementary groups of visitors or guests. This increases the chances of satisfying those markets and lessening conflict.

To further manage the behavior of guests and visitors, the tourism enterprise must establish norms of acceptable behavior for the tourist.[21] This can be accomplished by establishing and, when necessary, enforcing rules necessary for the safety and comfort of guests and visitors. Whenever possible, it is better to establish the norms of acceptable behavior up front in order to avoid the need for enforcement. Signs, daily newsletters, and employees themselves can remind the guest of proper behavior. In addition, the management of guest activities can keep tourist interactions on an even keel. A resort should separate diverse guest groups or incompatible activities by time and by space in order to prevent conflict.

The management of tourist-to-tourist interactions has several additional marketing implications. First, the lack of conflict enhances tourist satisfaction and supports repeat business and longer stays. Second, part of the image of a tourism business is generated by its clientele; first-time visitors will be impressed by people, like themselves, having a good time. Third, well-managed interactions can foster good word-of-mouth promotion.

Finally, people like to know that they are not alone in how they feel about their vacation, or how they choose to spend their money. Tourists who are made to feel confident and comfortable with their decision by staff and by other tourists are more likely to have a good time, stay longer, spend more, and in the end, think and speak well of the place to others.

Tourist and Setting Interactions

A setting can be described as follows:[22]

1. A place where social or individual behavior occurs on a regular or prescribed basis

2. A place where coordination occurs between the guests' behavior and the physical design and objects within the setting

3. A function for which people are substitutable.

4. An activity for which a minimum number of persons is required

5. A situation in which action is self-regulating

6. An activity or function determined by boundaries of time and place

The front desk is a setting where specified activities occur. The physical design is meant to facilitate registration behavior, and that behavior is determined by the location and the hours of operation. Front desk staff are required to make the desk function. Several employees may be trained to operate the front desk so that substitutes for all shifts are readily available. The front desk is also self-regulating: if forms are missing or if staff are short of cash, a system is in place to correct these deficiencies.

Settings have other characteristics that influence the tourism experience. These include design and appearance, and feel and orientation.

Design and Appearance. Well-designed attractions, destinations, hotels, and resorts are important to the tourist in several ways. An aesthetic setting projects an image to the traveler. A well-designed and well-maintained facility reflects an image of caring, professionalism, success, and quality. Designs should be both beautiful and functional. Functional designs enhance the effectiveness of behavioral settings. Poor design can create settings that are awkward and disruptive and that lead to unsatisfied customers and disgruntled employees. Busy hotel lobbies that are too small and amusement parks with too few benches and shaded areas are two examples of ineffectively designed settings. Since so much of the tourism experience is intangible, the appearance and functionality of a facility becomes an important tangible characteristic which a tourism business can control.

Atmosphere and Orientation. Setting design and appointments provide a certain atmosphere and orientation for the tourist. The atmosphere is created by appropriate design of the physical environment—including the design and arrangement of furniture and other physical objects within the setting. The appearance and dress of employees and guests also contribute to the atmosphere within the setting. Settings, too, are places of orientation. Routine settings such as the front desk, the information desk, admission counters, dining areas, and pools should be accessible and easy to recognize and find. Disorientation creates discomfort; this can be diminished by functional design and appropriate and easily readable signs.

An important example of tourist and setting interaction is barrier-free design for the handicapped guest. Recent legislation in the United States has made it imperative that public tourism attractions accommodate the disabled. Many private facilities, attractions, hotels, and even campgrounds are making their facilities accessible to wheelchair users or other individuals with special mobility needs.

Tourist and Community Interactions

No tourism business is an island. Experiences along the way set the stage for the impression a traveler has of the final destination. The hospitality of surrounding communities and businesses near the final destination is important and contributes to

An aesthetic guestroom reflects care, professionalism, and quality, and provides a pleasant atmosphere for the traveler. (Courtesy of Di Leonardo International, Inc., Hospitality Design, Warwick, Rhode Island)

overall satisfaction. Hostility, on the other hand, shortens the length of stay, lessens the amount of money spent in the community, diminishes the likelihood of tourists returning, and creates negative word of mouth.

Tourism businesses must be sensitive to and involved in their communities and assist with the management of community responses to tourism. Tourism businesses have a vested interest in making sure that community residents understand the importance of tourism to the community as a whole. The gas station attendant who provides faulty directions does a disservice not only to the visitor but to the entire community.

Internal Marketing

If tourist satisfaction depends on good service and good service depends on people, then it follows that employing top-notch people is one of the keys to success in the tourism industry. Employees and management staff make up that part of the marketing mix referred to as internal marketing. The process of internal marketing focuses on employees as customers—in effect, "selling" employees on the values important to management.[23]

There are two important aspects of internal marketing. First, the primary purpose of internal marketing is to foster a strong customer orientation among management and employees, from top to bottom within the organization. Second, internal marketing seeks to recruit and retain high-quality employees. Both are essential to the success of any tourism business. Internal marketing has its own marketing mix, elements of which are customer service philosophy, employee training, service-oriented personnel policies, and organizational communications.[24] The recruitment and retention of qualified employees is also important to internal marketing.

Customer Service Philosophy

A tourism business has to create an environment conducive to customer orientation. Such an environment starts at the top; top management must be true believers in the primacy of service and customer satisfaction. An effective customer service philosophy is not just something that is talked about or issued as a directive in the company newsletter; it is a vital, day-to-day process which constantly encourages employees to go "the extra mile" in providing service for customers. Management should not only reinforce employees' efforts in the area of customer service, but should lead by example. For instance, a manager should not wait around when a customer needs help, but be prepared to step in and perform tasks ordinarily handled by line employees.

To be effective, a customer-oriented philosophy must be instilled in all members of the organization—not just those dealing directly with customers. The bookkeeper, the dishwasher, the airline baggage handler—all must be able to relate every aspect of their job to the philosophy. To successfully implement a truly customer-oriented philosophy, the spirit of service must be contagious; it must permeate and be reflected in the actions *and* attitude of every employee—not only toward customers, but toward each other.

Employee Training

Typically, employee training in tourism businesses is limited to providing the technical skills necessary to do the job, along with a brief "pep talk" on customer service-orientation. Management can and should instill concrete techniques—such as listening, and recognizing verbal and non-verbal cues—in new employees as an integral part of the training process.

One of the most effective training tools used by progressive organizations today is the presentation of an introductory videotape designed to inform new employees about the organization and its values. Larger organizations will often hire video production companies to create customized videos for training purposes. However, many firms and non-profit organizations such as the Educational Institute of the American Hotel & Motel Association offer many useful instructional resources including videotapes which dramatize the importance of customer service.

Yet another important facet of customer-oriented training should be a personal talk with new employees—either singly or in small groups—by the C.E.O., president, or general manager. This is perhaps the most effective way of establishing top management's dedication to customer service. It will also reinforce the new employee's perception that he/she is truly important to the customer-oriented success of the business.

Important to any internal marketing program is the one-on-one training provided to employees.

Personnel Policy

Within the framework of internal marketing, personnel policy should reinforce customer orientation. Good service should not only be encouraged, but rewarded. This means that management should establish clearly understood performance criteria and appropriately reward the meeting of such criteria with wage increases, bonuses, and special non-financial recognition such as employee-of-the-month parking spaces, incentive travel packages, or other such celebrations of employee dedication.

Typically, tourism businesses—especially hotels, motels, resorts, and restaurants—offer only low wages to their frontline employees and often experience high rates of turnover. While low wages may continue to be a factor in this highly competitive industry, personnel policy must address the significant cost of employee turnover. Management must balance the cost of retaining loyal and effective employees through frequent wage increases against the cost of breaking in new employees and the cost of losing customers by the actions of poorly trained employees.[25]

Organizational Communication

Communication with employees should not end with training, and it should not be limited to giving orders. Positive verbal communication between supervisors and employees and between employees and other employees should be frequent and systematically encouraged. Frequent pats on the back reward employees in important ways above and beyond wages; no one gets tired of hearing that he or she is doing a good job.

Sharing information with employees about policy changes before they take place, or about new services and products, will not only help employees better serve the customer, but will also give employees a sense of "ownership" in the business. Verbal communication should be supplemented by newsletters, bulletin boards, and regular information meetings.

Another objective of organizational communication is to lift and sustain high employee morale and help employees acquire a greater sense of connection with the organization and other employees. The annual company picnic is a traditional example, but there are many other, more inventive ways to achieve such objectives.

New and constructive activities will not only maintain high employee morale, but may very well benefit customer and community relations.

Recruitment and Retention of Employees

Recruiting and retaining talented employees is another important function of internal marketing. While the connection between recruiting and retaining good employees with maintaining high levels of customer service has been well-documented, another factor currently confronts the tourism business: a serious and growing labor shortage. This labor shortage—especially of unskilled and semi-skilled laborers such as housekeepers, food handlers, and other frontline staff—is now world-wide. While the United States still has a reservoir of people for these positions, many European countries and Japan are bringing in thousands of foreigners on work visas.

An improved wage structure alone might relieve the labor shortage, but other actions may also have some favorable impact. One internal marketing perspective maintains that: "Jobs are bundles of benefits that people pay for through their labors."[26] Tourism businesses have to market their job openings not only to potential employees, but to those employees already on staff. One of the better ways to retain good employees is to promote from within—even if such promotion requires a lengthy and expensive training period.

Positions have to be made attractive in ways other than wage-and-benefit packages. Job value can be enhanced by other features such as perceived prestige, flex time, job autonomy, job variety, and pleasant working conditions. Enhanced job value can be developed through three key categories: content, work relationships, and working conditions.[27]

Content. Content is what an employee does on a job—the specific everyday tasks and work routine. Some content is inherently routine, repetitive, and unfulfilling to most workers. The resulting boredom can negatively affect customer service. Other jobs are stressful by nature—such as serving large numbers of people during peak periods. The resulting "burnout" is detrimental to quality customer service. Management can ameliorate both boredom and burnout by creating positions with a balanced mix of activities. Even better, management can cross-train employees for several different positions within the organization. Such practice has the added benefit of producing a cadre of adequately trained employees who are ready to fill in for others during sudden absences or an unexpected rush of customers.

Working Relationships. People appreciate jobs more when they like the people they work with and for. Accordingly, one of management's more important responsibilities is to monitor the social relationships among workers. Management must be alert to the quality of relationships among employees and constructively address problems as soon as they are observed. A supervisor upset by a problem at home can "take it out on" his/her staff. Staff members often pass such negativity on to their customers—meaning that literally *hundreds* of customers could be affected during a busy day.

Working Conditions. Working conditions are those conditions created by the physical environment—including lighting, temperature control, and work area furnishings; they are also conditions surrounding how a particular job is organized—or how well it serves its purpose and how well it is integrated with other jobs. For instance, if management is poorly organized with respect to handling large crowds, employees who have to constantly deal with disgruntled customers or take on additional responsibilities will soon seek other employment.

The elements of internal marketing will go a long way toward creating and managing a successful, cohesive, and, ultimately, profitable organization. Without it, money spent on external marketing will be money down the drain.

Market Research

Market research is the systematic study of any issue, problem, or phenomenon related to the marketing of a product or service. Systematic study may include an analysis and detailed study of a problem or the gathering of statistics to better understand it. Applied to tourism, market research may be as simple as reviewing demographic information to see if a restaurant, or a certain *kind* of restaurant, will attract the nearby population. A simple profile of guest registration addresses and zip codes is another example. Market research can be used to describe the competition, forecast potential demand, monitor and evaluate promotional efforts, or measure customer satisfaction. Whether simple or complex, market research is a prerequisite to effective marketing: "Without good marketing information, managers have to use intuition or guesses—and in our fast-changing and competitive economy, this invites failure."[28]

Market research provides information for the marketing manager—the person who makes decisions about potential markets, prices, and supply. It helps the marketing manager solve problems, capitalize on opportunities, estimate or be aware of potential or undiscovered markets, and understand the loss of customers or customer dissatisfaction. This type of information enables the business to "change and develop with its customers."[29] Such research is needed because, as management consultants will tell you: "In working with service organizations, we often find that managers have only the vaguest notions about what really counts in the mind of the customer."[30]

Sources of information and data are plentiful. Internally, the hotel guest list, the monthly or weekly sales reports, guest comment cards, as well as tax, utility, or other internal files can be good sources of marketing research data. Externally, the business or marketing manager may use the local library or a governmental planning unit. Many government offices such as the Census Bureau have large sources of data which can be useful to a tourism business. Sometimes it is necessary to talk to the customer directly to gather the needed information. This would be the case when gathering information on satisfaction levels or visitor travel patterns.

Solid research supports not only market analyses and planning, but feasibility analysis and situational analysis.[31] **Market analysis** assesses potential markets, demand, size, and location. A **feasibility analysis** includes the market analysis as well as a study of pricing, costs, development, and potential return on investment. In both cases, these types of research are conducted before a new enterprise is established. A **situational analysis** helps develop marketing strategies for improving and expanding existing businesses. All too often, situational analyses are initiated only during an economic downturn, either in the business itself or in the economy.[32] Market research must be a consistent component of successful marketing strategies for both existing and new businesses.

Private and Public Tourism Marketing

Marketing is a necessary function of tourism organizations in both the public and private sector. Private businesses and local, state, or national tourism agencies must make marketing an important day-to-day function. Tourism businesses, such as retail travel agencies, may market directly to the tourist. Other tourism businesses, such as hotels or resorts, may market their services to an intermediate supplier, such as a tour operator, in order to be included in a tour package.

A marketing orientation is no less important to public sector agencies and associations than it is to the private sector. The U.S. National Park System markets its attractions, services, and accommodations not only to promote visitation and ensure satisfied visitors. The foreword of a recent marketing book written for the U.S. National Park Service notes that:

> Meeting the challenge of today's leisure service market has prompted many park and recreation agencies to adopt private sector business practices. Increasingly, successful managers are turning to marketing as a means of providing their clientele (the public) with more relevant services at fairer prices, more efficient delivery of these services, and enhanced program awareness.[33]

This situation also applies to many state travel offices. As more and more state travel offices meet new marketing challenges, they must not only prepare and distribute quality promotional materials, but must also account for their efforts and for their expenditure of public funds on behalf of tourism.

This unique relationship between public and private sector tourism is somewhat different from the relationship between government and other private businesses. Few state governments put up millions to promote a private business. Not so for tourism. Increasingly, state governments and other public sector agencies spend millions of dollars to promote tourism. These public sector marketing efforts may include assistance with development or market research and promotion.

There are several reasons why public and quasi-public agencies become involved in tourism promotion and other direct assistance to the industry.[34] First and foremost is the fact that visitors tend to boost the overall economy in a city, state, region, or country. Second, tourist businesses lack the resources for a massive promotion of a state or region. Third, the government is responsible for the development and maintenance of the infrastructure. Roads, bridges, and water and sewage systems are all vital to the success of tourism. In many countries, the airlines and rail systems are owned by the government. Some resorts and national park concessions are government-owned as well.

Unquestionably, the public has a vested interest in promoting travel. For many countries and for certain states within the United States, tourism is critical to the economy and governmental spending reflects its importance. Not counting other types of direct assistance for tourism, the 50 U.S. state travel offices alone spent nearly $291 million in 1987–88, with a projected total budget of $317 million for 1988–1989.[35]

Marketing is more than advertising, promotional budgets, and public relations. It involves a range of areas—from training to product development. Marketing that occurs in isolation represents marketing that is poorly planned—and virtually useless. Marketing is a comprehensive, dynamic, and holistic discipline—one that cuts straight to the heart of any tourism business.

Endnotes

1. Edward M. Mahoney, "Recreation Marketing: The Need for a New Approach," *Visions in Leisure Business* 5 (Winter 1987), pp. 57–58.

2. E. Jerome McCarthy and William Perreault, Jr., *Basic Marketing: A Managerial Approach,* 9th ed. (Homewood, Ill.: Irwin, 1987), p. 36.

3. Alastair M. Morrison, *Hospitality and Travel Marketing* (Albany, N.Y.: Delmar, 1989), p. 256.

4. Robert L. Catlin, "Service Business Is People Dealing with Other People," an interview with Gary Knisely, in *Advertising Age,* 1979. Reprinted in *Service Marketing: Text, Cases, and Readings,* edited by Christopher H. Lovelock (Englewood Cliffs, N.J.: Prentice-Hall, 1984), p. 25.

5. Morrison, p. 256.

6. Morrison, p. 256.

7. Walt Disney World and Delta newspaper ad appearing in the *Detroit Free Press,* August 27, 1989, p. 7J. Additional information obtained through the Delta 800 number.

8. Mary J. Bitner and Bernard H. Booms, "Trends in Travel and Tourism Marketing: The Changing Structure of Distribution Channels," *Journal of Travel Research* 20 (Spring 1982), p. 40.

9. This discussion on suggested pricing policy is based on Morrison, p. 468; Robert W. McIntosh and Charles R. Goeldner, *Tourism: Principles, Practices, Philosophies,* 5th ed. (New York: Wiley, 1986), pp. 378–379; McCarthy and Perreault, pp. 492–503.

10. Edwin P. Hollander, *Principles and Methods of Social Psychology,* 2d ed. (New York: Oxford University Press, 1971), p. 213.

11. *Trends in Travel and Tourism Advertising Expenditures in the United States Measured Media 1984–1988,* A Special Report for Ogilvy and Mather, July 1989, p. I-2.

12. Douglas C. Frechtling, "Overview of U.S. Domestic Travel," in *Travel and Leisure's World Travel Overview—1988/1989* (New York: American Express Publishing Corporation, 1988), p. 77.

13. Somerset R. Waters, *Travel Industry World Yearbook—The Big Picture—1988* (New York: Child and Waters, Inc. 1988), p. 65.

14. Frechtling, p. 76.

15. "Characteristics of International Travel Markets," in *Travel and Leisure's World Travel Overview 1988/1989* (New York: American Express Publishing Corporation, 1988), pp. 45; 48.

16. Richard R. Perdue, "The Influence of Unplanned Attraction Visits on Expenditures by Travel-Through Visitors," *Journal of Travel Research* 25 (Summer 1986), p. 17.

17. Arch G. Woodside and Ellen M. Moore, "Competing Resort Hotels: Word-of-Mouth Communication and Guest Retention," *Tourism Management* 8 (December 1987), p. 16.

18. Karl Albrecht and Ron Zemke, *Service America: Doing Business in the New Economy* (Homewood, Ill.: Dow Jones-Irwin, 1985), p. 27.

19. Albrecht and Zemke, p. 37.

20. Mahoney, 1987, p. 63.

21. Mahoney, 1987, p. 65.

22. Allan W. Wicker, *An Introduction to Ecological Psychology* (Monterey, Calif.: Brooks/Cole, 1979), pp. 8–12.

23. James H. Donnelly, Jr., Leonard L. Berry, and Thomas W. Thompson, *Marketing Financial Services: A Strategic Vision* (Homewood, Ill.: Dow Jones-Irwin, 1985), p. 231.

24. Edward Mahoney, "Marketing Parks and Recreation: The Need for a New Approach," unpublished report, Department of Park and Recreation Resources, Michigan State University, East Lansing, Mich., 1987. An expansion of the article published in *Leisure and Business,* 1987.

25. Mahoney, 1987, p. 26.

26. Donnelly, Berry, and Thompson, 1985, p. 233.

27. Donnelly, Berry, and Thompson, p. 234.

28. McCarthy and Perreault, 1987, p. 124.

29. Albrecht and Zemke, p. 58.

30. Albrecht and Zemke, p. 59.

31. Morrison, p. 89.

32. Morrison, pp. 104–107.

33. National Park Service, *Marketing Parks and Recreation* (State College, Penn.: Venture Publishing, Inc., 1983), p. iii.

34. G. A. Schmoll, *Tourism Promotion* (London: Tourism International Press, 1977), p. 36.

35. *Survey of State Travel Offices 1988–89* (Washington, D.C.: U.S. Travel Data Center, 1988), p. 9.

Key Terms

attribution
credibility
encoding
feasibility analysis
interactive marketing
internal marketing
market analysis
market research

marketing mix
P-mix
packaging
programming
service cycle
situational analysis
word of mouth

Discussion Questions

1. What are the traditional four "Ps" of marketing? What "Ps" are added to make the "P-mix" for tourism marketing?

2. How does service marketing differ from product marketing?

3. What is programming? packaging? a marketing partnership?

4. What are some of the complexities and factors to consider when establishing a price for tourism products and services?

5. What are some of the promotion techniques used in marketing?

6. What is the difference between publicity and public relations?

7. What is interactive marketing? internal marketing?

8. What are four key interactions that influence tourist satisfaction?

9. What are the elements of the internal marketing mix?

10. How are market analysis, feasibility analysis, and situational analysis used in market research?

REVIEW QUIZ

When you feel you have covered all of the material in this chapter, answer these questions. Choose the *best* answer. Check your answers with the correct ones found on the Review Quiz Answer Key at the end of this book.

True (T) or False (F)

T   F   1. One of the most critical factors in the tourism business is consistency.

T   F   2. Programming combines a range of services and programs into one package for one price.

T   F   3. Frequent flyer programs are examples of fully integrated and connected marketing partnerships.

T   F   4. The perceived value of a service is just as important as its actual price in motivating travelers to make a purchase.

T   F   5. Tourism promotion primarily targets tourists and intermediate audiences like travel agents.

T   F   6. Encoding is the process of putting a message into language or visual symbols.

T   F   7. Word-of-mouth promotion occurs when a product or service is mentioned in the news media.

T   F   8. Management can best reduce job boredom and burnout by monitoring employees' social relationships.

T   F   9. External sources of information for market research include tax and utility records.

T   F   10. Marketing is an important function of both public and private sector tourism organizations.

Alternate/Multiple Choice

11. The "four Ps" traditionally include all of the following *except*:

    a. product.
    b. promotion.
    c. partnership.
    d. price.

12. Salient motives are:

    a. always obvious.
    b. generated by wants and desires.

13. Moments of truth are:

    a. a consumer's instantaneous emotional reactions.
    b. encoded advertising messages.

14. One of the four key interactions in the interactive marketing mix is:

   a. tourist and setting.
   b. tourist and transportation.

15. The internal marketing mix includes all of the following *except*:

   a. employee training.
   b. personnel policy.
   c. organizational communication.
   d. feasibility analysis.

Chapter Outline

Research and Tourism
    Product Research
    Place Research
    Price Research
    Promotion Research
    Monitoring and Forecasting
Types of Research
    Primary Research
    Secondary Research
The Research Process
    Sample Research Steps
Research Consultants
    Selecting a Consultant
    Investigating a Consultant
    Working with a Consultant

Learning Objectives

1. Summarize product and place research.

2. Summarize price and promotion research.

3. Contrast basic and applied research.

4. List three primary research techniques.

5. Explain observation and experimentation research.

6. Describe the advantages of using personal interviews as a research technique.

7. Describe the advantages of using telephone surveys as a research technique.

8. Explain the advantages and disadvantages of mailback surveys.

9. Give examples of secondary research.

10. Summarize a sample research process.

11. Describe three sources of research consultants.

12. Identify ways to investigate and work with a research consultant.

12

Research and Measurement

This chapter was written and contributed by Donald F. Holecek, Ph.D., Professor, Department of Park and Recreation Resources, and Director, Michigan Travel, Tourism and Recreation Resource Center, Michigan State University, East Lansing, Michigan.

"RESEARCH" IS A TERM that strikes fear in the minds of many people who have no experience with this fundamental business tool. Yet, all of us are involved in some form of research almost every day. Maybe you carefully searched stores, newspaper ads, and magazines for an item of clothing to complement your wardrobe; or perhaps you investigated the types of equipment you needed for a weekend camping trip. In either case, you conducted research.

Clearly, all you need to know about research cannot be presented in a single chapter. It takes years to train a highly skilled researcher. But you do not need extensive training to conduct effective research. Many large tourism firms employ research specialists to provide assistance to managers conducting research. In addition, the services of outside research consultants can be obtained for a fee. Much useful research is published in professional magazines, journals, and newsletters as well as in a wide array of business-oriented publications such as the *Wall Street Journal*, *Travel Weekly*, and *Business Week*. Research findings are also part of the agenda for many professional meetings you are likely to attend.

This chapter is designed to introduce you to the role research plays in the tourism industry. It will discuss research and tourism, types of research, a sample research process, and explain how you can select and work with research consultants.

Research and Tourism

Professionals in all industries rely on research to some degree. Tourism industry managers rely most directly on marketing research for both long-range plans and short-range operational decisions. Marketing research is not always easy to gather, analyze, or use. There are two basic reasons for this. First, the subject of tourism's marketing research is people—current and potential customers or guests. People are complex, and their behavior is difficult to measure and predict. Second, the most useful marketing research is that which is customized to fit the unique characteristics of a particular problem or opportunity. A hotel manager in Los Angeles would hesitate to make decisions based on research conducted by a hotel in Atlanta, for example.

Exhibit 1   Important Areas of Tourism Research

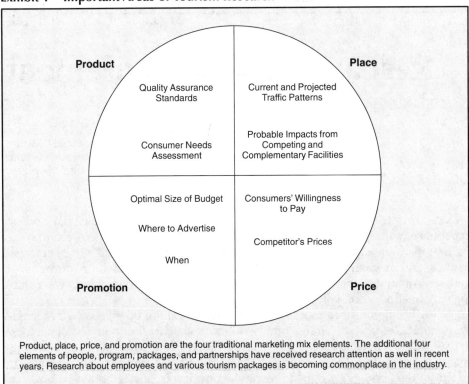

Product, place, price, and promotion are the four traditional marketing mix elements. The additional four elements of people, program, packages, and partnerships have received research attention as well in recent years. Research about employees and various tourism packages is becoming commonplace in the industry.

Because of the inexact nature of marketing research and the need to tailor research as closely as possible to the particular situation, as a tourism industry manager you will often be directly involved in developing a marketing research project for your own firm and analyzing and applying the information learned from the research. Therefore, the quicker and better you master the research facet of your job, the more you will be able to contribute and the more valuable you will be to your employer.

Today, the tourism firms with the best information hold an edge over the competition. The more you know about your guests' wants, needs, and preferences, the better prepared you are to offer the right product, at the right place, at the right price, and to promote it in the right way. Today's travelers have high-quality expectations and widely varying needs. The tourism industry has responded by expanding research programs that investigate the four traditional marketing mix elements critical to almost every tourism business: product, place, price, and promotion (see Exhibit 1).

Product Research

Research is commonly used in the tourism industry as a basis for increasing, decreasing, or altering the product offering. For example, a *Wall Street Journal* article described how research saved a failing Chicago restaurant with a high-priced Euro-Asian specialty menu. Research suggested that the restaurant's guests and potential guests were more interested in traditional oriental food at moderate prices. Once menu items and prices were changed, the restaurant's popularity grew rapidly.

An important part of most tourism firms' "product" is service. Many tourism firms attempt to differentiate their firm from competitors by providing higher quality service. What if your research shows that most of your guests are willing to pay for higher quality service? The question then becomes, What is "high-quality service" and how can it be measured and monitored to assure that the targeted level of quality is maintained?

First, you must realize that *your* definition of high-quality service is not as important as your guests' definition. It is your guests' perception of quality that must somehow be measured. Current and prospective guests must be identified and their preferences for types of services and levels of quality must be assessed. The most desired types of services and levels of quality—as revealed by your research—can then be incorporated into the firm's product offering.

At some point—even after they have changed their product, and quality service programs have been implemented—many firms begin to fail. Why? Because they become complacent. They relax, because they know that they are producing what their guests demand—at least, what their guests demanded when the guest research was conducted. Successful managers know that guest expectations change over time. Ongoing research must be conducted to ensure that current guest expectations are being met.

Even without ongoing research, it will eventually become obvious when guest expectations aren't being met. However, neither you nor the owners want to wait until declining occupancy rates and/or falling profits provide the first indications that the firm's product is losing favor with guests. By then, correcting the problem will be costly, if not impossible. And you may not get the chance to turn things around—owners tend to hire new managers when profits fall. Therefore, it is best—for personal as well as professional reasons—to employ an effective, ongoing, guest-oriented product research program at your firm.

Place Research

Many tourism businesses fail. Poor location choice is a common factor underlying many of these failures. It is common for the profitability of otherwise identical businesses to vary significantly simply because of differing locations. The difference between profit and loss can be a matter of a few miles, as in the case of motels located at different interchanges along a major highway. It can even be a matter of a few feet! Identical souvenir shops on different sides of an east-west street during hot summer days may post markedly different sales simply because the majority of potential buyers travel down the shady side of the street.

Location decisions must be made with extreme care because poor location choices are very costly to correct. For this reason, most major corporations rely on highly trained and experienced research teams for information about markets, economic trends, real estate values, and traffic patterns before choosing a location. Even small independent firms should reserve a significant portion of their development budgets for location research and should hire experienced consultants if expertise within the firm is not available.

Price Research

Intense competition is common within the tourism industry, but many individual firms have considerable flexibility in what they can charge for their products. Why? Because travelers have different wants, needs, and preferences—as well as varying abilities to pay for tourism products. Firms that can identify and quantify these differences have knowledge that can be exploited by providing products tailored—and priced—to fit the needs of specific travel market segments. Good research can help a firm identify under-served travelers or products and services for which higher prices can be charged.

Promotion Research

In the 1989–1990 fiscal year, state travel promotion offices in the United States expected to spend more than $126 million on travel advertising, and reported total overall promotion budgets of well over $300 million.[1] Total travel promotion expenditures by airlines, car rental corporations, hotels and motels, travel agencies, and other sectors of the tourism industry are unknown but most certainly exceed the states' total by a factor of ten or more. Clearly, tourism businesses invest considerable amounts of money each year in promotion.

Promotion research can help a firm determine which types of promotions will work best. However, most small firms and even some larger organizations fail to conduct research to help them design promotional campaigns or to evaluate the effectiveness of the campaigns they implement. For example, research can be used to establish how much should be spent on a promotion, yet promotion budgets are often determined arbitrarily. Many firms use a simple formula to determine how much money to spend on promotions—for example, 1% to 2% of total sales. State travel office promotion budgets are often linked to the state's overall budget circumstances; when tax revenues begin to fall behind expenditures, many states spend less money on travel promotion. Cutting promotion budgets when sales or tax revenues decline may very well be exactly the wrong response under certain market conditions. However, without supporting research, managers have little basis for supporting one level of investment in promotion over another.

Once the decision about how much to spend on promotion has been made, research can provide guidance into when, where, and for what the money should be spent. The effectiveness of any promotional strategy depends on good answers to these three questions.

Promotion research often draws on the literature and methods of applied consumer psychology for clues for timing the release of promotional messages. Understanding when targeted guests make travel plans for different types of trips will help to time promotional messages to arrive when the market is most receptive and interested; that is, when promotion is most likely to have the desired impact on consumer behavior.

It is equally, if not more important, to know *where* to promote. Here the choices are many, including radio, television, newspapers, magazines, brochures, billboards, and newsletters. Because the cost-effectiveness of these media is highly variable, an investment in research that narrows the media options even slightly can yield an attractive return. Research can help to establish which media should be used at the beginning of a promotional campaign and identify if and when media should be changed as the campaign progresses.

Sometimes, one feature or aspect of a firm's services should be emphasized over others. For example, research might show that a hotel's profits could be increased by promoting the in-house restaurant or by introducing and promoting a new feature of the restaurant such as 4:00 P.M. "high tea."

Monitoring and Forecasting

There is a tendency for many tourism managers to seek solutions to their problems from outside their organizations. This perspective should be balanced by a focus on information available from within the organization.

Monitoring is designed to provide information on a firm's current performance and its progress toward meeting operational goals and objectives. Daily sales reports, guest counts, meals-sold-per-meal-period reports, and other management reports are examples of the kinds of monitoring engaged in by tourism businesses. Monitoring produces vast volumes of data—much of which is not used in research applications. This is unfortunate, since this data can be analyzed to provide useful information. For example, state governments monitor tax collections from tourism businesses, yet few tourism managers draw on this data to spot important trends in tourism industry development throughout the state. Hotels and motels collect information from guests during the reservation process primarily for operational purposes, but this data can be used for many research purposes as well. For example, registration data can be analyzed to provide information about the geographical market or markets being served. This information can help managers give direction to the firm's promotional activities. Guest registration forms can be modified to gather research information too. For example, the form can ask guests to identify the purpose of their trips. This data can be analyzed to determine the share of sales attributable to business travelers, non-business travelers, tour groups, conventioneers, and so on. Among other things, this would tell managers which categories of guests they should promote to.

Data generated by a firm's monitoring systems can also be used for **forecasting**. A firm's recent sales records are a good base from which to forecast sales for the coming year. Forecasted sales can be adjusted up or down to reflect expected changes in the coming year's operating environment. Many firms have found this simple approach to forecasting to be as effective as more sophisticated and expensive alternatives. Many firms are also projecting sophisticated forecasts from their sales and other financial records by using "spreadsheet" computer software.

Types of Research

There are two fundamental types of research: basic and applied. There is often considerable overlap between these categories and many research projects are designed to contribute both basic and applied research information. **Basic research** tends to focus on new problems or on developing new approaches to old problems. It is more theoretical in the sense that both the success of the project and its potential applications are uncertain. **Applied research** tends to focus on problems that have been studied before, using approaches that have proven to be successful in the past. The expectation is that an applied research project will contribute to a specific problem's solution.

There are strong relationships between basic and applied research. Applied researchers rely heavily on basic researchers to upgrade and enhance the applied researchers' ability to successfully solve an expanding range of problems. For example, the silicon chip was a product of many years of basic research, and applied researchers successfully incorporated the technology into many products that solve problems or make life easier for people in a wide range of industries, including tourism. In turn, applied researchers serve basic research scientists in significant ways. For example, they thoroughly test basic research products, identifying their strengths and weaknesses. This information is, in turn, fed back to basic research scientists and helps them to better target their basic research.

The United States leads the world in both the quantity and quality of information discovered in its basic research programs. But this lead has diminished in recent years as other industrialized countries have increased their investments in basic research while we have not. This does not bode well for the strength of the U.S. economy in the long run. However, the greater and more immediate challenge faced by the United States is that the country is relatively slow in finding applications for basic research products. The potential competitive edge from basic research programs is being lost because overseas competitors are proving far better at finding applications for U.S. ideas. The tourism industry can do its part to correct this situation by supporting basic research and becoming more involved in seeking applications for basic research information.

Research is also categorized based on the source of the data used in the analysis. **Primary research** uses original data collected specifically for a particular research project. **Secondary research** uses data collected by others, often for purposes other than the particular research project in question. It is not unusual for researchers to employ data from both primary and secondary sources in analyzing a problem or opportunity.

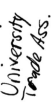

Primary Research

Many different techniques are used to gather primary research information. Selected primary research techniques with which you should be familiar include:

- Observation

- Experimentation

- Surveys

Observation. Observation is one of the most popular and reliable data collection techniques that tourism researchers use. Observation is especially accurate because it studies the actual behavior of research subjects rather than their statements. Observation may be direct or indirect.

The **time and motion** direct observation technique has long been a popular method of improving employees' efficiency. As the name implies, a researcher carefully observes and records employee actions as they perform assigned tasks. Results of time and motion research are used to: (1) redesign facilities to eliminate bottlenecks, (2) reassign employee tasks to improve the flow of work, and (3) train employees to handle their tasks more efficiently.

The **garbage survey** is an indirect observation technique that can be used to monitor consumer preferences for menu items served in a restaurant. A systematic tally of which items are being eaten and which are being thrown away can be very useful for managers. Even garbage can be a source of valuable primary research data.

These and other observation techniques yield exceptionally accurate results. However, observation is one of the most costly primary research methods. Costs are high due to factors such as the degree of observer training required, the amount of time required, and in some cases the equipment and facilities that must be used. Despite the costs, observation can be profitably employed in solving many challenging situations encountered in the tourism industry.

Experimentation. **Experimentation** is a primary research technique in which one or more independent variables are allowed to change and the impact of this change on a dependent variable is then measured.

Experimentation is by far the most common primary research choice of researchers in the natural and engineering sciences. There are many opportunities to employ experimentation in the tourism industry as well. For example, experimentation can be used to determine which brochure cover will be most effective. Two or more brochure covers can be designed (the dependent variables), and guests' reaction to them (the independent variable) can be measured. However, experimentation is not often used by tourism researchers, in part because of its relatively high cost.

Often, experimentation is not employed simply because tourism researchers are not familiar with experimental research methods and their potential applications. As tourism research becomes more advanced, experimentation will become a more common tool in addressing some of this industry's most vexing problems.

Surveys. **Surveys** are the primary data collection technique employed most often by tourism researchers. This is understandable, given the people-oriented nature of tourism. The best source of information needed to help tourism managers make decisions are their current and potential guests or consumers.

Surveys can be classified based on the amount of interaction between the research subjects or respondents and members of the survey team. Three common types of surveys include:

- Personal interviews
- Telephone surveys
- Mailback surveys

Exhibit 2   Three Survey Research Methods

	Personal Interview	Telephone Interview	Mailback Survey
Relative Cost	High	Medium	Low
Expected Rate of Response	High	Medium	Low
Flexibility	High	Medium	Low
Time to Complete	High	Low	Medium
Quality Control Costs	High	Medium	Low

A personal interview research team in action along a Michigan highway. (Courtesy of the Michigan Department of Transportation)

The degree of interaction between subjects and the research team is greatest in the personal interview and least in the mailback survey. Each approach has strengths and limitations that must be understood in order to select the method or methods most suitable to the situation being studied (see Exhibit 2). Frequently, situations are encountered in which one of the three alone will not produce the quality of primary data required at an affordable price. In such situations, the research team may use two or even all three approaches to collect quality data within established budget constraints.

Personal interviews. The personal interview, as its name implies, involves an interviewer talking face-to-face with selected respondents. The interviewer may ask questions and record responses, present a questionnaire and ask the respondent to complete it, or do a little of each. The personal interview technique allows the interviewer to help the respondent understand difficult questions. It is also common practice to show respondents photos, models, and other aids to illustrate products or product concepts.

This high degree of flexibility comes at a rather high cost. Interviewers must be carefully selected, trained, and supervised. They must be transported to the site where the interview will be held and often are paid even while they are idle waiting for the next respondent to arrive.

Rates of response are generally highest with personal interviews. Personal interviews also yield a higher percentage of fully completed questionnaires. The personal interview is the most expensive survey technique, but it provides data of the highest quality. It may be the only satisfactory approach when the issues under consideration are complex or require significant interviewer assistance, actual demonstrations, or models.

The focus group and the in-depth interview are variations of the personal interview that have become very popular in the tourism industry. A focus group involves a discussion between a facilitator and a carefully selected group of respondents, while the in-depth interview is a one-on-one extended discussion between the interviewer and a single respondent. Both techniques permit researchers to probe deeply to uncover the what, when, and why of consumer tastes and preferences. The focus group approach often includes a panel of outside observers hidden behind a one-way mirror, or the sessions may be videotaped for later analysis.

The principal advantage of focus groups and in-depth interviews is the opportunity to explore an issue in depth from the perspective of a group of specially selected individuals. The principal disadvantages include the relatively high cost, small number of subjects, and less structured questions and responses. Focus groups and in-depth interviews can be good sources of new ideas and insights, but it is usually wise to follow up with a more structured survey of a larger and more representative sample.

Telephone surveys. New technology has had the greatest impact on telephone surveys. Even the most poor and remote households in the United States now have reliable telephone service. Computers have replaced many telephone operators, thereby reducing long-distance charges. Computers are also used to: (1) select respondents through random digit dialing, and (2) to place the call, thereby reducing unproductive interviewer time between calls. Survey questions are displayed on interviewers' computer screens, and responses are entered directly into computer data files by the interviewers.

Speed is a major advantage of telephone surveys. Under ideal conditions, a well-equipped and experienced telephone survey firm can complete a national telephone survey and provide results in a matter of a few days. However, the typical project encountered in the tourism industry requires more time to complete because questionnaire development and pretesting are time-consuming, and because few clients are willing to pay a premium price for fast service.

Reaching targeted respondents can be a problem for telephone interviewers. More and more households have answering machines for screening out unwanted calls, and many targeted respondents simply aren't at home to take phone calls. The latter may be the very subjects you want to reach; they may not be at home because they work long hours, earn high incomes, and travel often.

The telephone interview technique is moderately expensive despite the cost reductions experienced in recent years. It is more flexible than the mailback survey, since some degree of interaction takes place between the respondent and the interviewer. But it is not as flexible as the personal interview, since no physical object—a photo, for example—can be exchanged. This may change somewhat as telephone fax technology advances and becomes more widespread; we may soon see creative applications of fax technology in telephone interviews.

Another disadvantage is that it is difficult to maintain the respondent's attention for a lengthy interview or to elicit responses to complex questions over the telephone. Telephone surveys work best when the questions asked are relatively simple.

Mailback surveys. Despite today's technology, the "old-fashioned" mailback survey remains an important vehicle for collecting information. With mailback surveys, there is no direct contact between the research team and targeted respondents; the subjects receive all materials by mail and respond by mail. Therefore, the survey must be carefully written, since there is no opportunity to assist respondents who encounter something that is confusing. The survey must also include an effective plea or incentive to convince the respondent to complete the questions. Reminder mailings and special incentives such as prizes and gifts have proven to be effective.

The mailback survey's principal advantage is its relatively low cost. No interviewers must be paid and no travel or telephone charges are involved. However, mailback surveys are the least flexible of the three types of surveys and generally yield the lowest rate of response and the highest rate of skipped questions.

While the quality of mailback data tends to be low because of non-response problems, consistency is far easier and less expensive to maintain than in personal interviews or telephone surveys. Incorrect interviewer behavior (including, on occasion, interviewers who complete questionnaires themselves) can severely bias personal and telephone interviews unless rigorous quality controls are followed.

Because of significant cost advantages, the mailback survey merits serious consideration when speed is not a priority. Mailback surveys are also a good choice when the information requested may require respondents to check their records or to take time to reflect before responding.

Secondary Research

Many problems or opportunities encountered in the tourism industry can be addressed without collecting primary data. Secondary data is information collected by others for other purposes. Secondary data is often available from within the organization and from external sources. When properly analyzed, secondary data may provide all the information you need to make effective decisions. In such instances, considerable cost and time can be saved.

Government agencies and private firms collect huge volumes of data—for example, data to support and document taxes owed and paid. This secondary data can be used by tourism managers and researchers. For example, tax data can be analyzed to identify trends in tourism industry revenues by geographic region. Other commonly collected data with many uses in tourism include: arrivals and departures at airports; highway traffic volumes; bridge and tunnel crossing traffic counts; number and nature of construction permits issued; licensed campgrounds, marinas, and bars in the area; national and state park use; weather statistics; census statistics; and so on. Trade magazines often publish surveys of restaurant guests and hotel or motel guests, as well as financial information reported by state, region, and country. Trade associations and universities are also good external sources of secondary data.

Exhibit 3 Sample Research Process

1. Identify the Problem and Establish Objectives
2. Evaluate Possible Approaches
3. Develop the Research Proposal and Budget
4. Develop and Pretest Research Instruments
5. Develop a Plan for Analysis
6. Select the Sample
7. Collect Data
8. Process and Analyze the Data
9. Report Results

The advantages of secondary data are that it is available at little or no cost and is already collected, saving you time and money. There are several disadvantages. The quality of the data is often suspect. Since the secondary data was collected for other purposes, it may not be exactly what is needed.

Careful evaluation of secondary data is mandatory before using it in an analysis. You must avoid the trap of believing everything that is in print or in a computer memory bank. While the quality of secondary data is beyond your control, it is possible and necessary to assess its quality before deciding whether it should be used in your research.

The Research Process Quality Control

Research is a systematic process for solving problems or for testing new ideas. Researchers use many different procedures to deal with research problems. There is no one best set of steps to follow to conduct good research.

Sample Research Steps

The sample research approach presented here includes nine steps (see Exhibit 3). A degree of interaction and overlapping between steps is unavoidable because research is an exploratory process. The research process may not always proceed directly from one step to the next, and it is common to return to an earlier step as one gains insight later in the research process.

Step 1: Identify the Problem and Establish Objectives. The problems you encounter as a tourism industry professional are rarely simple and directly researchable. Problems tend to be masses of symptoms in which one or more researchable problems are embedded.

Setting out to do research without a well-defined problem and one or more objectives is like taking an automobile trip without an established destination. Even though you may have a complete set of road maps (research tools), they can't be used effectively unless you know where you want to go (the research problem) and, of course, you won't know when to stop without established objectives.

Exploration is often a primary goal of a travel experience and is an element of research as well; however, most tourism organizations don't initiate research to derive pleasure from the process itself. Rather, information is sought for the purpose of making better management decisions, enhancing profits, or achieving other organizational objectives. Well-defined problems with clearly stated research objectives are the key to effective and efficient research projects.

Step 2: Evaluate Possible Approaches. Once the problem has been defined, you can begin to evaluate possible approaches to its solution. During this step, you should visit a library to determine how others have approached similar problems in prior research studies. Background data should be evaluated for its quality and relevance. This preliminary assessment will help you determine the research approach most likely to succeed and will help you identify whatever additional information you will need for your study.

Step 3: Develop the Research Proposal and Budget. You should incorporate the information you gathered during your preliminary assessment into a proposal specifying what will be done during your research study, when it will be done, by whom, and at what cost. Considerable interaction between you and your research staff (or outside research consultant) and upper management occurs during this step. These interactions lead to: (1) refinements in how the research problem is stated, and (2) refinements of your research objectives. This, in turn, may lead to a second preliminary assessment and a rewrite of the proposal. This process should be repeated until a proposal emerges that meets your needs, your budget, and the capabilities of your research staff or consultant.

Part of your research proposal involves outlining the target population of the research—which consumers or potential consumers you wish to question, how many, and how they will be chosen. The proposal should also include a brief description of how you propose to analyze the information that is gathered.

Step 4: Develop and Pretest Research Instruments. Most tourism research studies involve collecting information from a targeted population identified in the proposal—business travelers, tourists from neighboring states, and so on. The research method or methods—personal interviews, telephone surveys, mailback surveys, etc.—for collecting information will have been specified in the proposal, but the actual **research instruments**—the questionnaires you'll use—must be developed and pretested during this step.

Questionnaires are designed to provide more objective and consistent data than can be obtained through informal, unstructured contact with guests. While frequent, courteous contact between employees and guests is encouraged by most tourism businesses, these contacts seldom produce reliable information. An employee who asks, "Did you enjoy your stay with us?" will usually get the expected "yes" rather than a frank assessment. The few guests who answer otherwise are unlikely to represent the majority, and their comments usually are not recorded or reported by employees.

Your information needs must be converted into questions that most respondents will understand and are willing to answer. As questions are written, you and your research staff or consultant must interact to ensure that all of the high-priority questions are asked and the low-priority questions are deleted. It is important to develop research instruments that are as brief as possible to ensure high response rates and minimize costs.

Pretesting can help you identify and correct unanticipated problems with your questionnaire. Pretesting involves administering your questionnaire to respondents, using procedures identical to those that will be used during your proposed research project. The basic purpose of the pretest is to determine if the questionnaire to be employed actually does what it is designed to do. Are the questions understandable? What questions are skipped by respondents? Why? Are the questions presented in the proper order? Does the order of questions make any difference in how subsequent questions are answered? Because designing an effective questionnaire is both an art and a science, even the most experienced researcher cannot be certain that a questionnaire will perform as expected without subjecting it to a rigorous pretest.

The pretest often includes a debriefing session during which respondents are asked many questions about the design and layout of the questionnaire itself. Results of the pretest are incorporated in a revised questionnaire that may again be pretested if major changes were made in the first questionnaire. Pretesting is expensive and takes valuable time. But it can be even more expensive and time-consuming not to pretest, since the entire study may have to be repeated if significant faults in the questionnaire are not discovered until analysis is underway.

Step 5: Develop a Plan for Analysis. As mentioned in Step 3, your research proposal should contain a general plan for analyzing the information you gather. During Step 5, your plan should be refined. You should conduct a more in-depth review of relevant literature to make sure that the latest basic research findings are fully understood and, where appropriate, are incorporated into your analysis plan. Whatever computer software is needed should be acquired or developed during this step. Staff needs must be assessed and, if necessary, new personnel hired and trained. The structure of the research report should be developed. In combination, these activities help ensure that the analyses of the information you gather will proceed correctly and quickly.

Step 6: Select the Sample. In this very important step, the sampling plan outlined in your research proposal (Step 3) should be refined and implemented. How a sample is chosen from the population you want to study varies with the survey research method or methods selected and the research environment.

Whatever research method is selected, you must select a **representative sample** of the targeted population. If the sample drawn is not representative, the data collected will not be accurate. For example, a community tourist council decided it needed information about tourists visiting the community in order to design a marketing plan. Local hotels and motels agreed to cooperate by distributing a well-designed questionnaire to a random sample of guests. Results were tallied and a profile of the community's tourists was subsequently reported to the council. One astute member of the council objected, stating that the results were not representative of the community's tourist population. Why? Because tourists who did not spend a night in a local hotel or motel were not represented in the sample.

You must also determine the optimal sample size. A number of factors must be known or estimated to make this determination. For example, the optimal sample size should be increased when the variability among individuals within the sample population being studied increases. Sample size should also increase when a higher degree of accuracy is required. If only a rough estimate is required to support a decision, a relatively small sample is probably adequate. A smaller sample size is also appropriate where members of the population being studied are relatively similar. Guidelines for determining the right sample size can be found in survey research texts, but even accomplished researchers often consult a statistician for advice before undertaking major studies.

When you are involved in a research project, you must keep in mind that there is a trade-off between costs and the precision of research information. Beyond a certain point, very large samples increase precision only sightly. Only you can decide at what point a slight increase in precision justifies a major increase in cost.

Step 7: Collect Data. Data collection involves implementing the procedures for gathering information that were defined in your research proposal (Step 3). Quality control is your (or your research consultant's) chief task during the data collection phase of the research project. Quality control is simplest in a mailback survey because there are no intermediaries between you and the respondents. However, you still must monitor the process to ensure that no unexpected problems arise. If response rate lags behind expectations, for example, it may become necessary to institute more intense follow-up procedures than called for in the proposal.

Quality control is more of a challenge in personal interviews and telephone surveys because you rely on others to administer the questionnaire. Interviewers may perform perfectly during training but may not adhere fully to what they learned as the project advances. The exact repetition required to ensure consistency from interview to interview can lead to boredom and sloppy interviewer behavior. Therefore, you must monitor interviewers closely and take corrective action as needed to ensure that all interviewers adhere to proper procedures.

It is also important to check on interviewers to be sure that they are following the prescribed sampling plan. Problems to watch for include:

- Reporting a "no contact" as a "refusal" so the interviewer doesn't have to return to complete the interview.

- Interviewing whoever may be at home rather than a specified member of a household.

- The interviewer rather than the respondent filling out all or a portion of the questionnaire.

Checkpoints and incentives can be incorporated in the survey design to control lapses in interviewer performance, but these add to overall study costs. You must be willing to pay these added costs or risk wasting research dollars on results derived from faulty databases.

Step 8: Process and Analyze the Data. Quality control is also important in this step of the research process. Completed questionnaires are often screened before coding for computer analysis. Obviously unreliable or incomplete questionnaires should be eliminated. The remaining questionnaires can be coded and entered into a computer file. Coding and entry errors may affect the accuracy of subsequent analyses. For this reason, you should carefully oversee the coding and entry process to keep such errors to an acceptable minimum. Where feasible, a double-entry method is best and should yield an error-free database. This approach essentially doubles the cost of data entry, and some researchers use a less rigorous spot-checking system. It is also important to employ appropriate questionnaire storage and computer file backup procedures to avoid loss of data.

Once data is entered into a computer, it is common practice for the database to be "cleaned." The purpose of cleaning a database is to eliminate data items that may have resulted from: (1) coding and/or entry errors, or (2) from respondents incorrectly answering a particular question.

Once the database has been entered and cleaned, analysis proceeds according to the plan outlined in the research proposal and refined in Step 5. For the researcher, this is the step that holds the most excitement: the fruits of many weeks and months of labor finally begin to emerge. You must remain alert for the unexpected, since anything unexpected suggests a previously undetected problem in the database, or—more happily—a much-hoped-for new discovery. In any case, the unexpected is reason for further analysis and verification of its cause.

Step 9: Report Results. As analysis draws to a close, the final step in the research process begins. From your perspective (and the perspective of your superiors), a comprehensive and understandable research report is essential to a successful research project. A good report begins with a well-structured introduction that clearly states your original problem and your research objectives. You should explain these in terms that are meaningful to those reading your report. The main body of your report may be long or short, but all significant research findings should be highlighted. A complete research report will include detailed sections on all aspects of the project, including pretesting, sampling, data processing, analyses, and results. Ideally, enough detail should be provided to fully evaluate the reliability of the results and to duplicate the study if necessary.

Your report should include an executive summary. Many people will only read this section of the report, so it should include the most important findings as well as a discussion of all significant limitations in the data or the analyses that were performed.

Research Consultants

While many tourism professionals regularly engage in some form of research regularly, it is also clear that no one individual can be adequately trained in all facets of tourism research. Therefore, for some research projects it will be necessary to seek the services of consultants inside or outside your firm. Knowledge of some basic principles will aid you in selecting and working with research consultants.

Before seeking the services of outside consultants, it is advisable to meet with in-house researchers if your firm employs them. They can assist you in several ways:

- They can provide background data to help formulate research objectives and establish data requirements.

- They can help in structuring the research problem.

- They may be willing and able to meet your research needs at little or no direct cost.

- They can help you identify a reliable outside consultant and provide examples of research proposals and contracts.

- They can help in screening consultants and their proposals.

Check with your organization's research staff even if you know in advance that they do not have the time or expertise to help you. Why? Because it is good management practice to keep them informed. They are on your team and will help you look out for your firm's interests.

Selecting a Consultant

Identifying and selecting a research consultant may be the most important research task you address in your career. Consultants offering tourism research services are readily available, but their capabilities, fees, and reliability vary greatly. Because of the nature of research and the research industry, there are no standards or certification programs to protect research clients. The research industry is not regulated by the government in any significant way. The industry is dominated by small firms because it is a relatively simple matter to start a research consulting business. Business failures for research firms are as common as they are for all small businesses. Thus, the adage "buyer beware" must be followed in selecting research consultants.

In most situations, it is desirable to seek several estimates from reliable research consultants before awarding a research contract. You must write a well-structured **request for research proposal (RFP)** if you want to obtain comparable proposals from consultants. A vague RFP is likely to elicit widely varying proposals, especially with respect to estimated costs. Much of this variation will be due to different guesses about such things as the sample size you want rather than to cost differences to perform the same set of research tasks.

There are three basic sources of research consultants:

- In-house
- Private firms
- Colleges and universities

In-House. If your firm is large enough to have a research department, use it to conduct your research or to assist you in selecting an outside consultant. However, even when in-house research services are available, your role as an actively involved research client will not differ markedly.

Private Firms. Research is the business of private research consultants, and their primary motive is to profit from the services they sell. The profit motive works as well in the research industry as it does in the tourism industry, yet it introduces pitfalls that you should avoid.

Satellite technology makes it possible to receive or transmit data from around the world. (Courtesy of Michigan State University)

For example, some types of research are more profitable than others. A consultant whose firm is well-equipped to conduct telephone surveys may need to subcontract with another firm to conduct focus group research. It is clearly in this consultant's interest to steer you toward using more telephone surveys and fewer focus groups, even though the opposite may be more effective in solving your research problem. Most consultants are ethical people and would not knowingly mislead a client for profit; however, it is natural to steer clients toward what a consultant knows best, which, more often than not, is research methods which the consultant finds most profitable.

Another potential pitfall involves the number of services offered by a private consultant. The more research services the consultant provides to clients, the higher will be his/her profit. The tendency, therefore, is for consultants to try to sell more services than the minimum required to satisfactorily address a research problem. Again, this is not necessarily unethical, since you will receive added services for the added costs, but the added costs may not always represent a good investment, given your needs. It is primarily your responsibility to determine what benefit you will derive from your research investment, but a good research consultant should fairly present the alternatives from which you can choose.

Colleges and Universities. Colleges and universities can be excellent sources for research services. Many faculty members work as consultants to supplement their salaries, sharpen research skills, and maintain ties to the "real world." Students can also be involved; applied research experience is a requirement in many courses and for many advanced degrees.

While you should expect exceptions, a few general advantages and disadvantages in using colleges and universities can be noted. Since overhead and student stipends are low, academic research can be relatively inexpensive. Academic researchers often have highly specialized and advanced research skills developed in their basic research programs and from intense monitoring of the research literature. Many academic institutions are home for tourism research institutes. These may have extensive libraries and secondary data files as well as staffs that are highly skilled and experienced in dealing with the tourism industry. Academic institutions are especially good choices when your research needs may call for an innovative or advanced approach.

An often cited disadvantage of research conducted by academics is that it takes more time to complete than is typical for projects conducted by private consultants. All researchers have a tendency to underestimate how long a research program will take to complete, in part because unexpected delays are inherent in the nature of research. At a college or university, research may assume a lower priority than teaching or taking classes, so be sure to negotiate a firm completion date if you intend to employ an academic researcher.

A more unique problem often encountered with academic research involves the issue of sharing the research information that results from your study. Education and sharing knowledge as widely as possible is the fundamental purpose of academic institutions, while it is often to your firm's advantage to restrict who has access to your research information. Academics usually want to publish their research findings and use them as teaching aids in the classroom. However, provisions to protect your interests can be negotiated with the consultant. Concerns with proprietary issues are often exaggerated by research clients who do not recognize how quickly findings become dated and useless to competitors. Within reason, some sharing of research findings are part of your responsibilities as a professional in the tourism industry, since such sharing helps to advance the state of industry knowledge. There are times when you will benefit from the knowledge shared by others in the industry.

Investigating a Consultant

It is necessary to thoroughly investigate a prospective outside research consultant's qualifications, regardless of whether he/she is with a private firm or an academic institution. The investigation usually begins by reviewing a consultant's resume and/or a research firm's statement of qualifications. The educational background and relevant research experiences of the research consultant are of major importance. Good tourism researchers can be found with remarkably differing educational backgrounds. Tourism researchers may hold degrees in expected fields like business, marketing, or economics, or in unexpected fields like communications, mathematics, or park and recreation resources. The institution awarding the degree is less important than the consultant's knowledge of courses taken.

The extent of a consultant's research experience is probably the best measure of his/her ability to perform. Ideally, the consultant will have successfully completed many projects similar to the one you have in mind. It is also important to note the research facilities available to the research consultant, and their proximity to where you are located. Even with a growing array of electronic communications devices, face-to-face contact between you and the consultant will benefit your research project.

All experienced research consultants know the importance of presenting themselves to a prospective client in the best possible light. Obviously, their written and verbal testimony will emphasize their strengths and downplay their limitations. They will showcase their most successful projects and list their most satisfied clients as references. Therefore, it is important to seek out additional information about a consultant. The best source of such information is the consultant's client list. Both very satisfied and less satisfied clients should be interviewed. The following are a few questions you should ask:

- Was the consultant accessible?

- Were deadlines met? If not, why not?

- Did the consultant work with you to achieve your goals?

- Did a good atmosphere of trust develop over the research process?

- Were the research reports clearly written?

- Did the reports meet your expectations and were they actually used?

- Was the price charged a fair one?

- How responsive was the consultant to questions, especially after the project was completed?

- If you were to work with the consultant again, what changes would you make?

No research consultant will meet all the criteria you establish, but a careful investigation will narrow the field to the best prospects.

Working with a Consultant

Regardless of whether in-house or outside consultants are selected, the first principle in working with research consultants is that you must retain possession of your research problem. Consultants can and should provide assistance in framing a research problem, but don't let them move you to an entirely different problem than the one you want to research.

A detailed research contract is the key to working successfully with a research consultant. A detailed contract ensures that you and the consultant have a good understanding of how the research will be conducted and the reports that are expected. It is important to be realistic in your expectations. The research process involves making trade-offs. A good research contract strikes a balance between your costs and the benefits you will receive.

Research involves a degree of exploration and some uncertainty. Therefore, even a good research contract may not cover everything that arises. Regular communication between you and the research consultant is important to a research project's success. Both parties learn from the exchanges of information, and mutually agreeable solutions to unexpected problems can be quickly developed. To avoid misunderstanding, any agreed-upon changes should be incorporated into the contract.

Good research takes time, often *a lot* of time. You and your consultant may differ with respect to what constitutes a reasonable amount of time to complete a research project. You may be in a hurry, because the sooner you have access to research results, the sooner those results can be used to guide management decisions. The research consultant, on the other hand, is likely to be serving a number of clients simultaneously, or may place a higher priority on taking time for quality control.

Several actions can be taken to keep the research project on an acceptable schedule. First, the contract should clearly specify when each phase of the project should be completed and provide penalties for not meeting deadlines. Incentives for early completion can be an effective motivation. Second, a higher-priced contract can be negotiated that: (1) calls for your project to receive priority over others, and (2) provides the funds necessary to employ the quickest means available to complete all tasks involved. Third, the consultant can provide you with interim reports. In most cases it is fairly simple for consultants to perform preliminary analyses of the data they have received to date. Although preliminary results are subject to change as the database grows and is subjected to more in-depth analysis, they are better than no information at all if they can help managers with decisions that must be made before a research project is completed. Be prepared to pay extra for this service if it is not specified in the original contract.

All research consultants are anxious to please their clients. This can be harmful in situations where the consultant does not perceive the client as being receptive to unpleasant research results. If a research consultant senses that you are looking for results that support a particular point of view, he/she may be inclined to deliver what is expected rather than alienate a client. If you want a totally objective research report, you must make this clear to the consultant from the beginning.

Endnotes

1. U.S. Travel Data Center, *Survey of State Travel Offices 1989-1990* (Washington, D.C., February 1990).

Key Terms

applied research	representative sample
basic research	research
experimentation	research instruments
forecasting	request for research proposals (RFP)
garbage survey	secondary research
monitoring	survey
observation	time and motion research
primary research	

Discussion Questions

1. Why is research important to tourism firms?
2. What is product research and how often should it be conducted?
3. Why is promotion research valuable to a tourism firm?
4. What is basic research? applied research?
5. What are three primary research techniques?
6. What are the advantages and disadvantages of personal interviews?
7. Should research instruments be pretested? Why or why not?
8. What is involved in selecting a population sample?
9. Quality control is especially important in which steps of the research process?
10. What are some guidelines for investigating and working with a research consultant?

REVIEW QUIZ

When you feel you have covered all of the material in this chapter, answer these questions. Choose the *best* answer. Check your answers with the correct ones found on the Review Quiz Answer Key at the end of this book.

True (T) or False (F)

T   F   1. The profitability of identical businesses can vary significantly because of different locations.

T   F   2. The cost-effectiveness of promotional media such as radio, television, and magazines is highly stable.

T   F   3. Applied research tends to focus on new problems or on developing new approaches to old problems.

T   F   4. The observation data collection technique is especially accurate because it studies the actual behavior of research subjects rather than their statements.

T   F   5. A major advantage of telephone surveys is that it is easy to maintain the respondent's attention for a lengthy interview.

T   F   6. The research process may not always proceed directly from one step to the next.

T   F   7. Data collected for a research study will still be accurate even if the target population sample is not representative.

T   F   8. A good research report begins with highlights of all significant research findings.

T   F   9. When in-house research services are available, it is not necessary for the client to be actively involved.

T   F   10. An advantage of research conducted by academics is that it generally takes less time to complete than projects conducted by private consultants.

Alternate/Multiple Choice

11. The garbage survey is an example of a/an _____ observation technique.

  a. direct
  b. indirect

12. A chief task during the data collection phase of the research project is:

  a. analyzing the data.
  b. quality control.

13. The section of the research report which discusses the most important findings and all significant limitations in the data or analyses that were performed is the:

  a. executive summary.
  b. main body.

14. Checking on interviewers to be sure they are following the prescribed sampling plan is an example of:

    a. direct observation.
    b. debriefing.
    c. quality control.
    d. primary research.

15. The key to working successfully with a research consultant is:

    a. a detailed research contract.
    b. infrequent communication.
    c. continual reassessment of deadlines.
    d. allowing no changes to be made after the contract is signed.

Chapter Outline

Policy Defined
    Public Versus Private Sector Policy
    Reasons for Tourism Policy
U.S. Tourism Policy
    Policy at the Turn of the Century
    The War Years and Afterward
    Recent National Tourism Policy
    Pending Policy Issues
    State-Level Tourism Policy
    Local-Level Tourism Policy
    Other Tourism Policymakers
Tourism Policy Around the World
    Canada
    Europe
    Asia
International Tourism Organizations
    European Travel Commission
    Pacific Asia Travel Association
    Organization for Economic
       Cooperation and Development
    World Tourism Organization
    Organization of American States

Learning Objectives

1. Distinguish between policy in general and tourism policy.

2. Compare public sector tourism policy and private sector tourism policy.

3. Identify four reasons for tourism policy.

4. Trace U.S. tourism policy from the turn of the century to post-World War II.

5. Explain the significance of the National Tourism Policy Act and the United States Travel and Tourism Administration.

6. Outline several policy bodies, decisions, and pending issues which affect tourism.

7. Describe the nature of state-level tourism policy.

8. Describe the nature of local-level tourism policy and identify typical participating organizations.

9. State the role of the Travel Industry Association of America.

10. Describe basic tourism policy issues and activities in Europe.

11. Identify several associations, organizations, and compacts which advance international tourism policies and agreements.

13

Tourism Policy

TOURISM IS AN INDUSTRY composed of public and private interests. Given its range, it is crucial for tourism to be recognized by people who formulate policies, regulations, and laws.

Public interests are served via government policies for tourist safety such as standards and codes for food service sanitation, building construction, or business licensing. The private sector develops tourism policies to guide commercial interests. A well-thought-out written policy assists owners and business managers in tourism planning, development, and marketing. It states business goals and objectives with respect to tourists and the provision of tourism services, experiences, and facilities.

Public or private, a tourism policy sets the direction of any planning, development, or marketing effort. On a government level, the policy may actually dictate what a state, region, or tourism entity may or may not do. Policies may foster tourism development, protect the tourist, or control development to preserve the environment and the quality of the attractions.

When well-executed, a tourism policy enhances the appeal of a region for tourists and businesses. But when policy is lacking or is poorly executed, an area or region can suffer. Seedy tourist traps, strip development, and other inferior tourism products can result.

Policy Defined

The actions of governments, agencies, and businesses imply that some type of policy is in place. **Policy** is a guideline for the future or a course of action to meet stated goals and objectives. Policy tends to create or generate consistent behavior and actions over a period of time.[1] Policy is dynamic; policymakers, business leaders, and citizens may change, replace, or eliminate policies as needed. For example, Congress passed legislation in 1978 that deregulated the U.S. aviation system. Years of airline regulation were set aside, allowing a competitive marketplace to prevail.

Tourism policy refers to guidelines and decisions designed to assist in meeting tourism goals and objectives. Local, state, national, or regional governments set tourism policies for their respective regions, businesses, and residents. Tourism trade associations, tourism marketing groups, chambers of commerce, and convention and visitor bureaus also influence tourism policy.

Tourism businesses set their own policies, often within a general business and marketing plan. Such policies recognize tourists as a critical market, and may include companies not directly tied to tourism. For example, a manufacturing company may have a policy regarding visitors to its plants. The company's policy might be stated this way:

> All visitors must be identified, registered at the reception desk, and invited in by an employee in attendance the day of the visit. On the second and fourth Saturdays of each month, group tours of the physical plant will be conducted for groups of 30 or fewer who register an interest with the company by Thursday of that week.

Official visitor and tour policies have very direct implications for the economy of a city, region, and state. Plant tours represent good public relations, and can become a tourist attraction or part of a tour package offered by the region or community. For example, brewery and winery tours are popular in many parts of the United States and Europe.

Public Versus Private Sector Policy

Several groups influence and create U.S. public policy. These include the three branches of government: the executive (the President, Cabinet, and independent agencies), the legislative (Congress), and the judicial (the federal court system).

Public sector tourism policy in the United States evolves through negotiation and compromise. For example, the House of Representatives or the Senate may propose a bill that fosters the development of U.S. tourism attractions. After members of Congress compromise and agree on the bill, the bill is sent to the President for signature. The President may sign the bill—making it law—or veto it—sending it back to Congress. If Congress feels strongly about the bill, it may override the presidential veto—making the bill law. The executive branch of government checks the actions of the legislative, and vice versa. The judicial branch may also be involved in the interpretation of the law, once passed.

U.S. policy is often influenced by lobbyists, special interest groups, and various agencies, professional organizations, and associations. Many—if not all—of these groups take an active role in shaping policy and subsequent laws, regulations, interpretation, and implementation.

Lobbyists and special interest groups reflect the interest of their sponsors. These groups usually support their argument with relevant data that Congress reviews and reacts to. The tourism industry has lobbied for pertinent issues on more than one occasion. During the energy crisis of 1979 and the early 1980s, government policy was drafted around fuel conservation needs—including the use of fuel for the family car. Representatives from the industry and related associations banded together to argue that tourism businesses would be severely damaged if weekend driving was prohibited.

Private sector tourism policy is usually specific to the company or tourism enterprise. Markets often differ from company to company, calling for a different set of policies. The tourism policies of an airline will be different from those of a hotel chain. Domestic hotel chains may have different tourism policies than chains that operate on an international scale.

Some businesses have several types of policies. For example, airlines involved in freight and passenger service will establish different—but complementary—policies for each type of business activity. One set of policies would guide the freight end of the business, another the business traveler, and maybe a third the tourist. A resort, however, with 90% of its business coming from tourists, would focus its policies on tourists as opposed to business travelers or local guests.

Reasons for Tourism Policy

Not all countries, regions, states, or communities have a tourism policy. Tourism is often pursued as a way to diversify the economy when economic conditions change or if a major sector of the economy fails. Establishing policy should be one of the first steps that a community takes as tourism becomes a reality—and a priority. As one researcher states:

> A tourism policy declares a clear intent to develop the tourism industry. It indicates community goals related to tourism, and may highlight a wide range of priority concerns.... A policy's purpose is to indicate direction and perform an initiating and stimulating role in achieving that direction.[2]

There are several good reasons for tourism policy, public or private.

1. **Economic Benefit**. Countries around the world develop and implement tourism policies, believing that an active, successful tourism industry benefits the economy, expands the job market, and assists with balancing deficits of payments. The government often creates an agency or unit to foster and protect tourism, and to promote tourism from other countries.

2. **Regulation and Control**. Policy can place regulations and controls on the industry for the safety and benefit of tourists and the general public. Regulations represent a type of consumer protection and range from food to airline safety. In the United States, most regulations come from agencies outside the tourism industry.

3. **Visibility, Recognition, and Support.** Policymakers can better assist an industry when it has visibility, recognition, and support provided by a tourism policy, agency, or unit of government at the national, state, or local level.

4. **Self-Interest**. Governments usually have a vested interest in tourism. First, taxes and economic expenditures directly result from tourism activity. Second, most policymakers appreciate the large investment involved in developing a tourism infrastructure, and recognize that heavy tourism volume can offer a return on this investment. Third, governments are sometimes very active partners in tourism. The amount of activity and investment varies from country to country, according to the philosophy of the government. The national airlines of Germany, France, and, until recently, the United Kingdom are partly owned by the government. The trains in France, the state-owned hotels in Spain, and the city- or state-owned museums in many parts of the United States reflect the government's investment in tourism.

U.S. Tourism Policy

National tourism policy in the United States has been fragmented, inconsistent, and very political. There was little national travel or tourism policy activity before

World War II. Most government policies pertained to lands, railroads, and natural resources. In Florida in the late 1880s, developers were building hotels, new towns were blossoming (like West Palm Beach), and rail and steamship lines were expanding to carry tourists and new businesspeople to the area.[3] While these events were occurring in the South, railroads were expanding to the West. These lines stimulated the growth of new prairie towns and mountain villages—all needing hotels to accommodate the business traveler or curiosity seeker.

Policy at the Turn of the Century

Awe-inspiring natural resources were among the attractions which drew tourists to the West in the late 1800s. Tourist demand to see unique landscapes was central to the formation of national parks. Initially, park lands could be set aside with little effect on the economy. When the first national park—Yellowstone—was established in 1872, the monetary value of the lands was not yet known. There was little economic threat in "locking up" thousands of acres rich in minerals and lumber, since these resources were available elsewhere. The public's demand to see and be in nature was reason enough to put aside the lands for public use.

As western lands developed, the government became actively involved in tourism policy—if not by plan, then by default. The National Park Service was founded in 1916 within the Department of the Interior to administer the National Park System. Limited policy was initiated through the park service. In 1917—just one year after its inception—the park service capitalized on the increasing use of the personal auto for travel by handing out auto guidebooks to promote the parks; by 1920, a million visitors had come to the parks.[4] Land grants for railroads and roadways became more than just land development policies—they became policies that permitted settlers and tourists easy access to the mountains, valleys, and parks. The government not only provided land tracks for rail, but provided the labor of the U.S. Army Corps of Engineers to build access roads to the parks.[5]

The War Years and Afterward

Ideas for a general national tourism policy remained diffused after the turn of the century. Some suggest that Charles Hatfield offered the idea for a national office of tourism in 1931.[6] Hatfield was the secretary and general manager of the St. Louis Convention, Publicity, and Tourist Bureau, and vice president of the American Travel Development Association. Hatfield felt that a tourism office could provide the national leadership needed by the tourism industry. Yet, it was some time before Congress passed a legislative mandate. Tourism policy was set aside as the government struggled through World War I and the Great Depression. In 1940, the National Park Service was charged with encouraging travel within U.S. borders through the *Domestic Travel Act*.[7]

Most tourism efforts were put on hold during World War II. After the war, the United States seesawed between encouraging travel to Europe—to re-energize destroyed economies—and restricting travel—to protect the U.S. economy. But as discretionary leisure time and money increased, so too did the appetite for travel. Year after year, international travel expenditures of U.S. citizens accumulated into billion-dollar deficits. The government proposed two ways to stop the drain on the economy: reduce travel abroad and increase the number of foreign visitors to the United States.

In 1958, the *Office of International Travel* was created within the Department of Commerce, but Congress provided very little funding for its operation. Some Congressional members felt it was not the government's job to promote the United States as a tourism destination; rather, they felt that private interests should pay for such promotion and marketing. Without adequate funding, the newly created office could not perform as planned and quickly fell into further disfavor with Congress. As one researcher notes, the promotional program, *Visit U.S.A.*, had difficulties from the beginning:

> The first Visit U.S.A. Year was a flat fizzle. The increase in foreign spending for the first half of 1960 indicated a gain that was less than the year before. Indeed it was the lowest gain in all but one of the previous six years. It failed because Americans, so expert at selling soap, underarm deodorants, and breakfast cereals, proved totally inept at selling themselves. It fell flat because United States visa requirements were too difficult and too insulting. Even the Russians didn't ask the kinds of questions demanded on a visa for the United States. It fell flat because the members of America's tourist plant were insular and provincial.... It fell flat because the United States needed travel offices abroad, of the type foreign countries long ago established in the United States.[8]

Despite this failure, Congress passed the *International Travel Act* in 1961. Out of this act grew the *United States Travel Service*. The goals of this unit were to: promote travel to the United States; encourage the positive reception of foreign guests; cut down on the barriers to their entrance into the country; and facilitate the collection of tourism statistics and information.[9]

The effort to foster, build, and legislate a national tourism policy was unsuccessful through the 1960s. As the 1960s progressed, the national psyche became more and more focused on the conflict and war in Vietnam. However, young families traveled whenever they were able, making use of their leisure time and spending their discretionary income. A new expressway system and fast jet airline service took Americans across the country and overseas.

Recent National Tourism Policy

In 1970, the International Travel Act was modified; out of that process came the **National Tourism Resources Review Commission**. Created by Congress, this commission was charged with assessing tourism needs through the 1970s and into the 1980s. This effort represented the first large-scale, government-sponsored tourism study in the United States. By the study's completion, 11 task forces had been created to address important industry issues.

[handwritten margin note: Guidelines and decisions to make tourism grow]

Specifically, the study looked at tourism supply and demand in the United States. It examined facilities, national parks, airlines, resources and institutions, the environment, transportation, and information quality and supply; and the needs of minority, handicapped, and foreign tourists.[10] The results were compiled in a six-volume report: *Destination USA*. The publication provided useful information about the tourism industry, and suggested that a national tourism bureau replace the U.S. Travel Service. That was not to be.

Despite cyclic concerns surrounding gas prices and availability, travelers have always taken to sight-seeing on the open road. (Courtesy of the Alaska Division of Tourism)

National Tourism Policy Act. Not satisfied with the results of the National Tourism Resources Review Commission, the Senate initiated the *National Tourism Policy Study* in 1974. This study reiterated the need for an expanded tourism presence at the federal level; it recommended that a bureau be established within the federal government, or that a combined tourism and recreation agency be created.[11] Despite these studies, a national policy was not enacted until the early 1980s. President

Exhibit 1 Foreign Offices of the U.S. Travel and Tourism Administration

Country	Cities
Australia	Sydney
Canada	Toronto, Montreal, Vancouver
France	Paris
Germany	Frankfurt
Italy	Milano
Japan	Tokyo
Mexico	Mexico City
Netherlands	Amsterdam
South America	Miami, Florida
United Kingdom	London

Source: USTTA Resources Handbook, "Charting a Course for the Nineties" (Washington, D.C.: U.S. Department of Commerce, United States Travel and Tourism Administration, 1990), pp. 7–35.

Ronald Reagan signed the **National Tourism Policy Act** in 1981—the first comprehensive national tourism policy for the United States. A copy of the National Tourism Policy Act is contained in the chapter appendix. The policy recognized the importance of tourism and recreation to the American public, stating that:

> The tourism and recreation industries are important to the United States, not only because of the numbers of people they serve and the vast human, financial, and physical resources they employ, but because of the great benefits tourism, recreation, and related activities confer on individuals and on society as a whole.[12]

Under this legislation, a new office—the **United States Travel and Tourism Administration (USTTA)**—was created, replacing the U.S. Travel Service. The responsibilities of that new office were to:

- Promote the United States as a destination for foreign tourists
- Develop marketing plans and strategies working with the regional offices located in nine foreign countries
- Assist state travel offices with attracting foreign tourists
- Reduce the national travel deficit
- Promote understanding and an appreciation of the United States abroad

This new initiative elevated the stature of tourism within the government. The USTTA would be headed by an under secretary of commerce on a level equal with other under secretaries within the Department of Commerce.[13] Exhibit 1 shows the location of the ten USTTA regional offices—nine of which are outside the United States.

Other Policy Bodies. The National Tourism Policy Act also provided for two additional bodies to assist with U.S. tourism policy. The *Tourism Policy Council* was created to coordinate federal policy as it relates to tourism. The council is an inter-agency coordinating body chaired by the secretary of commerce. The council includes the under secretary of commerce and representatives from the Office of Management and Budget, the International Trade Administration, and the Secretaries of Energy, State, Labor, Interior, and Transportation. This council ensures that tourism and recreation policies, needs, and concerns are considered in other government sectors, and that these policies and initiatives complement each other. The council also seeks input from the state and local levels of government—but does not regulate or monitor policies beyond the federal level.

The second body created was the *Travel and Tourism Advisory Board*. This board consists of representatives from industry, academia, labor, and the public and private sectors. This body advises the Secretary of Commerce and USTTA on the yearly development and implementation of international marketing plans, and relays industry concerns to the Tourism Policy Council for their consideration.

Other Policy Decisions. Recent policy decisions that have shaped U.S. tourism include the 1970 decision to set up Amtrak: the National Railroad Passenger Corporation. Around the same time, Congress elected not to fund a prototype of a supersonic jet. This trans-Atlantic jet would have carried more passengers and flown faster than the supersonic transport planes (SSTs) of England and France. However, the idea for this jet coincided with the birth of the modern-day environmental movement. Strong protests concerning the environmental consequences of the jet helped defeat this national effort. When the bill did not pass the Senate, the United States abandoned supersonic transport to the British, French, and Russians.[14] Despite environmental concerns, French and British SST flights to the United States became regular events by the end of the 1970s. Within this same period—1978 to be exact—the United States deregulated the airline industry, sparking rapid change in the manner and costs of doing business in American skies.

Finally, restrictions on travel can be and are used to make points to other countries. U.S. citizens are warned against traveling to countries that are considered "dangerous" for U.S. citizens. Governments across the world restrict visas and boycott travel to countries in disfavor. After the Soviet Army invaded Afghanistan in 1980, the United States urged Americans not to attend the Olympic Games in Moscow. Soviet and Eastern Bloc countries did the reverse by boycotting the Olympics in Los Angeles in 1984.[15]

Pending Policy Issues

A number of tourism issues will require policy change and consideration in the next few years. Some of these will come from the USTTA, others from Congress and the executive branch.

Transportation is an issue on the domestic scene. Airport congestion due to limited capacity is a problem in many U.S. markets. This means—at least in the short term—that new airports will need to be approved and constructed. A sound, safe, and efficient freeway system has always been a boon to the tourist. But America's highways are getting old and in need of repair—which requires the attention and action of policymakers. Air pollution and auto congestion will force policymakers to look at improved, efficient, and speedy rail travel in certain corridors. Cyclic concern surrounding energy costs, availability, and crisis will bring transportation issues to the forefront.

International issues are pending as well. New and emerging markets in Europe, Asia, and South America call on the United States to address foreign tourism flows and trends. In 1986, the United States and Canada entered a five-year agreement which permitted the USTTA and Tourism Canada to jointly conduct marketing studies in most of Western Europe, Japan, Mexico, and several countries in South America.

Removing visa requirements is another important step in enhancing the image of the United States as a travel destination. Work still needs to be done on improving the often embarrassing, humiliating, and confusing procedures for screening foreign tourists as they pass through U.S. customs. The Immigration Reform and Control Act of 1986 permitted—on a trial basis—the waiver of visas for visitors from seven European countries plus Japan.[16] The waiver expired in 1991; many advocate that the waiver be extended and become a permanent change in visa requirements.

State-Level Tourism Policy

Each individual state is responsible for its own policy and tourism marketing effort. In effect, each state is a separate entity with its own plans, goals, and objectives for its respective tourism destinations.

Tourism-related policy is carried out through state travel offices. These offices have different names and locations within state government. Most states —76%—have one unit responsible for tourism policy and programs: usually a Department of Commerce or Economic Development. Three states—Hawaii, Texas, and Alaska—have two different units responsible for tourism.[17] Exhibit 2 breaks down the location of state travel offices within the 50 state governments. A number of different agencies are responsible for tourism, but only 8% of the states have a cabinet-level tourism administration unit. Another 8% of the states have combined tourism with the administration of parks, recreation, and cultural activities.

Many states have a unit within their highway program to administer highway information centers and facilities. These units come in touch with millions of auto-based tourists each year to assist them with travel plans, orient them to state roads and attractions, and answer questions they may have.

State travel offices usually have a promotional budget. Some states conduct marketing research in-house, but most contract with consulting firms or academic institutions. Very few states foster a statewide policy or development effort. Only 65% of the 50 states report having a travel development plan—or even a policy statement.[18] Of the 32 states that do, most of the plans are marketing-oriented and focus on media advertising for the state.

Common policy issues at the state level include defining the state as a destination, clarifying the role state government will play in tourism development and promotion, and defining what type of tourism to encourage. The tourism industry is well aware that the economic benefit of tourism is underestimated and underrated. The industry counts on state travel offices to enlighten government officials

Exhibit 2   Location of U.S. State Travel Offices

Agency or Entity	No. of States	Percentage
Department of Commerce, or Economic Development	39	76%
Department of Parks and Tourism, or Culture, Recreation, and Tourism	4	8
Department of Local Affairs	1	2
Cabinet Level Unit, Bureau	4	8
Commission on Tourism	1	2
Department of Tourism	1	2
Highways	1	2
Total	51	100

Note: The total is 51 states because Texas has two different agencies administering tourism.

Source: *Survey of State Travel Offices 1989–1990* (Washington, D.C.: U.S. Travel Data Center, 1990), General Administration Table 2, pp. 24–27.

regarding the important role that tourism plays in generating jobs, revenue, and improving the quality of life for all citizens—not just tourists.

However, state-level planning is often plagued by politics. Certain parts of a state are sometimes selected for development over others—which can cause political problems for the state agency. The nature of the appointments of state travel directors makes the state tourism agency subject to the whims of local politics and executive officers. It is difficult to foster a continuous tourism policy when changes in political will and interest may reverse decisions made by the previous administration. Among state travel offices, 70% of the directors are appointed to the position; 63% of these directors are appointed by the Governor. Only 20% of the 50 state directors are covered under civil service.[19]

Local-Level Tourism Policy

In the United States, each city, community, town, or village determines its goals and objectives for tourism by making its own tourism policy. The state may assist with, but rarely leads, such an effort. The nature and characteristics of tourism policy at the community level are as varied as are the communities. One city may produce policy that fosters cultural attractions, others may build policy around historical sites, unique city architecture, natural resources, or resorts. Communities, too, may work together to develop a regional tourism policy, assuming that, collectively, they will be able to stretch their financial and human resources.

Developing Local Tourism Policy. Many U.S. cities have strong tourism policies which attempt to attract visitors from around the globe. San Francisco, New York, and Las Vegas are prime examples of cities with strong tourism development and marketing campaigns. All communities have to decide what attractions, amenities, or resources can foster tourism for their unique situation. For example, gaming

Cable cars figure prominently in most images created by San Francisco tourism development and marketing campaigns. (Courtesy of the San Francisco Convention & Visitors Bureau)

and night life became the centerpiece of Las Vegas's tourism marketing efforts. Developing a community tourism policy rallies community members around an agreed-upon goal. A statement should be simple and to the point, and should address more than revenue. The policy should voice concern about the negative impacts that tourism development may have.

Simple as it may seem, getting community members to endorse the policy statement is critical to the long-term success of tourism. An approved tourism policy statement means that the community is united behind tourism development and promotion. Such a policy influences thousands of other community decisions. For example, bankers deciding on loans will know that the community supports tourism—and may seek out and support businesses that fulfill the tourism mission. Businesspersons may train their employees to be extra sensitive to the tourist. The businesses on main street may be kept neater—and even remodeled—when owners know that image and appearance affect the tourism effort. Residents, too, are influenced by the policy through their day-to-day contact with visitors.

Local tourism policies should complement the policies of the state and surrounding regions. While such an approach to tourism at the local level makes sense, many communities around the country do not have a tourism policy at all. Tourism development without policy often leads to fragmented, disruptive, and unprofitable tourism development. The lack of policy and planning at the community level is partly responsible for the development of policy and planning manuals by the U.S. Department of Commerce through the USTTA.[20]

Local Organizations. Several local-level organizations can pull a community together and address tourism potential. This list is representative:

- **Chamber of Commerce.** Most cities have a Chamber of Commerce. Chamber members often initiate discussions on community tourism policy.

- **Convention and Visitors Bureau.** In most communities, the local Convention and Visitors Bureau (CVB) has been the only entity that pays attention to tourism. The local CVB brings an understanding of tourism markets, necessary services, and marketing expertise to tourism development efforts.

- **City Council and Special Tourism Subcommittees.** The elected or appointed city council should represent community citizens and be involved in tourism policy-making and planning. The city council may create a subcommittee to foster discussion and policy for community tourism development.

- **Regional Tourism Offices or Councils.** A number of states have regional tourism offices that are partially supported by the state travel office and through their own membership fees. These organizations often have contacts within state government, marketing and planning expertise, and a broad-based knowledge of tourism that can be useful in planning community or regional tourism.

- **Special Tourism Districts.** In some states, local organizations and businesses form new tourism promotional districts that encompass several cities or counties. These special districts are funded in different manners, but usually through a special self-assessment tax. Members are usually experienced business-persons heavily involved in tourism.

Other Tourism Policymakers

Many other organizations are involved in developing tourism policy in the United States. For example, the **Travel Industry Association of America (TIA)** started out as a small organization of travel officials. Today, TIA is one of the largest and broadest-based industry organizations in the United States. TIA is a large association which represents all segments of the tourism industry, from hotels and restaurants to convention and visitors bureaus to major attractions and amusement parks. TIA promotes the professional advancement of the members through conferences. Through its various councils, TIA plays a role in developing national policy by working closely with key members of Congress and the executive

Convention and Visitors Bureaus help tourists to easily find the "must sees and dos" in the community. (Courtesy of the Alaska Division of Tourism)

branch—especially the Department of Commerce and state travel directors. TIA created and supports several councils that focus upon the needs of particular industry sectors. These include the:

- National Council of State Travel Directors

- National Council of Urban Tourism Organizations

- National Council of Travel Attractions

- National Council of Area and Regional Travel Organizations

In addition, TIA sponsors the *Travel and Tourism Government Affairs Council* which consists of representatives from travel and tourism organizations and associations. This council provides a means for the industry to address the government on issues affecting tourism.

In 1972, TIA created the *U.S. Travel Data Center*—a research affiliate in Washington, D.C. The center's national and state-level research focuses on the economic impact of tourism, travel trends, selected markets, and special issues.

Other organizations that address travel and tourism related issues include the:

- American Hotel & Motel Association (AH&MA)
- National Tour Association (NTA)
- Air Transport Association (ATA)
- Travel and Tourism Research Association (TTRA)
- American Automobile Association (AAA)
- American Bus Association (ABA)
- Cruise Lines International Association (CLIA)
- American Society of Travel Agents (ASTA)
- National Restaurant Association (NRA)
- International Association of Amusement Parks and Attractions (IAAPA)
- National Recreation and Parks Association (NRPA)
- American Recreation Coalition (ARC)
- Recreation Vehicle Industry Association (RVIA)
- Council on Hotel, Restaurant, and Institutional Education (CHRIE)
- International Association of Convention and Visitor Bureaus (IACVB)

Tourism Policy Around the World

Most countries with any amount of tourism have developed a modest amount of tourism policy at the national and regional level. The nature varies according to the type of government and the tourism resources available. For example, the limited amount of tourism policy in the United States reflects a tenet of capitalism: that it is best when government intervenes the least in the private sector. In contrast, the Mexican and French governments have provided direct aid to the tourism industry to develop and plan huge resort complexes and facilities. The level of support has often gone beyond loans for developing the infrastructure to include grants and federal decisions that cleared the way for development.

Canada

Canada created an active national tourism office in 1935 to promote tourism: the Canadian Travel Bureau. The name of this bureau has changed several times, from the Canadian Government Travel Bureau to the Canadian Government Office of Tourism to what it has been called since 1983: *Tourism Canada*.[21] Tourism Canada is housed within the branch of government called *Industry, Science and Technology Canada*. Tourism Canada has four primary units: product development; market development; research; and management services and liaison.

Canadian tourism policy and administration is broader than that of the United States, including domestic as well as international marketing and promotion. Since 1975, national tourism policy has had a strong domestic orientation. Communities and provinces have received millions of dollars for developing tourism facilities, large-scale planning efforts, research, and marketing campaigns. To support domestic and international tourism, Tourism Canada has field offices abroad and 12 within Canada. A research unit—the *Canadian Tourism Research Institute*—was developed in 1987 to support policy, product development, and marketing.

The policy objectives of Tourism Canada clearly spell out the role of the federal government as a coordinating and stimulating force that reaches into the provinces and communities and across public and private sector lines. Federal leadership for tourism is pervasive and backed by development, marketing, and research funds.

Europe

The recent political and economic changes in Europe will have dramatic implications for tourism—many of which are unknown. Coupled with a restructured European market, the changes in Eastern Europe will call older national tourism policies into question or review. These policies will provide the foundations on which new national tourism policies will be built in the next five to eight years.

Since Europe is not politically united, the structure and administration of national tourism policy varies from one country to the next. The level of government involvement also differs from country to country. Several countries—Holland, Austria, and West Germany—jointly administer national tourism policy with the private sector. Others—France, Spain, and Belgium—designate branches of government to lead national tourism policy.[22]

Europe has several common tourism policies that are similar to those of Canada and the United States. These policies are summarized as follows:[23]

- Stimulate the national economy through tourism in terms of jobs, tax income, and direct expenditures; as much as possible, distribute the positive benefits across different regions, provinces, and counties.

- Encourage a positive foreign exchange of the funds brought in and taken out of the country by tourists.

- Improve the quality of life for European citizens.

- Protect tourists as consumers of host country services.

- Protect and encourage the use of cultural and natural resources and the environment.

- Foster a positive image of the host country and promote international friendliness and cooperation.

Most countries put a high priority on attracting visitors from other countries. Many national tourism offices have initiated extensive marketing studies that target primary markets in each particular country. Yet, most European countries focus a portion of their research and development efforts on domestic tourism. In France, sizable funding has gone into developing resorts and the national tourism infrastructure. In Germany, the government aims to improve tourism facilities for the benefit of German citizens. The United Kingdom, Denmark, France, Austria, and Sweden have similar objectives in place.

Tourists and residents alike enjoy the convenience and beauty of the Amsterdam canals.
(Photos by Joseph D. Fridgen)

The complexities and the breadth of policy across the European continent are too difficult to capture here. For our purposes, it is better to briefly review some of the current key policy issues and activities.[24]

Staggered Holidays. In many countries and most occupations, it is not unusual for employees and school children to have as many as four or five weeks of vacation a year—mostly in prime summer months. As these vacationing Europeans pour from their homes, severe crowding results along major European highways and in popular resorts. To counter such problems, most countries—in cooperation with industry and labor representatives—have tried to change school and working schedules to stagger employee vacations and holidays. For example, each of the three regions in Holland has a different starting and ending time for their major summer holidays. France began varying the school calendar in 1990. Sweden staggers the winter school holiday across four weeks in February and March. In Switzerland, there are no particular periods when schools and businesses are closed; individuals choose their own holiday times, resulting in a "natural" staggering of holidays. Norway and Portugal differentially price tour packages and vacations to entice citizens to take holidays at different times of the year. In Portugal, banks have gone so far as to double the monthly salary for employees who take vacations in January and February.

Tourism Training and Vocational Education. The shortage of labor and skilled workers is hitting the European tourism industry in much the same way as it is in Canada and the United States. Several countries are developing strategies to deal with the problem. In 1988, the French Ministry of Tourism began funding the training of entry-level employees in hotel, restaurant, and other tourism-related positions. The Ministry also focused on continued on-the-job training. Several other countries have turned their attention to training, including Austria, Norway, Denmark, Finland, Sweden, and Greece.

Impacts. A major theme of government policy across the world is studying and understanding economic, social, cultural, and environmental impacts of tourism. Economic impacts will continue to receive policy attention. Concern for social and environmental impacts has grown and is reflected in the national tourism policy of several European countries including Norway, France, and Austria.

Tourism Attractions and Facilities. Most European countries have a policy provision reflecting the intention and interest of government to fund tourism via loans or matching grant programs. Monies are usually targeted at special projects which will enhance tourism in a particular region or community. Most of Europe also values quality. As facilities age and tourist preferences change, it becomes increasingly important and difficult to maintain quality tourism facilities and services. Many countries target economic aid for renovating or modernizing tourism facilities. In 1987, the French Ministry of Tourism introduced the *Fonds d'aid au Conseil et a l'Innovation Touristique*—or the *Tourism Counseling and Innovation Fund*. The fund provides money to help tourism business leaders renovate their firms, update their operating procedures, and assist with modernizing their businesses.[25]

Asia

The policies of Asian countries are as varied as the countries themselves. The standard of living in Japan and Taiwan supports tourism through the leisure time and discretionary income available to many people. China moved beyond the cultural revolution and began to nurture tourism as an economic and cultural addition to their society. The 1989 student protests and massacre in Tiananmen Square did not close the doors on Chinese tourism, but did slow it down. The governments of South Korea, Singapore, and Thailand have been strongly involved in tourism development. National tourism policies guide the location, extent, and character of tourism resorts, entry and exit policies, and broad international marketing programs.

Politics and Tourism. Any social or political disturbance—big or small—concerns the tourism industry. Stability and security are the watchwords of international tourists and their travel agents. Once a negative political or social event hits the international news, it is difficult to convince many tourists to *not* change their travel plans.

Politics played a pivotal role in Chinese tourism. The dramatic changes in Chinese politics over the last twenty years opened China to the Western World. Today, most tourism is a government function. The government cares for and markets the nation's tourism attractions. Tourism planning and services are the direct responsibility of the central government at the national, provincial, and community level. The government manages major attractions, travel agency services, tourism schools, and training programs. China has limited partnerships with private enterprises from other countries. Major hotel chains from different parts of the world have built hotels in China in cooperation with the Chinese government. Similar types of arrangements have occurred between the government and private interests in Japan, Taiwan, and Singapore.

Leisure Time and Spending. Japan has one of the strongest and most direct national tourism policies among Asian countries. Aside from developing a tourism system at home and supporting domestic tourism, Japan actively supports travel abroad.[26] The government has made it public policy to encourage international travel to: (1) reduce the excessive balance of payments received by Japan from other countries; (2) generate understanding of other nations among Japanese tourists and international hosts; and (3) foster the well-being of its citizens in terms of encouraging the pleasurable and relaxing use of leisure time. Much of this effort was contained in the *Ten Million Program*: a five-year program begun in 1986 with the goal of sending 10 million tourists abroad. The Ministry of Transport sent missions to other countries in an effort to remove travel barriers to various countries. The government also sponsors publicity campaigns to stimulate and support travel abroad and the idea of taking longer vacations.[27] In fact, the Ministry of Health recently informed the Japanese people that taking more and longer vacations was a healthy thing to do.

International Tourism Organizations

Tourism success in the next decade rests on the continuation of old international agreements and the development of new mutually beneficial agreements between countries. International agreements can ensure smooth international air travel, currency exchange, and tourist safety. Several associations, organizations, and compacts advance international tourism policy and agreements.

European Travel Commission

The European Travel Commission (ETC) was created in 1948 to help rebuild the economies of Western Europe after World War II. The ETC coordinates national tourism organizations across Europe. Presently, 23 countries are represented through the officers of respective national travel offices. The commission's functions include research, marketing, and a range of allied tourism policy issues.[28]

Pacific Asia Travel Association

The Pacific Asia Travel Association (PATA) was organized in 1951 and promotes tourism in Asia and the Pacific Rim. The association enjoys full representation across the entire tourism industry and conducts research in support of tourism. Through annual meetings, conferences, and marts, the association creates a forum for exchanging ideas on tourism in the Pacific and across Asia.

Organization for Economic Cooperation and Development

The Organization for Economic Cooperation and Development (OECD) was created in 1961 to foster economic growth and development for member countries in a non-discriminatory international business climate.[29] Over the years, members have worked together to advance people's freedom to travel across borders—with a minimum number of barriers. The OECD carries out most of its efforts through its tourism committee. Headquartered in Paris, OECD has 24 country members, plus one associated member. These policymakers and analysts influence their respective governments about the nature and direction of tourism in major industrial countries. Each year the OECD publishes the report *Tourism Policy and International Tourism in OECD Member Countries*. This report reviews current tourism issues and records the trends in tourism activity for each country on a yearly basis.

World Tourism Organization

The World Tourism Organization (WTO) is the only worldwide organization focusing upon international tourism. Started in 1975 and headquartered in Madrid, Spain, the WTO has 109 country members.[30] The organization acts as a worldwide clearinghouse for tourism statistics, technical information, and reports. WTO sponsors global conferences on international tourism and issues yearly publications—including an annual statistical report on worldwide tourism that is printed in three languages. The WTO General Assembly also issued the *Tourism Bill of Rights and Tourist Code*. This document encourages tourists and tourism providers to protect the environment and host communities around the world.

Organization of American States

The Organization of American States (OAS) focuses on tourism development in North and South America. Members assist each other in sharing development expertise, policy formation, and promotion campaigns. A program in 1992 drew world attention by celebrating the 500th anniversary of Columbus's discovery of the Americas.[31] OAS explores broad tourism policy implications within the region, going beyond economic issues to social, cultural, and environmental matters.

The continuation and development of tourism policy signifies the important role that tourism plays in today's world. As an industry, tourism stands to benefit from the increased recognition of its influence and contribution in public and private circles.

Endnotes

1. Charles O. Jones, *An Introduction to the Study of Public Policy*, 3d ed. (Monterey, Calif.: Brooks/Cole, 1984), p. 26.

2. Uel Blank, *The Community Tourism Industry Imperative: The Necessity, the Opportunities, its Potential* (State College, Penn.: Venture Publishing, 1989), p. 182.

3. Horace Sutton, *Travelers: The American Tourist from Stagecoach to Space Shuttle* (New York: Morrow, 1980), pp. 76–77.

4. John A. Jakle, *The Tourist: Travel in Twentieth-Century North America* (Lincoln, Neb.: University of Nebraska Press, 1985), pp. 68–69.

5. Jakle, p. 70.

6. Chuck Y. Gee, James C. Makens, and Dexter J. L. Choy, *The Travel Industry*, 2d ed. (New York: Van Nostrand Reinhold, 1989), p. 115.

7. Gunn, *Tourism Planning*, 2d ed. (New York: Taylor & Francis, 1988), p. 33.

8. Sutton, pp. 263–264.

9. Gee, et al., p. 115.

10. Gunn, *Tourism Planning*, p. 33.

11. Gee, et al., p. 116.

12. *National Tourism Policy Act* Title I, Sec. 101. (a) (1) (1981).

13. David L. Edgell, Sr., *Charting a Course for International Tourism in the Nineties: An Agenda for Managers and Executives* (Washington, D.C.: U.S. Department of Commerce—U.S. Travel and Tourism Administration and Economic Development Administration, 1990), p. 6.

14. Sutton, p. 275.

15. Edgell, p. 24.

16. Edgell, p. 44.

17. *Survey of State Travel Offices 1989–1990* (Washington, D.C.: U.S. Travel Data Center, 1990), p. 2.

18. *Survey of State Travel Offices 1989–1990*, pp. 80–86.

19. *Survey of State Travel Offices 1989–1990*, General Administration Table 1, pp. 19–23.

20. Deirdre K. Hirner, Glenn Weaver, Craig W. Colton, Glenn A. Gillespie and Bruce T. Cox, *Tourism USA—Guidelines for Tourism Development* (Washington, D.C.: U.S. Travel and Tourism Administration and Economic Development Administration, Department of Commerce, 1986), p. iii.

21. Robert W. McIntosh and Charles R. Goeldner, *Tourism: Principles, Practices, Philosophies*, 6th ed. (New York: Wiley, 1990), p. 59.

22. Martinus Jan Kosters, "Tourism Research in European National Tourist Organizations," in *Travel, Tourism, and Hospitality Research: A Handbook for Managers and Researchers* edited by J. R. Brent Ritchie and Charles R. Goeldner (New York: Wiley, 1987), p. 129.

23. This discussion on European tourism policy is based on: *Tourism Policy and International Tourism in OECD Member Countries* (Paris, France: Organization for Economic Cooperation and Development, 1989); and Stephen Wheatcroft, "Strategic Planning for Tourism: Governmental View," in *Tourism Marketing and Management Handbook*, edited by Stephen F. Witt and Luiz Moutinho (Englewood Cliffs, N.J.: Prentice-Hall, 1989), p. 433.

24. The major themes for this section of key policy issues is drawn from the policy review provided in *Tourism Policy and International Tourism in OECD Member Countries* (Paris, France: Organization for Economic Cooperation and Development, 1989).

25. OECD, 1989, p. 43.

26. *Tourism in Japan 1989* (Tokyo, Japan: Japan National Tourist Organization, Ministry of Transport, 1989), p. 21.

27. *Tourism in Japan 1989*, p. 21.

28. Kosters, pp. 137–138.

29. OECD, 1989, p. 2.

30. Edgell, p. 28.

31. Edgell, pp. 27–28.

Key Terms

National Tourism Policy Act
National Tourism Resources Review Commission
policy
TIA
tourism policy
USTTA

Discussion Questions

1. How would you define policy in general? tourism policy?

2. What is the difference between public sector tourism policy and private sector tourism policy?

3. What are four reasons for establishing tourism policy?

4. What was the nature of U.S. tourism policy at the turn of the century? throughout the two world wars and afterward?

5. What is the significance of the National Tourism Policy Act? the United States Travel and Tourism Administration?

6. What is the nature of state-level tourism policy?

7. What is the nature of local-level tourism policy? What local organizations assist with formulating tourism policy?

8. What other organizations assist with the development of U.S. tourism policy?

9. What are some of the major themes affecting tourism policy around the world?

10. What are some of the associations, organizations, and compacts which advance international tourism policy and agreements?

Chapter Appendix ———————————————

United States National Tourism Policy Act

PUBLIC LAW 97-63—OCT. 16, 1981

Public Law 97-63
97th Congress

An Act

To amend the International Travel Act of 1961 to establish a national tourism policy, and for other purposes.

Oct. 16, 1981
[S. 304]

Be it enacted by the Senate and House of Representatives of the United States of America in Congress assembled.

National Tourism Policy Act.

SHORT TITLE

SECTION 1. This Act may be cited as the "National Tourism Policy Act".

22 USC 2121 note.

NATIONAL TOURISM POLICY

SEC. 2. (a) The International Travel Act of 1961 (hereinafter in this Act referred to as the "Act") is amended by striking out the first section and inserting in lieu thereof the following: "That this Act may be cited as the 'International Travel Act of 1961'.

22 USC 2121 note.

"TITLE I—NATIONAL TOURISM POLICY".

"SEC. 101. (a) The Congress finds that—

22 USC 2121.

"(1) the tourism and recreation industries are important to the United States, not only because of the numbers of people they serve and the vast human, financial, and physical resources they employ, but because of the great benefits tourism, recreation, and related activities confer on individuals and on society as a whole;

"(2) the Federal Government for many years has encouraged tourism and recreation implicitly in its statutory commitments to the shorter workyear and to the national passenger transportation system, and explicitly in a number of legislative enactments to promote tourism and support development of outdoor recreation, cultural attractions, and historic and natural heritage resources;

"(3) as incomes and leisure time continue to increase, and as our economic and political systems develop more complex global relationships, tourism and recreation will become ever more important aspects of our daily lives; and

"(4) the existing extensive Federal Government involvement in tourism, recreation, and other related activities needs to be better coordinated to effectively respond to the national interest in tourism and recreation and, where appropriate, to meet the needs of State and local governments and the private sector.

"(b) There is established a national tourism policy to—

"(1) optimize the contribution of the tourism and recreation industries to economic prosperity, full employment, and the international balance of payments of the United States;

"(2) make the opportunity for and benefits of tourism and recreation in the United States universally accessible to residents of the United States and foreign countries and insure that present and future generations are afforded adequate tourism and recreation resources;

"(3) contribute to personal growth, health, education, and intercultural appreciation of the geography, history, and ethnicity of the United States;

"(4) encourage the free and welcome entry of individuals traveling to the United States, in order to enhance international understanding and goodwill, consistent with immigration laws, the laws protecting the public health, and laws governing the importation of goods into the United States;

"(5) eliminate unnecessary trade barriers to the United States tourism industry operating throughout the world;

"(6) encourage competition in the tourism industry and maximum consumer choice through the continued viability of the retail travel agent industry and the independent tour operator industry;

"(7) promote the continued development and availability of alternative personal payment mechanisms which facilitate national and international travel;

"(8) promote quality, integrity, and reliability in all tourism and tourism-related services offered to visitors to the United States;

"(9) preserve the historical and cultural foundations of the Nation as a living part of community life and development, and insure future generations an opportunity to appreciate and enjoy the rich heritage of the Nation;

"(10) insure the compatibility of tourism and recreation with other national interests in energy development and conservation, environmental protection, and the judicious use of natural resources;

"(11) assist in the collection, analysis, and dissemination of data which accurately measure the economic and social impact of tourism to and within the United States, in order to facilitate planning in the public and private sectors; and

"(12) harmonize, to the maximum extent possible, all Federal activities in support of tourism and recreation with the needs of the general public and the States, territories, local governments, and the tourism and recreation industry, and to give leadership to all concerned with tourism, recreation, and national heritage preservation in the United States".

DUTIES

SEC. 3. (a) The following heading is inserted before section 2 of the Act:

"TITLE II—DUTIES".

(b) Section 2 of the Act (22 U.S.C. 2122) is amended by striking out "purpose of this Act" and inserting in lieu thereof "the national tourism policy established by section 101(b)".

Ante, p. 1011.

(c) Section 3(a) of the Act (22 U.S.C. 2123(a)) is amended by striking out "section 2" and inserting in lieu thereof "section 201", by striking out "and" at the end of paragraph (6), by striking out the period at the end of paragraph (7) and inserting in lieu thereof a semicolon, and by adding after paragraph (7) the following new paragraphs:

"(8) shall establish facilitation services at major ports-of-entry of the United States;

"(9) shall consult with foreign governments on travel and tourism matters and, in accordance with applicable law, represent United States travel and tourism interests before international and intergovernmental meetings;

"(10) shall develop and administer a comprehensive program relating to travel industry information, data service, training and education, and technical assistance;

"(11) shall develop a program to seek and to receive information on a continuing basis from the tourism industry, including consumer and travel trade associations, regarding needs and interests which should be met by a Federal agency or program and to direct that information to the appropriate agency or program;

"(12) shall encourage to the maximum extent feasible travel to and from the United States on United States carriers;

"(13) shall assure coordination within the Department of Commerce so that, to the extent practicable, all the resources of the Department are used to effectively and efficiently carry out the national tourism policy;

"(14) may only promulgate, use, rescind, and amend such interpretive rules, general statements of policy, and rules of agency organization, procedure, and practice as may be necessary to carry out this Act; and

"(15) shall develop and submit annually to the Congress, within six weeks of transmittal to the Congress of the President's recommended budget for implementing this Act, a detailed marketing plan to stimulate and encourage travel to the United States during the fiscal year for which such budget is submitted and include in the plan the estimated funding and personnel levels required to implement the plan and alternate means of funding activities under this Act.

(d)(1) Paragraph (5) of section 3(a) of the Act is amended (A) by striking out "foreign countries." and inserting in lieu thereof "foreign countries;", (B) by striking out "this clause;" and inserting in lieu thereof "this paragraph.", (C) by inserting the last two sentences before the first sentence of subsection (c), and (D) by striking out "this clause" in such sentences and inserting in lieu thereof "paragraph (5) of subsection (a)". 22 USC 2123.

(2) Paragraph (7) of section 3(a) of the Act is amended by striking out "countries. The Secretary is authorized to" and inserting in lieu thereof "countries; and the Secretary may" and by striking out "this clause" and inserting in lieu thereof "this paragraph".

(3) Section 3 of the Act is amended by striking out "clause (5)" each place it appears and inserting in lieu thereof "paragraph (5)".

(e)(1) Sections 2 and 3 of the Act are redesignated as sections 201 and 202, respectively, and section 5 is inserted after section 202 (as so redesignated) and redesignated as section 203. 22 USC 2122, 2123, 2123a.

(2) Section 203 of the Act (as so redesignated) is amended by striking out "semi-annually" and inserting in lieu thereof "annually". 22 USC 2123a.

(f) The following section is inserted after section 203 of the Act (as so redesignated):

"SEC. 204. (a) The Secretary is authorized to provide, in accordance with subsections (b) and (c), financial assistance to a region of not less than two States or portions of two States to assist in the implementation of a regional tourism promotional and marketing program. Such assistance shall include— Regional assistance. 22 USC 2123b.

    "(1) technical assistance for advancing the promotion of travel to such region by foreign visitors;

    "(2) expert consultants; and

    "(3) marketing and promotional assistance.

"(b) Any program carried out with assistance under subsection (a) shall serve as a demonstration project for future program development for regional tourism promotion.

"(c) The Secretary may provide assistance under subsection (a) for a region if the applicant for the assistance demonstrates to the satisfaction of the Secretary that—

"(1) such region has in the past been an area that has attracted foreign visitors, but such visits have significantly decreased;

"(2) facilities are being developed or improved to reattract such foreign visitors;

"(3) a joint venture in such region will increase the travel to such region by foreign visitors;

"(4) such regional programs will contribute to the economic well-being of the region;

"(5) such region is developing or has developed a regional transportation system that will enhance travel to the facilities and attractions within such region; and

"(6) a correlation exists between increased tourism to such region and the lowering of the unemployment rate in such region.".

ADMINISTRATION

United States Travel and Tourism Administration, establishment.

SEC. 4. (a)(1) The first sentence of section 4 of the Act (22 U.S.C. 2124) is amended to read as follows: "There is established in the Department of Commerce a United States Travel and Tourism Administration which shall be headed by an Under Secretary of Commerce for Travel and Tourism who shall be appointed by the President, by and with the advice and consent of the Senate, and who shall report directly to the Secretary."

(2) The second sentence of section 4 of the Act is amended by striking out "Assistant Secretary of Commerce for Tourism" and inserting in lieu thereof "Under Secretary of Commerce for Travel and Tourism".

(3) Section 4 of the Act is amended by striking out the last sentence and inserting in lieu thereof the following: "The Secretary shall designate an Assistant Secretary of Commerce for Tourism Marketing who shall be under the supervision of

the Under Secretary of Commerce for Travel and Tourism. The Secretary shall delegate to the Assistant Secretary responsibility for the development and submission of the marketing plan required by section 202(a)(15).".

Ante, p. 1012.

(4) Section 5314 of title 5, United States Code, is amended by striking out "Under Secretary of Commerce" and inserting in lieu thereof "Under Secretary of Commerce and Under Secretary of Commerce for Travel and Tourism".

(b) Section 4 of the Act is amended by inserting "(a)" after "Sec. 4.", and by adding at the end the following:

"(b)(1) The Secretary may not reduce the total number of foreign offices of the United States Travel and Tourism Administration or the number of employees assigned to the offices of the Administration in foreign countries to a number which is less than the total number of employees of the United States Travel Service assigned to offices of the Service in foreign countries in fiscal year 1979.

"(2) In any fiscal year the amount of funds which shall be made available from appropriations under this act for obligation for the activities of the offices of the United States Travel and Tourism Administration in foreign countries shall not be less than the amount obligated in fiscal year 1980 for the activities of the offices of the United States Travel Service in foreign countries.".

(c)(1) The following heading is inserted before section 4 of the Act:

"TITLE III—ADMINISTRATION".

(2) Section 4 of the Act is redesignated as section 301 and the following new sections are inserted after that section:

"Sec. 302. (a) In order to assure that the national interest in tourism is fully considered in Federal decisionmaking, there is established an interagency coordinating council to be known as the Tourism Policy Council (hereinafter in this section referred to as the 'Council').

"(b)(1) The Council shall consist of—

"(A) the Secretary of Commerce who shall serve as Chairman of the Council;

22 USC 2124.

Tourism Policy Council, establishment. 22 USC 2124a.

Membership.

"(B) the Under Secretary for Travel and Tourism who shall serve as the Vice Chairman of the Council and who shall act as Chairman of the Council in the absence of the Chairman;

"(C) the Director of the Office of Management and Budget or the individual designated by the Director from the Office;

"(D) an individual designated by the Secretary of Commerce from the International Trade Administration of the Department of Commerce;

"(E) the Secretary of Energy or the individual designated by such Secretary from the Department of Energy;

"(F) the Secretary of State or the individual designated by such Secretary from the Department of State;

"(G) the Secretary of the Interior or the individual designated by such Secretary from the National Park service or the Heritage Conservation and Recreation Service of the Department of the Interior;

"(H) the Secretary of Labor or the individual designated by such Secretary from the Department of Labor; and

"(I) the Secretary of Transportation or the individual designated by such Secretary from the Department of Transportation.

"(2) Members of the Council shall serve without additional compensation, but shall be reimbursed for actual and necessary expenses, including travel expenses, incurred by them in carrying out the duties of the Council.

Compensation; travel expenses.

"(3) Each member of the Council, other than the Vice Chairman, may designate an alternate, who shall serve as a member of the Council whenever the regular member is unable to attend a meeting of the Council or any committee of the Council. The designation by a member of the Council of an alternate under the preceding sentence shall be made for the duration of the member's term on the Council. Any such designated alternate shall be selected from individuals who exercise significant decisionmaking authority in the Federal agency involved and shall be authorized to make decisions on behalf of the member for whom he or she is serving.

Alternate designation.

"(c)(1) Whenever the Council, or a committee of the Council, considers matters that affect the interests of Federal agencies that are not represented on the Council or the committee, the Chairman may invite the heads of such agencies, or their alternates, to participate in the deliberations of the Council or committee.

Meetings.

"(2) The Council shall conduct its first meeting not later than ninety days after the date of enactment of this section. Thereafter the Council shall meet not less than four times each year.

Functions.

"(d)(1) The Council shall coordinate policies, programs, and issues relating to tourism, recreation, or national heritage resources involving Federal departments, agencies, or other entities. Among other things, the Council shall—

"(A) coordinate the policies and programs of member agencies that have a significant effect on tourism, recreation, and national heritage preservation;

"(B) develop areas of cooperative program activity;

"(C) assist in resolving interagency program and policy conflicts; and

"(D) seek and receive concerns and views of state and local governments and the Travel and Tourism Advisory Board with respect to Federal programs and policies deemed to conflict with the orderly growth and development of tourism.

"(2) To enable the Council to carry out its functions

"(A) the Council may request directly from any Federal department or agency such personnel, information, services, or facilities, on a compensated or uncompensated basis, as he determines necessary to carry out the functions of the Council;

"(B) each Federal department or agency shall furnish the Council with such information, services, and facilities as it may request to the extent permitted by law and within the limits of available funds; and

"(C) Federal agencies and departments may, in their discretion, detail to temporary duty with the Council such personnel as the Council may request for carrying out the functions of the Council, each such detail to be without loss of seniority, pay, or other employee status.

"(3) The Administrator of the General Services Administration shall provide administrative support services for the Council on a reimbursable basis.

Policy committees, establishment.

"(e) The Council shall establish such policy committees as it considers necessary and appropriate, each of which shall be comprised of any or all of the members of the Council and representatives from Federal departments, agencies, and instrumentalities not represented on the Council. Each such policy committee shall be designed—

"(1) to monitor a specific area of Federal Government activity, such as transportation, energy and natural resources, economic development, or other such activities related to tourism; and

"(2) to review and evaluate the relation of the policies and activities of the Federal Government in that specific area to tourism, recreation, and national heritage conservation in the United States.

Report to President.

"(f) The Council shall submit an annual report for the preceding fiscal year to the President for transmittal to Congress on or before the thirty-first day of December of each year. The report shall include—

"(1) a comprehensive and detailed report of the activities and accomplishments of the Council and its policy committees;

"(2) the results of Council efforts to coordinate the policies and programs of member agencies that have a significant effect on tourism, recreation, and national heritage preservation, resolve interagency conflicts, and develop areas of cooperative program activity;

"(3) an analysis of problems referred to the council by state, and local governments, the tourism industry, the Secretary of Commerce, or any of the Council's policy committees along with a detailed statement of any actions taken or anticipated to be taken to resolve such problems; and

"(4) such recommendations as the Council deems appropriate.

"Sec. 303. (a) There is established the Travel and Tourism Advisory Board (hereinafter in this section referred to as the 'Board') to be composed of fifteen members appointed by the Secretary. The members of the Board shall be appointed as follows:

Travel and Tourism Advisory Board, establishment. 22 USC 2124b. Members, appointments.

"(1) Not more than eight members of the Board shall be appointed from the same political party.

"(2) The members of the Board shall be appointed from among citizens of the United States who are not regular full-time employees of the United States and shall be selected for appointment so as to provide as nearly as practicable a broad representation of different geographical regions within the United States and of the diverse and varied segments of the tourism industry.

"(3) Twelve of the members shall be appointed from senior executive officers of organizations engaged in the travel and tourism industry. Of such members—

"(A) at least one shall be a senior representative from a labor organization representing employees of the tourism industry; and

"(B) at least one shall be a representative of the states who is knowledgeable of tourism promotion.

"(4) Of the remaining three members of the Board—

"(A) one member shall be a consumer advocate or ombudsman from the organized public interest community;

"(B) one member shall be an economist, statistician, or accountant; and

"(C) one member shall be an individual from the academic community who is knowledgeable in tourism, recreation, or national heritage conservation.

The Secretary shall serve as an ex officio member of the Board. The duration of the Board shall not be subject to the Federal Advisory Committee Act. A list of the members appointed to the Board

5 USC app.

shall be forwarded by the Secretary to the Senate Committee on Commerce, Science, and Transportation and the House Committee on Energy and Commerce.

(b) The members of the Board shall be appointed for a term of office of three years, except that of the members first appointed—

"(1) four members shall be appointed for terms of one year, and

"(2) four members shall be appointed for terms of two years, as designated by the Secretary at the time of appointment. Any member appointed to fill a vacancy occurring before the expiration of the term for which the member's predecessor was appointed shall be appointed only for the remainder of such term. A member may serve after the expiration of his term until his successor has taken office. Vacancies on the Board shall be filled in the same manner in which the original appointments were made. No member of the Board shall be eligible to serve in excess of two consecutive terms of three years each.

"(c) The Chairman and Vice Chairman and other appropriate officers of the Board shall be elected by and from members of the Board other than the Secretary.

"(d) The members of the Board shall receive no compensation for their services as such, but shall be allowed such necessary travel expenses and per diem as are authorized by section 5703 of title 5, United States Code. The Secretary shall pay the reasonable and necessary expenses incurred by the Board in connection with the coordination of Board activities, announcement and reporting of meetings, and preparation of such reports as are required by subsection (f).

"(e) The Board shall meet at least semi-annually and shall hold such other meetings at the call of the Chairman, the Vice Chairman, or a majority of its members.

"(f) The Board shall advise the Secretary with respect to the implementation of this Act and shall advise the Assistant Secretary for Tourism Marketing with respect to the preparation of the marketing plan under section 202(a)(15). The Board shall prepare an annual report concerning

Margin notes:

Terms of office.

Compensation; travel expenses.

Meetings.

Ante, p. 1012.
Report.

its activities and include therein such recommendations as it deems appropriate with respect to the performance of the Secretary under this Act and the operation and effectiveness of programs under this Act. Each annual report shall cover a fiscal year and shall be submitted on or before the thirty-first day of December following the close of the fiscal year".

AUTHORIZATIONS

Sec. 5.(a) Section 6 of the Act (22 U.S.C. 2126) is redesignated as section 304 and the first sentence is amended to read as follows: "For the purpose of carrying out this Act there is authorized to be appropriated an amount not to exceed $8,600,000 for the fiscal year ending September 30, 1982.".

Repeal.
22 USC 2121
note.

(b) Section 7 of the Act (22 U.S.C. 2127) is redesignated as section 305 and sections 8 and 9 of the Act (22 U.S.C. 2128) are repealed.

EFFECTIVE DATE

22 USC 2121
note.

Sec. 6. The amendments made by this Act shall take effect October 1, 1981.

Approved October 16, 1981.

REVIEW QUIZ

When you feel you have covered all of the material in this chapter, answer these questions. Choose the *best* answer. Check your answers with the correct ones found on the Review Quiz Answer Key at the end of this book.

True (T) or False (F)

T   F   1. Policymakers, business leaders, and citizens may change, replace, or eliminate policies as needed.

T   F   2. Tourism businesses rarely set their own policies; they rely on government to do so.

T   F   3. Private sector tourism policy is quite general in nature and rarely differs from company to company.

T   F   4. Tourism is often disregarded as a way to diversify the economy when economic conditions change or if a major sector of the economy fails.

T   F   5. Policymakers can better assist an industry when they work behind the scenes and out of the limelight.

T   F   6. National tourism policy in the United States has been fragmented, inconsistent, and very political.

T   F   7. Most tourism efforts were put on hold during World War II.

T   F   8. Recent policy decisions that have shaped U.S. tourism include the 1970 decision to set up Amtrak.

T   F   9. Europe has several common tourism policies that are similar to those of Canada and the United States.

T   F   10. International agreements can ensure smooth international air travel, currency exchange, and tourist safety.

Alternate/Multiple Choice

11. Governments usually have a vested interest in tourism activity because of:

   a. resulting taxes and economic benefits.
   b. low investment requirements.
   c. negative returns on investments.
   d. lack of ownership and control.

12. Some suggest that the idea for a national office of tourism was first presented by:

   a. President Hoover.
   b. the National Park System.
   c. Charles Hatfield.
   d. Congress.

13.   One important step in enhancing the image of the United States as a travel destination is:

    a.   removing visa requirements.
    b.   strengthening visa requirements.

14.   Certain parts of a state are sometimes selected for tourism development over others. This is often the result of:

    a.   tourism agency priorities.
    b.   politics.

15.   Special tourism districts are usually funded through:

    a.   Federal grants.
    b.   F.I.C.A. tax.
    c.   self-assessment taxes.
    d.   state income tax.

Glossary

A

ADJUSTMENT MODEL

A tool used by social scientists and other researchers to explain the social impacts of tourism by focusing on the passive and active responses of residents toward tourists.

ADVENTURE TOURISM

A growing portion of the nature-based tourism around the world. Adventure tourism frequently tests the tourist's skills, and places the tourist in an unusual, remote, and exciting environment or culture. There are three categories: high-risk adventure tourism, soft adventure tourism, and cultural adventure tourism.

ALLOCENTRIC

A term used to describe a person who is more adventurous and willing to travel to exotic destinations, and who travels more frequently and by more modern or unusual forms of transportation. Allocentric travelers are apt to spend more money than psychocentric travelers.

ALTERNATIVE TOURISM

A form of tourism that advocates smaller scale tourism in terms of the number of tourists and the dimensions of tourism development. Sometimes called *responsible* or *green* tourism.

AMBIENCE

A feeling or mood associated with a particular place, person, or thing.

AMTRAK

An acronym drawn from the words "American travel by track" which is the trade name for the National Railroad Passenger Corporation. The U.S. Congress established Amtrak in 1970 to take over intercity passenger operation from railroads that desired to drop passenger service. Amtrak is subsidized in part by federal funds appropriated yearly by Congress and administered through the Department of Transportation.

APPLIED RESEARCH

Research which focuses on previously researched problems for the purpose of developing practical solutions (applications). Applied research is practical rather than theoretical.

ATTITUDES

Intellectual, emotional, and behavioral responses to events, things, and persons which people learn over time.

ATTITUDINAL MODEL

A tool used by social scientists and other researchers to explain the social impacts of tourism by focusing on the positive or negative attitudes that residents actively or passively display toward tourists.

ATTRIBUTION

The process of ascribing qualities and characteristics to people or objects in order to understand behavior in a range of situations.

AUTHENTICITY

A dimension of a tourism setting that refers to the concept or state of experiencing what a culture or society is *really* like—now or historically—through attention to authentic detail in artifacts, costumes, activities, attractions, and lifestyles.

B

BASIC RESEARCH

Research that focuses on new problems or developing new approaches to old problems. Basic research is theoretical in nature since the success of the project and its potential applications are uncertain.

BEHAVIOR

The manner in which a person conducts him/herself; the response of an individual or group to an action, stimulus, or environment.

BEHAVIORAL SETTING

A smaller subset of the environment that regularly surrounds the person—usually a familiar situation. Behavioral settings usually contain people. Sometimes referred to simply as **setting**.

BUSINESS PLAN

A formal document which assesses a business's strengths and weaknesses, analyzes the competition and marketing conditions, and provides various strategies for success; often required by lending institutions as documentation for new business loans.

C

COGNITIVE MAP

A mental representation of the world; a collection of information that an individual uses to orient him/herself within an environment or a setting.

COMPARATIVE ADVANTAGE

In economics, the concept that the overall output and standard of living rises when economies produce what they produce most efficiently and then trade with other economies.

COMPETITIVE CRITERIA

An analysis of how well a new product or service meets the preference of consumers in relation to existing competition.

CONFORMITY

The correspondence of an individual's behavior to the norms and expectations of the group.

COOK'S TOUR

The precursor to the modern all-inclusive group tour, developed by Thomas Cook in England in the late 1800s.

CREDIBILITY

The reputation of a person or business for providing honest and reliable information.

CRUSADES, THE

A series of several military expeditions between 1095 and 1291 in which Christian powers attempted to regain the Holy Land from the Muslims.

CULTURAL IMPACT

The effects of tourism activity or development on the culture of a locality or region—on its arts, artifacts, customs, rituals, architecture, and, in particular, the cohesiveness and cultural identity of the residents.

CULTURAL TOURISM

A form of tourism in which the culture of the area is the primary attraction.

CULTURE

A complex set of learned beliefs, customs, skills, habits, traditions, and knowledge shared by members of a society.

D

DEMAND CURVE

A graphic depiction of the relation between the amount of demand for a product or service and its price.

DEMOGRAPHICS

The study of groups of people, particularly the characteristics and trends of various groups *within* a population or *compared to* other populations.

DEREGULATION

The process of removing or relaxing legal regulations restricting the activities of business; particularly relevant to tourism through federal laws enacted in 1978 which eliminated government regulation of the airlines in regard to fares and routes, thereby increasing—theoretically—competition.

DIRECT IMPACT
The first-round effect of tourist spending.

DIVERSIFICATION
A corporate strategy by which a company seeks to spread the risk of a market downturn for its principal product or service by purchasing other companies or interest in other companies with different products or services or to, simply, increase its overall earnings.

DOMESTIC TOURISM
Travel people take within their country of residence.

E

ECONOMIC BENEFIT/COST
A microeconomic issue reflecting how consumers make decisions about what to buy and how firms can remain profitable.

ECONOMIC BENEFIT/COST ANALYSIS
A basic economic tool used to examine microeconomic issues reflecting how consumers make decisions about what to buy and how firms can remain profitable.

ECONOMIC IMPACT
A macroeconomic effect on the aggregate number of jobs and amount of income that a region can expect from economic development of various industries such as tourism.

ECONOMIC IMPACT ANALYSIS
A basic economic tool used to examine macroeconomic concerns about the aggregate number of jobs and amount of income a region can expect from economic development of various industries such as tourism.

ECONOMIC MODELS
Simplified, small-scale versions of some aspect of the economy used to explain and predict major economic events and consequences.

ECOTOURISM
Ecology-oriented tourism in which tourists seek out environmentally sensitive travel and/or tours or vacations which in some way improve or add to the knowledge of an environment.

EFFICIENCY
In economics, the absence of waste of resources.

EMERGING AUTHENTICITY
The result obtained when current artifacts and cultural activities replicate historic or older artifacts and, in time, become "authentic" artifacts of the community.

ENCODING

The process of putting into a message certain language or visual symbols designed to move or persuade the receiver—in other words, a message which is *encoded* within the message.

ENERGY-LETHARGY DIMENSION

A measurement used in conjunction with allocentric-psychocentric traits to understand consumer behavior.

ENVIRONMENT

That which surrounds an individual—both social and physical. A common perspective on the environment is that environment includes everything beyond a person's body, such as the air, the water, the land, buildings, and other people.

ENVIRONMENTAL DEGRADATION

The erosion of the quality of the environment, especially when caused by people.

ENVIRONMENTAL PERCEPTION

A holistic approach to perception which considers how an individual translates and interprets information from the environment.

EQUILIBRIUM PRICE AND QUANTITY

The point where the quantity of a good or service that buyers demand and purchase is just equal to the quantity that sellers supply and sell.

EXPERIMENTATION

A primary research technique in which one or more independent variables are allowed to change and the impact of this change on a dependent variable is measured.

EXTERNALITIES

Costs or benefits of a transaction affecting third parties not directly involved in the transaction. These costs or benefits escape the control of the market system.

EXTRINSIC MOTIVATION

Motivation which causes an individual to carry out a behavior for external reward.

F

FAMILY LIFE CYCLE

A series of stages used to distinguish between types of travelers; variables used to determine family life cycle stages are age, marital status, and presence and age of children.

FEASIBILITY ANALYSIS

A type of **market analysis** which includes a study of pricing, costs, development, and potential return on investment—everything, in short, which could help determine whether introducing a new product or service is feasible.

FEEDER AIRLINES
Small, regional airlines which meet commuter needs in less populated areas by making connecting flights to areas served by larger airlines.

FIRST IMPRESSION
What a person thinks about another person after a first encounter.

FLYCRUISING
A travel trend in which tourists fly to a destination to begin a cruise; generally as part of a travel package.

FORECASTING
An educated guess about future trends, events, sales levels, etc., based on data collected both within and outside a tourism operation.

G

GARBAGE SURVEY
An indirect observation technique used for monitoring consumer preferences for menu items. It involves keeping a systematic tally of which menu items are thrown away rather than eaten by guests.

GEOGRAPHY
In reference to tourism, the science of locating tourism destinations, routing vacations, and moving people from one place to another.

GRAND TOUR, THE
A trip taken by the sons of the English aristocracy for educational purposes. A typical tour began in England and had the major cultural cities of Italy as its destination. In its early years, a tour could last as long as 40 months. By the end of the Grand Tour era, the age of the traveler had increased, and the length of the tour decreased; individuals traveled more for pleasure than for an extended educational tour. The Grand Tour era lasted from about 1500 to 1820.

GREEN MOVEMENT
Environmentally-oriented movement or political party composed of concerned citizens who call for less destructive methods in agriculture, community development, rural development, and tourism.

GREENS
Members of the Green Movement or Green Party.

GROUP
A collection of people who regularly have contact, share structured interaction, have a common feeling of togetherness, and work toward a common set of goals and objectives.

I

IMAGE
The perceptions one has of some thing, place, or event which is carried in one's memory.

INCOME MULTIPLIER
A tool used to estimate the effect of an injection of new money on income in an economy.

INDIRECT IMPACT
The effect of tourist spending as the money passes through various stages of recirculation.

INDUCED IMPACT
The effect on an economy of employees spending their tourist-derived incomes.

INFRASTRUCTURE
The physical necessities and supporting systems that must be supplied for human activity and communication. Generally, the infrastructure includes all forms of construction on and below the ground such as roads and conduits for electricity, gas, water and sewage, telephones, and so on.

INJECTIONS
In economics, new dollars "injected" into a local economy by the spending nonresidents (such as tourists).

INPUT-OUTPUT MODELS
A means of calculating Keynesian-type multipliers that derive employment and income multipliers for specific sectors of the economy instead of just the aggregate effect on the whole destination region.

INTERACTIVE MARKETING
A form of marketing based on the premise that marketing doesn't stop when a tourist arrives at a destination. Interactive marketing contends that effective marketing includes managing and optimizing interactions between tourist and employees, tourist and other guests, as well as other pertinent interactions.

INTERNAL MARKETING
A type of marketing that focuses on employees as customers—in effect, "selling" employees on the values important to management.

INTERNATIONAL TOURISM
Travel people make abroad—or outside their country of residence.

INTRINSIC MOTIVATION
Motivation which causes an individual to carry out a behavior for internal satisfaction or reward.

IRRIDEX MODEL

A tool used by social scientists and other researchers to explain the social impacts of tourism by focusing on various stages of feeling which residents experience in dealing with tourists.

K

KINESICS

The study of the relationship between communication and non-verbal body motions such as blushes, shrugs, and eye movements.

L

LANDMARKS

Distinguishing features that stand out and provide a reference point for orientation; landmarks also provide travelers with information about direction and distance.

LEAKAGE

The amount of money that leaves an economy as it moves through various spending rounds. Also, an economic term describing the situation when monies are drawn from the economy of one nation to pay for imported goods from another nation, resulting in a net gain for the exporting nation (also referred to as *trade imbalance*).

LEARNING

A process by which a person acquires knowledge, experiences, and skills that result in changed behavior.

LIBERALIZATION

European legislation similar to U.S. deregulation of the airlines.

LIFE CYCLE

Stages which tourism developments go through in the course of their business life, similar to those stages experienced by a consumer product. Life cycle stages include the start-up stage, growth period, maturation, and decline stage.

LIFESTYLE MEASURES

A marketing tool used to examine a person's way of life; often used in conjunction with psychographic measures. Lifestyle measures look at a person's interests, activities, and opinions regarding a range of national and personal issues.

LINKAGE

In economics, the underlying connections which explain many observed causal relationships.

M

MACROECONOMICS

The branch of economics which deals with and analyzes a whole economy or a large sector of it.

MARGINAL COST

The change in total costs associated with producing one more unit of output.

MARKET ANALYSIS

A part of the market research that analyzes aspects of the marketplace to determine the potential of a product or service.

MARKET MIX

The combination of all the kinds of customers—market segments—to which a product or service will be marketed. (Compare with **MARKETING MIX**.)

MARKET RESEARCH

The systematic study of any issue, problem, or phenomenon related to the marketing of a product or service.

MARKET SEGMENTATION

The process of defining or identifying smaller, distinct groups or "segments" within the larger marketplace—"corporate business travelers," for instance, as a segment of "business travelers."

MARKETING

Traditionally, marketing has meant the process of exchange between buyer and seller; today, it also means identifying potential customers' needs and desires, developing products and services to meet those needs and desires, and using advertising and other tools to persuade customers.

MARKETING CONDITIONS

The social and economic context within which a product or service is marketed or exchanged.

MARKETING MIX

The total combination of marketing tactics and tools employed to ensure a product or service's success. (Compare with **MARKET MIX**.)

MARKETING ORIENTATION

A business orientation which focuses on and emphasizes the needs and desires of customers.

MARKETING PLAN

A plan which provides the results of market research in analyzing market conditions and competition, and details a strategy to reach particular market segments and persuade them to purchase a product or service.

MASS TOURISM
Wide-scale travel by a large number of people—not just the elite—brought about by the increase in leisure time, discretionary income, and reliable and inexpensive modes of transportation such as the automobile and airplane.

MASS TOURISTS
Travelers participating in wide-scale travel designed for large numbers of people.

MICROECONOMICS
The branch of economics which deals with and analyzes individual units or markets in an economy.

MIDDLE AGES
The period of European history dating from about A.D. 400 to 1500. Sometimes called the Dark Ages.

MONITORING
Consists of daily sales reports, guest counts, and other management reports designed to provide information on a firm's current performance and its progress toward meeting operational goals.

MOTIVATION
Anything which moves people to change their thinking or behavior; can be negative or positive, and can come from without or within.

MULTINATIONAL CORPORATION
A corporation having divisions in two or more countries.

MULTIPLIER
A tool used in economic impact analysis to express the impact of a given investment in terms of change in employment, income, or sales.

N

NATIONAL TOURISM OFFICE
Primary government agency responsible for implementing national goals and public policy with respect to tourism, and for providing information services to international travelers.

NATIONAL TOURISM POLICY ACT
The first comprehensive national tourism policy in the United States; enacted by the Reagan Administration in 1981.

NATIONAL TOURISM RESOURCES REVIEW COMMISSION
A commission created by Congress in 1970 and charged with assessing tourism needs through the 1970s and into the 1980s; represents the first large-scale, government-sponsored tourism study in the United States.

NEOLITHIC AGE

The latest period of the Stone Age characterized by polished stone implements. Human activity during this era focused on the formation of agricultural communities and elementary cultures.

NON-VERBAL CUES

Perceptual information provided in a social exchange through a person's dress, personal appearance, hand gestures, body movement, stance, and facial expressions.

O

OBSERVATION

A primary research technique. Observation is especially accurate because it relies on the actual behavior of research subjects rather than on statements about their behavior.

OPPORTUNITY COST

In economics, the cost of foregoing another cost—if we forego the cost of cleaning up air pollution, the added cost incurred by increased healthcare, lost workdays, etc.

ORGANIZATION FOR ECONOMIC COOPERATION AND DEVELOPMENT (OECD)

An association of 25 countries promoting economic development and cooperation among nations.

P

P-MIX

The **marketing mix** is often said to include four "Ps"—product, price, place, and promotion. Since tourism is so experiential and service-oriented, one researcher combined the traditional four "Ps" with four additional "Ps"—programming, packaging, partnership, and publicity (including public relations)—to create the P-mix.

PACKAGING

The practice of combining a selected number of products and services (often from different companies) into a single package for one price. Travel packages, for instance, often include airfare, hotel, and meals for one price.

PALEOLITHIC AGE

The second period of the Stone Age, dating from 32,000 B.C. to 10,000 B.C., characterized by rough or chipped stone implements. Human activity during this era was nomadic and focused upon day-to-day survival.

PERCEPTION

The process by which an individual translates sensory data into meaningful information that can be used and acted upon.

PERSONALITY
The totality of an individual's mental and emotional characteristics expressed through his/her behavior—especially as such behavior is perceived by others.

PERSUASION
The act or process of using information in a manner designed to convince others to change their attitudes toward some object, person, or event.

PILGRIMAGE
A journey undertaken by individuals during the Middle Ages to religious sites for the purpose of divine forgiveness, adventure, learning, and merriment.

POLICY
A guideline for the future or a course of action to meet stated goals and objectives; policies usually result from the actions of governments, agencies, organizations, and businesses.

POSITIONING
A marketing strategy which attempts to "position" a product or service favorably in comparison with the competition or "position" it to better serve particular market segments.

PRICE CEILING
An artificially imposed maximum price which is below the true market equilibrium price.

PRICE SUPPORT
An artificially imposed minimum price which is above the true market equilibrium price.

PRIMARY RESEARCH
Uses original data collected specifically for a particular research project.

PRODUCT LIFE CYCLE
A series of stages used to distinguish between different phases in the life or duration of a product; the stages of a product life cycle are *introduction, growth, maturity,* and *decline.*

PRODUCT ORIENTATION
A business orientation that concentrates more on the manufacture and distribution of a product or service than on the needs of customers.

PROGRAM
The format within a setting that determines behaviors. Programs are supported by the physical design, people, and objects within the setting.

PROGRAMMING
The practice of resorts and other tourism enterprises to create and schedule (program) a combination of activities designed to attract visitors and maximize their enjoyment of the facilities.

PROXEMICS

The study of the spatial orientation of individuals in social and interpersonal situations.

PSYCHOCENTRIC

A term used to describe a person who is more likely to travel to familiar destinations, and who travels less frequently and by more traditional or standard means of transportation. Psychocentric travelers are apt to spend less money than allocentric travelers.

PSYCHOGRAPHICS

The measurement of personality traits, attitudes, interests, activities, and values from a marketing perspective.

PSYCHOLOGY

The study of human behavior; specifically, the study of thoughts, feelings, and actions of the individual.

PUBLIC GOODS

Goods provided by the public sector because they are considered too important to the public at large and/or too big for the private sector to deal with adequately (national parks, for example).

R

RATIO MULTIPLIER

An economic mathematical modeling tool which can be used to indicate the extent of a region's economic self-sufficiency.

RECEIPTS

Money spent by international travelers.

RENAISSANCE, THE

A transitional age between medieval and modern times, lasting from the fourteenth to the seventeenth century. The Renaissance is characterized as a time of renewed interest in arts and literature and the beginning of modern science.

REPRESENTATIVE SAMPLE

A small sample of a targeted population group that is designed to represent, as accurately as possible, the entire targeted group.

REQUEST FOR RESEARCH PROPOSALS (RFP)

A written document sent to outside research consultants to request their proposals on how they will approach the research problem and what they will charge for their services. An RFP should be specific so that researchers can make accurate estimates of their costs.

RESEARCH
A systematic process for solving problems or testing new ideas.

RESEARCH INSTRUMENTS
Questionnaires and other forms used to survey a selected group of people.

ROLE
The prescribed or expected behavior of a person with a certain status.

ROMANTICISM
A literary, artistic, and philosophical movement originating in the eighteenth century, characterized by an emphasis on the virtues of the natural world.

S

SALES MULTIPLIER
A tool used to estimate the effect of an injection of new money on total sales in an economy.

SALES ORIENTATION
A business orientation that focuses more on increasing sales and promotional efforts than on the actual needs or desires of customers.

SCIENCE TOURISM
A subgroup of ecotourism in which laymen and laywomen travel with scientists and students to help with scientific work at various sites throughout the world; the phenomenon is that people *pay* for vacations in which they often work very hard, long hours but also make a contribution to a body of scientific knowledge.

SECONDARY RESEARCH
Uses data collected by others, often for purposes other than the particular research project in question.

SERVICE CYCLE
A series of impressions and activities which start with a tourist's first impression of a destination—whether first sight or advertisement—and includes every service interaction with the facility thereafter.

SETTING
See **BEHAVIORAL SETTING**.

SITUATIONAL ANALYSIS
A type of market analysis aimed at improving or expanding an already existing business.

SOCIAL IMPACT
The effects of tourism activity and development on the social fabric of residents of destination communities—as individuals, as families, and as members of social organizations.

SOCIAL NORMS

Guides to behavior within groups and particular cultures which describe how a person is expected to act in various situations.

SOCIAL PERCEPTION

The process by which an individual perceives and interprets information about another person within the context of the other person's social standing or social environment.

SOCIAL STRATIFICATION

The perception of and, oftentimes, adherence to a hierarchy of layers or strata within a society. Among the elements which differentiate social strata are wealth, income, prestige, and power.

SOCIALIZATION

The process by which a person learns to act and interact in social situations according to certain socially accepted norms.

SOCIETAL ORIENTATION

A business orientation that focuses on the needs of customers but, in addition, tries to assure that a product or service is not harmful to society as a whole.

SOCIETY

An organized, independent, continuing number of people living in a specific area.

SOCIOLOGY

The study of the development and organization of societies.

SPECIALIZATION OF LABOR

The division of skills within a society which permits individuals to master one particular craft or trade.

STAGED AUTHENTICITY

The result of using the environment to enhance or support the authentic or to give the appearance of authenticity through imitations or re-enactments.

STATUS

The perceived position of an individual within a social hierarchy or strata.

STEREOTYPES

A standardized, oversimplified, and erroneous mental picture or classification held by one group of people to be true about all or most members of another group of people, certain places, or things. Such erroneous classifications are created by prejudice, bigotry, and insufficient information.

SUPERSTRUCTURE

Forms of construction above ground which are supplied for human activity. The superstructure is supported by the infrastructure and includes such facilities as hotels, shopping malls, restaurants, and tourism attractions.

SUPPLY CURVE
A graphic depiction of the relation between the amount of supply of a product or service and its price.

SURVEY
The primary research technique employed most often by tourism researchers. It involves getting information from people by using carefully designed questionnaires and other survey forms. Three types of surveys are personal interviews, telephone surveys, and mailback surveys.

T

TARGET MARKETS
Distinctly defined groupings of potential buyers (market segments) at which sellers aim or "target" their marketing efforts.

TEN MILLION PROGRAM
An administrative program developed by the Ministry of Transport in Japan to promote overseas travel by Japanese residents.

TIA
The Travel Industry Association of America; a large, broad-based industry organization in the United States, representing all segments of the tourism industry. Promotes professional advancement of members, and plays a role in developing national policy by working with the government.

TIME AND MOTION RESEARCH
A direct observation technique researchers use to observe and record employee actions as they perform tasks.

TOURISM DEVELOPMENT
The long-term process of preparing for the arrival of tourists; entails planning, building, and managing attractions, transportation, accommodations, services, and facilities that serve the tourist.

TOURISM ENCLAVES
Self-contained resort complexes that cater to all the needs of tourists who arrive as part of a tour or other type of package.

TOURISM PLANNING
The process of preparing for tourism development; a tool for addressing the choices associated with tourism development.

TOURISM POLICY
Guidelines and decisions designed to assist the tourism industry in meeting goals and objectives; tourism policies usually result from the actions of government, agencies, organizations, and businesses.

TRAVEL SURPLUS

Expenditures by travelers over and above those projected by the economy of a destination.

U

USTTA

The United States Travel and Tourism Administration; responsible for promoting and marketing tourism to the United States; assisting state travel offices; reducing national travel deficit; and promoting the United States abroad. Replaced the U.S. Travel Service as a result of the National Tourism Policy Act.

V

VALS

A comprehensive marketing system of studying values and lifestyles which places consumers into four value categories and nine lifestyle categories.

VALUES

A set of beliefs, often socially and culturally defined, which attempt to guide behavior—either of an individual or of a group.

VERBAL CUES

Perceptual information provided in social exchanges through the tone and method of speech delivery, as well as the content.

W

WORD OF MOUTH

A term used to describe people talking to each other about their experiences as consumers.

Index

TOURISM AND THE HOSPITALITY INDUSTRY

REVIEW QUIZ ANSWER KEY

The numbers in parentheses refer to the page(s) where the answer may be found.

Chapter 1	Chapter 2	Chapter 3	Chapter 4
1. F (3)	1. T (31)	1. F (54)	1. T (77)
2. T (4)	2. F (32)	2. T (54–55)	2. F (79)
3. T (7)	3. T (33)	3. F (57)	3. T (81–82)
4. F (11)	4. T (35)	4. T (57)	4. F (82)
5. F (13)	5. T (37)	5. F (59)	5. T (85)
6. F (17)	6. T (39)	6. T (61)	6. T (86)
7. T (19)	7. T (39)	7. T (62)	7. F (86)
8. T (23)	8. F (42)	8. T (66)	8. F (86)
9. F (25)	9. T (43)	9. T (69)	9. F (88–89)
10. T (26)	10. F (44)	10. T (72)	10. F (91)
11. b (10)	11. a (32)	11. b (54)	11. d (77)
12. a (17)	12. a (35)	12. a (54)	12. c (78)
13. a (24)	13. a (42)	13. a (57)	13. b (82)
14. d (17)	14. a (44)	14. b (61)	14. b (83)
15. a (19)	15. c (45)	15. d (71-72)	15. a (95)

Chapter 5	Chapter 6	Chapter 7	Chapter 8
1. T (101)	1. F (133)	1. T (158)	1. F (182)
2. T (103)	2. T (134)	2. T (162)	2. T (182)
3. T (105)	3. T (139)	3. T (163)	3. F (183)
4. T (108)	4. F (141)	4. F (164)	4. T (186)
5. F (108)	5. F (141)	5. F (167)	5. F (194)
6. T (116)	6. F (141–142)	6. F (171)	6. T (201)
7. F (119)	7. T (143)	7. F (171)	7. T (201)
8. F (120)	8. F (146)	8. F (172)	8. F (201)
9. T (121)	9. T (148)	9. F (172)	9. T (202)
10. T (123)	10. T (150)	10. F (174)	10. T (204)
11. a (103)	11. b (133)	11. b (158)	11. a (187)
12. a (104)	12. a (134)	12. c (159)	12. c (187)
13. b (107)	13. a (137)	13. b (164)	13. b (189)
14. a (113, 115)	14. d (140)	14. a (167)	14. a (194)
15. b (119)	15. a (143)	15. a (171)	15. a (195)

Chapter 9	Chapter 10	Chapter 11	Chapter 12
1. T (209)	1. T (233)	1. T (259)	1. T (287)
2. F (212)	2. F (234)	2. F (262)	2. F (288-289)
3. T (215)	3. F (235)	3. F (263)	3. F (289-290)
4. T (218)	4. T (237)	4. T (264)	4. T (290)
5. F (219)	5. F (243)	5. T (266)	5. F (294)
6. T (221)	6. F (246)	6. T (266)	6. T (295)
7. T (221)	7. F (247)	7. F (270)	7. F (297)
8. T (221)	8. T (248)	8. F (278)	8. F (299)
9. F (222)	9. F (251)	9. F (279)	9. F (300)
10. T (222)	10. F (253)	10. T (280)	10. F (302)
11. a (210)	11. a (235)	11. c (257)	11. b (291)
12. b (212)	12. b (242)	12. b (267)	12. b (298)
13. a (215)	13. b (245)	13. a (271)	13. a (299)
14. a (220)	14. a (242)	14. a (270)	14. c (298)
15. b (221)	15. b (251-252)	15. d (276-277)	15. a (303)

Chapter
13

---

1. T (307)
2. F (307)
3. F (308)
4. F (309)
5. F (309)
6. T (309)
7. T (310)
8. T (314)
9. T (321)
10. T (324)
11. a (309)
12. c (310)
13. a (315)
14. b (316)
15. c (318)